Voices In Flight: The Wellington Bomber

Voices In Flight: The Wellington Bomber

Martin W. Bowman

Pen & Sword
AVIATION

First Published in Great Britain in 2014
and reprinted in this format in 2022 by
Pen & Sword Aviation
an imprint of
Pen & Sword Books Ltd
47 Church Street, Barnsley, South Yorkshire S70 2AS

Copyright © Martin W Bowman, 2014, 2022
ISBN 9-781-39907-489-6

The right of Martin W Bowman to be identified as author of this work
has been asserted by him in accordance with the Copyright,
Designs and Patents Act 1988.

A CIP catalogue record for this book is
available from the British Library.

All rights reserved. No part of this book may be reproduced or transmitted
in any form or by any means, electronic or mechanical including
photocopying, recording or by any information storage and retrieval system,
without permission from the Publisher in writing.

Typeset in 10/12pt Palatino
by GMS Enterprises

Printed and bound in England by
CPI Group (UK) Ltd, Croydon, CR0 4YY

Pen & Sword Books Ltd incorporates the Imprints of Pen & Sword Aviation,
Pen & Sword Family History, Pen & Sword Maritime, Pen & Sword Military,
Pen & Sword Discovery, Wharncliffe Local History, Wharncliffe True Crime,
Wharncliffe Transport, Pen & Sword Select, Pen & Sword Military Classics,
Leo Cooper, The Praetorian Press, Remember When, Seaforth Publishing and
Frontline Publishing.

For a complete list of Pen & Sword titles please contact
PEN & SWORD BOOKS LIMITED

47 Church Street, Barnsley, South Yorkshire, S70 2AS, England
E-mail: enquiries@pen-and-sword.co.uk
Website: www.pen-and-sword.co.uk

Contents

Acknowledgements		6
Introduction		7
Chapter 1	Opening Gambit	21
Chapter 2	Coastal Command	37
Chapter 3	Night Offensive	63
Chapter 4	'How Deep Is The Night'	85
Chapter 5	They Sowed The Wind	119
Chapter 6	Desert War	145
Chapter 7	Mad Dogs and Englishmen	165
Chapter 8	African Adventure	173
Chapter 9	Mediterranean Missions	191
Chapter 10	Maritime Operations	209
Appendices		219
Index		222

Acknowledgements

I am indebted to all the contributors for their words and photographs. I am most grateful to the following: Les Allington; Wing Commander E. E. M. Angell; Les Aspin RCAF; Len Aynsley; Mike Bailey; Andy Bird; Theo Boiten; David K. Brearey; G. Stuart Brown RCAF; Don Bruce; Jim Burtt-Smith; John Callander; Arthur 'Chan' Chandler; K. Clement; Norman Child; L. W. Collett; Bob Collis; A. J. Cook; Gerald F. Cooke; Rupert 'Tiny' Cooling; Gary Cooper; E. M. Cox; Noel C. Croppi AFC; D. Cumming; Eric Day; G. B. Dick; Fred Dorken RCAF; Dr Colin Dring; Huby Fairhead; Henry Fawcett; Harvey Firestone; the late Charles Fox; Dr Paul A. Fox; Malcolm Freestone; Brian French; Peter Frost; Wally Gaul; Michael L. Gibson; Roy Gristwood; Gordon E. Haddock; Les Hallam; B. Hammond: Harold J. Hamnett RCAF; Captain T. A. Hampton AFC; the late Raymond Harding; S. Harle; Flight Lieutenant Keith Haywood RAF; Robin T. Holmes of the Loch Ness Wellington Project; Johnny Hosford; Alfred Jenner; Arthur Johnson; the late Group Captain Jones: R. Kirk; John O. Lancaster; Legion magazine; Tom Leonard RCAF; Squadron Leader Geoffrey N. W. MacFarlane; Reg Mack; J. A. Ian Mackay RCAF; Robert G. MacNeil RCAF; G. H. S. Malcolmson; the late Leslie Marlow; Eric A. Masters; Squadron Leader Rem Merrick, RAF Marham; Ian McLachlan; Nigel McTeer; Tomas Nagy; Des Norris; Major Stephen A. Oliphant USAF; Ernie Payne; Jeremy Petts; Stella Poynton; Charles Ray; A. H. Rawlings; Edward N. Reynolds RCAF; the RCAF Association; Albert E. Robinson; Flight Lieutenant W. 'Rusty' Russell RAF; Hans-Heiri Stapfer; Terence Mansfield the Lord Sandhurst DFC; Maurice 'Scats' Sandell; *Sentinel* magazine; Group Captain M. J. A. Shaw DSO; Squadron Leader R. C. Shepherd DFC; Leslie Sidwell; Alan G. Smith; Charles Stephens; Reg Thackeray DFM; Geoff Thomas; J. Tipton; Bryn Watkins; Jack Weekley; Brian Wexham of Vickers Ltd; Group Captain John N. Williams OBE DFC; Fred Wingham; James Woodruff.

Thanks also go to my fellow author, friend and colleague, Graham Simons, for getting the book to press ready standard and for his detailed work on the photographs; to Pen & Sword and in particular, Laura Hirst; and to Jon Wilkinson, for his unique jacket design once again.

Introduction

My heart is heavy, its throbbing pulsation soon to sink into the quiet of death. My skin is already torn, soon to express the symmetrical form of my skeleton, to expose it to the elements which will render it back into the fabric of the earth. Soon I shall be forgotten, both by those who had my welfare at heart and by those who feared my very existence. The moon is high, the night sky a canvas of blue; beneath me the earth is like a patchwork quilt of many colours. I am a Wellington, a crippled aircraft alone in the sky with no human pilot at my controls, no navigator at my chart table and no sound from my radio. My guns are now mere symbolic sentinels of defence. No sensitive fingers will nurse my descent into that watery grave that I know lies ahead; my last hour is now at hand, and I face it alone. An air lock in my fuel lines cut both my engines simultaneously and caused my crew to abandon me, as I twisted and convulsed, before I was able to regain the circulation of my life fluid. The automatic pilot had been engaged and my throttle set at cruising speed, so that when my engines started again I was able to level out and fly on - alone. My heart is broken, for they lost faith. From the first day of my working life I have been dependable, and no airman has ever lost his life or been injured by my inefficiency. I have survived over a hundred return journeys from Hell's suburbs, and always they had faith in me ... until tonight. My controls move slowly and methodically, the stick making deliberate and precise movements as if held by unseen hands. I am tangible proof of man's skill and ingenuity, proof of his conquest of the air, but at the same time useless without the guidance of my creators. I shall be mentioned on the news bulletin in the morning, as one of our aircraft that failed to return. If only they could learn the truth, that here in a moonlit sky a lonely lady is trying to reach the shores of England, if only to prove that she did get back. I am losing height at the rate of one thousand feet per minute, and my altimeter is slowly moving back. A slight vibration has started throughout my geodetic fuselage; one of my engines needs synchronising. These are the first presentiments of the end, my course becoming more and more erratic as the off-beat motor pulls me against the automatic pilot.

I'm well across the Channel now. The moon's reflection in the water is accompanied by the shadow of a big bird in a futile migration. As I see the coast of England I have less than a hundred feet of space beneath me, and white-topped waves appear like sharks' mouths awaiting their prey. It seems bitterly strange to me, that my end should be like this. Tonight I should have proved all that my scientific machinery was capable of achieving, but at the time when it was needed most, my crew had shown no faith. As my flying sped drops to a stall my tailfin and rudder still retain their graceful dignity, even after the first impact with the water which rips open my belly. My engines are silent now. In a few seconds the hissing of salt water against red hot metal will cease, and I shall sink to my final resting place.

Lonely Lady by D.A. Dugard, writing in Intercom; The Official Quarterly Magazine of the Aircrew Association, autumn 1983.

It was in March 1911 that the name of Vickers first became associated with heavier-than-air craft when an aviation department was formed in Vickers' plant at Erith in Kent. By 1919 Vickers had consolidated its aircraft production solely at Weybridge and the design office was moved there from Imperial Court, Knightsbridge, where it had been since 1916. In the twenties the company built a single-engined civil transport and an amphibian aeroplane and biplane bombers and troop carrying aircraft for the RAF. In 1928 Vickers and Armstrong Whitworth merged into a new company called Vickers-Armstrongs Ltd and Supermarine Aviation Company of Southampton was also acquired. Four years' earlier, in 1924, Vickers had established the Airship Guarantee Company and Mr. Barnes Neville Wallis became its Chief Engineer. After World War I Wallis felt that governmental attitudes to aviation left little scope for his advanced ideas for aircraft capable of establishing long-range routes and he had turned his back temporarily on aviation matters. On his return to the fold he was entrusted with the design of the airship which became known as the R100, in which he utilised for the first time the principle of geodetic construction. This form of lightweight, robust and seemingly-complex lattice structure was capable of withstanding severe punishment without its structural integrity being destroyed. At various times between 1908 and 1929 Vickers had produced a number of large airships for the Government, the last being the R100. This was intended for an experimental air service between the UK and the Commonwealth countries but it was scrapped following the crash of the R101 in October 1930.

Dr. (later Sir Barnes) Wallis had first come to prominence in aviation in 1913, when, in conjunction with H. B. Pratt he designed Britain's second rigid airship, the R9, which was completed by Vickers in 1917. Wallis was painstaking and academic in his approach to aeronautical design and whenever possible, he tested his ideas before passing the final design for construction. In January 1930, when design work on the R100 had already been completed, Wallis joined Vickers' aeroplane division at Weybridge as chief engineer (structures) and evolved a novel geodetic aeroplane structure which was inspired by the wire-netting envelopes containing the balloons, or gasbags of the R100. In his new lattice-like construction system, loads were transferred from member to member by the shortest distance, or as near to it as external configuration would allow, on a criss-cross route and it led to a considerable advance in weight/strength characteristics with a fabric-covered aeroplane. After experiments with a geodetic wing for the Viastra, Wallis used geodetic construction for the first time in a heavier than air aircraft, when it was incorporated in the Type 253 single-engined biplane built by Vickers to meet a 1931 Air Ministry specification for a general-purpose aeroplane. Then, in a private-venture Vickers went further and designed a low-wing monoplane of high aspect-ratio to the same Air Ministry specification but with Wallis's system applied to the entire airframe. This machine first flew in June 1935 and the improvement in performance was such that the Air Ministry ordered this two-seat monoplane bomber, subsequently named the Wellesley, in place of the biplane. A total of 176 Wellesleys was built. The Wellesley demonstrated clearly the excellent weight/strength ratio of such structures when, in November 1938, two specially-prepared Wellesleys flew from Ismailia, Egypt to Darwin, Australia, non-stop in just over 48 hours and setting a new world long-distance record of

7,157.7 miles. Wellesleys entered service with Bomber Command in the spring of 1937. The 2,000lb bomb load was carried in streamlined nacelles to avoid breaking up the internal geodetic pattern of the fuselage. The bomb stowage problem would be overcome in 1936 in Vickers' next geodetic-structure type to appear, a medium bomber conforming to the Air Ministry specification B9/32.

On 20 October 1932 the Air Ministry had invited Vickers, Bristol, Gloster and Handley Page to submit a design study for an experimental twin-engined day bomber capable of carrying a bomb load of 1,000lb for 720 miles and with a range of 1,500 miles. Handley Page offered the unorthodox HP 52 Hampden which, with its sleek, long tapered boom and twin tail might have been considered unconventional for its day. At Vickers Rex Pierson and his design team applied all that was best in a succession of previous company models and the ingenious and immensely strong geodetic framework devised and developed by Barnes Wallis.

A comparison of the respective performance details of the Bristol Pegasus IS2 or IIS2 and the Armstrong Siddeley Tiger engines was settled in favour of the Pegasus for the air-cooled engined version of the bomber. For the liquid-cooled engined variant of the basic project, the Rolls-Royce Goshawk I was selected. These two versions were submitted in tender designs on 28 February 1933. In September the Air Ministry placed a pilot contract for a bomber with Goshawk engines. By this time the revised specification included front, rear and midships gun mountings with wind protection. The proposed aeroplane was also altered from a high to a mid-wing configuration, to give a better view to pilots flying in formation, which modification also improved the aerodynamic characteristics. The revised specification also called for the modification of bomb undershields and the incorporation of spring-loaded bomb doors. The oil system was also revised and permission to raise the tare weight to 6,798lb was requested. This increased weight was accepted in principle, so the detail design proceeded while the ancillary installations became progressively more complicated, as a result of production and operational requirements. The fixed weight penalty became apparent and by June 1934, the Air Ministry had cancelled the prohibitive upper weight limit of 6,500lb.

In March 1933 R. K. Pierson envisaged that the Type 271 should employ a high wing monoplane design with a fixed undercarriage and be powered by either two Bristol Mercury VIS2 or the Rolls-Royce Goshawk evaporatively-cooled power-plants. By October he had come down in favour of a retractable undercarriage and he proposed using geodetic construction throughout the aircraft because the geodetic latticework construction had reached such a stage by late 1933 that it could be incorporated in the airframes of large aircraft. The Vickers proposal was accepted and in December 1933 the Air Ministry placed an order for a single prototype Type 271 with Goshawk engines, which proved to be one of the few Rolls-Royce failures. In August 1934 Vickers submitted proposals for using the more powerful Bristol Pegasus or Perseus air-cooled engine in place of the Goshawk, which promised considerable improvement in speed, climb, ceiling and ability to fly on one engine, without a correspondingly serious increase in all-up weight. It was also hoped that the delivery date of the first aircraft could be brought forward. The Air Ministry quickly accepted these proposals and took the opportunity to increase the fuel load to provide a range of 1,500 miles at 213 mph at 15,000 feet. The Pegasus engines were to be fitted with variable pitch propellers and following wind tunnel tests conducted by Vickers, their own nose and tail turrets were also accepted. The loaded weight by this time was increasing rapidly and another design study using Rolls-Royce Merlin engines was carried out for the Air Ministry at an all-up weight of 17,850lb.

The prototype finally made its maiden flight at Brooklands on 15 June 1936 with Vickers chief test pilot Captain J. 'Mutt' Summers at the controls, accompanied by Barnes Wallis and Trevor Westbrook. It was powered with two conventional air-cooled 915hp Bristol Pegasus X engines which gave a speed of 250 mph at 8,000 feet at an all-up weight of 21,000lb. The span of the aeroplane was 85 feet 10 inches and the length 60 feet 6 inches. Fitted with a Vickers-Supermarine Stranraer-type fin and rudder to save on design time, the model bore scant resemblance to later models. Both front and rear gun turrets were glazed over with Plexiglas and no armament was carried. A crew of four was provided for, with allowances for one supernumerary for special duties. The bomb load was nine 500lb bombs or nine of 250lb for long range operations. Nose and tail gun stations were fitted for single guns in each. These 'cupolas' were hand-operated, but there was provision for a third gun with a retractable shield to be mounted in a dorsal position half-way along the fuselage. The B.9/32 was successful during a series of trials and was exhibited in the New Types Park at the annual RAF display at Hendon on 27 June. The new aircraft enthralled the RAF and public alike and the former were particularly impressed with its ability to carry double the bomb load and cover twice the range (3,000 miles) to that originally specified. In August the Air Ministry placed an initial production order for 180 of the Vickers Type 271. Vickers suggested the name 'Crecy' but the more famous name of Wellington was later adopted, on 8 September.

On 29 January 1937 Specification 29/36 was issued to cover the first production run of 185 Wellington Is. This specification could be described as an interim measure to provide as quickly as possible the aircraft required for the rapidly expanding Royal Air Force. The production Wellington I was a complete redesign and went hand in hand with the detail design of the larger and heavier B.1/35 (Warwick) twin-engined bomber. As a result, large portions of the two aeroplanes were common to one another, an engineering operation made easier by the singular features of the geodetic structure with its special member-forming machinery. This parallel detail design suited the Wellington admirably, for a deeper fuselage emerged which nicely accommodated the larger bomb load required with associated equipment. It also provided better disposition for the regular aircrew who were increased in number to five. The nose was lengthened to accommodate the revised gun turret and bomb aimer's position. A redesigned horizontal tail unit of high aspect ratio saw the deletion of the horn balances of the B.9/32. Constant speed propellers and a retractable tail wheel were fitted and the Air Ministry requested the replacement of the Vickers ventral turret mid ships with one of Frazer-Nash design. This was heavier than the Vickers type and Pierson produced data showing that the aeroplane C of G position with this alternative turret was extremely critical so the F-N turret was fitted to the first production aircraft only, compensating by ballast to obtain the required flying characteristics during handling trials. On 19 April while undergoing Service tests the prototype crashed at Waldringfield, 1½ miles east of the A&AEE station at Martlesham Heath, during diving trials. Excessive load caused the failure of the horn balance and the aircraft turned on to its back. The pilot was thrown through the roof of the cockpit and escaped by parachute but the flight engineer was killed in the crash.

The first production Type 285 Wellington B Mk I had revised fuselage and tail surfaces and flew for the first time from Brooklands on 23 December 1937. Power was provided by Pegasus XVIIIs but subsequent production Wellington Is were powered by 1,000hp Pegasus XVIII engines. (The Mark II was to be fitted with Rolls-Royce Merlin Xs and the Mark III with Bristol Hercules IIIs). Vickers power-operated nose and tail turrets and a Nash and Thompson ventral retractable and revolving turret mid-ships were all armed with two 0.303 inch Browning guns with 600 rounds of ammunition for the front turret and for 1,000 rounds for each of the mid and rear turrets. The tail-wheel was retractable and the bomb bay was enlarged. Elongated side windows were built in the fuselage, which was increased in length. Wingspan was also extended slightly and the crew positions increased from four to five members.

On 10 October 1938 99 Squadron became the first in Bomber Command to receive the Wellington I. In 1939 production of 189 examples of the Type 408 B.IA began. Both Vickers turrets were replaced by Nash and Thompson and each was equipped with two .303 inch machine-guns (as was the existing ventral position). Various other improvements were made and the crew complement was increased to six. A Mk.IA (P2516) was converted at the end of 1939 to carry a large electrically energised hoop of 48 feet diameter as an enemy magnetic mine destroyer and the type, known as Directional Wireless Installation (DWI) was successfully used for this duty in British coastal waters and later in Mediterranean harbours and the Suez Canal. British scientists had devised two methods of neutralization. A passive method of neutralizing the mines lay in equipping ships with degaussing gear to nullify the magnetic attraction of the ship's steel hull; ironically Professor Gauss was a German. An aggressive method of dealing with the mines was to destroy them by triggering their detonator by creating a magnetic field. Vickers was approached to modify a number of Wellingtons to carry equipment consisting of generators with which to create an electro-magnetic field generated from an aluminium coil encased inside a cumbersome circular 51 foot diameter balsa wood structure outside the aircraft. The balsa casing was constructed in sections and the assembly minus the aluminium coil was slung under a Wellington Mk IA (P2516) for flight testing.

After the flight characteristics tests proved satisfactory the aluminium strip coil was inserted. The nose and tail turrets were removed and faired into smooth conical positions, later some aircraft carried glazed tail positions. To save weight the interiors were generally stripped of all unnecessary equipment. The aluminium strip coils were initially powered with a Ford V8 engine driving 35kw Maudsley generators. Three more Wellington Mk 1As were modified straight off the Vickers Weybridge production line and conversion work on eleven additional Mk Is was carried out at Croydon with Rollasons performing airframe adaptation and English Electric producing the coils. The lighter, but more powerful Gypsy

Six motor driving a 95kw generator were installed in the Wellington DWI Mk II. The Gypsy's 95kw output generated a much greater magnetic field while saving over 1,000lbs of weight. Tests carried out on the magnetic section of a de-fused German mine located in the middle of the experimental airfield at Boscombe Down provided encouraging results but tidal depth affected the degree of magnetic field which could be directed at the mine. Another critical factor in searching out and destroying a mine was the height at which the aircraft could safely descend without the risk of being damaged by the mine's detonation. Initial operational flights were conducted at around 60 feet but 35 feet became the minimum altitude. The speed of the aircraft had to be slow enough that the magnetic field did not peak for too short a period of time to detonate the mine, but fast enough that detonation of a mine did not damage the aircraft. Also, the angle of incidence of the magnetic ring had to be co-ordinated with the trim of the aircraft in order to bring to bear the most effective electro-magnetic field on a mine. The first aerial detonation of a mine was achieved on 8 January 1940. A mine had been detonated by the specialist vessel Borde, but the ship was badly damaged in the process and the task of mine detonation was left to the Wellingtons of 1 GRU.

The second aerial success was recorded five days later on 13 January, but on this occasion the aircraft descended below 35 feet, the hatches were blown off and the accelerometer recorded ten Gs. The aircraft was grounded and checked by Vickers engineers for structural damage but none was found. Due to the presence of the DWI gear normal compasses were thought to be completely inoperable and recourse was to the use of the standard air-driven Gyro Direction Indicator (GDI). The GDI had to be set using a stretch of straight railway track laid out in the vicinity of the Manston base from which operations were conducted. Subsequently, P4 compasses were located in the aircraft tail well away from structural influences, doing away with dependence on the fallible GDI. After operations began a directional switch was installed which allowed a reversal of the direction of the coil's electrical current from the normal North-seeking thrust to South-seeking in order to detonate mines whose magnetism was so set. The two trial DWI Wellingtons (P2518 and P2521) carried out initial sweeps and were soon joined by the first Gypsy Six equipped Wellington DWI Mk.II (L4356) and plans were put into effect for a series of combined aircraft sweeps to increase the magnetic field. The rate of mine destruction was steady rather than spectacular and the inclusion of Wellington DWI Mk.IIs within the force was of definite advantage. In April a second GRU unit was formed and based at Bircham Newton in Norfolk. The operation of the generators produced heat discomfort for the actual operator, but the provision of air ducts did considerably reduce the temperature. Ducts were also used in cooling the smaller 48 foot diameter ring of the DWI Mk II. Since DWI aircraft were defenseless a fighter was assigned to protect, them with the Blenheims of 600 Squadron drawing the duty, however, in the event no recorded attack by the Luftwaffe was made. The enemy was advancing through the Low Countries and France in its successful May offensive. One of the Wellington DWI Mk Is (L4374) was detached on 20 May to the Middle East where its use after the Italian entry into the War was to lead to the conversion of several Mk IAs and a single Mk IC to DWI aircraft for sweeping duties around the Suez Canal. Parts were sent out from Britain for the conversions. Ironically, as the British advanced across the desert during 1942/43 DWI Wellingtons were used to sweep North African ports of not only German mines, but also of British mines!

The Type 409 IB did not enter production but the first of 2,685 Type 415 B.IC Pegasus XVIII powered versions began entering squadron service before the outbreak of war. Its airframe and systems in general formed the basis for later Marks. By now however, bombing by day had given way to night bombing only. Bitter experience revealed that the Vickers turrets had insufficient traverse, the 'dustbin' ventral turret was useless against beam attacks from above and self-sealing fuel tanks were essential.[1] In September 1940 Wellington production was at the rate of 134 a month and by the spring of 1941 was more than double this figure.

The B.IC was easily distinguishable by the addition of a pair of Vickers K machine-guns, installed to fire from each side of the fuselage, in place of the earlier ventral position; and the addition of larger main wheels which protruded from the engine nacelle when retracted. However, some problems remained. The Wellington IC required tremendous forward pressure on the control column to bring the nose down when going round again with flaps down. A characteristic of the Wellington was to drop its nose during turns.

The design of the Wellington II was begun in January 1938. Because of a delay in the production of the Merlin X, the prototype (L4250) finally flew on 3 March 1939. Armament was provided by Frazer-Nash turrets. By the end of the year the performance of the Mark II was superior to that of the IC. The Type 299 B.Mk.III prototype, with 1,400hp Bristol Hercules III engines-plants, flew for the first time on 16 May 1939. Both types entered production the following year as the Type 406 B.Mk.II and the Type 417 Mk III respectively and began service with Bomber Command in 1941. A total of 400 Mk.II Wellingtons was built and these were followed by 1,519 Mk.III models. A Mk.IC fitted with a pair of Pratt and Whitney R1830-S3C4-G Twin-Wasps was re-designated Type 410 to become the Mk IV prototype. A total of 220 production models were built. To increase Wellington production, Vickers established a new factory at Chester and later, another factory was producing the type at Squires Gate, Blackpool. Wellingtons were being produced at the rate of 134 a month in September 1940. By the spring of 1941 this had grown to more than double this figure.

A civil version of the Wellington was prepared as a design study for Mr. Nigel Norman of Airwork in May 1939 and in September of that year, two representatives of British Airways (the pre-war airline eventually merged with Imperial Airways to form BOAC) visited Weybridge to discuss a civil version for use on the West African route, with the possibility of an extension across the South Atlantic. Another study was submitted to the Air Ministry for a transport version, providing for a maximum of 13 troops without a navigator or, alternatively, 11 troops with a navigator. At that time the New Zealand Government was re-equipping its Air Force and ordered 18 Wellingtons.

Much has been made of the relative strength of the Wellington airframe but there were several accidents caused by outer mainplanes breaking away. During May 1942 Vickers co-operated with RAE Farnborough in an effort to improve the design of the main spar, which was prone to fatigue cracks. Eric Day, who was mostly involved with the Wellington Mk III at 91 Group Servicing Unit, recalls:

'In August 1943 we were suddenly posted to RAF Hemswell, Lines, which was temporarily closed while runways were being laid. 91 GSU were to be put into a unit of about 300 to work in groups of about seven men under a Corporal and supervised overall by civilians from Vickers on a big new mod, P1303, because of metal fatigue causing cracks in the main spar at the root of the main-plane where they joined the inner plane in the nacelle. All Wellingtons were to be checked, each OTU sending one aircraft and bringing back another when collecting the former. The procedure was as follows: with a Coles' crane in attendance the wings were removed. The aircraft was jacked up and the main wheels removed. A hefty beam of timber was bolted on to the oleos where the wheels had been, then the nacelle, complete with engine and propeller, was removed and stood aside, using a specially fabricated tubular metal tripod, which took the weight behind the propeller at the point of the engine reduction gear casing. The whole assembly would stand quite safely until rebuilding began. Imagine the amount of work involved in all this as everything had to be disconnected; flying controls, hydraulic, pneumatic, turret hydraulic, fuel pipes, etc, etc. Incidentally, when rebuilding it was sometimes extremely difficult to get all these items to line up and many four letter words were uttered. With the aircraft now lying around in very large pieces the Vickers men could examine the root end fixtures of main and inner planes using sophisticated optics and if anything appeared suspect, the wing would be written off and a brand new one fitted. A continuous supply of these was being delivered by the famous sixty feet long 'Queen Mary' vehicles.

'In many cases nothing sinister appeared. The main-spar was reinforced with a sleeve and taper pins. Wellington main-spars were based on tubular booms and were not box sectioned as on orthodox aircraft. After modification the aircraft was re-assembled and pushed out of the hangar six days later. The completed aircraft had to be thoroughly test flown. There was no telling how it would fly with its existing ailerons built into a new port or starboard wing, for example. The entire flying characteristics would be altered. We had Reception and Despatch flights for this purpose and from these the test flying was done. I went on quite a few test flights. We could only take off and land in one direction because of the runway construction. When major adjustments had to be made an aircraft would be test flown a second or even a third time. The entire P1303 job took the best part of a year to complete and this included a move to Upper Heyford when Hemswell became operational for Lancasters.

'When the Wellington was correctly rigged and in a stable flying condition it was a delightful aircraft. The control surfaces were actuated by push-pull rods which ran through roller guides at various stations in their travel. This gave a smooth and positive control, unlike the old method of using 15cwt steel cable running through fairleads and tensioned by turn-buckles. Of course, the Wellington was something of an oddity, or an in-between, coming as it did between the old Heyfords, Harrows and Hendons and the later, modern Lancasters and Halifaxes. The geodetic build was wonderful for lightness, strength and flexibility but the fabric covering was on a par with aircraft of World War I. There can be no doubt that stressed skin, monocoque construction, had to prevail for the new generation of aircraft. Nevertheless, the Wellington earned the laurels which it richly deserved. Viewed from the ground when in flight, a Wellington looked superb. The high aspect ratio wings gave it a graceful appearance. It was so adaptable it could be made to do almost anything, except tow a glider (for fear of stretching the fuselage like lazy tongs).'

The Wellington was often called the 'flying mod'. The most weird and wonderful mod of all had to be the high-altitude version. Late in 1939 Vickers produced two high-altitude prototypes in response to Air Ministry specification B.23/39, which called for the development of a high-altitude conversion of the Wellington. The specification stipulated that the type had to be capable of attaining an altitude of 40,000 feet, i.e., to put it out of reach of enemy flak and fighters. Both prototypes had a special cigar shaped fuselage with a pressurized cabin in the nose to simulate conditions at 10,000 feet. Originally, it was planned to fit two 1,650hp Bristol Hercules VIII engines but production difficulties dictated the use of the Hercules III power-plant.

The first of the two Mk.V prototypes (R3298) made its maiden flight in September 1940 and achieved a height of 30,000 feet. Only one Mk.V model (the second off the production lines) was completed and nineteen more were finished to Mk VI standard. Meanwhile, the first production aircraft was re-designed the Mk.VI prototype and as such, fitted with two 1,600 hp Rolls-Royce Merlin 60 RM6SM engines. In April 1941 this engine was bench tested with a two-stage supercharger. Without such a device, the Wellington had no chance of reaching the prescribed 40,000 feet.

On 19 August 1941 a further 100 VIs were ordered, although 56 were later cancelled. The majority of the survivors became VIs equipped with 'Gee' navigational systems. Late in March 1942 109 Squadron at Tempsford received four Wellington VIs - W5801, W5802, DR481 and DR285 - for commencement of trials with the 'Oboe' radar blind bombing device. Geoffrey MacFarlane, a wireless operator and 109 Squadron's first Signals Leader, flew with Squadron Leader Hal Bufton in W5801 on its first squadron air test on 30 March. He recalls:

'Flying in the Mk.VI was quite an experience in itself. It had a pressure chamber up forward, resembling a large boiler about five feet in diameter with a large valve at the front which had to be closed after the pilot, navigator and wireless operator (no gunner, naturally) had squeezed in through a just-large-enough, if we bent double, circular 'door' which had to be clamped closed with four very large and solid steel clips. Finally, a large wheel in the centre of the locking contraption had to be turned many times to close the main valve and so make the chamber airtight. Then pressure could be built up to a comfortable level. There was also a low cupola above the pilot's head out of which he only could just see - when the tail was down, so that taxiing was a rather 'hit or miss' affair. Getting out of the contraption in a hurry was seldom performed in less than 1½ minutes; then there was a forty-foot trot to the rear exit - hardly calculated to give one confidence in survival if the worst happened.

'Although the 'Oboe' blind bombing system was extraordinarily accurate it had two drawbacks, both related. Quite obviously the aircraft carrying the airborne component must be able to reach the Ruhr at least if it was able to be used to its full potential. Because of the frequencies on which it was operated and with the controlling ground stations in England (not until after D-Day could specially prepared mobile stations be deployed in Europe) a target range of at least

270 miles was a 'must'. High flying aircraft which could reach 30,000 feet plus were a minimum requirement. It was alleged that the VI was capable of reaching 35,000 feet with a load sufficient for our needs; cruising at 280 mph. (The VI underwent many changes and only by extending the wing by twelve feet was the Mk.VI finally able to reach the magic 40,000 feet.) My log book shows no record of any height reached in one above 30,000 feet, though I do have a vague recollection of once just making 32,000 feet.

'Our Wellingtons were fitted with the embryo airborne part of the Oboe system (nicknamed 'Broody Hen') thereby carrying out the initial trials of what later became the most accurate British blind bombing system of World War 2 when it was fitted to Pathfinder Mosquitoes of our squadron and 106 Squadron. Fortunately for us and for the two Oboe squadrons, a week before it was almost decided to use the Mk.VI operationally, it was rejected in favour of the Mosquito. The Mk.VI had proved too slow and had other disadvantages which made it unsuitable for use in the Oboe squadrons.'

During 1941 and 1942 109 Squadron (formerly the Wireless Intelligence Development Unit) was designated the Wireless Intelligence Special Duty Squadron. It had a number of different types of aircraft; all fitted with special radio intercept equipment. Wellingtons had been introduced in January 1941 and were used especially on the longer distance flights, both by day and by night. Geoffrey MacFarlane recalls: 'Wellingtons were invaluable in the radio-intercept role. These and Ansons were the main 'work-horses' of our squadron, which was the airborne unit initially tasked with finding and pinpointing German radio beams used in their blind bombing systems and other radio intercept duties which devolved upon us. On 8 May 1941 we were able to prove the existence of nine sites along the French coast of an advanced type of Fighter Control radar, capable of much greater accuracy than earlier models. This resulted in one, the site at Bruneval, being raided and dismantled by Combined Operations forces in 1942. We were also used in the interception of the German battleship Bismarck on 27 May 1941. Because the Wellington was such a rugged aircraft we were able to operate it in the radio countermeasures role, from late June 1941, for a few months in the Middle East with only one rigger as ground crew. Despite our best maintenance efforts, our port engine became so temperamental that we made several flights to Crete, Malta, Sicily and Gibraltar with the engine only about 25 per cent serviceable. On leaving Gibraltar for the UK when our detachment was over it became completely unserviceable but in spite of this we were able to fly for seven hours to Land's End on the other engine and were, I believe, the first Wellington to do this.'

Meanwhile, advances had been made in the technical field. Very early in the war Coastal Command had realised that its anti-submarine aircraft would need something more reliable than the quickly consumed flares they were using at night to illuminate U-boats during the last mile of the approach when ASV metre-wavelength radar was blind. As a result, in 1940 Squadron Leader Humphrey de Verde Leigh a personnel officer in Coastal Command was encouraged by the then Chief of Coastal Command, Air Chief Marshal Bowhill KCB CMG DSO, to develop the idea of an airborne searchlight. A pilot in the First World War, Leigh had flown many anti-submarine patrols and had experienced the frustrations of searching for the elusive underwater craft. Locating the U-boat had become considerably easier since the introduction of ASV radar; nevertheless, the difficulties of the last mile or two of the approach remained. The target simply dropped off the radar screen, leaving the aircrew literally in the dark. In October 1940 Leigh experimented with a 90cm searchlight in the nose or belly of a Wellington bomber because he knew that several Wimpys had been equipped with an extra motor and a heavy current generator to become the DWI Wellingtons used to explode magnetic mines. Leigh explained it all in a paper: 'The electrical generating equipment used in the DWI Wellingtons...consisted of either a Gipsy Queen engine and a 90kw generator or a Ford V-8 engine and a 35kw generator, either of which would give ample power for the searchlight... mounted in a swivel ring to allow at least 20 degrees downwards or sideways movement. The 15 cwt 90cm Army type searchlight as at present used for ground defence gives an effective beam of about 5,000 yards with 2 degrees dispersion. It is suggested that a searchlight of not less than this power...would be most suitable for this purpose.'[2] Despite early difficulties, Leigh had his prototype installation ready by January 1941.

The Royal Aircraft Establishment at Farnborough claimed that the type of searchlight specified by Leigh would be far too big to fit into a Wellington's turret - and tried to interest Bowhill in experiments carried out in 1928 with towed flares. Bowhill dismissed their suggestion out of hand and ordered Leigh to work full time on his idea. He soon abandoned the idea of using the 90cm searchlight, instead specifying the naval 24-inch, or 61cm, light. This could occupy the aperture in the floor of the Wellington fuselage originally intended for the 'dustbin' ventral gun position The Frazer Nash hydraulic-control-system gun turret was adapted to operate the searchlight so that the operator's eyes were six feet above the top of the four-degree-wide beam - later widened to twelve degrees - which could be steered from the nose of the aircraft. In March 1941 a Wellington began flight trials with ASV radar installed. After some disappointing trial runs against a RN submarine, Leigh occupied the bomb aimer's position, the ASV radar picked up the submarine and one mile from the target, Leigh switched on the light, left it on and found it quite simple to hold the beam on the target, clearly illuminating it. More trials followed. It was found that submarine crew could not hear the approaching aircraft until the last moments of the attack.

By May 1941 any weight problems were overcome by substituting batteries for the generator. The light would have to burn for only the final thirty seconds of an attack so Leigh replaced the motor-driven generator system, which was too large and too heavy, with a battery of seven standard 12-volt batteries, trickle-charged by a generator powered by the Wellington's engines. It weighed 600lb. However, the Leigh Light had a rival; the Turbinlite, which had been developed by Group Captain Helmore to illuminate enemy bombers during night raids over Britain. In mid-June 1941 Bowhill left to form Ferry Command and Air Chief Marshal Sir Philip B. Joubert de la Ferté KCB CMG DSO took over Coastal Command. He ordered Leigh to return to his duties as Assistant Personnel officer and asked for Helmore's invention to be installed on two ASV Wellingtons. The Turbinlite was thirteen times as powerful as Leigh's but it occupied the whole of the nose of the aircraft and required so much power that the batteries took up the whole bomb bay of a Douglas Boston. After two months Joubert found out that he had made a mistake. 'The Helmore Light was unnecessarily brilliant for use against U-boats and otherwise unsuitable. I then came to the conclusion that Leigh's light was preferable.' The operator had to switch on the light at the last possible moment just as the ASV reading was disappearing from the radar screen because the blip, which grows clearer up to about three quarters of a mile from the target, then becomes merged in the general returns from the sea's surface. The detached object was then trapped and held in the beam allowing the crew to release its bombs. At best, the device illuminated the target U-boat superbly, simultaneously dazzling its gunners and spoiling their aim. At worst, it dazzled the aircrew, leading to catastrophic crashes into the sea.[3]

The Leigh Light went into production but eighteen crucial months had elapsed between Leigh's original suggestion and the first use of the device on operations. On 7 August Joubert called for six Wellingtons and six Catalinas to be fitted with the Leigh Light. Three months later he called for another thirty Wellingtons to be so equipped. However, the Air Ministry had misgivings and needed the guarantee of successful trials by the first six Wellingtons before it would sanction more suitably equipped aircraft. Under pressure from Joubert they finally agreed, in February 1942, to the formation of a full squadron of Leigh Light Wellingtons. In April 1417 Flight at Chivenor was expanded to become 172 Squadron but suitably equipped aircraft were slow to arrive. By May the squadron could only call upon five Wellingtons.

In the spring of 1942 the first Wellington GR.VIIIs entered service with Coastal Command. Just over two years earlier, ICs had taken part in maritime operations for the first time when Wellington DWIs, fitted with 48 feet diameter dural hoops, had been employed in exploding enemy magnetic mines at sea. Altogether, 394 GR.VIIIs were built. As on the Mk IC the type was powered by the Bristol Pegasus XVIII engines. The GR.VIII differed from the Mk IC in being the first to be equipped with ASV.II radar and fitted with radar masts on top of the fuselage. Some versions also carried Leigh Lights. The GR.VIII was subsequently joined in Coastal Command service by a series of more advanced marks of Wellington. 180 XIs, built at Squires Gate, were followed on the production lines by 843 XIII models. 58 XII versions were produced at Chester and Weybridge. Squires Gate and Chester turned out a further 841 XIVs. Altogether, 3,406 Wellingtons were built at Blackpool, with the last leaving the production lines on 13 October 1945.

Both the XI and XII versions were powered by Hercules VI or XVI power-plants and carried no nose turret or radar masts on top of the fuselage. ASV Mk.III radar was housed in a chin radome beneath the nose. Beneath the wing provision was made for two 18-inch torpedoes and a retractable Leigh Light was installed in the bomb bay. ASV.II radar and masts and the nose turret were re-introduced on the XIII, which was fitted with two Bristol Hercules XVII engines. The final general reconnaissance version, the XIV, differed little from the XII but was powered by Hercules XVII engines. Some Coastal Command Wellingtons served as 'flying class-rooms' after conversion to T.XVII and T.XVIII standard.

The Wellington X, which entered service with RAF Bomber Command in 1943, was the final bomber version to see service in World War II and was the most-produced model of all. An improved version of the B.III, it was powered by two 1,675hp Bristol Hercules XVI engines and 3,804 examples were built. Flown by a crew of four or five, it had a twin-gun nose turret, a four-gun rear turret and sometimes carried two beam guns; bomb-load was 4,000lb. At one time the Wellington X equipped 25 OTUs (Operational Training Units) and the type saw widespread service in the Middle East. Post-war, the Wellington X was employed on training duties with no armament fitted for eight years until finally replaced by the Vickers Varsity, the veteran Wellingtons then being returned to Maintenance Command for disposal as scrap. The B.X had a maximum speed of 255 mph. Nos. 99 and 215 Squadron in India operated the Wellington X against Japanese targets and during the battle of Imphal in April-May 1944 they ferried much needed bombs to Hurricane fighter-bomber squadrons on the Imphal Plain. During August and September 1944, 99 and 215 Squadrons converted to the Liberator.

In 2nd Tactical Air Force 69 Squadron was unique in that it used Wellingtons for photo-reconnaissance at night. One cannot complete the Wellington's diversity of wartime operations without a mention of the role played by the Mk XV and XVI (most of which were converted from Mk ICs) in Transport Command. Their bomb bays were sealed and none carried armament.

In total, four aircraft that embodied geodetic construction were designed by Vickers, starting with the Wellesley and ending with the oval-section, all metal-bodied twin-engined Viking passenger airliner which initially embodied the Wellington's geodetic wing. The two other types, originally conceived as heavy bombers, were designed in parallel with the Wellington. The Warwick, a larger development of the Wellington, was first flown on 13 August 1939 and was powered by the troublesome Rolls-Royce Vulture engines. It did not enter into RAF service until spring 1945 and Pratt & Whitney Double Wasp and later, the Bristol Centaurus replaced the Vultures. A total of 843 Warwicks was built at Weybridge.

Fourth and last of the wholly geodetic line was the four-engined Windsor bomber, which first flew on 23 October 1943. An altogether novel and capacious aircraft, it included four main landing gear units, sparless wings and 20mm cannon in two remotely-controlled rearward-firing nacelle barbettes with a tail gunner's sighting station. Just three Windsors - all prototypes - flew and a fourth was almost complete when the programme was cancelled soon after the war ended.

With the end of hostilities Wellingtons soon all but completely disappeared from the RAF inventory, as L. W. Collett, an RAF regular since 1938, recalls: 'At the end of the war hundreds and hundreds of Wellingtons were flown to Little Rissington (not far from Cirencester) for disposal. They were better than the ones we had at Wellesbourne and we used to go and rob bits and pieces off them to maintain our serviceability.'

Several Wellington Xs were revamped by Boulton Paul for extended service as crew trainers with Flying Training Command. This version was known as the T.10 (one of which is on permanent display at the RAF Museum, Hendon) and earned the distinction of being the last Wellington in RAF service. The last Wellington T 10 was finally struck off charge in 1953. Both the T.10 and the T.19 were superseded in the Air Navigation Schools and at 201 Advanced Flying School at Swinderby by the Vickers Valetta T 3 and the Vickers Varsity respectively.

Vickers had started work on the design of the VC1 (Vickers Commercial One) as the Viking was originally known (the same name as the amphibian which was Vickers first complete post-World War I design) in the late autumn of 1944. The Viking was the first British post war airliner to fly, on 22 June 1945. After 19 Vikings had been built, a switch was made to all stressed-skin construction, but the Bristol Hercules remained the standard power plant of all Vikings, production of which eventually totalled 163. The Nene-powered Viking was the world's first jet transport and in July 1948 it was flown from Heathrow to Villacoublay, near Paris, in 34 minutes 7 seconds at a mean speed of 384mph - a record for a civilian transport aircraft. A redesign of the Viking led to the Valetta for the RAF - a machine first flown in June 1947 and which was really 'five aeroplanes in one' because it was capable of quick conversion to a troop carrier, freighter, ambulance, glider tug or paratroop transport. The Valletta was followed by the Varsity 'flying classroom', a specialised crew trainer which took the place of the Wellington T Mark 10, but on an expanded scale. In general it followed the lines of the Viking and Valetta but it differed in having a tricycle undercarriage, increased length and wingspan and a bomb-aiming pannier beneath the fuselage.

For seventeen years the Wimpy earned the undying affection of its air and ground crews. During the Second World War no other British bomber was built in greater numbers and the 11,461st and final Wellington, a T.10 built at Squires Gate, Blackpool, was delivered on 13 October 1945. No other RAF bomber saw greater and more widespread service. The Wellington's place in aviation history is thus assured.

Footnotes

1   When war was declared on 3 September 1939 No.3 Group of RAF Bomber Command was equipped with Wellington Mk Is and IAs in East Anglia and consisted of eight Squadrons (9, 37, 38, 99, 115, 149 and two Reserve Squadrons: 214 and 215). On 4 September fourteen Wellingtons of 9 and 149 Squadrons raided Brünsbuttel where two German warships had been reported by air reconnaissance. Bad weather and heavy anti-aircraft fire interfered with the action and two aircraft, which had penetrated 'the harbour, were lost. Others failed to locate the target while the bombs which did score hits were ineffective. In addition there was an embargo imposed by the War Cabinet on attacks on other than strictly military targets, which precluded the bombing of enemy ships in harbours, for fear of injuring civilians in the vicinity. On 3 December 24 Wellingtons attacked units of the German fleet at Heligoland from 'high' level in cloud, with almost negative results on either side. This action was taken to confirm that Wellingtons, could penetrate strongly defended areas but on 14 December when 12 Wellingtons of 99 Squadron penetrated the Schillig Roads near Wilhelmshaven at low level, five were lost and one crashed when almost home. Four days later when 24 Wellingtons attempted an attack on the German fleet and naval bases in the Schillig Roads and Wilhelmshaven over half the force was lost.
2   'In Great Waters: The Epic Story of the Battle of the Atlantic 1939-45' by Spencer Dunmore (Pimlico 2001)/ Aircraft versus Submarine by Alfred Price (William Kimber 1973).
3   Toward the end of the war, a Canadian pilot, John Brooks of Toronto, was still undergoing operational training over the North Sea when his ASV operator picked up a target. It seemed to be a good opportunity to practise the use of the Leigh light. Flying at low level, Brooks approached the target and at the appropriate moment switched on his Leigh light - to be confronted by the sight of Queen Mary, her immense hull filling his windshield. For an electric moment, he pictured himself crashing full tilt into the Allies' most valuable troop carrier. Applying full power, Brooks just managed to drag the sluggish Wellington over the huge ship's mast-tops.

Chapter 1

Opening Gambit

'Sometime during the early summer we were completely re-equipped, the Hendons disappeared and 115 Squadron received their Wimpys - a name for the Wellingtons that was to become universal.'
E. C. 'Johnnie' Johnson, Aircraftsman 1st Class, Fitter 2.

It was the first week in January 1939 when the bus from King's Lynn in North Norfolk deposited Aircraftsman 1st Class, Fitter 2, E. C. 'Johnnie' Johnson, complete with all his kit, including a very heavy kit bag, outside the guardroom at RAF Marham nine miles southeast of the coastal town. Construction of the aerodrome had begun in 1935 when the RAF expansion programme began. It was envisaged that a home-based force of 68 bomber and 35 fighter squadrons be ready by March 1937. One third of the bomber force was to equip with aircraft capable of reaching targets in the Ruhr from British aerodromes. In February 1936 fresh plans called for a front line force of 1,736 aircraft by 1939 and it was to include twenty heavy bomber squadrons. Modern aerodromes had to be constructed for the new bomber squadrons and Marham was one of these. The aerodrome opened as planned on 1 April 1937, as a heavy bomber station in 3 Group, Bomber Command. Marham was 19-year old 'Johnnie' Johnson's first adult RAF station. He had joined the Royal Air Force in 1936 as an aircraft apprentice and completed his three-year apprenticeship at No.1 School of Technical Training, RAF Halton and was now qualified on both engines and airframes. Marham in 1939 housed two Squadrons, 38 Squadron equipped with twin-engined Fairey Hendons, the RAF's first all-metal low-wing monoplane bomber, powered with two Rolls-Royce Kestrels and 115 Squadron with Handley Page Harrows. 38 Squadron was the only squadron ever to be equipped with Hendons and it was the RAF's first monoplane bomber. 'Johnnie' Johnson thought that it looked 'a large clumsy looking beast with a tall spatted undercarriage.'[4]

When 38 Squadron had first arrived at Marham on 5 May 1937 from Mildenhall they had been equipped with Handley Page Heyford biplane bombers. In June 38 Squadron's 'B' Flight was used to form 115 Squadron, which used some of 38 Squadron's Hendons to become operational until deliveries of Handley Page Harrow Is and IIs began. Even so the Hendon and the Harrow were vast improvements on the types that had soldiered on in RAF service long after World War One ended. 'Marham, after the last three years of rigid discipline of Halton, was to us heaven on earth' Johnnie' Johnson continues. 'We were gradually absorbed into the Squadron and worked regular hours and had most evenings and weekends off. So passed two or three months and life was very pleasant. It was really like being a member of an exclusive and free and easy flying club. Changes were in the air but how fast and far-reaching and how long-lasting they were to turn out; we had at that time no idea. The first change was a rumour soon to become a fact that 38 Squadron was to be re-equipped with Wellingtons and we would say goodbye to the lumbering old Hendons.[5] With the rumblings of war, the news was greeted with great pleasure. Not least by the pilots and aircrew, who were only too aware that their chances of survival in a modern war would be very slim indeed, in their old underpowered machines, with World War One Lewis guns for their defence. The news was also welcomed by us ex-apprentices because we had been trained on hydraulics, retractable undercarriages and radial engines and were now on a par with our long-serving colleagues to whom all these modem innovations were very strange and new.'[6]

Nos. 38 and 115 Squadrons spent two years working up and taking part in the pre-war exercises. In December 1938, 38 Squadron re-equipped with Wellington I bombers. 115 Squadron followed them in April 1939. 'Johnnie' Johnson remembers the arrival of the Wellingtons.

'Very soon the first Wellington Mk Is started to trickle in. Some of the landings left a great deal to be desired as the aircraft could bounce quite high if dropped too hard on the final flare-out. One of the early arrivals forgot he had a retractable undercarriage and landed without lowering it - although it's difficult to understand how he managed to ignore the loud klaxon horn that blew in his ear whenever the engines were throttled back with the wheels up. But he managed it! Sometime during the early summer we were completely re-equipped, the Hendons disappeared and 115 Squadron received their Wimpys - a name for the Wellingtons that was to become universal.[7] Indications of the coming war became stronger as summer went on. In August hundreds of reservists were called up and posted to Marham. The camp became crowded, tents appeared, the NAAFI canteen bulged at the seams - we'd always been served with tablecloths, cups, saucers and spoons and enjoyed personal service by the staff but with the sudden influx this obviously couldn't continue. Gradually the cloths and saucers disappeared and even broken beer glasses couldn't be replaced quickly enough. At times we were reduced to drinking out of jam jars. The exclusive flying club atmosphere was fast disappearing!'

During the evening of Wednesday, 23 August 1939 RAF units in Great Britain and abroad were secretly placed on a war footing and mobilization of the Auxiliary Air Force and 3,000 members of the Volunteer Reserve was begun. The British public, probably aware they were enjoying the last days of an August at peace for some time to come, went about their business knowing they too would soon be called into the Services. The fragile peace was quickly shattered during the early hours of 1 September. Poland was invaded by German armoured divisions supported by the Luftwaffe employing

'Blitzkrieg' ('lightning war') tactics developed from experience gained during the Spanish Civil War, 1936-39. In Britain full mobilization followed while units of Coastal Command began flying patrols over the North Sea. At bomber bases camouflage was liberally applied to buildings and aircraft alike and brown tape was stuck over every pane of glass in criss-cross patterns.

'I suppose the first effect of the war was that the aircraft were no longer put in the hangars at the end of flying each day' 'Johnnie' Johnson recalls. Daily inspections and rectifications were no longer undertaken in reasonable comfort, but carried out on the tarmac. Another shock was the appearance of a few WAAF mechanics who at that time, it seemed to us, were extremely toffee-nosed and never spoke to anyone below the rank of Squadron Leader. It was also around this time that our aircraft were returned to the manufacturers to have hydraulically powered gun turrets fitted in the nose and tail - then to be known as Mk ICs. Authority then decided that the aircraft lined up on the tarmac were very vulnerable to bombing and initiated a dispersal policy. Whoever thought of the idea of dispersing the aircraft every day to Little Rissington in Gloucestershire was obviously taking no chances! A one-and-a-half hour flight every evening for every serviceable aircraft was indeed dispersal! The disadvantages of this system soon became evident. Some pilots got lost and landed all over the place and then one of our aircraft landed at Rissington with a defective engine. On the day that this happened I'd been in bed less than an hour when I was shaken awake by the Sergeant engine fitter with the words, 'Get up and get dressed. I want you' and he named another couple of engine fitters, 'to go to Rissington to do an engine change'. We spent a large part of the rest of that night loading up a replacement engine with all the tools and equipment required, onto a lorry and in the early hours of the morning headed west to Gloucestershire. After what seemed to be endless hours of travelling, we refuelled at a nameless army base somewhere in Buckinghamshire and arrived in the Cotswolds at Rissington. With stops only for food we carried on with the removal of the defective engine, which took most of that day. Later on in the war we could do the same job in about quarter of the time. We then prepared the new engine, transferring the necessary components from the old engine, hoisted it up, bolted it into position, reconnected all the pipes and controls and locked all the connections, re-checked them and declared all ready for a test run. It was now full daylight on the second or was it the third day? We were too tired to be sure. We pushed the aircraft out and carried out a successful test run, refitted the cowlings, summoned the pilot and saw him off back to Marham. We then re-crated the bad engine, loaded up all the equipment, cleared up all the spilt oil, climbed aboard the lorry and headed back to Marham ourselves.

'It was obvious that dispersal required a rethink. Almost immediately, bulldozers appeared and opened up gaps in the hedges in the fields adjoining the aerodrome in the vicinity of what was then the bomb dump and thus began Marham's expansion. Aircraft were dispersed in these fields during daylight hours for servicing and refuelling. As winter advanced, my most vivid memory of this era is the cold and the mud. The mud was the worst, the aircraft bogged down, the petrol bowsers bogged down, lorries bogged down and they all had to be dug out. We were permanently covered with mud - eventually we had to have tractors fitted with tracks to move anything.

'The winter of 1939 and the early months of 1940 were subsequently known as the 'Phoney War'. Day after day our aircraft were loaded with bombs, stood by and were then unloaded. However, we loaded millions upon millions of leaflets into the aircraft to be dispersed from the flare chute, together with the odd house brick, that we put in for the sleeping 'fatherland'. In retrospect, neither the leaflets nor the house bricks seemed to do much good.

'On the camp itself another aspect of the war had made itself felt. Overnight all the airmen flying on operations were made up to Sergeant - airman one day, Sergeant the next. Imagine the effect of this on the Sergeants' Mess! It is doubtful if at that time any of its regular members had less than eighteen years' service and then overnight they were swamped with large numbers of youngsters, to whom Mess tradition mattered a lot less than tomorrow's bombing target. The exclusive flying club had gone forever. Meanwhile Marham was still expanding. 115 Squadron had opened up its own fields for dispersal and metal tracking had been laid down to combat the mud - servicing outside had become the norm. Reservists and National Service men had come to swell the ranks of both ground and aircrew and regular working hours and regular meals were definitely things of the past. It fell to the fitters and riggers to guard the aerodrome, on top of their other duties. I often patrolled alone around the bomb dump on the blacked-out station in the early hours of the morning, hoping that 'Jerry' wouldn't choose this moment to drop a bomb on it. We had had no experience of enemy bombs so we didn't know quite what to expect.'

At the outbreak of war the overall strength of Bomber Command stood at 55 squadrons. On paper this sounds a respectable figure but by the end of September it had been pared down to 23 home-based first-line squadrons. These consisted of six squadrons of Bristol Blenheim IV light bombers of 2 Group and six squadrons of Wellington Is and IAs of 3 Group (with two in reserve) stationed in East Anglia. The rest of the force comprised five squadrons of Whitleys of 4 Group based in Yorkshire and six squadrons of Handley Page Hampdens of 5 Group in Lincolnshire. Wellingtons were first-line equipment for 9 Squadron at Honington, Suffolk; 37 Squadron at Feltwell, Norfolk; 99 and 149 Squadrons at Mildenhall and Newmarket, Suffolk respectively and 38 and 115 Squadrons at Marham, Norfolk while 214 (Federated Malay States) Squadron and 215 Squadron (at Methwold) were similarly equipped in Reserve. On 1 June 1939 1 RNZAF Unit had begun forming at Marham to fly Wellingtons. A decision had been taken early in 1937 that the New Zealanders would have a complement of thirty Wellingtons, six of which would be ready to leave for the antipodes in August 1939. When war clouds gathered the New Zealanders were put at the disposal of the RAF and the unit moved to RAF Harwell where it became 15 OTU. Under the RAF Bomber Command 'Scatter' plan, the majority of bomber squadrons were immediately dispersed to satellite bases. For instance, Wellingtons of 115 Squadron were sent to the satellite airfield at Barton Bendish. By 2 September all of 99 Squadron's Wellingtons had been moved to the famous Rowley Mile racecourse on Newmarket Heath. The famous racecourse had been used as a landing ground for aircraft in World War I. HRH the Prince of Wales landed at the strip in 1935 before travelling by road to attend the Jubilee Review at Mildenhall. After the Munich Crisis, in 1938, the Air Ministry took an interest in the area as a satellite for bombers at RAF Mildenhall. The Rowley Mile course - 2,500 yards in an east-west direction - in about 300 acres north of the Beacon Course and Cambridge Hill provided the longest grass landing and take-off runs in Britain. A Wellington IA filled with 1,500lb of bombs and 720 gallons of fuel required a 1,080-yard run to become airborne which left little margin for error. Using the Rowley Mile strip a Wellington IA could operate safely carrying 2,000lb of bombs. Although long and flat, crews had to remember to hurdle the twenty foot high Devil's Dyke running along one boundary. Accommodation for air and ground crews was in the racecourse administration buildings, the grandstand and requisitioned housing locally until new huts could be built.

'Johnnie' Johnson recalls.[8]

'Memories of flying club days were by now a very distant dream. For night-time dispersal the aircraft were flown into a large field about three miles away at Barton Bendish. More cold and more mud. Starting the engines at Barton Bendish after they had stood out all night in the middle of winter was quite an experience and required a special and a very, very unofficial technique. The Pegasus engine was primed for starting by pumping raw petrol into the top three cylinders, by means of a key gas pump fitted to the aircraft. The engine oil was of course by now thick and viscous, so that the trolley batteries could hardly turn the engine. The trick was to get the engine to backfire into the carburettor, where it would ignite surplus petrol in the air intake, let it burn for the requisite number of seconds to warm up the carburettor and then extinguish it by placing your forage cap over the intake. All engine fitter forage caps had singe marks on them! If you misjudged it, you stood a good chance of burning up the whole aircraft but usually it worked pretty well.

'All stories, even non-fiction so I'm told, should contain an element of tragedy and romance, to hold the attention of the reader. The tragedy occurred on the afternoon of 5 November 1939. A close friend of mine, John Bailey, who was one of the ex-apprentices who came with us to Marham, was one of six riggers detailed aboard a Wimpy being dispersed at Barton Bendish. It was not his aircraft but for some reason its own ground crew couldn't go to cover it up and tie it down as was the normal procedure. Ten minutes after take-off we saw in the distance, in the general direction of the dispersal, a towering column of thick black smoke. It was obvious that the aircraft had crashed. Later it appeared that the pilot, indulging in a bit of low flying, had hit a tree with his tail and the aircraft crashed in flames burning and killing everyone on board.[9] Imagine my feelings when a few days later, together with another mutual friend, we escorted John's coffin to his home in Beccles. Here we found his grieving family and the undertaker, waiting in the sitting room with another coffin, to which the body was to be transferred, in front of them all. How I conveyed to the undertaker that injuries sustained in a crash in flames made it inadvisable to carry this out, I don't know. I was just nineteen years old, but I think I grew quite old that day.[10]

'Flying in those days was subject to virtually no restrictions whatsoever. Providing the flight was authorised by the Flight Commander or his Deputy, a pilot could take off and go more or less anywhere he wished. The favourite pastime was hedgehopping. Many times I have stood just behind the pilot, flying below the level of the Norfolk hedges, waiting for him to lift the aircraft above the line of trees rushing towards us and dropping it down the other side. It was a breathtaking thrill, but then we were all very young and foolish. In later years, when I could appreciate how little flying training some of those pilots had done, I shudder at the risks we took.'

On the afternoon of 2 September ten squadrons of Fairey Battles flew to France to take up their position as part of the Advanced Air Striking Force. It was a sombre Neville Chamberlain, the British Prime Minister, who announced his country's declaration of war over the air on the BBC the following morning, 3 September. His resigned tones had barely vanished into the ether when reconnaissance revealed German warships leaving Wilhelmshaven. At 1700 hours an order was sent to RAF Mildenhall for twelve Wellingtons of 99 Squadron to be made ready to attack them. No Wellingtons could be airborne until 1830 hours and then only three aircraft were operational. They took off but bad weather and oncoming darkness forced them to abort. They returned to Suffolk after jettisoning their bomb loads in the North Sea. It was evident that the RAF was not fully prepared for an immediate strike at the enemy. The President of the United States, Franklin D. Roosevelt, had appealed to the belligerent nations to refrain from unrestricted aerial bombardment of civilians. The British heeded this request but the RAF was prevented from using a direct passage to the German industrial heartland because of the strict neutrality of both Holland and Belgium. France also requested that Bomber Command did not attack land targets in Germany for fear of reprisal raids on French cities, which her bombers could not deter nor her fighters protect.

The only way to carry the war to Germany, then, was to make attacks on German capital ships. The task of bombing the German Fleet fell, therefore, to the Bristol Blenheim light bombers of 2 Group and Wellingtons of 3 Group in East Anglia, which were ideally placed to attack installations in the Heligoland Bight. However, British War Cabinet policy decreed that no civilian casualties were to be caused as a direct result of the bombing. RAF Bomber Command could strike at ships at sea or underway but vessels moored in harbours were not to be bombed for fear of injuring 'innocent' civilians. Plans were laid for the first RAF raid of the war to take place during the afternoon of 4 September. While fifteen unescorted Blenheims took off for a strike on the *Admiral von Scheer* at Wilhelmshaven, eight Wellingtons of 9 Squadron and six Wellingtons of 149 Squadron, also without escort, flew on over the North Sea towards Brünsbuttel. Their targets were the battle cruisers *Scharnhorst* and *Gneisenau*, which had earlier been spotted by a Blenheim reconnaissance aircraft from RAF Wyton. Squadron Leader Paul Harris was leading 149 Squadron this day. En route Harris ordered his gunners to test fire their Brownings. He was startled to discover that not one gun was in working order! However, not wishing to miss the first action of the war, he decided to press on to the target. Unfortunately, bad weather added to the problems beset by the crews and five of his squadron were forced to return early. Harris lost sight of the two remaining aircraft in thick cloud. As he flew over Tonning, his Wellington took a direct flak hit. Harris' bomb aimer aimed his bombs at a bridge over the Eder and turned for home. Harris nursed the ailing aircraft the 300 miles back to England and landed at Mildenhall six and a quarter hours after taking off.

Meanwhile, 9 Squadron had fared little better. Three Wellingtons, led by Flight Lieutenant Peter Grant, managed to reach the German battleships amid fierce anti-aircraft fire but although they succeeded in dropping their bombs, none struck the ships. A further three Wellingtons which succeeded in penetrating the harbour were attacked by Messerschmitt Bf 109s and two of the bombers were shot down. The day's losses reached seven when five Blenheims failed to return. Debriefing revealed that some aircraft had failed to find the warships. One crew mistook the River Elbe for the Kiel Canal and one even dropped two bombs on Esbjerg. Crews that had scored hits on the vessels had discovered to their dismay that the general-purpose bombs, fused for eleven seconds delay, had simply bounced off the armoured decks and fell into the sea without exploding. The only casualties suffered by the German Navy occurred when a stricken Blenheim crashed into the bows of the cruiser Emden. Despite the losses, 3 Group prepared for another shipping attack the following day, 5 September. Plans were quickly scrapped, however, when it was feared that the Luftwaffe was about to launch an all-out attack on bomber stations in East Anglia. The 'Blackout Scheme' was put into effect and squadrons were sent to safety further afield. 149 Squadron, for instance, flew their Wellingtons to Netheravon in Wiltshire and did not return to East Anglia until 15 September.

During a temporary respite from the shooting war the Wellington crews of 9 and 149 Squadrons licked their wounds while others carried the war, albeit tentatively, to the enemy. On the night of 8 September 99 Squadron flew its first operation when three Wellingtons were dispatched to drop propaganda leaflets over Hannover. One aircraft was forced to abort but the other two successfully completed the operation. The Wellington and Blenheim crews were rested while Hampden squadrons bore the brunt of bombing raids in East Anglia. Ground crews used the time to iron out the bugs and eliminate teething troubles inherent in the Wellington IA, which had been introduced almost overnight into squadron service.

A combination of bad weather and the lack of suitable targets as dictated by War Cabinet policy delayed squadrons from using their new Wellington IAs and during the next few weeks on several occasions aircraft took part in sweeps over the North Sea. Otherwise, they were mainly occupied in bombing and firing practice and formation exercises, some of them in co-operation with fighter squadrons. In 1939 the officially accepted theory was that fighters had such a small speed advantage over the 'modern' bomber that any attack must become a stern chase. It was also accepted that fighters attacking a section of bombers flying in 'Vic' would attack in 'Vic' formation. On 30 October three Wellington crews practiced evasive flying with fighters of 66 Squadron near

Honington. At 800 feet, just below the cloud base, the leading Wellington I, flown by Squadron Leader Lennox Lamb and a second Wellington flown by Flying Officer John Chandler collided. The propellers of Lamb's Wellington tore through the rear fuselage of Chandler's aircraft below, completely severing the tail unit, which spun away like a falling leaf. Chandler's tail-less Wellington then reared up into a steep climb, turned over onto its back and struck the leader's Wellington again with its port wing. Both aircraft plunged earthwards. Chandler's Wellington crashed against a large tree and caught fire on impact while Lamb's machine dived nose first into a dyke and completely disintegrated. Both landed less than fifty feet apart in marshy ground near Sapiston Water Mill, only three quarters of a mile from the Honington runway. All nine airmen from the two Wellingtons were killed in the tragedy. However, Sergeant Smith had cheated death. He had climbed aboard Lamb's aircraft and had taken his usual place in the rear turret but Flying Officer Peter Torkington-Leech, who was a South African, had come back and said that he would be rear gunner for the exercise. Smith had decided that if he could not be rear gunner he would not fly at all and promptly got out of the aircraft and returned to the crew room. The new Flight Commander was Squadron Leader Archibald Guthrie.

Meanwhile, the Air Ministry planners were still of the opinion that close-knit formations of Wellingtons, with their healthy defensive armament, could survive everything the enemy could throw at them and penetrate heavily defended targets. Recent heavy losses in British merchant shipping and pressure from Winston Churchill, the First Lord of the Admiralty, in particular, prompted the War Cabinet to order Bomber Command to mount, as soon as possible, 'a major operation with the object of destroying an enemy battle-cruiser or pocket battleship'. However, the directive added, 'no bombs are to be aimed at warships in dock or berthed alongside the quays'. The War Cabinet wanted no German civilian casualties. During the late afternoon of 2 December 1939, 115 and 149 Squadrons at Marham and Mildenhall were alerted that a strike would be mounted against two German cruisers moored off Heligoland. Immediately, 24 Wellington IAs were bombed up with four 500lb SAP (Semi Armour Piercing) bombs and 620 gallons of fuel, ready for a strike early the following morning. Leading the attack would be 34-year-old Wing Commander Richard Kellett AFC, a distinguished pre-war aviator, now Commanding Officer of 149 Squadron.[11]

On the morning of 3 December the weather had improved and at 0900 hours Kellett led his twelve Wellingtons off in four flights of three. He rendezvoused with three Wellingtons on 38 Squadron and nine on 115 Squadron from Marham and the force flew out over the North Sea towards Heligoland in four 'battle formations' of six Wimpys each.[12] At the head of the bomber force Kellett positioned his section well out in front. Following some distance behind and leading the remainder, was Squadron Leader Paul Harris. Off to his right and a little way behind and leading the remainder flew the third section led by a young Canadian, Flight Lieutenant J. B. Stewart. The fourth section, led by Flight Lieutenant A. G. Duguid, flew directly behind Stewart. Two cruisers were spotted at anchor in the roads between the two tiny rock outcrops that are Heligoland in the German Bight. Kellett prepared to attack from up sun. As a result of the early losses, the bombing altitude had been raised to 7,000 feet (considered 'high level' bombing altitude at this time). Harris claimed hits on one of the warships and Stewart attacked a large merchantman anchored outside the harbour but a cloud obscured the targets and results were unconfirmed.

Although 'Freya' radar had warned the German gunners of the impending raid the thick cloud at their bombing altitude fortunately had hidden the Wellingtons from view. Four Messerschmitt Bf 109Ds of 1 Gruppe Zerstörergecshwader 26 at Jever led by Hauptmann Dickore climbed and intercepted the bombers after they had bombed but their aim was spoiled by cloudy conditions. Even so, the two pairs of Bf 109Ds damaged two of the Wellingtons in the attack. One pair attacked from above and the other pair from below. Leutnant Günther Specht, who damaged one of the Wellingtons, was shot down by return fire from Corporal Copley the rear gunner on Sergeant Odoire's Wellington on 38 Squadron. One of the rounds from Specht's machine guns actually hit and lodged in the belt buckle of Copley's harness without injuring him. Specht ditched in the sea and he was later rescued. The German had been wounded in the face and later had to have his left eye removed.[13] Luckily for the Wellington crews, the three remaining Bf 109Ds were low on fuel and they broke off the engagement, while sixteen Bf 109D/Es and eight of I./ZG 26's new Bf 110Cs arrived too late to intercept the bombers.

Again the bombs were to fail miserably, although an enemy minesweeper was claimed sunk when one bomb went clean through the bottom of the vessel without exploding. It was however, a trawler, formerly the *Johann Schulte*, which did sink to the bottom. Back at the RAF bases hopes ran high now that the bombers had penetrated enemy air space, duelled with the Luftwaffe and escaped unscathed. These hopes were to be short-lived.

On 13 December, ten days after the disastrous RAF raid on Heligoland, running silent and deep the Royal Navy submarine HMS *Salmon* spotted the German cruisers *Nürnburg* and *Leipzig* in the cold waters of the North Sea. *Salmon* stalked its prey and fired a salvo of torpedoes, hitting the two cruisers. The submarine scurried away leaving the German ships to limp back to Wilhelmshaven. Coastal Command contacted Bomber Command to send bombers to finish them off. Flares were loaded into the Wellingtons for a night attack but this was later cancelled. By dawn the following day a force of Hampdens had taken off to intercept the battle squadron but they returned to base without having spotted the enemy. An armed reconnaissance by twelve Wellingtons on 99 Squadron at Newmarket Heath was ordered. Each aircraft carried three 500lb semi-armour piercing bombs and any large battle cruisers or cruisers seen were to be bombed if the weather allowed the aircraft to reach a height of 2,000 feet. Leading the formation were Squadron Leader Andrew 'Square' McKee, the New Zealander pilot[14] and the CO Wing Commander J. F. Griffiths. The formation, which consisted of four sections of three aircraft each, took off from Newmarket at 1143 hours and set course for Great Yarmouth. There the visibility was down to two miles just below 10/10ths cloud and crews peered into the thick sea haze in a vain search for a horizon. The weather deteriorated even further and at 1305 hours, when the formation reached the Dutch coast, the Wellingtons were flying at 600 feet in fine rain.

Griffiths altered course in the direction of Heligoland in order to give the enemy flak ships the impression that Heligoland was the objective. The weather continued to worsen and the formation was now down to just 300 feet. At 1347 hours course was altered for the Schillig Roads near Wilhelmshaven. Visibility was down to half a mile and the Wellingtons were now flying at only 200 feet. Despite the weather conditions the aircraft maintained a good formation and they flew on towards Wangerooge Island. They were spotted by five stationary trawlers, one of which fired off a red signal flare. Shortly afterwards a submarine was sighted and also fired a red flare. The leader replied by firing two red signal cartridges in rapid succession on the off chance that this might be the recognition signal. The submarine immediately did a crash dive and the formation turned on a north-easterly course.

At 1425 hours the *Leipzig* and *Nürnburg* were sighted. Griffiths attempted to carry out an examination to assess any possible torpedo damage but the fast closing speeds made this impossible. Griffiths swung the formation around and was about to try again when eight cargo boats were sighted. Immediately, they opened fire on the Wellingtons. A minute later three destroyers steamed up directly under Griffiths' bomber and opened fire. The Wellingtons were only 200 feet off the water and a barrage of light anti-aircraft fire from the ships below buffeted crews. Five minutes after the destroyers had opened fire, the *Leipzig* and *Nürnburg* added their pom-poms and other anti-aircraft firepower to the battle. Sergeant Richard Henry James Brace's Wellington was shot down in flames. Pilot Officer Norman Leonard Lewis, whose Wellington was thought to have been struck by flak, turned and crashed into the following aircraft flown by Flight Sergeant William Howarth Downey, causing both Wellingtons to crash in flames. Flight Sergeant James Ernest Kirby Healy's Wellington was also thought to have been a victim of flak. Griffiths turned the formation away and shortly afterwards a formation of three single-engined fighters was sighted approaching the bombers from Wangerooge, which came up out of the mist. The fighters, which were Bf 109Es of II./JG 77 that had taken off from Wangerooge together with four Bf 110s of 2/ZG 26 from Jever, closed and the RAF gunners responded with rapid firing. Fighters approaching in line astern from sea level made their attacks. Corporal A. Bickerstaff, the rear gunner in McKee's aircraft, fired at the attackers and saw a Wellington falling and believed it to be the Messerschmitt he had just shot down.[15]

Flying Officer John Arkell Harding Cooper's Wellington was seen to break away and enter the clouds. It was last seen heading towards the German coast with its undercarriage down, apparently under control. All the crew were lost without trace. Bf 110s badly damaged New Zealand Flight Lieutenant Eugene John Hetherington's Wellington and he was forced to jettison his bombs into the sea. He went into the clouds and was able to nurse his ailing Wellington back across the North Sea with petrol pouring from its tanks (the Wellingtons did not yet have self-sealing fuel tanks). Almost home, the machine crash-landed in a field near Newmarket racecourse. The aircraft was a write-off and Hetherington and two of his crew were killed. The injured were removed to Newmarket hospital. The loss of five Wellingtons was so disastrous that Air Vice-Marshal J. E. A. 'Jackie' Baldwin, AOC 3 Group was compelled to compare it to the Charge of the Light Brigade.

Despite the losses Bomber Command opined that the Wellingtons had survived repeated fighter attacks and faith in the old adage that 'the bomber will always get through' seemed as unshakable as ever. Indeed, the debriefing report was to state later, 'After careful analysis of individual reports by all members of crews, it seems almost possible to assume that none of our aircraft were brought down by fire from the Messerschmitts'. At Bomber Command the consensus was that in future, concealment was more important than defensive firepower. Henceforth bomber formations would fly at 10,000 feet and crews were urged to seek the safety of cloud cover whenever possible. In his report of the events of 14 December, the Senior Air Staff Officer at Bomber Command Headquarters, Air Commodore Norman Bottomley, wrote:

'It is now by no means certain that enemy fighters did in fact succeed in shooting down any of the Wellingtons…the failure of the enemy must be ascribed to good formation flying. The maintenance of tight, unshaken formations in the face of the most powerful enemy action is the test of bomber force fighting efficiency and morale. In our service it is the equivalent of the old 'Thin Red Line' or the 'Shoulder to Shoulder' of Cromwell's Ironsides… Had it not been for that good leadership, losses from enemy aircraft might have been heavy.' In complete contrast to the British version of the events the Luftwaffe report stated. 'German pilots registered five kills, plus one probable but unconfirmed kill. One German fighter shot down.'

On the evening of 17 December Wing Commander Kellett and Squadron Leader Paul Harris of 149 Squadron were summoned to Group Headquarters at Mildenhall, along with the squadron commanders and section leaders of 9 and 37 Squadrons for a briefing on another raid on Wilhelmshaven the following morning. Unfortunately, there would be little cloud cover for the weather forecast for 18 December predicted clear conditions. Harris was informed that Peter Grant would be flying with him, together with three of 9 Squadron's aircraft. This was the first time they had ever flown together and as they strolled away from the briefing, Harris put his hand on Grant's shoulder and said, 'Stay close to me whatever happens'. 9 Squadron was to supply nine aircraft for a force of 24, with nine on 149 Squadron and six on 37 Squadron at Feltwell. There were to be four groups of six aircraft: three of 149 and three of 9 in front, six of 149 to starboard, six of 9 to port and six of 37 in the rear. Targets were to be any German warships in the area of Heligoland or the Schillig Roads. Bomb loads were four 500lb general purpose bombs per aircraft.

9 Squadron was airborne from Honington at 0900 hours. At 1000 hours nine Wellingtons on 149 Squadron led by Wing Commander Kellett took off from Newmarket Heath and rendezvoused over King's Lynn with the nine Wellingtons on 9 Squadron. The six Wellingtons on 37 Squadron took off from Feltwell and flew straight across north Norfolk, falling in behind the rear elements of the formation while over the North Sea. The formation flew a dog

leg course over the North Sea, first flying northwards as far as possible from the concentration of enemy flak ships among the Friesian Islands and then they headed due east for the German island of Sylt. After fifteen minutes on this new heading Flight Lieutenant A. G. Duguid began to have trouble with one of his engines. As he lost speed and dropped back, he signalled by Aldis lamp to his two wingmen to close up on Kellett's Vic. Riddlesworth, his No.3 obeyed but Kelly, his No.2, apparently failed to pick up the Aldis signal. Kelly peeled away from the formation, followed his leader down and headed for home as well. At 1230 hours Kellett sighted Sylt about fifty miles ahead. The formation was still at 15,000 feet and there was not a cloud in the sky. It was an open invitation for enemy fighters. As the Wellingtons approached the German coast near Cuxhaven, Bf 109 and Bf 110 fighters of Jagdgeschwader 1, guided by radar plots of the incoming formation made by the experimental Freya early warning radar installation at Wangerooge and directed by ground control, were waiting.

Kellett led the formation through the flak-stained sky over Wilhelmshaven and each bomb aimer prepared to drop his three bombs on the ships below. Suddenly, Kellett gave the order not to bomb. All the battleships and cruisers were berthed alongside quays and harbour walls. His orders were precise: he was not to risk German civilian casualties. Bomb doors were opened but no bombs fell. Moored in the middle of the harbour were four large ships that appeared to be merchantmen. Heavy anti-aircraft fire was coming from them. It was all the encouragement Paul Harris needed. They appeared to be fleet auxiliaries so he dropped his bomb load on them. Another Wellington in his section did the same but the results were obscured by cloud. Kellett's formation had become strung out and disjointed. 9 and 37 Squadrons had become detached and had fanned out in the face of heavy barrage. The Wellingtons were easy pickings and the RAF crews were caught cold as the cunning German fighter pilots made beam attacks from above. Previously, attacks had been made from the rear but now the German pilots tore into the bombers safe in the knowledge that the ventral gun was powerless at this angle of attack. They knew too that the front and rear turrets could not traverse sufficiently to draw a bead on them.

Enemy fighters shot down five Wellingtons on 37 Squadron. One of these was N2936 flown by Sergeant Herbie Ruse, which was singled out North of Wangerooge by Oberstleutnant Karl Schumacher, *Geschwaderkommodore*, JG I, who shot out both the Wellington's engines and raked the aircraft with machine gun fire, killing Corporal Frederick James Taylor, the front-gunner. LAC Harry Jones, the rear gunner, wrote.

'You thought the flak was going to hit you straight between the eyes and then it veered off. We went through a huge barrage and you couldn't see anything except big puffs of black smoke. There was not a cloud in the sky; it was unreal. Wellingtons were scattered all over the sky. As we came through the barrage there were the Messerschmitts waiting for us. We hadn't got any guns at all. All our gadgets had packed in so we had no front gun, no rear gun or anything. We discovered afterwards that they got the wrong oil in our hydraulic system. During one of these attacks I was hit in the back and then through the ankle. I rang up the skipper and said, 'I've been hit and it bloody well hurts.' He told me to come to the front and get it dressed. I staggered to the front of the aircraft. The wireless operator [Sergeant Thomas William Holley] saw my ankle and got a hypodermic syringe and bunged this stuff through my flying trousers into my leg, which killed some of the pain. He was hit and killed immediately. He went a funny sort of grey and purple and died. A Messerschmitt sat on our tail and shot right through the aeroplane, through the rear turret and through the front of the aircraft. I was sitting on the bed behind the wireless operator's area watching the blood coming out of my foot. The second pilot [Sergeant T. May] had to stand with his legs astride the bullets going between his legs. Then a bullet hit him in the thigh. I heard the skipper say he had got to get down. We had caught fire. We were over an island [Spiekeroog] off the German coast and he found a bit of beach to land on. We were burning by now. I got to the hatch at the top and pulled myself up but I got stuck and I could feel the flames burning my rear end. They pulled me out and carried me to the sand dunes.'[16]

For almost half an hour 44 Luftwaffe fighters had torn into the Wellingtons. 9 Squadron, which had despatched nine Wellingtons, lost five aircraft shot down, including Squadron Leader Archibald Guthrie, one of the flight commanders. Thirty-five year old Sergeant John R. Ramshaw's crew with his rear-gunner, Leading Aircraftsman Walter Lilley dead were shot up by Oberleutnant Gresens of 2/ZG 76. The fuel tanks were holed but Ramshaw managed to nurse the ailing Wellington to the coast of Lincolnshire, where he ditched. He and the crew, which included the second pilot and navigator, 24-year old Sergeant Bob Hewitt, whose wife Helen Annie in Glasgow was expecting a baby, were picked up by the Grimsby trawler Erillas 100 miles from the Wash. On 13/14 June 1940 Hewitt was killed when his Wimpy crashed at Drosay, France on the operation on Pont de l'Arche. None of the crew survived.

Fighter attacks had continued until the bombers were only eighty miles from home. Kellett remembered Paul Harris' suggestion after the 3 December raid and 'flew a little slower' to allow the stragglers to keep up. Off to his right Peter Grant obediently stuck rigidly to Harris' Wellington. The tightly knit formation of ten aircraft on 149 Squadron fought their way through. 'B-Beer' piloted by Flying Officer James Heggie Cumming Speirs was shot down during a beam attack by a Bf 110. There were no survivors. 'P-Peter' piloted by Flying Officer Michael Franklin Briden ditched near Cromer Knoll. All of Briden's crew perished before they could be rescued by the Cromer and Sheringham lifeboats. Squadron Leader Harris circled the scene of the crash and attempted to drop a dinghy to the stricken crew but its attached rope snagged the tail of his Wellington and Harris was forced to land at the fighter airfield at Coltishall, near Norwich, which was still under construction. The one survivor on 37 Squadron, Flying Officer P. C. 'Cheese' Lemon, crash-landed at RAF Feltwell. There were no injuries and the Wellington was repaired.[17] 9 Squadron, which had lost five aircraft from the nine despatched, suffered another loss when Sergeant Frank Petts crash-landed on his return and the aircraft was written off.[18]

The survivors returned from ten day's special leave to discover that changes had been made. At Honington a new Flight Commander, Squadron Leader (later Air Commodore) L. E. Jarman joined 9 Squadron from Training Command. 'Shortly afterwards a new CO, Wing Commander McKee arrived from 99 Squadron. The RAF post-mortem into the disastrous raid on Wilhelmshaven had concluded that its Wellingtons and Hampdens could no longer cross German territory in daylight and expect to survive against Luftwaffe opposition. From thenceforth Blenheims, whose losses had been lower, were despatched singly or in pairs, to overfly the German North Sea bases. However, a few daylight bomber sweeps were flown over the North Sea. On 2 January 1940 twelve Bf 110s attacked three Wellingtons on 149 Squadron. Two of the bombers were shot down and a third had a lucky escape. Meanwhile, RAF ground crews at the Wellington and Hampden bases installed armour plate and applied self-sealing covering to fuel tanks.

Footnotes

4   *RAF Marham Transition To War* by E. C. 'Johnnie' Johnson. *West Norfolk Aviation Journal. No.2* (Summer 1994).
5   Marham's first Wellington (L4230) was delivered to 38 Squadron on 28 September 1938.
6   *RAF Marham Transition To War* by E. C. 'Johnnie' Johnson. *West Norfolk Aviation Journal. No.2* (Summer 1994).
7   The Vickers Armstrong Wellington was affectionately known as the Wimpy after the cartoon character 'J. Wellington Wimpy' in 'Popeye'. On 1 June 1939 1 RNZAF Unit began forming at Marham to fly Wellingtons. A decision had been taken early in 1937 that the New Zealanders would have a complement of 30 Wellingtons, six of which would be ready to leave for the antipodes in August 1939. When war clouds gathered the New Zealanders were put at the disposal of the RAF and the unit moved to RAF Harwell where it became 15 OTU.
8   *RAF Marham Transition To War* by E. C. 'Johnnie' Johnson. West Norfolk Aviation Journal. No.2 (Summer 1994).
9   With overcast at 400 feet and rain showers, the Wellington I was flown by 30 year-old Sergeant Edward Thoms 'Slim' Summers AFM, one of the most experienced pilots on 38 Squadron, having accumulated 1,102 flying hours, of which 167 hours were on Wellingtons. 'Slim' was a very colourful and ebullient character and he had earned his Air Force Medal earlier that year, on 2 January 1939. On 15 May he had saved the life of his rear gunner during a low-level bombing exercise in a Wellington. The starboard engine had failed and 'Slim' was unable to turn the aircraft against the port engine. A fire broke out between the tail and centre section and the aircraft was landed in a field near RAF Marham, on the port engine. A normal landing would have blown the flames into the area of the rear turret. After touchdown the bomber ran into a hedge and the undercarriage collapsed. The crew quickly vacated the aircraft, which was still burning but 'Slim', who was wearing an old style aircraft harness, became caught up in the side window. He extricated himself by releasing the harness and though the aircraft was burnt out, the crew escaped serious injury. 'Slim's' fame spread and he was known locally, for when he was not on duty Summers lived at the Whitington 'Bell' near Stoke Ferry with his wife. On 8 August 1939 he was asked if he would fly a Wellington out of a field at Roudham Heath near Thetford after it had crash-landed with the undercarriage retracted during a night exercise. The daredevil Summers successfully got the Wellington off and flew it back to Marham. On the fateful day of 5 November 'Slim' attempted a very dangerous manoeuvre near the ground (it is thought he was trying to fly wingtip low between two trees). It must be assumed that he did not allow for the keel action of a heavy aircraft in a steep turn; also he failed to judge the height of the trees. The aircraft crashed inverted at

Boughton killing all seven on board. Wellington: *The Geodetic Giant* by Martin Bowman (Airlife 1989 & 1998). Summers and LAC David George, one of the six fitters, are buried in Marham village churchyard, which contains 16 WWII and two WWI graves and six German graves in the main plot.

10 'The romance followed on from that funeral. John had been very friendly with one of the girls who worked in the NAAFI. She was a favourite with us all in that little band of friends. She was rather a shy girl but had a lovely smile. When the crash occurred, she had been at home for the weekend, so I had the unenviable job of breaking the sad news to her on her return and offering my sympathy. This same NAAFI girl and I married and we celebrated our Golden Wedding Anniversary in 1994. Well I did say she had a nice smile and she always did!' RAF Marham *Transition To War* by E. C. 'Johnnie' Johnson (West Norfolk Aviation Journal No.2 (Summer 1994). (Early in 1940 four Wellingtons of the New Zealand Flight were stored at Barton Bendish. On 20 November 1940 a Wellington Ic on 38 Squadron flown by Sergeant I. N. Robertson, made a belly-landing at Barton Bendish having failed to maintain height on take-off during a non-operational flight. The aircraft was repaired on site and returned to service. During this period the airfield was used as a decoy site with a flare-path in operation at night. From June to September 1941 detachments of 26 and 268 (Army Co-Operation) Squadrons were stationed at Barton Bendish with Curtis Tomahawk IIa low-level reconnaissance aircraft and a number of Westland Lysanders. 218 Conversion Flight followed with Wellingtons, before moving to Oakington on 2 October 1942. In 1942 Downham Market opened as Marham's satellite in place of Barton Bendish, which was unsuitable for 218 CU's Stirlings).

11 Kellett, the son of an Anglo-Irish Surgeon Rear-Admiral, joined the RAF rather than the Navy after being told that Cranwell cadets were given motorcycles to assist their training. In the late 1920s while serving in Iraq, he force-landed in the desert and was saved by a fellow pilot from capture by hostile tribesmen who were advancing on the rescuing aircraft as it took off. In 1936 he had the unusual experience of being seconded to the Imperial Japanese Army to advise on engineering for the Japanese Air Force, his services being recognised by the Emperor with the Order of the Sacred Treasure of Japan. He returned home in 1937 and took command of 148 Squadron equipped with Wellesleys. During 5-7 November 1938, as leader of the RAF's Long Range Development Unit, he flew one of two Wellesleys to establish a new long-distance record-breaking non-stop flight of 7,158.95 miles in just over 48 hours from Ismailia, Egypt to Darwin, Australia. Kellett was awarded the DFC in 1940 and in the autumn of 1942 in North Africa he was shot down in a raid on Tobruk and taken prisoner, being sent to Stalag Luft III where he was SBO at the time of the celebrated Wooden Horse escape. He was awarded the CBE in 1943. Air Commodore Kellett CBE DFC AFC died aged 84 in January 1990.

12 The Wellington and the Handley Page Hampden and the Armstrong Whitworth Whitley and Bristol Blenheim - all twin engined bombers - were the mainstay of Bomber Command early in the war. Following heavy Wellington and Blenheim losses in daylight the elderly Whitley squadrons in 4 Group were immediately employed in night leaflet dropping operations and made no appearance in daylight at all. the serious losses inflicted on 29 September, when a complete formation of five 144 Squadron Hampdens were destroyed over the German Bight between Heligoland and Wangerooge Island by Bf 109s of I./ZG 26, soon convinced the Air Staff that a profound change of its daylight policy was necessary.

13 Later, in May 1943, after a long convalescence and post in fighter training schools, Specht became *Gruppenkommandeur*, II./JGII. He scored 32 confirmed victories, including 15 four-motor bombers and was awarded the *Ritterkreuz* (Knight's Cross) before being reported MIA on 1 January 1945 during the disastrous *Bodenplatte* operation.

14 Later Air Marshal, Sir and C-in-C Transport Command.

15 Hauptmann Restemayer, pilot of a Bf 110 was wounded and his aircraft badly damaged. Feldwebel Friedrich Braukmeier, one of the Bf 109 pilots, was shot down and killed.

16 Ruse crash-landed in shallow water on a mud flat off Spiekeroog. He and May and Jones were captured. Oberleutnant Johann Fuhrmann, Schumacher's *Rottenflieger* (wingman) carried out three beam attacks on another Wellington without apparent result and was shot down making a pass from dead astern. He was shot down in the crossfire and ditched his Bf 109D in the sea but was drowned before he could be rescued. Flying Officer P. A. Wimberley was believed shot down by Leutnant Helmut Lent of I./ZG 76 in a lone Bf 110. Wimberley crash-landed on Borkum, his

Wellington bursting into flames. Wimberley survived but his crew perished. Australian Flying Officer Oliver John Trevor Lewis, Squadron Leader Ian Victor Hue-Williams and Flying Officer Arthur Telford Thompson piloted the three other 37 Squadron Wellingtons shot down. Lewis was Lent's second victim. There was only one survivor, AC1 George Warne Geddes but he too died of his wounds later. 2./ZG 76 led by the *Gruppenkommandeur*, Hauptmann Reinecke, claimed another Wellington, while Bf 109Es of 5./JG 77 claimed three bombers.

17 On 25/26 July 1942 Squadron Leader 'Cheese' Lemon DFC, now on 12 Squadron, was shot down over Holland on the operation on Duisburg and taken into captivity along with the rest of his crew. On 31 July he was awarded the DSO. (N2903 subsequently flew on 214 Squadron and 11 OTU before being SOC on 22 March 1943).

18 In addition to the 12 Wellingtons lost and the 2 written off in crashes, three others were damaged in crash landings in England. Canadian Flying Officer William John Macrae RCAF on 9 Squadron force-landed at North Coates with a damaged starboard wing, rear fuselage and rudder and two men wounded. (Macrae was KIA on 8.3.40). Wing Commander Kellett and Flying Officer Riddlesworth were the other two Wellingtons that crashed. Luftwaffe fighter claims for aircraft destroyed on the raid totalled 38, which later, were pared down to 26 or 27. Among these, Oberleutnant Johannes Steinhoff's claim for two destroyed was reduced to one. Only two of I/ZG 76's 16 claims were disallowed, one of which was 2./ZG 76's Hauptmann Wolfgang Falck's second. Falck was hit by return fire during an attack on one of the Wellingtons but managed to force-land on Wangerooge. His wingman, Unteroffizier Fresia, was credited with two confirmed destroyed. Leutnant Uellenbeck's claims for two destroyed was upheld, as was Leutnant Helmut Lent's claims for two bombers shot down. Uellenbeck's Bf 110 was hit 33 times by return fire but although he and his gunner, Unteroffizier Dombrowski, were wounded, they landed safely back at Jever. Though RAF crews claimed 12 German single and twin-engined fighters had been shot down, just three Bf 109 fighters were lost and a handful damaged or hit.

Chapter 2

Coastal Command

On 8th April 1940 at 2 o'clock in the afternoon, a Sunderland flying boat sighted a battleship of the 'Scharnhorst' class accompanied by two cruisers of the 'Leipzig' class and two destroyers. They were a hundred and thirty miles from the Alsboen Light off the West coast of Norway. The ships saw the Sunderland almost at the same moment and opened anti-aircraft fire which was both heavy and accurate. The Sunderland was hit almost at once; two of its tanks were holed and the hull gradually filled with petrol. When it landed at its base it had lost 300 gallons. That same day German destroyers had been seen at various times in the neighbourhood of the Horns Reef, steaming on a Northerly course. The German attack on Norway had begun.

Throughout the next day aircraft of Coastal Command were very busy reconnoitring the new area of battle. Before midday a London flying boat had reported the presence of a German cruiser of the 'Koln' class in Bergen. This intelligence was confirmed later by a Blenheim and a Wellington. A Sunderland reported one 'Hipper' class cruiser in Trondheim Fjord and Wellingtons enemy warships and possibly transports at Kristiansand (South). The cruiser at Bergen was attacked that afternoon by Wellingtons, which dropped thirty armour-piercing 500lb bombs from between 4,000 and 6,000 feet. They were met by heavy fire, but thought that they had scored one direct hit on her stern. On the next day a Hudson reported that after a further attack by naval Skuas from the aircraft carrier HMS Furious the cruiser had sunk. On 12th April a Wellington, put at the service of Coastal by Bomber Command, flew from an aerodrome in Northern Scotland over a thousand miles' of sea to the North of Norway. When it entered Narvik Fjord 'huge rocks towered up on either side of us,' reports the wireless operator. 'Snow drifted down so that we could see only a few yards ahead. The gusts were terrific, bouncing and throwing us about... By then we reckoned we were within about ten miles of Narvik, but we could not continue. Visibility was almost nil... We went about and picked our way down the fjord again... like a boat hugging the shore. Suddenly we saw once more the open sea.' They soon saw something else, a Ju 88 crossing their bows. 'We began to circle each other, two heavy bombers waiting to pounce.' Then the inevitable curtain of snow fell and they lost each other: Near Narvik the compass showed errors of between twenty and thirty degrees, but the Wellington set course for base and landed safely after a flight of fourteen and a half hours.

On the next day the Royal Navy entered the fjord and sank seven German destroyers. A second reconnaissance, made on 22nd April, also by a Wellington, covered 1,180 miles in eight and a half hours and photographed Trondheim. It saw, among much else of interest, twenty-two German aircraft on 'a frozen lake,' and its signal about this discovery was picked up by an aircraft carrier whose aircraft 'bombed the lake with excellent effect.'

By 14th April the German Air Force was in occupation of all the aerodromes in Norway and Denmark...'

Coastal Command: The Fight for Norway (Air Ministry 1942)

Until the spring of 1940 the war at sea had gone steadily in Britain's favour. Even the Germans' victorious campaign had cost the Kriegsmarine one-third of its cruisers and almost half its destroyers. However, in April the sea war flared up again. Units of Bomber Command found themselves called upon to bolster 18 Group Coastal Command, which was responsible for Britain's Northern Approaches. Germany's occupation of Norway, the subsequent overrunning of France and the Low Countries and Italy's intervention in the war changed the situation in the war at sea radically. U-boats and E-boats began operating with deadly effect from French Atlantic bases. Soon aircraft such as the four-engined Focke Wulf 200, an adapted commercial transport with a range of 2,000 miles, began to menace Britain's Western Approaches and reach out into mid-Atlantic waters previously immune from German intervention. RAF Coastal Command was at once confronted with a series of fresh problems ranging from anti-invasion patrols to long-range escort duties. In June 1940 Air Chief Marshal Sir Frederick Bowhill KCB CMG DSO could only call upon 500 aircraft for such diverse tasks and only 34 of these, the Sunderlands, could only operate beyond 500 miles from Britain's shores. The period between June and October, when U-boats sank 282 ships with only seven U-boats lost to all causes, became known to the U-boat crews as the 'Happy Time'. At first the U-boats attacked shipping in the South-West Approaches. During June sinkings by U-boats peaked at 63 ships. By August they became bolder, following up on the surface during the day and delaying closing in on convoys until nightfall. To escape detection by the Asdics [19] they remained on the surface and attacked under cover of darkness. Coastal Command did not have an answer to such tactics and from the beginning of June to the end of 1940 over 300 million tons of Allied and neutral shipping was sunk.[20]

The only salvation available to RAF crews was ASV (Air to Surface Vessel) radar. Relatively few aircraft in Coastal Command were fitted with the device and those that were did not always perform as efficiently as crews would like. Ideally, a U-boat had to be fully surfaced and no more than three miles distant for ASV to be effective. On 21 November 1940 221 Squadron re-formed at Bircham Newton, Norfolk, equipped with Wellington Is. Early in 1941 ASV sets were installed and in March 1941 the squadron began replacing its Mark Is and ICs with Mark VIII 'Stickleback' Wellingtons (so named because of the ASV.II aerials atop the fuselage), nicknamed, 'Goofingtons'.[21] By May 1941 the U-boats were largely reduced to operating off West Africa or in the central Atlantic, the latter being beyond the range of Coastal Command aircraft. In June 1941 when Air Chief Marshal Sir Philip Joubert de la Ferté KCB CMG DSO took over Coastal Command, he inherited a force of forty squadrons and more than half the aircraft were now fitted with ASV radar. Joubert's overriding task was to increase the effectiveness of his ASV aircraft and create airborne U-boat killers. He pressed for heavier types of anti-submarine bombs, bomb sights for low level attack and depth charge pistols which would detonate at less than fifty feet below the surface. He encouraged tests, first started by Bowhill, with various forms of camouflage, in order to render the attacker invisible for as long as possible. As a result all anti-U-boat aircraft were painted white on their sides and under-surfaces.

By September 1941 increased shipping losses again prompted the Admiralty to explore the possibility of employing bombers in the war at sea. Air Marshal

Harris had steadfastly refused to allocate any of his four-engined bombers to Coastal Command but had turned over large numbers of Wellingtons and other twin-engined types. In September 221 Squadron moved to Iceland, returning in December for transfer overseas. Three crews flew their Wellington VIIIs to Malta while the remainder of the squadron flew to Egypt in January 1942 to begin anti-shipping patrols from bases in the Canal Zone. Meanwhile, the shipping losses in October and November 1941 showed a reduction over those of September. During early 1942 Coastal Command was helped by the transfer of further aircraft from Bomber Command. In April a squadron of Whitleys, eight Liberators and a Wellington squadron (311 Czech) were transferred to Coastal Command. On 7 May Bomber Command relinquished control of 304 (Polish) Squadron, which flew to its new base at Tiree in the Inner Hebrides. Both squadrons were needed urgently and they took up their new role almost immediately. The Poles had a very eventful career in Coastal Command, moving on 13 June 1942 to Dale in South Wales where they joined 19 Group Coastal Command. They flew 2,451 sorties up until 30 May 1945 and attacked 34 U-boats out of 43 sighted. The Czechs also gave sterling service in Coastal Command. 311 operated the Wellington until June 1943 when it converted to the Liberator. 304 commenced operations on 18 May and 311 Squadron took off from its new base at Aldergrove in Northern Ireland on 22 May 1942 for its first operation.

The Bay of Biscay, 500 miles wide, which was the U-boat's route to the wider hunting-fields of the Atlantic Ocean, would become a happy hunting ground for the Wellingtons, Sunderlands, Liberators, Halifaxes, Whitleys and Hudsons of Coastal Command. All flew the Bay patrols and Coastal Command Beaufighters intervened against German long-range fighters which attempted to intercept the U-boat hunting aircraft. Leonard R. Gribble, a thriller writer of such works as *'The Scarlet Widow'* wrote Bombers Fly East for the Air Ministry in 1942 using his pen-name, 'Bruce Sanders'. He painted a prosaic propaganda picture of British air operations and *'Deep-Sea Hunters'*, his chapter on Coastal Command, was no exception: 'Hunting U-boats is a big-game sport for men with patience. One Wellington captain spent 1,300 hours on operational flying before he sighted and attacked his first under-sea victim. There had been plenty of other work and adventure crowded into that long flying period, so the captain, a former student of the Scottish School of Physical Education in Glasgow, was not bored. But he may be forgiven if at times he seriously doubted whether he ever would see a submarine. Another Wellington skipper, a Canadian, Sergeant A. S. Hakala from Sioux Lookout, Alberta got a submarine on the first patrol he made with his crew. It was not beginner's luck this case, for the U-boat's look-out spotted the plane and the aircraft could not arrive before the submarine crashed but the bombs went down to burst just ahead of the feather of foam betraying the sunken periscope. Hakala recalled. 'It was some explosion. The U-boat surfaced groggily until the conning tower and part of the hull were awash. The Wellington readily took this second opportunity, guns blazing away. To my surprise and joy flames and smoke poured from the conning-tower. The bombs must have started it, but I hope the bullets helped.' The U-boat was still on fire when a thick mist came down and the Coastal Command aircraft had to make for home...'

On 6 June 1942 a Spanish radio report asserted that an Italian submarine [the

Luigi Torelli of the 1,200-ton Marconi class commanded by Capitano di Corvetta (Lieutenant Commander) Augusto Migliorini] had been beached near Santander. The foreign radio reports that continued to mention the beaching added that two Sunderland flying-boats of Coastal Command, which had attacked the U-boat, had been forced down. The foreign radio reports were misleading. The Sunderlands were back at base. The episode involving the Italian submarine had all started on the night of 3/4 June. Air Marshal Sir Philip Joubert, knowing that only a successful operational demonstration of the capabilities of Leigh Light Wellingtons would carry the day had thrown caution to the wind and despatched four of the five Wellingtons on 172 Squadron into the Bay of Biscay. The *Luigi Torelli* was damaged by Squadron Leader Jeaff H. Greswell and the crew on a Wellington on 172 Squadron (one of five Wimpys fitted with the Leigh Light) picked up an ASV contact. His target was outbound from Bordeaux to the West Indies. Greswell homed on the *Luigi Torelli* by radar and then switched on the Leigh Light but owing to a faulty setting in his altimeter, his approach was too high and he saw no sign of the submarine. However, Migliorini, mistaking the Wellington for a German aircraft, fired recognition flares, precisely pinpointing his boat. On a second approach with the Leigh Light, Greswell got the *Luigi Torelli* squarely in the brilliant beam and straddled the Italian boat with four shallow-set 300lb Torpex depth charges from an altitude of fifty feet. The shattering effect that depth charges had on a submarine crew is described in frightening detail by Secondo Capo Mechanista Carlo Pracchi of the Regia Marina Velella: 'The sounds are coming from starboard, midships. Thuds in the water, three at a time, and a few seconds later you hear three rumbles followed by the inevitable shaking. Sound source from 10 o'clock and then from 7 o'clock, and louder thuds. It sounds as if every gauge in the control room is shattering. All the valves are shut down. The glass of the depth gauge breaks. From the telephone comes the voice of someone shouting 'Engines... signal leaks or other faults.' We get the boards up to look at the water-level in the bilge tanks. I can see water running down the sides... I look up. In the meantime the bombs go off. I look up again to see where that water is coming from. I can see from the cracks that fortunately it is the varnish peeling off! Higher up I can see drips on the heads of the rivets in the frames. I touch one with my finger, and water runs down my arm. Then we get another depth charge, and the drips start to run down themselves. That earlier charge exploded underneath and brought us up; one went off overhead, and pushed us down. Machine room crew informs: damage. Forward, with a lunatic grin on his face M.N. shows me a rope with knots he has been keeping a tally of the bombs with it. The main relays shut down. The lights have just gone. We'll have to use the emergency lighting. I feel my leg cramp up, then the tingling starts, then shaking. Maybe I'm tired after these hours of tension. I try to snatch a bit of rest sitting down the centre of the aft bulkhead door of the [salvage] box called by the name of the inventor: Garitta Girolami-Arata-Olivati... The effect on my legs doesn't stop; I use my arms to try to suppress it, holding my knees. It makes no difference ... I try to stop just one knee from trembling, but it carries on and only makes my arms shake. In desperation I say: 'Bloody hell I'm just panicking: can't get myself out of it ... I really panic.'[22]

Unsurprisingly, the blasts to *Luigi Torelli* forced Migliorini to abort and he headed to Aviles, Spain.

In the meantime Greswell and his crew spotted a second submarine nearby. It was submerging when spotted with ASV and searchlight. Greswell strafed the submarine with machine-gun fire, having used all its depth charges on the first attack. What saved the second submarine and the *Luigi Torelli* was the failure of the pursuer to get a signal of the attack to the other three Wellingtons on patrol in the area and home them to the place of the attacks. No doubt the coded signal which indicated 'Sighted sub. Am attacking' had been sent to Chivenor but it may not have reached them immediately because of the low level at which the Wellington was flying when the signal was sent or because of atmospheric disruptions. The three other Wellingtons sighted no U-boats but the ease with which they illuminated fishing vessels proved the merits of the Leigh Light.[23]

During the remainder of June the five Leigh Light Wellingtons sighted no fewer than seven U-boats in the Bay of Biscay. Whitleys using conventional methods failed to find any enemy vessels during the same period. The Leigh Light Wellingtons proved so successful that on 24 June Doenitz ordered all U-boats to proceed submerged at all times except when it was necessary to recharge batteries. The morale of U-boat crews slumped with the knowledge that darkness no longer afforded them protection. The work of the Leigh Light Squadrons was the keystone of the success in the air offensive against U-boats in the Atlantic. They enabled night attacks to be made on submarines when they surfaced to re-charge their batteries under cover of darkness. On the night of 5/6 July the Leigh Light Wellingtons chalked up their first true kill when west of La Rochelle in the Bay of Biscay, an American pilot on 172 Squadron, Pilot Officer Wiley B. Howell flying 'H-Harry' sunk the U-502, which was bound for the Caribbean on its third war cruise. Kapitänleutnant Jürgen von Rosenstiel and all 52 hands perished. It was described by 'Bruce Sanders' thus: 'H for Harry', a Wellington, spotted a U-boat surfaced eight miles distant and began stalking it. Closer and closer the Wellington crept out of the sun, handled very clearly by a pilot who was determined to get the submarine if it was at all possible. He proved that it was. He had covered the entire eight miles and was roaring down over the U-boat before its crew awoke to their danger. Three men were still struggling at the conning-tower hatch when the redskin of the skies charged overhead with machine-guns chattering. They tumbled this way and that like broken dolls and the bombs broke across the under-pirate's slim back.'

What Sanders could not mention was the Leigh Light. About a mile from the target, the crew switched the light on to reveal the Type IXC U-boat rolling gently on the surface. Four shallow set 250lb depth charges straddled the boat. When the water settled, the aircrew saw that the water around the submarine had become uncommonly dark. Six days later, Howell and his crew attacked U-159, again using their Leigh light. The U-boat skipper, Kapitänleutnant Helmut Witte, ordered his gun crew to shoot out the aircraft's Leigh light. The gunners, blinded by the intense glare, could not obey. U-159 escaped but suffered damage.[24]

From the twentieth day of June 1940 when Mirek Vild (Flight Lieutenant Miroslav Vild) set out with Alois Siska from Bordeaux bound for England in the good ship *Ary Sheffer* until 1 November 1944 when Mirek completed his last operational flight as a radio and radar operator, few men can have survived so many potential deaths. On his very first operation with 311 (Czech) Squadron from East Wretham, in Norfolk, the Bomber Command Wellington in which he was flying crashed soon after take-off, eventually accounting for five killed and three more seriously wounded. Vild's escape (he was literally blown to the ground from the aircraft) was providential. 25 May 1941 was his lucky day. After six months in hospital at Ely and another three on light duties, recuperating with the Squadron, he was back on the treadmill. Four months later, on 10 August 1942, after 311 had been transferred to Coastal Command and to the airfield at Talbenny in south-west Wales, he was the radio operator on Flying Officer J. Nyult's crew on Wellington HF922 'H-Harry' who claimed their first U-boat destroyed in the Battle of the Atlantic north of Cape Ortegal.[25]

Soon afterwards Vild was obliged to change crews. He joined the crew of Flying Officer J. Vella DFC. On their very next trip, Vild's former comrades were shot down on a patrol in the Bay of Biscay. None of Nyult's crew survived. Vild then had a strange dream about one of his lost friends. He dreamt that, over a glass of red wine, he asked his departed comrade how he found things and what he thought about life. The message that came back was clear: forget your cares and worries, and have a drink, for all will be well. Next, Vild was inquiring of his friend what had happened when he was shot down. Was the end very painful? He was anxious to know the answer. But, suddenly, Vild felt a strange sensation in his head; it seemed to become heavy and painful. What was this? he wondered. He wanted to rest and sleep - but he couldn't because someone was now shaking him, telling him he must wake up and get ready for the briefing... Now wide awake, the radio and radar operator found it was raining outside. He didn't at all feel like flying on what would be his 33rd operation. What is more, he noticed that the comrade sitting next to him in the crew-room was looking downcast and glum, whereas normally he was a jolly, spirited and talkative fellow. Vild asked him what was wrong. It turned out that he, too, had just been dreaming and was now apprehensive; dreams, he said, can so often come true. The two remained silent, content to nurse their own thoughts... As the crew were climbing aboard their Wellington, the front air gunner dropped his Thermos flask. It shattered in a dozen fragments on the tarmac. Vild looked down at the broken glass. His face came to life. 'Ah!' he exclaimed, 'broken glass! Broken glass is lucky. We shall be lucky today!'

That day they were patrolling in the Bay of Biscay, searching for U-boats leaving the south-west ports of France for the Atlantic, or returning after days at sea. Suddenly, down below, the crew spotted eight enemy aircraft, one of which was white. They were Ju 88s. Immediately bombs were jettisoned to make the aircraft safer and more manoeuvrable in a fight. The pilot climbed to 3,000 feet and headed west, out into the Atlantic, at full bore. Mirek radioed the bad news of the sighting back to base.

Meanwhile the 88s began climbing for their prey with the white aircraft positioning for the initial, frontal attack. But the Wellington pilot held his course steady, meeting the approaching German head-on. As they began to close, the Czech air gunner started blazing away from the front turret. Down went the 88, plunging seawards... How the 311 crew evaded the unequal attacks, none could truly say, but at the end of the engagement, which seemed like an eternity, the score sheet read: 311 Squadron - three German aircraft destroyed: the enemy - zero.

Back at base, the crew stepped down thankfully from the aircraft. Once on the ground Vild sought out the front-gunner. 'Are you superstitious?' he asked. 'No,' came the positive, monosyllabic response. Vild brushed the negative aside. 'Have no doubt,' he said, 'the broken glass from your Thermos brought us the luck...'[26]

During the war ferry flights were frequently fraught with danger not only from the elements but from hunting enemy aircraft. A mixed crew briefed to take a Wellington to the Middle East was attacked by a Junkers 88 off Cape Finisterre soon after their dawn take-off on 20 July 1942. The Ju 88 dived and at 500 yards opened fire, shattering the Wellington's rear turret and injuring the gunner with broken pieces of perspex. The fire holed the nacelle tanks, shot through the main spar and severed various controls. The rear gunner of the Wellington, his face streaming with blood and with a bullet in his leg, held his fire until the enemy was 150 yards away, then fired. The Ju 88 stopped firing immediately; smoke began pouring from the port engine. Flight Sergeant J. M. Rogers RAAF, who was in the astrodome, saw it go past the Wellington about thirty yards distant and swoop down into the sea. Half-way down it lifted a little as though the pilot were mortally wounded and someone else were trying to pull the aircraft out, but if so it was a vain attempt.

The Wellington landed at Gibraltar. As it touched down the port tyre collapsed, and petrol began to stream from bullet holes in the top of the tanks. Soon afterwards the same crew returned to England, where they were chosen to pioneer the West African route for Coastal Command Wellingtons. The first journey began on 3 October 1942 and the trip to Gibraltar was made without incident. On 14 October they left Gibraltar at dawn, flying past Casablanca, to which, a few months later, Australians, among other ferry pilots, were to bring important delegates. As the day progressed, visibility deteriorated and by the time the Wellington was off Dakar it was flying in thick haze, fighting against high winds and made sluggish by its heavy cargo. Seeking Bathurst, which the wireless operator was unable to pick up because of severe interference, the aircraft flew up and down the coast in the haze until night overtook them with almost empty petrol tanks, They sent out an SOS, and decided on a crash-landing on a beach. The pilot touched down and ran into a sand dune. There was a crash, and the aircraft burst into flames. The back of the aircraft was broken, and the fuselage opposite where Rogers, the Australian was sitting, split from top to bottom, enabling him to dive out of the fiery interior into the sand, although he was badly burned in doing so.

The second pilot escaped through the escape hatch in the rear of the fuselage. The wireless operator got out through the astrodome, and the pilot through his escape hatch. The pilot's hands were terribly burned in releasing himself from his harness. The rear gunner alone escaped burning, although he was stunned and bruised. He managed to salvage his parachute, tore the silk into strips and bandaged the burns of the others. It was a hot, tropical night, but all were cold from shock, and they huddled close to the burning aircraft.

About an hour later, in the darkness beyond the circle of fiery light, the crew saw several vague figures moving. Rogers and his English comrades staggered to their feet, calling out in the few words of Arabic and French they knew, and the figures materialized as scared natives who obviously had seen few, if any, white men before. 'By signs they were made to understand the airmen's need of water and half an hour later they came back with a big calabash full of warm, earthy water, and the crew drank deeply. Then the natives helped them along the beach to their fishing hut, warned the airmen by signs to beware of leopards and snakes, and went off to their village some distance away. The rear gunner kept the fire going through the night. None of them slept; their burns were too painful.

At first light came the roar of an aircraft and a Hudson aircraft appeared, circled, and in response to Very lights and a message written by the Australian and the rear gunner in the sand - 'Five, badly burned' - signalled by Aldis lamp that they were to stay by their aircraft and left. Thirty minutes later a Sunderland arrived. It had picked up the Hudson's signal to base. The Sunderland landed about three-quarters of a mile out. Then another Hudson arrived and dropped a dinghy and some food, and the Sunderland sent another dinghy in through the surf to take off the crew. The natives returned, collected the airmen's kit, and helped get it into the dinghy on a subsequent trip. Rogers thinks the crew left that tribe the richest in Africa. One of the natives, possibly, is still wearing the remains of the blue silk pyjamas he gave him. The crew was flown to a military hospital at Bathurst. There the second pilot died the following morning from fever and burns. The wireless air gunner died four days later. The rear gunner recovered rapidly and went on to the Middle East. Rogers and the pilot were in hospital for two or three months before they returned to Britain on 2 March 1942.

On 4 August 1942 meanwhile, in the Mediterranean, forty miles west of Jaffa, U-372, which had left Salamis on its eighth war cruise on 27 July, was attacked by Wellington HF913/M on 221 Squadron and Wellington N on 203 Squadron and depth charged and sunk by RN destroyers *Sikh* and *Zulu* and frigates *Croome* and *Tetcott* after a thirteen-hour hunt. The commander, 33-year old Hans-Joachim Neumann and his crew perished.

In September, a detachment on 172 Squadron, operating from Skitten, Caithness was expanded and became 179 Squadron. The primary task of the Leigh Light-equipped Wellingtons was to saturate the Bay of Biscay at night, forcing as many U-boats as possible, to dive and run submerged and then to surface in daylight hours to charge batteries. This tactic increased the effectiveness of the daylight air patrols of the Whitleys, Sunderlands, Catalinas and other aircraft fitted with less sophisticated radar, whose crews relied heavily on daytime visual spottings.

On 16 September 1942, Wellington 'E-Ela' on 304 Squadron was airborne at 0930 and within five minutes was setting out on its 140-mile leg to the Biscay area; briefed for a 'routine' U-boat search. The navigator, Flight Lieutenant Minakowski, takes up the story. 'As we approached position 'A' at 1612, six aircraft appeared; one starboard, three to port and two far astern. The sky was cloudless and the weather fine, with visibility between 25-30 miles from our altitude of 1,500 feet. Flying Officer Stanislas Targowski, our pilot, descended to 500 feet when the aircraft were sighted and, when we identified them as Ju88s, jettisoned our depth charges and went further down to 50 feet.'

The enemy fighters closed in rapidly. At 1615 three Ju 88s bore in from the port front quarter, one after another, and Targowski threw the Wellington into violent evasive manoeuvres, almost dipping the wings into the sea. Each time a Junkers came in, he turned to face it head-on, thereby presenting the smallest possible target. Both front and rear gunners opened fire as the first Ju 88 came on and hit one of them and saw it fall into the sea. The wireless operator, after transmitting a signal to base about the attack and the aircraft's location, manned the beam gun. Minakowski's report continues:

'Two Junkers - those originally farthest away - now closed in from starboard, passed us and then attacked. They nearly succeeded. As one attacked on the starboard beam, our Wellington turned head-on towards him and was struck by cannon shells and a machine-gun burst. One of the petrol tanks was damaged and the cabin was filled with smoke from the explosions. All our guns were banging away furiously. Another Hun was hit and pieces fell off him as he turned towards France with smoke streaming out of his starboard engine. Shortly after this a crash resounded in the Wellington and dense smoke filled the fuselage. There were no fumes, however and nobody was wounded. Some clouds appeared on the horizon just then and we made for them.

'Two fighters now attacked us time after time from astern. Both were hit by our gunners who greeted them with accurate fire as they got within close range. Thereafter the enemy's attacks were half-hearted. The clouds were by now much closer, about 1,500 feet up, so Targowski made for them at full speed. He reached them safely, and we finally broke away from the enemy. We fixed our position and informed base we would land at Portreath in Cornwall, owing to fuel shortage. The petrol in the starboard tank had all leaked out, and the auxiliary oil-delivery tank was damaged. We landed at 1750, having been airborne for 8hr 20min. None of us was hurt.'[27]

On 22 October 'B-Bertie', a Leigh Light-equipped Wellington on 179 Squadron piloted by Flight Sergeant A. D. S. Martin DFM sank the U-412, commanded by 26-year old Kapitänleutnant Walter Jahrmärker, as she entered the Atlantic northeast of the Faeroes, six days out from Kiel on her first war cruise. All 47 hands were lost. Early in November the Squadron was stood down from anti-shipping operations and by the end of the month had moved to Gibraltar. Meanwhile, 544 Squadron had formed at Benson on 19 October 1942 with two flights. 'A' Flight operated Ansons and Wellingtons from Benson while 'B' Flight operated Spitfires in the PR role from Gibraltar. 'A' Flight Wellingtons began flying experimental night photographic operations over France in January 1943.[28]

By January 1943 Coastal Command aircraft had almost ceased to locate U-boats by night. The only solution was to replace the ASV Mark II, which only had a 1½ metre wave-length, with the long overdue ASV Mark III of ten centimetre wavelength. This apparatus which had a PPI display was already in operation having originated from an adaptation of centimetric AI. An American version, developed with the help of British scientists, had been successfully tested in May 1942 although British models would not be available until spring 1943. The new model Leigh Light-equipped Wellington GR.XIV, which was fitted with ASV.III was powered by more powerful Hercules engines and propellers that could be feathered, which enabled the aircraft to fly on one engine in emergencies. Two Coastal Command squadrons - 172 and 407 Squadron RCAF - consisting of about fifteen aircraft each, received these new Wellingtons.

In 1943 Coastal Command underwent many changes to its Wellington squadrons. On 9 February 1943 U-268 commanded by 26-year old Oberleutnant zur see Ernst Heydemann was inbound to Brest returning from its fourth war cruise low on fuel and was found west of St. Nazaire by 'B-Bertie' a Leigh Light-equipped Wellington on 172 Squadron piloted by Flying Officer G. D. Lundon. He dropped four depth charges close to the U-boat and later, German aircraft and patrol boats could find no sign of U-268. The boat and all 45 hands had perished.[29] Ten days' later, on 19 February U-562, which had left La Spezia on its tenth war cruise on 7 February, was bombed north-east of Banghazi by Wellington LB177/S on 38 Squadron piloted by Flying Officer I. B. Butler DFC who was escorting Convoy XT.3 U-562 was also depth charged by RN destroyers Isis and Hursley. All 49 hands including the commander, Horst Hamm, perished.

In March 1943 one of the biggest convoy battles of the war took place when nearly fifty U-boats in six wolfpacks attacked four large eastbound convoys numbering 150 merchantmen and their escorts. U-333, which had been equipped with extra anti-aircraft guns, encountered a Wellington on 172 Squadron in the Bay of Biscay. When the Wellington attacked, the U-boat crew fought back instead of diving and shot the Wellington down in flames, killing the crew.[30] On 22 March it was thought that Wellington Z6950/Q on 10 OTU [31] flown by Sergeant J. A. Marsden had exacted some measure of revenge, finding U-665 with ASV-IV radar and sinking the submarine, which was returning to Kiel at the end of its first war cruise, west of Nantes. The U-boat, which was commanded by 32-year old Hans-Jürgen Haupt, was lost with all 46 hands.

Confirmation of claims for kills and identification of the actual U-boat 'victims' often posed difficulties. West of Nantes on 10 April 1943 an attack by a Leigh-Light Wellington, 'C-Charlie', flown by Pilot Officer G. H. Whiteley on 172 Squadron using ASV-IV radar, formerly credited with the destruction of U-376 commanded by 28-year old Kapitänleutnant Friedrich-Karl Marks, was actually directed against U-465, inflicting severe damage.[32] U-376 was outbound for a special operation code-named 'Elster' (Magpie) to take aboard German naval officers who escaped from a Canadian PoW camp at North Point on the northern tip of Prince Edward Island on the Canadian east coast. When it failed repeatedly to report its position after sailing, it was posted as missing in the Bay of Biscay effective 13 April 1943.[33] On 26 April U-437 commanded by Hermann Lamby left St Nazaire on its sixth war cruise bound for the mid-Atlantic but he was forced to return after being hit by a stick of Mark XI Torpex depth charges dropped by 'G-George' a Leigh-Light Wellington on 172 squadron piloted by Flying Officer Peter H. Strembridge. Almost immediately 'two separate patches of very large bubbles were seen' reported Strembridge but two flights of Ju 88s and another U-boat helped nurse the badly damaged submarine to safety at St. Nazaire on 30 April. U-437 wa heavily damaged and did not re-sail until 23 September when it set out for the North Atlantic.

North-west of Cape Ortegal in the Bay of Biscay in the early hours of 3 July Leigh-Light Wellington 'R-Robert' on 172 Squadron piloted by Flight Sergeant Alex Coumbis, a Rhodesian, picked up U-126 or U-154, which was close by, on radar. Coumbis lined up and attacked a U-boat that proved to be U-126 commanded by 26-year old Siegfried Kietz, which was returning from West Africa on its sixth war cruise. Nothing more was ever heard from U-126 which was lost with all 55 hands. West of Figueria six days' later the veteran U-435 commanded by Siegfried Strelow, which was returning from the Azores area having left Brest on its ninth war cruise on 20 May, was bombed by four depth-charges dropped by Wellington 'R-Robert' flown by Flying Officer E. J. Fisher on 179 Squadron. The U-boat was lost with all 48 hands.[34]

The U-459 commanded by 49-year old Korvettenkapitän (Lieutenant Commander) Georg von Wilamowitz-Mollendorf sailed from Bordeaux on 22 July bound for refuelling operations in company with two other U-boats, one of which soon developed a bad leak and aborted. On 24 July, late in the day, Flying Officer W. H. T. Jennings piloting Wellington 'Q-Queenie' on 172 Squadron found U-459 and attacked out of low clouds. U-459 remained on the surface and Wilamowitz-Mollendorf's new quad 20mm and twin 20mm guns opened fire. Jennings bravely flew into this very heavy flak barrage and crashed into the starboard side of U-459, demolishing the quad 20mm and other guns and killing or wounding half a dozen of U-459's crew. Utter chaos ensued. The Germans cut away the wreckage of the Wellington fuselage and pushed it into the sea. Upon doing so, they found three unexploded depth charges, two on the bridge and one on the afterdeck. Apparently unaware that the depth charges were fitted with shallow-set pistols, Wilamowitz-Mollendorf rang up full speed and ordered his men to roll them overboard. One or more of the charges exploded as designed beneath the stern of U-459, inflicting horrendous damage. A second Wellington, on 547 Squadron, piloted by Flying Officer J. Whyte arrived on the scene. Upon seeing U-459, which was slowly circling out of control stern down, he attacked, dropping eight depth charges at wave-top level in a close straddle. These explosions dashed any hopes the U-459 crew may have had of limping home. In a second attack run, Whyte dropped several more depth charges and raked the topside with machine-gun fire, killing and wounding more Germans and destroying some of the dinghies. Following this attack, Wilamowitz-Mollendorf ordered his men to abandon ship and scuttle. As the dinghies pulled away, he saluted his men and then went below and opened the vents. Observed by Whyte and his aircrew, the U-459 sank swiftly by the stern. This second Wellington and other aircraft directed the Polish-manned destroyer *Orkan* to the scene. Seven to eight hours after the first Wellington attacked, the Poles picked up forty-one Germans and one British airman, A. A. Turner, who had been blown out of the crashed Wellington and had climbed into his own dinghy. The Admiralty credited the kill to the first Wellington and in view of his 'high degree of courage' recommended Jennings for a posthumous Victoria Cross.[35]

During the great battle with U-boats in the Bay of Biscay on 30 July 1943 - subsequently officially described as 'the greatest single victory of the war against U-boats' - a formation of three U-boats was annihilated by aircraft of Coastal Command and the USAAF and by sloops of the Royal Navy, in a six hour's engagement. The U-614, commanded by 27-year old Kapitänleutnant Wolfgang Sträter sailed from St. Nazaire on 25 July 1943 on its third war cruise. On the fifth day out while still in Biscay, Wellington 'G-George' on 172 Squadron piloted by Wing Commander Rowland G. Musson found and attacked U-614, dropping six depth charges. Sträter remained on the surface to fight it out with his new quad 20mm and other flak guns, but the depth charges blew the boat to pieces. The Wellington aircrew saw survivors in the water, 'some wearing life jackets and yellow skull caps.' All waved or defiantly shook fists, but no German survived. About a month later, Musson was killed in the crash of another Wellington.[36]

The U-106, commanded by 24-year old Oberleutnant zur see Wolf-Dietrich Damerow sailed from Lorient in company with U-107, which planted a minefield in American waters. On the fifth day out, 1 August, Damerow reported that he had repelled an aircraft, but that it or another was shadowing the boat, doubtless calling in other planes. The shadower was a Wellington on 407 Squadron RCAF, piloted by a British officer, J. C. Archer, who had dropped six depth charges and had indeed given the alarm. Two Sunderlands responded on 2 August: one on 228 Squadron piloted by Flying Officer Reader D. Hanbury and one on 461 Squadron RAAF piloted by Flight Lieutenant Irwin A. F. Clarke. Both aircraft strafed and dropped six depth charges that wrecked U-106.[37]

On 24 August 1943, three days after an attack by a Wildcat-Avenger team from the carrier Croatan, escorting convoy UGS 14, a Leigh-Light equipped Wellington on 179 Squadron piloted by a Canadian, Flying Officer Donald F. McRae, found U-134 commanded by Kapitänleutnant Hans-Günther Brosin west of Vigo and attacked in the face of heavy flak. Brosin was returning from American waters and had shot down a blimp in the Florida Straits. McRae dropped six depth charges and claimed U-134 destroyed 45 miles south of Cape Finisterre but he was unable to provide positive evidence of a kill.[38] This was often difficult, to say the least. Sometimes crews did not return to file their claim. On 27 August, Flying Officer R. B. Gray on 172 Squadron attacked U-534 which was on its third war cruise and was shot down by return fire. The pilot was awarded a posthumous George Cross.

On 6 September Flying Officer Donald F. McRae attacked U-760 off Cape Finisterre and this time there was no doubt. The U-boat, commanded by Otto-Ulrich Blum, had left La Pallice on its second war cruise on 24 July and on 12 August had been damaged in an attack by an American B-24 and had to return to port. McCrae's attack put both diesel engines out of action and U-760 limped into El Ferrol in Spain two days' later only to be interned with its crew.[39] On the night of 18/19 November, 430 miles south-west of Cape Finisterre, McRae was flying Wellington 'F-Freddie' and escorting Convoys SL.139/MK S.30 when U-211 was detected on radar and bombed by Leigh-Light. The Type VIIC U-boat, which was commanded by 27-year old Karl Hause, had left Brest on 14 October, on its fifth war cruise, and was operating as a 'flak trap'. Type VII 'Flak boats' or 'flak traps' were introduced to lure and destroy anti-submarine aircraft. Their first success came on 24 May when west of Gibraltar, the veteran U-441, the first of eight such boats, which was armed with two quad 20mms on bandstands fore and aft of the conning tower and a rapid fire 37mm flak gun on a second, lower bandstand aft, plus nests of machine guns on the bridge and a team of highly trained gunners, shot down Sunderland EJ139 on 228 Squadron flown by Flying Officer H. J. Debden, who also damaged the U-boat's bow area by depth charges. None of the flying-boat crew survived. U-211 went down with all 54 hands.

On 7 September 1943 Pilot Officer E. M. O'Donnell DFC on 407 Squadron RCAF carried out an attack in 'W-William' on a U-boat believed to be U-669, commanded by Oberleutnant zur see Kurt Köhl, which was outbound for a special operation code-named *'Kiebitz'* to take aboard former U-434 Kapitänleutnant Wolfgang Heyda, who escaped from a Canadian PoW camp at Baie de Chaleurs, New

Brunswick on the Canadian east coast. The attack, in which O'Donnell dropped five depth charges, was actually directed against U-584 and they inflicted no damage.[40] On the night of 10 September a Leigh Light-equipped Wellington on 179 Squadron, piloted by a Canadian, Squadron Leader D. B. Hodgkinson DFC found U-617 commanded by Kapitänleutnant Albrecht Brandi about one hundred miles east of Gibraltar near the coast of Spanish Morocco. Attacking into 'heavy' flak, Hodgkinson dropped six depth charges that disabled U-617.[41]

Three hours later, in the early hours of 11 September, another Wellington on 179 Squadron, piloted by Pilot Officer W. H. Bronini, arrived and, in the face of 'intense' flak, dropped six more depth charges. These attacks so badly damaged U-617 that Brandi, could not dive. To avoid certain capture, he drove the boat into shallow water offshore and abandoned ship. After he and the 48 crew reached the beach, Spanish troops took them into custody.[42]

Among Australians serving in the Leigh Light Squadrons was Pilot Officer M. H. Paynter on 612 Squadron. At three o'clock on a black morning in October 1943, when the water was covered in a thick sea mist he piloted a Wellington in one of the many Leigh Light operations in the Bay of Biscay. The Wellington had been sent out to search for a dinghy previously reported in the Bay, and it was flying low when an unidentified object was picked up on the detector apparatus. Paynter switched on the Leigh Light and in a few seconds it swivelled round on to a fully surfaced U-boat. As soon as the light went on, red and white and green tracer bullets streamed up from the submarine's guns, and the glass of the Leigh Light was shattered and the tail of the aircraft hit. Paynter's navigator, Pilot Officer J. W. McKay RAAF had moved along to man the front gun, and at 300 yards could see the gun crew clearly. He opened fire and saw his tracer ricocheting off the deck. Then the Wellington swept in from the beam and dropped a stick of depth charges across the conning tower. McKay kept firing until they passed over and the fire from the submarine slackened and then died away. The last two depth charges straddled the U-boat. The rear gunner saw the explosion close to the conning tower and then there was nothing more in the pitch blackness. The Wellington stayed near the spot for another twenty minutes and then proceeded on patrol. An hour and twenty minutes later the crew found the dinghy floating 100 miles off the Spanish coast near Cape Finisterre. It illuminated the spot, reported its position and returned to base.[43]

Forty miles WSW of Cape Spartel at the mouth of the Gibraltar Strait in the early minutes of 1 November U-340 was damaged in a bombing attack by Leigh-Light Wellington piloted by Flying Officer Arthur H. Ellis DFC on 179 Squadron. Ellis dropped six depth charges but an engine malfunction forced Ellis to abort. Later in the day RN destroyers HMS *Active* and HMS *Witherington* and HMS *Fleetwood* found the U-340 with sonar and attacked with depth charges. The U-boat, which had left St Nazaire on its third war cruise on 17 October, was abandoned by its commander, 28-year old Hans-Joachim Klaus, after passing through the Straits due to extensive damage. Forty-eight hands were rescued by Spanish fishermen but were then taken off by HMS *Fleetwood* and taken into captivity.[44] In the early hours of 10 November 1943 the U-966, commanded by 25 year old Oberleutnant zur see Eckehard Wolf, which sailed from Trondheim on 5 October, was found by a Leigh Light-equipped Wellington on 612 Squadron piloted by Warrant Officer Ian D. Gunn while inbound to France via the northern Spanish coast south-east of Punta Estace. Gunn attacked U-966, dropping six depth charges, all of which fell short. After an exchange of gunfire, U-966 dived.[45]

On the night of 26 November 'H-Harry', a Leigh Light-equipped Wellington (HF146) on the Azores-based 179 Squadron piloted by Flight Sergeant Donald M. Cornish found the U-542, commanded by Oberleutnant zur see Christian-Brandt Coester north of Madeira. The boat was on its first war cruise, having left Kiel on 21 October for the Azores area. Cornish and his crew had earlier sunk U-431 in the Mediterranean east of Cartagena on 21 October[46] and three days' later forced Kapitänleutnant Hans Hornkohl to scuttle U-566 in the North Atlantic thirty miles west of Porto after a bombing attack as the steering gear failed and the screws were ruined.[47] Flying into heavy flak, Cornish dropped six depth charges that destroyed U-542, which was lost with all hands.[48]

In November 547 Squadron converted to the Liberator. On the 15th 415 (Swordfish) Squadron RCAF moved to Bircham Newton, Norfolk, for operations using Leigh Lights to illuminate targets for its Albacores to attack E-boats. The Royal Navy was also involved, as Fred Dorken, a WOp/AG on the squadron, recalls: 'The Navy would stay a few miles beyond the convoy route in their MTB and MGBs and when the E-boats were within range, working singly we would drop flares and illuminate them for the Navy. The E-boats had impressive armament and we longed for bombs instead of flares. We flew eight-hour patrols against enemy convoys and several ships were destroyed. (We carried 500lb bombs on these trips.) All told, it was hours of boredom and every once in a while, wild excitement.' The North Sea in wartime is a cruel place and a goodly number of crews just disappeared.'

Derek Bielby, a Coastal Command pilot recalled the experience of a Polish crew on 304 Squadron at Chivenor near Barnstaple in north Devon, one black night in the Bay of Biscay in the winter of 1943. It proved again the rugged durability of the Wellington aircraft.

'The night-aircraft of Coastal Command were navigated, in those days, by dead reckoning. The method depended on the constant measuring of drift[49] by taking back bearings on flame floats dropped overboard. These devices ignited on contact with the sea. As drift-taking took place with monotonous frequency, the sea was often dotted far and wide with the flame-float pattern of other aircraft of 19 Group flying parallel courses in the saturation search for surfaced U-boats. Indeed, on a moonless night with a heavy overcast, it appeared as though the heavens and the sea had changed places.'

Flying one night in such conditions, the captain of one of 304's Wellingtons was suddenly puzzled to see four glowing red dots just in front of him. Equally suddenly the apparition vanished, and the aircraft shuddered with the stupefying shock of hard contact. Baffled by the swiftness of the phenomenon, the captain realized that there had been a collision of some sort and though the aircraft vibrated uncharacteristically, it was manageable and still flew. As the patrol was reaching its limit, the pilot at once turned for home and the long, lonely haul over six hundred miles of hostile sea. It was only after the aircraft had been safely parked and the engines shut down that the ground crew discovered that the Wellington's fin and rudder were missing. And when a Coastal Command

Liberator returned to its 19 Group base the same morning after an all-night Biscay sortie, minus the outer part of a wing, the realization of what had actually happened gradually dawned. The patrolling Polish pilot had seen the red-hot exhausts of the four-engined Liberator as it closed on a collision course. Inches only must have averted the sudden and total loss of both aircrews and aircraft. Chance had, yet again, played a fateful hand...'[50]

1944 brought fresh hopes of improving the U-boat kill ratio, although the early success of Leigh Light operations was now very much reduced due to U-boats being fitted with *Schnorkel* equipment enabling them to re-charge their batteries at periscope height. After getting through Gibraltar Strait, late in the evening of 8 January 1944, a Wellington on 179 Squadron piloted by Flying Officer W. F. M. Davidson, found U-343 south of Sardinia by radar and a full moon. Attacking into heavy flak, Davidson dropped six depth charges on the U-boat, which was commanded by Oberleutnant zur see Wolfgang Rahn. Riddled by flak, the Wellington crashed into the sea, throwing Davidson clear, but the rest of the airmen perished. Davidson found a raft, climbed in and was later rescued by Allied forces.[51]

North-east of the Azores on the night of 13 January the U-231 commanded by 33-year-old Kapitänleutnant Wolfgang Wenzel was located by aircraft from the aircraft carrier USS *Block Island* which brought up Wellington HF168 'L-London' on 172 Squadron piloted by a Canadian, Pilot Officer W. N. Armstrong DFC who was on a night escort patrol over a convoy. In two runs into flak, 420 miles northeast of the Azores, Armstrong dropped six depth charges that wrecked the U-231 beyond saving. 'There was a brilliant blue flash after my depth charges had gone down' recalled Armstrong 'and I think one of them must have hit the sub. We stooged around for a while and then saw him again. It looked as if he was too damaged to dive, and my gunners opened up immediately, raking the sub from end to end. This time, however, he was ready for us and gave us everything he had. The flak was terrifying and it's a near-miracle we weren't hit then.

'I came round for my third attack run. The U-boat was clearly silhouetted in the moon-light and I could see that the hull aft of the conning tower was under water, with the bows clear of the sea. My own gunners kept up so effective a barrage that the Jerry gunners only got off one shot before ducking for cover, but it was an unlucky shot for us. It hit our rear turret, smashing it and exploding right in front of the gunner, Flying Officer H. B. W. Heard. I didn't know about this at the time and only first learned what had happened when I asked over the intercom what the rear gunner had seen of our attack. Back came the answer, 'Sorry, but I'm afraid I must come out. I've been hit.' He showed amazing courage and managed to lever himself out of the turret with his arms - he'd been hit badly in the legs. Despite his pain, he insisted on writing up his own report during the return journey - just in case he didn't make it, as he said - and was laughing and joking. At base, as soon as we landed, they rushed him to hospital where he underwent amputation, but he lived.'

With his boat flooding heavily aft, Wenzel ordered abandon ship. An American intelligence reported that: 'Sometime during the abandoning of his boat, Wenzel, probably in a fit of despondence, attempted suicide by firing a revolver bullet into his mouth.' The bullet 'lodged harmlessly...in the back of the neck and most crew members were unaware of the event.' All fifty men on U-231 escaped from the sinking boat in rafts and dinghies, but seven soon died of exposure. About thirteen hours later, on 14 January, two aircraft found the survivors and two American destroyers, the USS *Parrott* and the USS *Bulmer* picked up the forty-three Germans and transferred them to the *Block Island*, which arrived in Norfolk on 3 February. A doctor on *Block Island* removed the bullet in Wenzel's neck.[52] Flying Officer Heard and Armstrong were each awarded a DFC.

Identification and confirmation of claims for kills were still posing problems. West of Bordeaux on 31 January 1944 Wellington MP813/K flown by Flight Sergeant L. D. Richards on 172 Squadron using a Leigh Light for a night attack, was thought to result in the destruction of U-364 but it was actually directed against U-608, inflicting no damage. The Wimpy was shot down in the attack without being able to drop its depth charges.[53] In moonlight west of the Butt of Lewis/Hebrides on 1 February Pilot Officer Max Paynter on 612 Squadron and another Wellington on 407 Squadron RCAF attacked U-545 commanded by 34-year old Kapitänleutnant Dr. Gert Mannesmann, which was on its first war cruise. The 407 Squadron Wimpy was shot down by the U-boat's 37mm AA gun. U-545 was crippled in the battle and one crewmember of the gunnery crew was killed before the boat was scuttled by her crew, 56 of whom were rescued. Paynter and his navigator, Pilot Officer J. W. McKay RAAF were awarded the DFC.[54] On occasion identification was easier. In the North Atlantic 180 miles south-west of the Faeroes on 11 February, U-283, which was on its first war cruise, having left Kiel on 13 January, was bombed in a night attack by Wellington MP578 'C-Charlie' flown by Flying Officer P. W. Heron DFC on 407 Squadron. The night before, U-283 had shot down a Wellington on 612 Squadron. Heron dropped six depth charges on the boat which was lost with all 49 hands including the commander, 21-year old Günther Ney, the youngest officer yet to command a U-boat at sea. In the Bay of Biscay on 3 March while U-525 was homebound to Lorient, another Leigh Light-equipped Wellington on 172 Squadron, piloted by J. W. Tweddle, bombed and severely damaged the U-boat, which was skippered by 35-year old Kapitänleutnant Hans-Joachim Drewitz. U-525 limped into Lorient, escorted by two Junkers Ju 88s and several small vessels. The boat was out of action until April.[55]

On 10 March 380 miles west of the mouth of the River Shannon on 10 March the gunners on U-625 and U-741 shot down Wellington HF311 on 407 Squadron RCAF flown by Pilot Officer E. M. O'Donnell. Sunderland EK591/U on 422 Squadron RCAF flown by Warrant Officer W. F. Morton, who was on his first operational sortie as captain and Flight Lieutenant Sidney W. Butler DFC along as check pilot, who were en route to their patrol area to escort Convoy SC.154, spotted U-625, which was commanded by 25-year old Siegfried Straub, a standard 517-tonner without the forward gun and she carried two twin 20mm mountings on the upper platform and one on the lower, the latter being well shielded. Butler, who was at the controls at the time, avoided flak by frequent alterations of height and dropped six depth charges. U-625 sank by the stern and all 53 hands perished.

Next day a Leigh Light-equipped Wellington 'H-Harry' flown by Flying Officer H. C. Sorley on 407 Squadron RCAF found and attacked the U-256 and U-741, which ran into difficulties while racing to locate and rescue shipwrecked Germans. U-256 suffered 'severe' damage. British and Canadian sources state that U-256 shot down 'H-Harry' but Oberleutnant zur see Wilhelm Brauel the U-boat commander, reported that the aircraft 'crashed 1500 metres off before own fire opened up.' Oberleutnant zur see Gerhard Palmgren in the outbound U-741 also reported an air attack. When he later surfaced, he said, he was attacked again, this time by 'four carrier aircraft and three destroyers,' which pursued him for hours, but inflicted only 'slight' damage. No trace of the U-625 crew was ever found by friend or foe. U-256 reached Brest on 22 March;[56] the U-741 continued her patrol. Meanwhile, the U-629, commanded by 27-year old Oberleutnant zur see Hans-Hellmuth Bugs, which sailed from Brest on 4 March was damaged the following day by DCs dropped by a Wellington on 304 Squadron which forced him to return to Brest on 7 March.[57] After repairs Bugs re-sailed on the 9th, but in the early hours of 12 March, 'C-Charlie', a Leigh Light-equipped Wellington on 612 Squadron piloted by D. Bretherton attacked into heavy flak and dropped four depth charges. These inflicted so much damage that Bugs was compelled to abort to Brest a second time, arriving on 15 March. The boat did not re-sail until 8 June when Bugs put to sea on a war cruise bound for the Plymouth area.[58]

In the North Atlantic in the early hours of 13 March U-575 commanded by Wolfgang Boehmer was attacked into heavy flak by Leigh-Light Wellington HF183/B piloted by Flying Officer John P. Finnessey DFC on 172 Squadron. Finnessey attacked with depth charges, dropped float flares, gave the alarm and broadcast beacon signals. At dawn Fortress FA700/R flown by Flight Lieutenant A. David Beaty DFC on 206 Squadron arrived on the scene and attacked into heavy flak and dropped four close depth charges. When the automatic feed of the U-boat's 37mm gun failed and it had to be loaded by hand. Boehmer decided to submerge. Overhead it looked to Beaty that U-575 went down stern first with her bow sticking up at a steep angle. Beaty climbed, broadcast an alarm and circled the position for five hours, sending beacons. Fortress 'J' piloted by Flying Officer Wilfred R. Travell DFC on 220 Squadron soon arrived. Seeing a large oil slick, Travell dived and dropped two depth charges into its middle. He then climbed and broadcast homing signals for the benefit of an American hunter-killer group which included the 'jeep' carrier USS *Bogue* with Grumman Avengers of VC-95 on board. One of the Avengers, piloted by John F. Adams came on the scene that morning, found the oil slick and dropped sonobuoys. A hunt was commenced by USN destroyers *Haverfield* and *Hobson* and RCN frigate HMCS *Prince Rupert* escorting Convoy Outbound North 227, backed by aircraft on the *Bogue* led to depth charge and Hedgehog attacks which finally forced U-575 to the surface. All three warships opened fire with main guns and an Avenger piloted by Donald A. Pattie attacked with rockets and bombs. These finally destroyed U-575 which sank with the loss of sixteen hands. Fourteen survivors were rescued and taken prisoner by *Prince Rupert* and took them to Newfoundland and 24, including the commander, were picked up by USS *Hobson*, which took them to Casablanca for eventual transfer to the United States.[59]

In the Bay in the early hours of 28 April 1944 the Admiralty believed that U-193, captained by Oberleutnant zur see Dr. Ulrich Abel, which had sailed from Lorient on 23 April to report weather and to serve as a provisional refueller if needed, came under air attack by 'W-William', a Leigh Light-equipped Wellington on 612 Squadron piloted by the Australian, Flying Officer 'Max' Paynter, a veteran of the

U-boat wars. Paynter reportedly picked up U-193 on radar and from wave-top level, dropped a salvo of depth charges that destroyed the boat west of Nantes. Paynter reported 'about ten small bluish lights in the water,' evidently illuminants on the life jackets of the German survivors.[60]

On 4 May in the North Atlantic Flight Lieutenant L J Bateman DFC RCAF on 407 Squadron RCAF piloting a Leigh-Light equipped Wellington (HF134/M) bombed U-846 in bright moonlight north of Cape Ortegal. Attacking into heavy flak, Bateman released six depth charges. Nothing more was ever heard from the boat, which presumably was sunk at this time and with the loss of all hands.[61] It was sweet revenge, for U-846, which was commanded by Berthold Hashagen on its second war cruise, had shot down Halifax HR741/H on 58 Squadron into the sea two days' earlier with no survivors on Flight Lieutenant D E Taylor's crew.

By June Coastal Command operations had reached a peak, with priority task of keeping the English Channel free of German shipping in preparation for the imminent invasion of Europe. Included in Coastal Command's Order of Battle were seven Wellington squadrons: 172, 304 (Polish), 407 'Demon' Squadron RCAF and 612 AAF at Chivenor while 179, returned from Gibraltar were at Predannack. 415 RCAF, and 524 at Davidstowe Moor were the remaining two squadrons. In Biscay on the early hours of 7 June, several aircraft of 19 Group attacked U-989 commanded by Kapitänleutnant Hardo Rodler von Roithberg. Coastal Command gave credit for the damage to a Leigh Light-equipped Wellington on 179 Squadron piloted by W. J. Hill. A Liberator and a flight of Mosquitoes also participated in the attack. Wounded in the thigh by Mosquito gunfire, von Roithberg aborted to Brest for medical attention.[62]

On the night of 6/7 June - the night of D-Day - Coastal Command reported the loss of a Wellington on 407 Squadron RCAF flown by Squadron Leader Farrell, and three Liberators, but it is not known which U-boats made which kills. In the early hours of 7 June a Leigh Light-equipped Wellington and/or a Liberator and perhaps other aircraft as well hit the U-415, newly commanded by 24-year old Oberleutnant zur see Herbert Werner. At a briefing he and fourteen other U-boat captains had been informed that their directive was to 'attack and sink the invasion fleet with the final objective of destroying enemy ships by ramming'. Werner wrote: 'Was suicide the purpose for which we had been trained so long? Was this futile gesture the greatest glory and satisfaction we were permitted to take down with us to our wet graves? Werner described the air attacks in his book *Iron Coffins*:

'00.30: Radar impulses chirped all around the horizon, their volumes shifting rapidly from feeble moans to high-pitched screams. The Tommies were obviously flying at various distances around our absurd procession. They must have thought we had lost our minds. Sometimes I could hear aircraft engines at fairly close range, but could not spot a plane. The hands of my watch crept slowly ahead while the British waited for reinforcement; our eyes sharpened and our hearts beat heavy under our breasts.

'01.12: The battle began. Our leading boats were suddenly attacked. Tracers spurted in various directions and then the sound of gunfire hit our ears. Fountains reached into the sky.

'01.17: One of the enemy aeroplanes caught fire. It flashed comet-like towards the head of our file, crossed over one of the boats, dropped four bombs and then plunged into the ocean. The bombs knocked out Sachse's U-413. With helm jammed hard-a-port, the boat swerved out of the column. She lost speed rapidly and sank below surface.'

U-415's 37mm flak gun crew then claimed a Liberator shot down.

'Open fire!' I screamed. Five barrels, all that we had available, blazed away at the Liberator as it dropped four depth charges ahead of U-256 and roared past us. Four giant water columns leaped skywards behind the riddled aircraft as it tried to escape our fire. But some shells from our 37mm gun hit the plane broadside. It exploded in mid-air and then plunged into the sea.'

Of the eight U-boats that had sailed out together, only U-415 and two others limped back to Brest with several wounded and severe battle damage. Werner dry-docked U-415 for emergency repairs and went to a hospital to have a slight head wound dressed.[63]

On the night of 8 June Flight Lieutenant L. Antoniewicz, captain of Wellington HF331 'A-Able' on 304 (Polish) Squadron claimed to have destroyed U-441 40 miles north of Ushant. The veteran boat's commander, 31-year old Kapitänleutnant Klaus Hartmann and all hands was thought to have perished. U-441 was a Type VII, the first of Kapitänleutnant Klaus Hartmann and all hands was thought to have perished. U-441 was a Type VII, the first of eight 'Flak boats' or 'flak traps' armed with two quad 20mms on bandstands fore and aft of the conning tower and a rapid fire 37mm flak gun on a second, lower bandstand aft, plus nests of machine guns on the bridge and a team of highly trained gunners, to lure and destroy anti-submarine aircraft. Their first success had come on 24 May when they shot down Sunderland EJ139/L on 228 Squadron flown by Flying Officer H. J. Debden, who also damaged the U-boat's bow area by depth charges. None of the flying-boat crew survived.

On 8 June west of Gibraltar, U-441 was nearing the end of a two-weeks patrol and 50 miles from its intended haven at Brest when it had the misfortune to cross the path of Antoniewicz's Wellington; the aircraft having had a complete breakdown in its radar-search equipment and merely relying on the 'Eyeball Mk I' for the completion of its patrol in the bright moonlight. Antoniewicz had been about to alter course to investigate a thin trail of vaporous grey smoke on the sea when he sighted at three miles distant, a black object which he identified almost immediately as the conning tower of a surfacing U-boat. He turned to port to get on an attacking course. At the same time he lost height. When one mile away, the 2nd pilot and radar operator in the astrodome sighted another U-boat, which had apparently just surfaced 1½ miles away. Antoniewicz kept on his course to attack first U-boat, which then started to submerge slowly. At 2257 hours six depth charges were dropped from 100 feet, spaced sixty feet and set to 14-18 feet. The rear gunner distinctly saw the first two hitting the water to starboard quarter of the U-boat about ten yards from hull and the remainder across the U-boat and on its port bow. Then he saw them explode and the explosions and plumes completely obscured the U-boat. He also saw a long black pipe-like object blown about 100 feet into the air with the depth charge explosion. When the explosion plumes subsided there was no sign of the U-Boat and the conning tower was only just visible when the DCs were dropped. Antoniewitcz's attack however, had probably been directed against U-988 commanded by 24-year old Oberleutnant zur see Eric Dobberstein which was lost with all fifty hands.⁶⁴

There were several Wimpy losses at sea during June. On the night of 12/13 June Wellington 'K' on 179 Squadron flown by Flight Lieutenant Walmsley was lost over the Channel and all the crew perished. On 13 June a Liberator on 53 Squadron hit the U-270 commanded by Kapitänleutnant Paul-Friedrich Otto. The German gunners, who had earlier destroyed a Fortress on 206 Squadron, shot down this aircraft as well. On the same day 'Y-Yorker', a Leigh Light-equipped Wellington on 172 Squadron piloted by L. Harris, hit U-270 and caused such damage that Otto aborted to Lorient.⁶⁵ A 415 Squadron Wellington with Pilot Officer G. H. Krahn and crew went missing from Ostend.

Early in September 1944 Arthur Rawlings joined 179 Squadron at Predannack. He recalls: 'My position was that of wireless operator-air gunner in Squadron Leader E. E. M. Angell's crew. Most of our operations in the Wellington Mk XIV were night sorties, using radar search and homing procedures, descending to fifty feet (using radio altimeter to inspect suspect contacts. The Leigh Light was switched on at about a quarter mile range.'

Squadron Leader Angell himself recalls: 'With overload tanks and carrying six depth charges, we used to patrol at about 1,500 feet for up to ten hours. We were given set areas to patrol from Predannack in the Bay of Biscay and from Benbecula and Limavady in the North Western Approaches. On making a radar contact the drill was to home in going down to sixty feet on the radio altimeter and illuminating with the Leigh Light at three quarters of a mile. In preparing to attack, the bomb doors would be opened and the depth charges armed. The Leigh Light would be lowered and lined up with the target in accordance with radar reports by the second pilot who had remote controls in the nose. He would switch on and search for the target on the instruction, 'Leigh Lights on!' from the captain. The front guns would be manned by the navigator sitting astride the second pilot and he would open fire if the submarine was surfaced. The pilot would release the DCs by eye, spacing them 60 to 100 feet apart. The rear gunner would be ready to fire at the submarine after the aircraft had passed over it. The wireless operator would already have sent a sighting report before the attack and would be preparing to send an attack report. Like so many aircrew on anti-submarine operations, I never actually saw a U-boat.'

Flying Officer 'Gord' Biddle's crew on 407 'Demon' Squadron RCAF, one of the few all-Canadian squadrons serving with Coastal Command, were also involved in anti-submarine operations in September 1944 stationed at Wick in north Scotland. Flight Sergeant Harvey Firestone, one of the wireless-operator-air gunners, recalls. 'Shortly after midnight on Tuesday 26 September we were briefed for a routine patrol off the coast of Norway. We feared that the trip would be cancelled because of persistent bad weather. A few days earlier we had missed an operation when Biddle had come down with a very high fever. We did not want to miss two trips in a row, so we hurried to board 'S-Sugar', a Leigh Light-equipped Wellington. Despite the wild and stormy weather we were given the green light to take off. With visibility down to about a quarter of a mile and with a fifty-knot wind from the west, we managed to become airborne at 0050 hours. We headed out over the North Sea and proceeded to our patrol area. We were about thirty miles out from the Norwegian coast on a course roughly parallel to it, when suddenly, at 04.52 hours, our starboard engine coughed and spluttered but commenced running smoothly again. Biddle climbed hurriedly to 3,000 feet. A short time later it coughed once and a large fireball gushed out of the exhaust. Biddle throttled back immediately. George Deeth, the second pilot, feathered the propeller and pushed the automatic fire extinguisher on. He switched the engine off and closed the fuel cocks and gills. 'George Grandy, at the wireless set, sent out a QDM-S (SOS) signal to Group. Fortunately, radio reception was good but Group informed us that the headwind we faced was not expected to abate but rather increase. They suggested we should try to reach the Shetlands and told us to continue sending signals so they could plot our course and attempt to monitor our position.

'Everything that we could do without was thrown out of the aircraft to maintain height and reduce strain on the one engine. Deeth and Neil threw the batteries that powered the Leigh Light out of the forward hatch. Graham threw out the radar equipment. Even the Leigh Light went, after quite a struggle for Graham and me. We rid ourselves of the ammunition through the opening where the Leigh Light had been. The parachutes went too. Meanwhile, Neil and Deeth got rid of the ammunition for the single nose gun. Biddle, who had turned for home, had jettisoned the depth charges but we were still losing altitude.

'At 1,000 feet Biddle decided, after consulting with Neil and Deeth, that as we had about 5,000lb of petrol still in the wing tanks, we could jettison about three quarters of it and still reach the Shetlands. The jettison valve was open for about twenty seconds, then closed but Graham, watching from the astrodome, reported that petrol was gushing from the wing outlet even after the jettison valve had been closed. Biddle and Deeth tried several times to stem the flow but the meter finally showed no petrol in the wing tanks. We could no longer hope to reach the Shetlands against the fifty-knot head-wind. We had only 92 gallons of petrol in our reserve tanks. We were over 100 miles from Sumburgh, the nearest British base and less than that from the Norwegian coast. Group ruled out an ASR operation for many hours and that to attempt to ditch in the raging sea would be suicidal. We all agreed, very reluctantly, that our only hope would be to turn round and head for Norway. Group were advised. They acknowledged and wished us luck. Our ground speed picked up considerably with the wind at our back and at the break of dawn we sighted the mountainous coastline of Norway. We heard Ken Graham softly praying over the intercom as we neared land.

'We could see nothing but mountains with low hanging clouds obscuring the tops. Biddle spotted an entrance to a fjord and headed towards it. We could see some ships escorting a submarine. We had little choice but to fly over the small convoy as our petrol at this time was just about all gone. As we neared the ships we were met by heavy machine-gun fire. Biddle took what little evasive action he could. I fired off a Very cartridge in the hope that we would confuse the gunners into thinking that we were a friendly plane. They stopped firing momentarily but started to fire again when they realised our deception. I fired off another but fooled no-one. Tracers entered just beside Graham in the astrodome. Our good engine had also been hit. Biddle and Deeth searched for a place to put the plane down as we had lost all power. They told me to tell Grandy and Graham to take crash positions. Grandy sent a final message and tied down the key. He strapped himself in at the wireless set. Neil was on the navigator's table. Biddle was in the pilot's position. Deeth, after first pumping down the flaps and opening the top hatch, took up his place behind the door. Graham and I braced ourselves on the floor behind the main spar. Silently, we turned to each other, shook hands and waited, wondering if we were going to make it.

'Biddle swung the plane around into the wind and without power, at over 100 knots per hour, attempted a wheels up landing on what appeared to be the only spot possible. We hit some trees with our port wing, shearing some branches about four feet from the ground. Biddle brought the tail down first to slow us up and then jammed the nose in. We slewed around and came to a very sudden stop, having landed in just about 65 feet. Grandy and the radio fell on top of Deeth, Neil was thrown from his table and had a gash in his head and a cut on his hand. Biddle was jolted but not hurt physically. The astro hatch, which had been removed in order for us to leave the plane and which had been thrown to the rear of the aircraft, came plummeting forward toward Graham and me. I instinctively ducked and when we hit the second time I hit my head on the main spar, dazing myself momentarily. Graham and I fully expected to see water come pouring into the aircraft but we had made it safely to land. As we jumped to the ground I saw that we had attracted a small crowd of people.'

Biddle's crew had crash-landed at Haughland on the outskirts of Os (Osoyra), three kilometres south of Bergen. They destroyed their maps and detonated the IFF equipment before burning their aircraft and headed in a south-easterly direction. Fortunately, they fell into the hands of the 2nd Company of the Milorg Resistance in Os and were later aided by the Norwegian SOE. On 6 October the Canadians witnessed at first hand the first all-Canadian daylight bomber raid, on U-boat bases at Bergen and Hattvik. The six airmen and the Norwegian sailor were picked up in a motor launch on the night of 11 October and taken to a waiting Norwegian naval vessel. Next day they were landed at Scalloway in the Shetland Islands, a distance as the seagull flies of 220 miles, via Leif Larson's 'Shetland Bus'; a service run by Norwegians in exile. Next day, the BBC broadcast *'Coconuts on holiday'* to tell their Norwegian friends that the Canadians had reached England safely.

The war continued for other crews in Coastal Command. On 21 October 1944 Squadron Leader E. E. M. Angell's crew was posted to 172 Squadron at Limavady, Northern Ireland and on 14 November Angell was posted to command a Halifax squadron. Flying Officer Chambers took over as pilot. Arthur Rawlings recalls: 'We had only one sighting of a U-boat just before the end of the war. We saw a periscope which was immediately submerged when we turned to attack. This was in the area of the Mull of Kintyre and the coast of Northern Ireland. At this time the enemy was increasingly entering the vicinity of the Clyde and North Channel in a last ditch effort against our shipping. Although Liberators and Sunderlands did most of the convoy escort duties' we once did an escort for the *Queen Elizabeth* on one of her troop carrying trips. She was too fast for the convoy system and both she and the *Queen Mary* were always independently routed. Of course, we had to keep a respectful distance but we could see the decks covered with thousands of GIs.'

Apart from enemy action, changing weather was a constant source of anxiety to Wellington crews on long, over water patrols. Icing could cause severe problems, as Gordon Haddock, a WOp/AG on 36 Squadron recalls: 'With radar being somewhat primitive it was deemed one man should not have to gawk at the screen for more than 1½ hours at a time. So, by having three people in the same category, one could play musical chairs every hour or so from being radar operator, to the wireless operator, to the rear gunner. Invariably, we would toss a coin as to who would choose the position for take-off. While on an anti-U-boat course at RNAS *Maydown*, Northern Ireland, on 26 December, I was lucky in winning the toss and choosing to start the trip as rear gunner. In flight the carbs iced up and we crashed into Way Moors Wood in Devon. The radar operator was killed and the wireless operator was facially burned. Neither he nor the captain ever flew again.'

The new U-927, commanded by 28-year old Kapitänleutnant Jürgen Ebert, sailed from Kristiansand to the English Channel on the last day of January 1945. Off the Lizard on the evening of 24 February, 'K-King', a Leigh Light-equipped Warwick on 179 Squadron piloted by Flight Lieutenant Antony G. Brownsill, got a radar contact on U-927's snorkel. He attacked from an altitude of seventy feet, dropping six depth charges at the snort in a perfect straddle. Nothing further was heard from U-927. Brownsill was later awarded the DFC.[66] The successes of the Leigh Light Wellingtons were to continue until the final victory in Europe in May 1945; with the final confirmed U-boat sinking by a Wimpy occurring on 2 April 1945 when southwest of Ireland, Warrant Officer R. Marczak piloting Wellington 'Y-Yorker' on 304 (Polish) Squadron sank the U-321. Oberleutnant zur see Fritz Berends and 41 crew perished.[67]

Arthur Rawlings concludes, 'We had the pleasure of escorting in a surrendering U-boat off the west of Ireland a few days after hostilities ended on 4 May.' Then Coastal Command was quickly run down. During June, 14, 36 and 407 RCAF Squadrons disbanded at Chivenor while 172 disbanded at Limavady in Northern Ireland. On 14 June 304 (Polish) Squadron was posted to Transport Command. By 7 July 524 and 612 AAF Squadrons had disbanded at Langham, Norfolk.

Footnotes

19   Term applied to Sonar equipment used for locating submerged submarines. ASDIC (an acronym for 'anti-Submarine Detection Committee' the organization that began research into this device in 1917) emitted a distinct 'ping' when locating the target.

20   The second 'Happy Time' for the U-boats came with the entry into the war by America following the Japanese attack on Pearl Harbor on 7 December 1941. The US Navy failed to learn from the bitter experience suffered by the Royal Navy and shipping losses off the American eastern seaboard 'grew to ridiculous proportions'. Between January and June 1942 567 ships were sunk at a cost of 21 U-boats. *U-boat Fact File* by Peter Sharpe (Midland Publishing Ltd 1998).

21   ASV radar, developed in parallel with Airborne Interception radar, was first demonstrated in trials in 1938. The first operational ASV sets were fitted to Hudson and Sunderland aircraft of Coastal Command but were only capable of looking directly forward and consequently were of limited value. The first ASV to be fitted to Wellingtons was the sideways-looking ASV MK.II. In trials, aircraft flying at 2,000 feet ASL detected a 10,000 ton ship at 40 miles range, a destroyer at 20 miles and a submarine at 8 miles. ASV Mk.II required four antennae on each side of the rear fuselage and a further four antennae on the spine of the rear fuselage. Wellingtons so equipped included the GR VIII, GR XI, GR XII and GR XIII variants and were known as 'Sticklebacks' or, on Malta, as 'Goofingtons'. Combined with Yagi antennae beneath the wings and lower nose of the aircraft, ASV MK.II provided the radar operator with information on both range and bearing of surface vessels. Aircraft equipped with ASV Mk.II proved so successful at detecting submarines that in August 1942 the Germans introduced the 'Metox' receiver to warn of approaching aircraft equipped with ASV. In late 1942 the Mk.III centimetric radar appeared.

Comparable with the H$_2$S navigation radar used by Bomber Command, in calm seas it was even capable of detecting a 'schnorkel' device from a submerged U-boat. The 'Stickleback' and Yagi antennae were replaced by a single rotating scanner housed in a radome beneath the nose of the aircraft, which in turn necessitated the replacement of the front gun turret with a Perspex cupola. Wellingtons equipped with ASV Mk III included late production GR XI's GRXIIs and the GRXIV. It was not until the closing months of the war that the Germans introduced 'Naxos', a warning receiver operating on centimetric wavelengths. Even so, Naxos had a maximum range of just 5,000 metres or less than one minute's warning of an attack.

22   *Submarine: An anthology of first-hand accounts of the war under the sea, 1939-1945* edited by Jean Hood (Conway Maritime 2007).

23   On 5 June the *Luigi Torelli* was hastily repaired and left Aviles the next day. Sunderlands on 10 Squadron RAAF found the U-boat and after circling it realized that the Italian commander was unable to submerge. A total of 15 depth charges were dropped on the submarine by the two Sunderlands and they hounded the boat into Santander. A month later the *Luigi Torelli* 'escaped' 'internment' at Santander and limped into Bordeaux. In 1943 the *Luigi Torelli* went to the Far East, was taken over by the Kriegsmarine after Italy's surrender and retitled UIT-25. After Germany surrendered in May 1945 UIT-25 was used by the Japanese who titled her RO-504. Four months later she fell into American hands and was finally scuttled in 1946.

24   See *'In Great Waters: The Epic Story of the Battle of the Atlantic 1939-45'* by Spencer Dunmore (Pimlico 2001). U-159 was bombed by a Martin Mariner of VP-32 210 miles ESE of Jamaica on 12 July 1943 and was lost with all 53 hands. *U-boat Fact File* by Peter Sharpe (Midland Publishing Ltd 1998).

25   They were formerly credited with the destruction of U-578, which was outbound for an operation in the North Atlantic, which was lost with all 49 hands and including 40-year old Korvettenkapitän (Lieutenant Commander) Ernst-August Rehwinkel. When U-578 failed repeatedly to report its position, it was posted as missing in the Bay of Biscay effective 11 August 1942. However, research by Axel Niestlé (*German U-boat Losses During WWII*, Greenhill Books 1998) states that the attack was actually directed against U-135 commanded by Kapitänleutnant Friedrich- Hermann Praetorious, inflicting minor damage. U-135 was sunk in a naval action on 15 July 1943. See *U-boat Fact File* by Peter Sharpe (Midland Publishing Ltd 1998).

26   *Miroslav Vild, Flying With Fate* by Alois Siska quoted in *Thanks For The Memory: Unforgettable characters in Air Warfare 1939-45* by Laddie Lucas (Stanley Paul and Co Ltd 1989). In June 1943 311 were re-equipped with four-engined B-24 Liberators, altogether more formidable aircraft for the long Atlantic or northern waters patrols. On 24 June 1944 Flying Officer J. Vella DFC and crew attacked the U-971 which crash-dived and hit the seabed and then surfaced out of control during a depth charge attack by two TN destroyers. U-971 was scuttled and all except one of the crewmen were taken prisoner. When Miroslav Vild and the crew flew their 30th operation on 1 November 1944, their tour was over; for the radio and radar-operator it was his 106th mission. Siska was shot down three times, the third into the North Sea in midwinter while piloting a 311 Squadron Wellington. The ditching, on 28/29 December 1941, and six days in an open dinghy in arctic weather, had left him with but two companions as they were finally blown into captivity on the Dutch coast. Frostbite and gangrene had forced the German surgeons' decision to amputate his legs. A heart attack stopped the operation as he was about to be wheeled to the theatre. Other treatment brought limited recovery. Three years later, Siska was taken by the Gestapo from Colditz to Prague, there to face trial by court-martial for 'treason and espionage' against the Third Reich. Only liberation by US forces thwarted the inevitable death by firing squad.

27   Wellington 'E-for- Ela' had sustained almost 40 bullet or cannon strikes, the starboard petrol tank had a six-inch square hole; the auxiliary oil tank was damaged; a jagged three feet by six feet hole had been ripped out in the wing fabric; wing ribs were damaged; airscrew spinners, engine nacelles, astro-dome, aerial and the length of the fuselage all bore strikes and ruptures. Exactly one month later, on 16 October 1942, Flying Officer Stanislas Targowski set off in high spirits on yet another trip over the notorious Biscay. That morning he had received his first letter from his wife, still in Poland - his first since 1939 - while only two hours after he left the squadron received notification of an award of the DFC for Targowski and immediately set about preparing a celebration party for his return. The squadron waited in vain - somewhere over the Bay that day Targowski and his crew, including four of 'E-Ela's crew on 16 September, were shot into the sea by the Luftwaffe.

28   In February the squadron handed its Wellingtons over to 172 and 179 Squadrons and reverted to the Whitley, which it flew until April 1943 when it was re-equipped with Wellingtons again.

29   *Axel Niestlé: German U-boat Losses During WWII* (Greenhill Books 1998)/ *U-boat Fact File* by Peter

Sharpe (Midland Publishing Ltd 1998). On 3 March 1943 Flying Officer Lundon and crew were shot down by U-333 during an attack.

30   U-333 was sunk on 31 July 1944. *Hitler's U-boat War: The Hunted, 1942-1945* by Clay Blair (Random House 1998). Another 172 Squadron Wellington attack by 'G-George' on 22 March 1943, formerly credited with the destruction of U-665 commanded by Kapitänleutnant Adolf Dumrese, was actually directed against U-448 commanded by Oberleutnant zur see Helmut Dauter, inflicting no damage. U-448 was sunk during a naval action on 14 April 1944. *Axel Niestlé: German U-boat Losses During WWII* (Greenhill Books 1998).

31   In a post-war reassessment the Admiralty credited the kill to a Whitley on 10 OTU. *Hitler's U-boat War: The Hunted, 1942-1945* by Clay Blair (Random House 1998).

32   West of St Nazaire on 2 May 1943 Flight Lieutenant E. C. Smith on 461 Squadron RAAF piloting a Sunderland, attacked U-465 commanded by 35-year old Korvettenkapitän Heinz Wolf, which was bound for the Atlantic. The conning tower was sighted and a flame float was dropped, followed by an aluminium sea marker and marine marker. At 1124 Smith sighted the U-boat on the surface and attacked with six depth charges. U-465 sank horizontally and then the stern emerged and disappeared vertically. Of the 48 crew, fifteen or more were seen to abandon ship but none were rescued. *U-boat Fact File* by Peter Sharpe (Midland Publishing Ltd 1998).

33   *Axel Niestlé; German U-boat Losses During WWII* (Greenhill Books 1998).

34   *U-boat Fact File* by Peter Sharpe (Midland Publishing Ltd 1998)/*Hitler's U-boat War: The Hunted, 1942-1945* by Clay Blair (Random House 1998).

35   *Hitler's U-boat War: The Hunted, 1942-1945* by Clay Blair (Random House 1998).

36   *Hitler's U-boat War: The Hunted, 1942-1945* by Clay Blair (Random House 1998).

37   *Hitler's U-boat War: The Hunted, 1942-1945* by Clay Blair (Random House 1998).

38   *Hitler's U-boat War: The Hunted, 1942-1945* by Clay Blair (Random House 1998). U-134 was lost with all 48 hands. *U-boat Fact File* by Peter Sharpe (Midland Publishing Ltd 1998).

39   *U-boat Fact File* by Peter Sharpe (Midland Publishing Ltd 1998).

40   After research by *Axel Niestlé (German U-boat Losses During WWII,* Greenhill Books 1998) who attributes the loss of U-669 to unknown causes. When U-669 repeatedly failed to report its position after sailing, it was posted as missing effective 8 September 1943. U-584 was lost with all 53 hands on 31 October 1943 when it was sunk by American Avenger torpedo bombers.

41   After dawn on 11 September, swarms of Hudsons and Swordfish of 48, 233, 833 and 886 (based at Gibraltar) located the abandoned hulk of U-617 and attacked with bombs and rockets. HMS *Hyacinth*, a corvette; British trawler *Haarlem* and Australian minesweeper *Woollongong* then arrived to destroy U-617 with shellfire. Hodgkinson, the Canadian who originally found and disabled U-617, was awarded the DFC. *Hitler's U-boat War: The Hunted, 1942-1945* by Clay Blair (Random House 1998).

42   Brandi was later given command of U-380. *Hitler's U-boat War: The Hunted, 1942-1945* by Clay Blair (Random House 1998).

43   See *RAAF Over Europe* edited by Frank Johnson (Eyre & Spottiswoode London November 1946).

44   *Hitler's U-boat War: The Hunted, 1942-1945* by Clay Blair (Random House 1998)/*U-boat Fact File* by Peter Sharpe (Midland Publishing Ltd 1998).

45   Later that morning, a US Navy PBY4-1 Liberator of VB 103, piloted by Lieutenant Kenneth L. Wright, found U-966 near El Ferrol. Wright made two attacks, dropping six depth charges and killing some Germans by gunfire. A PBY4-1 of VB 105 piloted by Leonard E. Harmon joined the attack. Soon there arrived yet another PBY4-1 of VB 110 piloted by Lieutenant J. A. Parrish, who dropped six close depth charges in spite of the heavy flak. Lastly, a Liberator on 311 Czech Squadron piloted by Flight Sergeant Otakar Zanta attacked U-966 with rockets about 3 miles off the Spanish coast. These attacks killed eight Germans and wrecked the boat. Wolf ran her aground off Punta Estaca and then blew her up. He and 41 other Germans reached shore in dinghies. *Hitler's U-boat War: The Hunted, 1942-1945* by Clay Blair (Random House 1998).

46   Cornish was flying Wellington MP741 'Z-Zebra' when he attacked the U-boat in the Mediterranean east of Gibraltar. All 52 hands including the commander, Oberleutnant zur see Dietrich Schöneboom perished. *U-boat Fact File* by Peter Sharpe (Midland Publishing Ltd 1998).

47   The crew were rescued by the Spanish fishing boat *Fina* and landed in Spain for return to France. *U-boat Fact File* by Peter Sharpe (Midland Publishing Ltd 1998).

48   It was previously believed that U-542 was sunk on 28 November 1943 by Wellington 'L-London' on 179 Squadron. The original assessment was changed in September 1990 following research by *Axel*

Niestlé (*German U-boat Losses During WWII*, Greenhill Books 1998).
49 The variation in an aircraft's intended track over land and sea due to winds.
50 Quoted in *Out of the Blue: The Role of Luck in Air Warfare 1917-1966*, edited by Laddie Lucas (Hutchinson & Co Publishers Ltd 1985).
51 On 10 March 1944 U-343 was sunk in a naval action.
52 *Hitler's U-boat War: The Hunted, 1942-1945* by Clay Blair (Random House 1998)/ *U-boat Fact File* by Peter Sharpe (Midland Publishing Ltd 1998).
53 Axel Niestlé; *German U-boat Losses During WWII* (Greenhill Books 1998). When the U-boat failed repeatedly to show up or to signal its position, it was posted as missing, effective 31 January 1944. All 49 hands perished.
54 *U-boat Fact File* by Peter Sharpe (Midland Publishing Ltd 1998).
55 U-525 was sunk with all 54 hands on 11 August by a Wildcat-Avenger team from the carrier USS 'Card'. *Hitler's U-boat War: The Hunted, 1942-1945* by Clay Blair (Random House 1998).
56 On 23 October 1944 U-256 was decommissioned at Bergen and cannibalised. In May 1945 the boat was captured by British forces.
57 U-629 had been damaged in an attack on 4 January 1944 by Wellington 'C-Charlie' on 304 Squadron. *U-boat Fact File* by Peter Sharpe (Midland Publishing Ltd 1998).
58 At 2214 hours on 7 June Flight Lieutenant Kenneth Owen 'Kayo' Moore, a Liberator pilot on 224 Squadron, took off in 'G-George' and at 02.11 hours on the 8th a radar contact was made dead ahead at twelve miles. At three miles a U-boat was sighted on the surface in the moonlight. Moore did not need to switch on his Leigh Light and he attacked from about fifty feet with six depth charges, which straddled the conning tower. U-629 disappeared leaving wreckage and oil on the sea. It was lost with all 51 hands.
59 *U-boat Fact File* by Peter Sharpe (Midland Publishing Ltd 1998)/ *Hitler's U-boat War: The Hunted, 1942-1945* by Clay Blair (Random House 1998).
60 According to *Axel Niestlé; German U-boat Losses During WWII* (Greenhill Books 1998) it was subsequently thought that the attack by Punter was directed against U-802, inflicting no damage. U-193 failed to report its position after sailing from Lorient and it was posted as missing in the Bay of Biscay after 6 May 1944 with the loss of all 59 hands. U-802, which was presumed lost in October 1944, surfaced and surrendered on 9 May 1945. *U-boat Fact File* by Peter Sharpe (Midland Publishing Ltd 1998).
61 *Hitler's U-boat War: The Hunted, 1942-1945* by Clay Blair (Random House 1998).
62 *Hitler's U-boat War: The Hunted, 1942-1945* by Clay Blair (Random House 1998). U-989 was lost in a naval action north of the Shetland Islands on 14 February 1945. All 47 hands perished. *Axel Niestlé; German U-boat Losses During WWII* (Greenhill Books 1998).
63 *Submarine: An anthology of first-hand accounts of the war under the sea, 1939-1945* edited by Jean Hood (Conway Maritime 2007).
64 *U-boat Fact File* by Peter Sharpe (Midland Publishing Ltd 1998) which also states that U-988 was previously believed to have been sunk on 28 June 1944 off Start Point. *Axel Niestlé (German U-boat Losses During WWII*, Greenhill Books 1998) claims the 'U-boat' that Antoniewicz sank was probably 'a whale'! The Admiralty later credited a Liberator on 224 Squadron piloted by Flight Lieutenant Kenneth Owen 'Kayo' Moore with the sinking of U-441, which restored his unprecedented claim of two sinkings in a single sortie, justifying the award of the DSO. *Hitler's U-boat War: The Hunted, 1942-1945* by Clay Blair (Random House 1998). Later, another U-boat was sighted, actually U-373 commanded by Oberleutnant zur see Detlef von Lehsten, which was on its twelfth war cruise, from La Pallice, bound for the Invasion Front. Moore attacked with six depth charges and sank the vessel. (Moore had sunk both boats within 20 minutes). He took 'G-George' in again and turned on his Leigh Light to pick out three dinghies on the surface of the sea and a few survivors swimming in the oil and wreckage. (U-373 was lost with six hands, 47 survivors being rescued by French fishermen). Moore received an immediate DSO, while DFCs were awarded to Warrant Officer Johnston McDowell, one of the navigators and Warrant Officer Peter Foster, the WOP/AG. Sergeant John Hamer the flight engineer received a DFM.
65 *Hitler's U-boat War: The Hunted, 1942-1945* by Clay Blair (Random House 1998).
66 *Hitler's U-boat War: The Hunted, 1942-1945* by Clay Blair (Random House 1998). U-927 was lost with all hands.
67 In total 304 Squadron flew 2,451 sorties, attacking 34 U-boats and sighting nine others, had 31 combats with German fighters and lost 106 aircrew men killed or missing. Two U-boats were claimed destroyed and a third seriously damaged.

Chapter 3

Night Offensive

The tail-light of the last Wellington vanished for a moment in a dip in the runway and appeared again, dwindling as it climbed steadily, to be lost at last among the stars. 'Well, that's the last one away.' The airfield control pilot turned and climbed back into the caravan which was his movable headquarters. The little group that had been watching the take-off dispersed. 'Hope it's Berlin,' growled one of the flare-path party and the other nodded agreement. 'Do the Hun good, some of that will,' he added.

'Who's cold?' inquired the WAAF driver, reaching in under the seat of her Fordson and producing a flask of coffee. They were all cold, for the flare path had been laid early and they had been standing around in the still, frosty air for some time. The hot drink was welcome. One of the men pocketed the empty flask to refill it for her when he went off for his supper. The night dragged a little, for it was some hours before the raiding bombers could be expected back.

The moon was just going down behind a hump of the Downs when the faint hum of the first returning bomber brought the sleepy group alive again. The sound of the approaching engines grew steadily, until the signaller's quick eyes picked out a navigation light. 'There she comes!' They stood watching, until suddenly the signal light flashed out from the aircraft, to be answered promptly by the green Aldis lamp. The aircraft roared by overhead, circled the airfield and came in to land, settling down smoothly, with the familiar 'crumph' of tyres meeting the hard runway. They came steadily then, with hardly a pause and within an hour all but one were in.

The almost continuous roar died away at last, the dispersal lorry was signalled safely back around the perimeter track to the dispersal point to await the last crew and silence settled down again. But it was a restless, uneasy silence. The ACP and the driver retreated to the lee-side of the caravan and stood, shoulders hunched against the cold, hands in her pockets, watching the bright starlight sky. They stood in silence for a long time, till the driver jerked her head up, listening intently.

'D'you hear anything?' she asked; and they both stood, straining their ears in a silence that was almost tangible.

'I don't know. Don't think so.'

At last she turned and stubbed out her cigarette and silence settled again to be broken, minutes afterwards, by the man's voice. 'Johnny's in that crew. We've been together since we joined.'

'It's a rotten war,' said the girl. And then: 'How much longer can we give them?'

'They should have been back before now.'

Neither would say what they both knew - that it was already too late. They just stood there, hardly aware of the bitter cold, waiting. It was half past five when the telephone rang and the officer reached forward and picked it up. 'ACP speaking... No, sir... Yes, we've been listening... There's not, sir ... No, nothing...' He set the instrument slowly back on its rest and picked up his book again, but he did not read.

Outside a grey dawn crept up over the empty sky.

They Also Serve by Sergeant N. A. Varley.

Early operations against German shipping had proved, at the cost of many valuable crews, that unescorted daylight bombing was out of the question. The losses seemed to have shaken the War Cabinet out of its chivalrous attitude towards the German civilian population but it would not be until March 1940 that the so called 'niceties' of war were dispensed with and Bomber Command was allowed to bomb land targets for the first time. The RAF night offensive had opened in February 1940 with 'Nickel' raids with propaganda leaflets or 'Bumphlets', being dropped on Germany. 'Nickelling', while of doubtful value as propaganda warfare, did, however, provide some training for the crews under operational conditions and the British cabinet were anxious that the RAF be seen to be operating with impunity against Germany and so leaflet dropping became of major importance. Later, in *'The RAF The Second Year'* Wing Commander W. T. S. Williams DSC reminded his readers that Generalleutnant von Metzsch, German authority on total war, 'has said '500,000 pamphlets (weighing 1 ton) may be more effective than an air raid with 100 tons of explosives.' Forthright as ever, Air Chief Marshal Sir Arthur Harris said it was 'Nonsensical, absolutely nonsensical. I always said that the only thing leaflet raids would achieve would be to supply Germany with toilet paper for the rest of the war!'

Unfortunately, the darkness was to prove no greater ally than daylight had been. On 2 March a Wellington on 149 Squadron intending to drop leaflets over Bremen crashed shortly after take-off when one engine developed trouble and the other cut out altogether. All the crew perished in the crash. The following night a Wellington IA on 99 Squadron crashed at Barton Mills, killing all six crew, after being recalled from a 'Nickel' sortie to Hamburg. In March 1940 the first Wellington ICs were issued to the squadrons. The Mk.IC had re-designed hydraulics and a 24-volt electrical system, which permitted the use of the new directional radio compass. Crews, ever mindful of the beam attacks made by the Luftwaffe; soon installed hand-held machine-guns in the long narrow side windows. In March significant changes occurred at RAF Mildenhall. The headquarters of 3 (Bomber) Group moved from Mildenhall to Harraton House at Exning, near Newmarket. On 3 March the first Wellington ICs were issued to 149 Squadron, quickly followed by 99 Squadron. The Mk.IC had re-designed hydraulics and a 24-volt electrical system, which permitted the use of the new directional radio compass. Crews, ever mindful of the beam attacks made by the Luftwaffe; soon installed hand-held machine-guns in the long narrow side windows. Mark ICs were first used on 20 March during a sweep over the North Sea. Next day Wellington ICs on 149 Squadron made a night reconnaissance over Germany. Then, on 23 March, Wellingtons reconnoitred the River Elbe and the port of Hamburg. One crew, which lost its way, was shot down by anti-aircraft fire near Dunkirk. All the crew managed to abandon their aircraft and reach the safety of Allied lines.

On 2 April 9 Squadron was dispatched to Lossiemouth and 115 Squadron began operating from Kinloss. The moves came none too soon. In total secrecy, on 3 April, Germany mounted 'Weserubung Nord' and supply ships sailed for the invasion of Norway. The British and French, not least the neutral Norwegians and Danes, were caught off balance. The Wellingtons were finally brought into action on 7 April. During the afternoon Blenheims attacked but their bombs missed and another attempt by six Wellingtons on 9 Squadron and another six on 115 Squadron was thwarted by bad visibility. On the way home flying close to broken cloud off Denmark, 115 Squadron was jumped by Bf 110s. Two Wellingtons piloted by Canadians, Pilot Officer Estelles Arthur Wickenkamp MBE and Pilot Officer Roy Allen Gayford were shot down with no survivors and three others were damaged.

Next day the Wimpys attacked and claimed hits on a cruiser in Bergen harbour. On 11 April six Wellingtons on 115 Squadron operating from Kinloss attempted to bomb Sola airfield at Stavanger. Three aircraft bombed the airfield. Pilot Officer Frederick Edward Barber was shot down and Flight Sergeant G. A. Powell's Wellington was seriously damaged and he had to belly-land back at Kinloss without hydraulics. He was later awarded the DFM for this operation. On 12 April six Wellingtons on 149 Squadron took off from Mildenhall and followed in trail behind six Wellingtons on 38 Squadron from Marham as part of a force of 83 aircraft seeking German shipping at Stavanger. No warships had been sighted when the Wellingtons were intercepted by Bf 110s. The enemy pilots, again employing beam attacks to excellent advantage, shot down two bombers on 149 Squadron and Squadron Leader Maurice Nolan's Wellington on 38 Squadron. All were killed. Twelve Wellingtons on 9 and 115 Squadrons, which were ordered to make a bombing attack on two cruisers, the *Köln* and the *Königsberg* in Bergen harbour, fared little better. None of their bombs did any lasting damage.

Operating from Wick on 13/14 April Pilot Officer George Lesley Crosby ditched 22 miles off Whitby. All the crew perished. Wellingtons on 38 Squadron also operated against Sola airfield and flew the first of three operations to Stavanger on the 16th. The next bombing operations against German forces were made at night on the airfield at Aalborg in Denmark where the Luftwaffe had established a large supply base for their Norwegian campaign. On the night of 17/18 April 75 Squadron despatched three Wellingtons to Stavanger for its maiden bombing operation.[68] On the Stavanger operation two aircraft managed to bomb the target. Then on 25 April, six Wellingtons on 149 Squadron took off late at night in another attempt to bomb Stavanger. It proved abortive. Thereafter, the Wellingtons were again employed on North Sea sweeps and night reconnaissance operations over the island of Sylt to prevent mine-laying seaplanes from operating.

On 2/3 May 24 aircraft including twelve Wellingtons bombed Stavanger, Rye and Fornebu. In all, the Marham Wellingtons flew 173 sorties during the month to Norway, Waalhaven and oil targets in Germany with the loss of five aircraft and crews. On 9 May a Wellington on 38 Squadron at RAF Marham was brought to readiness for a security patrol to Borkum in the German Friesian Islands. The front-gunner, LAC G. Dick, recalls.

'The object was to maintain a standing patrol of three hours over the seaplane base to prevent their flarepath lighting up and thus inhibit their mine-laying sea-planes from taking off. We carried a load of 250lb bombs in case a discernible target presented itself. We took off at 2130 hours. Holland was still at peace and their lights, though restricted, were clearly visible, the Terschelling lightship in particular, obliging by giving a fixed navigational fix. After three hours monotonous circling and seeing next to nothing, I heard Flying Officer Burnell, our Canadian pilot, call for course home. The words always sounded like music to a gunner in an isolated turret with no positive tasks to take up his mind, other than endless turret manipulation and endless peering into blackness. I heard the navigator remark that the lightship had gone out and the pilot's reply, 'Well give us a bloody course anyway'. One only had to go west to hit Britain somewhere, or return on the reciprocal of the outward course - drift notwithstanding. After an hour's flying with the magic IFF box switched on for the past thirty minutes, I gave the welcome call, 'Coast ahead!' Much discussion occurred as to where our landfall really was. I told them I thought north of the Humber, which was 150 miles north of our proper landfall at the Orfordness corridor. I was told to 'Belt up'. As a gunner, what did I know about it? (I had flown pre-war on 214 Squadron for two years up and down the East Coast night and day and was reasonably familiar with it.) Probably pride would not let them admit that they were 150 miles off course, in an hour's flying. Eventually, a 'chance light' showed up and we landed on a strange aerodrome, which turned out to be Leconfield. Overnight billets were arranged at 0400 hours for the visiting crew. However, others were on an early start. They switched on the radio at 0600 hours and gave us the 'gen' that at around midnight Germany had invaded Holland, Belgium and France - hence the extinguished lightship. The odd thing was, we had returned with our bombs, as it wasn't the done thing to drop them indiscriminately. We returned to base later on the tenth to be greeted with 'We thought you'd gone for a Burton'. Good news was slow in circulating in those days.'

On 10 May, after eight months of inaction, the front in France erupted. German forces were sweeping into Holland, Belgium and Luxembourg. Parachute and glider troops had seized the forts and crossings of the Meuse. The balloon had truly gone up. At Honington Wing Commander Andrew McKee, the New Zealander CO of 9 Squadron could tell his crews little more than they had gleaned from their wireless sets. As expected, all crews were on standby; all aircraft were to be checked; any air tests must be completed before noon. They were to reassemble at 1430 hours unless a call went out to order otherwise. It was back to the mess for breakfast, to shave, to dress properly and then to go to dispersal. Clean the guns, talk to the fitters and tune up the wireless; keep busy; try not to think of the hours ahead.

Rupert 'Tiny' Cooling was second pilot in Sergeant 'Duggie' Douglas' crew, one of two new crews who had arrived on the base barely three days before. Their pilots were among the first of the RAF Volunteer Reservists to reach an operational unit. Behind them were exhilarating hours of weekend flying in Harts and Hinds and Audaxes, the pleasures of buzzing about in Blackburn B.2s and Tiger Moths. A 12-week course on Oxfords had been interesting; conversion to the Wellington a challenge. Ten tons of aircraft, two 1,000-horsepower engines, a wingspan of more than 86 feet; to a youth just days out of his teens it seemed as if someone, somewhere, had made a man-sized mistake. Now, six weeks later, he was to discover the purpose to which it had all been directed, as Cooling recalls.

'Honington, the home of 9 Squadron, lay in the flat fields of Suffolk. Bury St Edmunds, a bus ride away, was a pleasant, quiet, uncluttered town. It had good pubs, a cinema or two and even a theatre. The squadron, part of 3 Group, Bomber Command, was regarded as most happily housed; Feltwell and Marham were somewhat isolated and Newmarket was a racecourse. A peacetime station, Honington had sound brick buildings and a crescent of three hangars fronting the grass landing area - the standard layout of RAF stations in the late 1930s. Now those hangars were draped with nets, disguised with irregular scraps of dun and dark green canvas. The enclosed air smelt of tar. Within them stood some of the squadron's aircraft - Wellington Mk IAs and a single Mk I to use for training. They were aeroplanes which had already gone to war. From Lossiemouth, on the shores of the Moray Firth, the bombers had thrust through darkness to strike at the German invaders of Norway. To some of the crews Stavanger was as well known as a nearby town

'With coming summer shrinking the hours of darkness, the Wellingtons withdrew. They had been deployed in daylight before, on 18 December 1939. On that occasion the Group had gone to Wilhelmshaven. Twenty-four Wellingtons on Nos. 9, 37 and 149 Squadrons set out. Two were forced to return shortly after take-off. The other 22 pressed on. Ten were shot down over the target; two ditched on the way home. Only seven made it back to base; three were forced to land shortly after crossing the Norfolk coast. It was an occurrence much in the mind of the aircrew as they made their way to the briefing rooms beside the hangars that Friday morning.

'The mess was quiet at lunchtime. Serious groups gathered round the radiogram, listening silently to the news. A lot was said but little was learned: things did not seem to be going well. It was all far from reassuring.

'Word went around - briefing at 1500 hours. Tension eased fractionally; at least here was something positive, even if it left two hours to conjure with, to fill with 'ifs' and 'maybes'. Lunch lay in the stomach like a warmed weight of unkneaded dough; there was a slightly greasy feeling in the bowel. Unwilling though they might be, none of the aircrew would have opted out if given any choice. Each was impatient only with semi-stagnant time which stretched its sinister prospect into unfocussed future. At a few minutes before three, small groups began to walk slowly, casually, towards the hangars. Sergeant Douglas said little. His uniform was well pressed and his buttons shone. This would be his first operation in command. Jock Gilmour was the observer, a Scot from Glasgow, extrovert, friendly to the new boy flying as second pilot. Both had a dozen or so trips behind them but both were quiet as they considered the events which were to unfold. They passed the parade ground upon which, only yesterday, the squadron had been drawn up in serried ranks. Young blond LAC Frank Horry, in best blue, had marched forward to receive the Distinguished Flying Medal from the Air Officer Commanding. Frank Horry, rear gunner, a survivor of 18 December, would be airborne again on this sortie.

'The murmur of voices stilled as McKee walked briskly into the crew room, followed by his flight commanders. The target was the aerodrome at Waalhaven; Rotterdam's airport. It had been seized by German troops. Junkers Ju 52s were flying in men, munitions and supplies.

The operation had cost the Luftwaffe dearly. Large numbers of airborne troops attempting to capture the airfields of Ypenburg and Valkenburg were annihilated by Dutch forces and the German plan to capture the Dutch Royal Family and Government in The Hague was a complete failure. The transport aircraft suffered heavily, anti-aircraft fire destroying many of the lumbering, low-flying Ju 52/3M tri-motors. Others stuck in the soft soil and mud when attempting to land on the uncompleted airfield of Valkenburg, while Dutch fighters strafed and destroyed many more transports that had landed on the beach north of The Hague. Although fearfully outnumbered, the Army Air Service fought valiantly and immediately after the occupation of Waalhaven by the German airborne forces three T.V bombers of 1st Air Regiment attacked the transport aircraft packed on the airfield. Only one returned to base.[69]

Dutch troops were to counter-attack at last light. The Wellingtons would crater Waalhaven airfield, destroy the transports and soften up the defences. Each was to carry sixteen 250lb bombs, nose and tail fused for maximum fragmentation. Weather was forecast to be fine; the winds south-westerly. Flak, said the intelligence officer, would be light stuff, mainly 20mm. The Germans had had no time to bring in heavy anti-aircraft weapons. Single-engined fighters were unlikely but there were reports of Bf 110 activity. He did not mention that five out of six Blenheims had been shot down by 110s earlier in the day and over the same target. Take off time was 1730 hours; aircraft would proceed independently.' In all, 36 Wellingtons would be despatched by Bomber Command.

'The hot mahogany-coloured sweetened tea was welcome, but no one really felt like food. With relief the crews returned to the locker room to sort out flying kit, clip on parachute harnesses and pull on flying boots. I followed Sergeant Douglas around, going through the motions, keeping out of the way. Jock Gilmour laid out the tracks, measured distances, computed courses and estimated flight times. It was reassuring to see that he had done so for the trip both out and home. We were to fly a Mark IA, 'U for Uncle'.

'Pilot, second pilot and observer stood beneath the jutting chin, the bulbous panelled Perspex nose. Bomb doors gaped; 16 ovoid shapes, the colour of damp sand, nestled against the matt black bomb beams; 32 bright steel arming wires snaked to the safety slides on nose and tail pistols. Observer and armourer checked the circuits; there was no point in taking them to Holland and dropping them 'safe'. Sergeant Douglas climbed the wooden ladder and settled in the green leather seat, fixing his Sutton harness. Jock Gilmour followed him to disappear into his gloomy compartment beyond. LAC Oliver, squirrel-like, was stowing equipment about his Marconi W/T set. I boarded last; looked down at the oblong square of grass framed in the open hatchway, reached for the proffered ladder which linked me with the safe and solid ground beneath and stowed it behind the batteries. The hatch shut with a thud. England, beneath my feet, was now another world. To reach it would require a journey beyond my current comprehension.

'The starter motor whined; the port engine stuttered and bellowed into life. Another jerky whine as the starboard propeller slowly rotated; more hesitant pops and another bellow. 'U for Uncle' trembled like a dog waiting to be unleashed. Full throttle; check each magneto, the pitch control, the boost, oil pressure and temperature. Throttle back, chocks away; the Wellington heaved into motion and rolled over the soft green grass. There was a brief pause as the man ahead took off. Raps to 15°, cowling gills all but shut, into wind and roll forward to straighten the tail wheel. Thin attenuated voices crackled in the earphones. 'Rear gunner, OK', 'Centre gunner, OK', 'Navigator and wireless op, OK'. Sergeant Douglas looked at me, nodded and then steadily opened the throttles. The respiratory rumble of the engines swelled to a roar as the Wellington began to move. The tail rose and the lumber accelerated to a scurry. The twin Pegasus engines raised their pitch to a plangent howl, the big balloon tyres spun over the grass, left it for an instant, touched once, touched once again and then the safety and security of Suffolk dropped away beneath. A squeeze on the brake levers and the wheels stopped. The detente which held the undercarriage selection at 'safe' was snapped down, the short stubby lever pulled up. On the instrument panel green lights went out, red ones replaced them. The H-frame legs swung slowly rearwards until the undercarriage doors, matt black below the engine nacelles, closed them in a tight concealing embrace. In response to the gentlest rearward pressure on the stick, 'U for Uncle' lifted her nose, thrust her chin above the horizon and heaved her heavy belly into the calm evening air. Honington lay a thousand feet below; behind the sun was low; ahead stretched Suffolk fields to Orfordness, then the separating sea, Holland and the unknown hazards of a hostile sky.

'The light was perfect; a butter-yellow glow irradiated the green of growing grain. Small herds of cattle grazed or lay content, indifferent to the drone of the aircraft overhead. From their lofty aspect the pilots and rear gunner watched the wide familiar vista flow past. Ahead, a stripe of gold and a glint of silver: the sandy shore gave way to the sea. An angry vibrato drummed through the airframe and a smell of burnt cordite seeped back as the guns were tested. Below, the polished grey waves lay frozen into immobility; the Wellington's height and speed had stilled their restless motion. Away to starboard, England was reduced to a dark shadow, separating sea from sky. Within a few moments it had vanished. With it, strangely, went those last niggling doubts; those faint tremors of fear were swamped by a rising tide of excitement. The sombre shadow now lay straight ahead. Another strand and the dark green of shoreline scrub gave way to fields and shining panes of glass. Straight skeins of water chequered the flat landscape. 'Wireless operator to front turret. Second pilot to the astrodome.

'Beyond the Wellington's bulbous nose, the deep grey shroud of night was being lifted above the horizon. Against it and still distantly, danced a curtain of dainty coloured lights, apple green, fuchsia pink, starry white. As 'U for Uncle' closed upon them, I saw, peering through the Perspex dome amidships, the flickering curtain of flak was hemmed with orange flame and rolling curls of dense black smoke. Jock Gilmour's voice over the intercom caused him guiltily to draw his fascinated gaze from the rising ribbons of glittering sequins to scan the sky for fighters. 'Bomb doors open. Target in sight. Right a little, right.' The last word was drawn out and then chopped as the nose came round to the required heading. Now the lights were directly ahead. The pattern seemed to part; to open up a pathway before closing in behind. Slowly at first the bright stars rose, gathering speed to race towards the aircraft and pass beyond the wing-tips and the tail. 'Left, left. Steady. Bombs gone.' The Wellington jerked perceptively, as 4,000lb of metal and high explosive plunged from the gaping belly.

'There was a sharp 'twack' like some large and floppy fly swat striking the fabric skin. A triangle of the camouflage covering leapt up to dance upon the upper surface of the starboard wing.'

Surprised at his own calm and composure, Cooling said, 'Pilot, we've been hit. Starboard mainplane. There's a patch of fabric flapping just outboard of the engine.'

The curtain of flak fell away behind. Another aircraft stood out in silhouette against the darkening sky. Cooling's heart thumped almost painfully and then subsided as he recognised another Wellington. A lazy line of grey surf hemmed the dun-coloured sands, suggesting the margin of comparative safety, the Dutch coast. 'U-Uncle' flew on past the Dutch coast. Out over the North Sea Sergeant Douglas handed over control to 'Tiny' Cooling before going aft to see the damage for himself.

'It was dark when 'U for Uncle' crossed the Suffolk coast. Electric blue flashes from Honington beckoned to within sight of the flickering gooseneck flare path. Undercarriage selector down; on the instrument panel, green lights lit up. Pitch levers to fully fine, and the engine note rose an octave. Line up, full flap; trip out the rearward pressure in the stick. The Chance light poured a pool of ghostly brilliance across the grass, draining into the surrounding darkness. The flares slipped past as U for Uncle felt, once more, for solid ground. With a gentle bump the wheels touched, the tail settled. Then the Wellington tugged determinedly to starboard. Brake, rudder, engine could not hold the aircraft straight. It came to a stop all but facing downwind, the tail partly across the line of flares. In the light of the downward recognition lamp the flattened starboard tyre was clearly visible. A figure appeared within the luminous pool, studied the wheel, and then dissolved into the draughty darkness. A hollow knocking noise sounded on the hatch in the bomb aimer's position below the pilot's feet. Then it rose, framing a face. The second pilot handed down the wooden ladder and the flight sergeant fitter climbed aboard. Sergeant Douglas pushed back his flying helmet to listen to the report. Then, with a brief burst of power on each engine, he brought back the propeller pitch to fully coarse and snapped off the ignition switches. A hoarse whistling sounded, as the two Pegasus wound down to a stop. Stiffly, the second pilot descended the ladder to feel again the springy soil of England beneath his flying boots. Still hot, the engine exhaust rings ticked and cracked above our heads in the cool night air as we examined the wing, the wheel and the undercarriage doors by the light of torches. A ragged patch of torn fabric as big as a dinner plate dripped intermittently, exuding the sweet smell of high octane petrol. One undercarriage door, perforated like the surface of a cheese grater, reflected a scatter of silver streaks on the matt black paint.

'Next day, we all went to see 'U for Uncle'. Overnight, the maintenance crew had removed the starboard wing; the self-sealing tanks had been extracted and lay on a line of wooden trestles. On one, above and below, sticky pustules of gunge, big and burgundy coloured had erupted to seal the punctured metal. Probing with my index finger, I found the aluminium nose-cap of a 20mm shell which had hit us. It seemed almost weightless.

'Sergeant Douglas was allotted the next aircraft delivered to Honington; 'U for Uncle', repaired, returned to a training unit. The brand new Wellington was a Mk IC, T2468, 'Y for Yorker'. She was a beauty. After another few dozen trips in her it was Sergeant Douglas' turn to retire to a training role; he had finished his operational tour. Yet another new crew arrived from the OTU. I took over 'Y for Yorker'. By a strange coincidence, our first trip together was again to the aerodrome of Waalhaven, this time in the mother-of-pearl light of a full moon. I wonder if my second pilot, on that occasion, felt as tense and nervous, as excited and exhilarated as I had been. Did he, too, find addictive that sensation of fear and self-induced dread? What had begun as a beautiful morning had developed into a day to remember. But it was the night which offered the reassurance that it could all be done again.'

Six Wellingtons on 149 Squadron bombed Waalhaven. The German violation of Dutch and Belgian neutrality had opened up a path for British bombers to fly directly from England to the Ruhr where sixty per cent of Germany's industrial strength was concentrated. However, political infighting between the French and British commands delayed matters. The French, with their hands full trying to repel an enemy force from its borders, were alarmed at the repercussions of such an action and Bomber Command, with its sixteen squadrons of Wellingtons, Whitleys and Hampdens, was prevented from carrying out the action.

On the night of 10/11 May 115 and 38 Squadrons contributed twelve and six Wellingtons respectively to the raid by 36 Wellingtons on Waalhaven airfield in Holland. The Wimpys carried twelve 250lb bombs in their bomb bays and all the attacks were carried out in dives from 4-6,000 feet down to 1,200-1,500 feet. Flight Sergeant L. Boore was unable to bomb when he found observation partly obscured by smoke from fires in the town and he returned with his bombs. On the night of 14/15 May Wellingtons on 149 Squadron bombed Aachen and the following day the War Cabinet authorized Bomber Command to attack east of the Rhine. On the night of 15/16 May Bomber Command began its strategic air offensive against Germany when 99 bombers, 39 of them Wellingtons, bombed sixteen different oil and steel plants and railway centres in the Ruhr area. No aircraft were lost over Germany but a 115 Squadron Wellington failed to return. Flight Lieutenant Alec Edward Pringle DFC had originally taken off at 2055 hours but the aircraft developed engine trouble and landing back at Marham the crew took off in another Wellington minus Aircraftsman Butler who had gone sick. On the return trip the Wellington was blown off course by an unexpected wind and it crashed at Bernay near Rouen with the loss of all the crew. By the end of the month Marham had lost another four Wellingtons.[70]

By early morning of 2 June the remaining troops of the BEF (British Expeditionary Force) had been evacuated from the shores around Dunkirk. Thousands of French troops had still to be evacuated and during the daylight hours of 3 June Wellingtons stood ready, bombed up, to attack German positions near Dunkirk. 'Tiny' Cooling at Honington recalls.

'9 Squadron were to wait by the Wellingtons, prepared to take off at 1530 hours. The target had yet to be decided. We lay on the grass by our allotted aircraft in the warm sunshine. A daylight operation was a daunting thought. Take-off was delayed by two hours; hopes rose. Take-off would be 2000 hours; the target Bergues, German positions on the southern edge of the Dunkirk perimeter. 'For God's sake,' said McKee with uncharacteristic emotion, 'make sure you drop your bombs over enemy occupied territory. Our troops have enough to cope with without the added burden of someone's misdirected aim. And keep well away from the Channel. The Navy will fire at anything overhead. In present circumstances, who can blame them?' Sergeant Douglas decided 'Tiny' Cooling would carry out the take-off and approach to the target. 'It was still daylight when I took off. As the coast appeared at Orfordness, I looked to port. A few hundred feet ahead was another Wellington, beyond it a third.' The moment of pride to be in such company made Cooling recall Shakespeare's *Henry V* before another famous battle in France. 'We few, we happy few, we band of brothers', he thought. The navigator's voice sounded over the intercom. 'Set course one-seven-one from Orfordness. ETA target 42 minutes.'

'The starboard wing dipped; the other aircraft were lost to sight. The turreted nose travelled round the horizon until, within the cockpit, the compass grid wires were aligned with the north-seeking needle. Level out, on course, the light is draining and darkness, like sediment, deepens in the Eastern Hemisphere. The sun has set and yet, due south beyond the bulbous nose, there is another sunset, a golden glowing arc resting upon the distant skyline. It is puzzling for a moment until we realize the glow is above Dunkirk; the light is from fires blazing ninety miles away.

'Douglas took over the controls; it was the second pilot's job to drop the bombs, whilst the navigator kept track of our wanderings as we sought out 'targets of opportunity.' From the bomb aimer's position the sight was awesome. Six thousand feet below, Dunkirk was a sea of flame glinting like a brightly spot lit plaque of beaten copper. We turned and flew south, avoiding the coast; skirting the column of smoke like a deep grey stake into the heart of the town. A flare ignited and drifted above a pale grey sea of smoke. We might have been flying over a lake of milky water. Spot a gun flash in that sea of featureless mist; line up its imagined position to track down the aiming wires of the bombsight and then let go a stick of three or four. Did we deceive ourselves? Scatter enough bombs about and chance will ensure that something is hit. It was time we were buying, fragments of time to load another boat; to allow another ship to sail. We left the burning beacon behind and headed home'.

Meanwhile the battle was joined in Belgium and France. Possible uses for the British bombing force had been carefully considered and discussed with the French as far back as the spring of 1939, when the seizure by Hitler of Czechoslovakia had made the prospect of a German attack in the West almost inevitable. On the night of 10/11 May 36 Wellingtons went to Waalhaven airfield and nine Whitleys to bomb bridges across the Rhine at Rees and Wesel and columns of road transport near Goch and Geldern. There were no losses. Two nights' later six Wellingtons and six Whitleys set out for the area between the Rhine and the Dutch border. All twelve aircraft returned safely. On the night of 15/16 May the first bombs were dropped in accordance with the British plan of strategic bombing. The major effort until the end of the fall of France was naturally to delay the advance of German troops, to bomb moving columns on the roads, to destroy bridges which should have been demolished by other means, or which the Germans had repaired, to attack aerodromes and to cause confusion at focal points of communication behind the enemy's lines. But on the night of 15/16 May bombers from England attacked east of the Rhine for the first time. Altogether, 99 aircraft - 39 Wellingtons, 36 Hampdens, 24 Whitleys – went to 16 different targets in the Ruhr area. Factories at Dortmund, Sterkrade and Castrop-Rauxel were designated as targets for nine aircraft each; all other targets had fewer aircraft. Eighty-one aircraft reported bombing at their primary targets or at alternatives over a wide area. This was the first strategic bombing of German industry in the Second World War. No aircraft were shot down over Germany but a Wellington, on 115 Squadron, blown off course by an unexpected wind, crashed into high ground at Burney near Rouen in France. Flight Lieutenant Alec Edward Pringle DFC and his four crewmen were all killed; the first RAF casualties of the strategic bombing war. Twelve further aircraft - six Wellingtons and six Whitleys - attacked German communications in Belgium without loss. This brought the total number of aircraft operating on this night to 111, the first time that more than 100 bombers were dispatched on one occasion since the war began.

On the night of 17/18 May more concentrated attacks were made on oil refineries and storage tanks at Hamburg and Bremen by 48 Hampdens and 24 Whitleys and six Wellingtons attacked railway yards at Cologne. A further 46 Wellingtons and six Hampdens attacked German troop communications in Belgium. There were no losses from the 130 aircraft dispatched. On 18/19 May sixty aircraft – 24 of them Wellingtons – attacked various oil refineries and railway yards in Germany and German troop concentrations in Belgium. One Whitley was lost. The night following, 78 aircraft - thirty of them Wellingtons - carried out widespread attacks on German troop communications in France and Belgium and on rail and industrial targets in Germany. Two Whitleys failed to return. On the night of 21/22 May 124 aircraft - 47 of them Wellingtons - attacked German railways leading to the battle front at many places between Mönchengladbach and Eukirchen, particularly in the Aachen area. Six aircraft; four of them Wellingtons on the operation on Dinant, were lost. A 99 Squadron

Wellington crashed near Belval killing all six crew and two Wellingtons on 115 Squadron at Marham also failed to return. One of these crews, who crashed in the target area were taken prisoner but the other crew, who crashed near Le Havre, were killed. Stan Brooks on 75 (New Zealand) Squadron was the wireless operator of Wellington Ic R3157 shot down over Froyennes, Belgium by ack-ack; the very first of 193 aircraft lost by the squadron during the war, which had the second highest losses in Bomber Command.

'My parachute had only just opened fully before I hit the ground. Shells were exploding and machine-gun and rifle fire was going on all around and I had no idea whether I was with friend or foe. I crawled to the edge of the field hoping to find a ditch in which to hide till daylight. There didn't appear to be a ditch so I continued crawling along the edge of the field. Suddenly a brilliant light picked me out and figures ran towards me ordering *Hande Hoch*! I knew I was very much in enemy territory. After spending the night in a cottage cellar with German army types, at 8am I was put on the pillion of a BMW motor-cycle combination, guard in the sidecar and taken on a hair-raising journey of about fifteen miles to a farm where two other members of my crew were being held prisoner. The three of us were then conveyed another twenty miles to a beautiful chateau where we were handed over to the Luftwaffe. Here the pilot officer [L R. R. Hockey] who had been flying as our rear-gunner was taken up the wide staircase. After about a half-hour he returned and the observer [Sergeant G. Thorp] was taken up. The pilot officer told me he had been interrogated by a flak regiment major and when my turn came, to give only name, rank and number. Eventually our observer returned and I was taken up the stairs and into a huge room.

'The interrogating officer was seated behind a desk chatting to two young Luftwaffe pilots. As one had a bandaged leg and the other an arm in a sling, they were obviously convalescing. Both smiled at me and said, 'Good Morning' in English before moving out to the balcony of the room that overlooked a lake. The interrogating officer bade me sit down and then pushed a box of 50 Players towards me. I took one and he lit it with a lighter. Then he commenced to ask me all sorts of questions to which I would give no answers other than those laid down by the International Red Cross Geneva Convention. This carried on for twenty minutes with the major becoming more annoyed and exasperated. I was not exactly pleased myself. All the time I was aware the two Luftwaffe fliers were taking a keen interest in the proceedings and from their reactions I was fairly sure they understood English. Suddenly, in his rage the major opened his desk drawer, took out a Luger and pointed it at my chest saying, 'If I don't get answers to my questions I will shoot.' At this point the two officers hurried in from the balcony and one pushed the major's revolver arm tight on the desk while they appeared to admonish him for his action. The major replaced the gun in the drawer and the two officers returned to the balcony.

'The questioning continued with, 'We know you were the pilot of the Blenheim we shot down last night and we know the airfield you came from in England.' I was a humble AC1 at the time and I then realized that as I had no flying brevet on my uniform they had assumed I was the pilot. As the

Wellington exploded in the air and only three men of the crew had apparently been captured, the Germans assumed the aircraft to be a Blenheim. When I was eventually returned to the others and we had a chance to compare notes I learned their interrogation had been on similar lines. We hoped the pilots had managed to escape and the 2nd pilot [Pilot Officer Francis Albert Gabriel Joseph de Labouche-Sparling] who had spent his early years in Belgium, had a good chance of going underground. Only after the war did I learn that he had been hit by ground fire while descending by parachute. Our skipper (Flying Officer John Noel Collins RNZAF] was killed in the aircraft.'

On the night of 3/4 June, the last night of the evacuation from the beaches of Dunkirk, a force of 142 bombers - 46 of them Wellingtons - made widespread attacks on German factories and oil plants from Hamburg to Frankfurt and a few of the Wellingtons made a last attack on German positions near Dunkirk. But bombers built for night attack could do little to check advancing Wehrmacht and by now their attacks on communications could do little to prevent the arrival of supplies on the Western Front.

All the Wellingtons and Whitleys out on the night of 9/10 June were engaged solely on impeding the German advance against the French armies; they were bombing crossings of the River Somme, northern entrances to Amiens, crossings of the Meuse, communication centres at Neuf Chateau and Libramont and troop concentrations in woods. Though there were much fewer casualties among the bombers which attacked by night, these night attacks, on German troop concentrations and communications were certainly not without hazard and adventure.

A Wellington went out from England one night to bomb a crossroads which had become a focal point of the German advance. At the time of the attack there were many convoys along the roads and all were heavily guarded by anti-aircraft guns. The Wellington swept through the defences and then came down low to bomb. As it turned away there were shells exploding all round and several fragments hit the bomber and badly damaged the petrol tanks. The pilot set course for base, but he soon found that he had scarcely enough petrol left to get him there. Then a Messerschmitt 110 appeared and much of the small stock of petrol had to be used in outmanoeuvring it. Before the fighter had a chance to open fire it fell, away; it had been caught in the German barrage. The Wellington's petrol lasted as far as Ostend; then it gave out and the pilot had to make a forced landing on an aerodrome there. This was difficult, as there was no wind-sock on the aerodrome to show the direction of the wind and the Wellington's speed indicator had been shot away. Worst of all, the Belgian troops had dug trenches, two feet deep and two feet wide, right across the flying field to prevent Germans from using it. There was nothing to do but to 'hang on and cover our heads,' as the rear gunner said afterwards. As the bomber touched the ground it turned over on its nose; the front turret was almost smashed to pieces. The whole crew were badly shaken but no one was seriously injured. They dismantled the instruments and guns and then set fire to the bomber.

But while they were doing this German raiders came over and began to bomb Ostend. They dropped four bombs on the aerodrome itself. But the aerodrome was still in Belgian hands and the Wellington crew were sheltered for a time and then were told that a ship would be leaving for England that night - it was now an hour or two after dawn. The crew made their way to the harbour and saw the captain of the ship. He told them that he would take them to England and that he would be leaving at midnight if he could get his cargo discharged in time. They said that they would wait in the ship. In the afternoon the Germans bombed Ostend again; this raid lasted for two hours and put a stop to all work in the docks; clearly the ship would not be ready to sail that night, so the airmen went ashore and slept in some wagons at a farm outside the town. At four o'clock in the morning the German bombers returned, but the airmen stayed in the wagons and got what sleep they could. At 9.30 they went down to the harbour again to find out what time the captain hoped to get away. The Germans were still overhead and one bomb fell so near to the rear gunner that the blast lifted him off his feet. Soon after this he was arrested by two Belgian army officers; they thought he was a German parachutist and would not let him go until he had got the captain of the ship to vouch for him. As the day drew on the bombing became even more intense and the airmen, who were now with two wounded men from the ship, got out of the town and took cover in a wood. There they stayed until some bombers flew over the wood and set it on fire with incendiary bombs. They went back to the farm where they had sheltered before. 'While we were there nothing very exciting happened,' the wireless operator said, 'except that four bombs fell close to the farm-house.' The captain of the ship came to tell them that he would be ready to sail at eight o'clock that night. But it was at five to ten that the ship sailed.

There were hundreds of refugees on board and as the ship moved out of the harbour a German aircraft came over and dropped a flare, which at the time everyone thought was a signal to submarines waiting a few miles off the coast, At 1 am the ship was attacked by a submarine; the captain changed course very sharply and the first torpedo missed the ship by three feet. The attack was at once reported by wireless and the captain gave orders to take a zigzag, course. Then another torpedo was fired, but this was two hundred feet wide of the mark. The submarines fired two more torpedoes at the same time; one of them missed, but the other hit amidships and cut the ship in two. The airmen had already, by good fortune, taken off their flying-boots to be ready for the water. They had the rest of their clothes on. The rear gunner, as soon as he was in the water, caught hold of a Belgian girl. He held her up as long as he could, but she did nothing to help herself. He found that she was dead. For half an hour the airmen were in the water and then they found the ship's wireless cabin still floating and climbed on top of it. There they joined an RAF fighter pilot and a soldier sitting in his greatcoat. A few minutes rest on top of the cabin and the submarine came to the surface and machine-gunned the men and women who were still in the water. They kept up shooting for about a quarter of an hour. The four men lay flat on the cabin top and were not seen. After about four and a half hours of drifting a man who had been clinging to some wreckage close by scrambled on to the cabin - it was the second mate of the torpedoed ship. The men found an oar, tied the soldier's greatcoat to it and used it as a flag. They fired the fighter pilot's revolver, which he still had and blew the mate's whistle. But any ships they saw were too far away to see or hear. At last they were seen by three British aeroplanes. These came quite low and then flew off to fetch help. Then destroyers came to the rescue and at 7am took everyone on board from the cabin. The airmen learnt that the captain's message from the ship had been received and that the destroyers had come out to help and to look for the submarine.

Italy's decision, at midnight on 10 June to declare war on Britain and France caused Bomber Command to re-direct its bombing strategy. Mussolini's intentions had already been anticipated and it was agreed that as soon as Italy joined the war Wellingtons and longer-range Whitleys would bomb her heavy industry in the north of the country. Accordingly, on 3 June, preparations were begun to transform Salon in the Marseilles area into a refuelling and operational base. At 1530 hours on 11 June Wellingtons of 99 Squadron flew in from England and landed at the forward base. Behind the scenes chaos reigned as first one order to bomb Italy was given, then countermanded by the French. Finally, an exasperated Group Captain R. M. Field, the CO of 'Haddock' force at Salon, ordered the Wellingtons off (a force of Whitleys, having refuelled in the Channel Islands, was already en-route to Turin and Genoa). The Wellingtons were prevented from taking off when at the last moment a procession of French lorries were driven directly into their path and left there! When the political shenanigans had been sorted out, more Wellingtons made the seven-hour flight from England to Salon. On 11/12 June Turin, a distance of 1,350 miles there and back was bombed by Bomber Command. Marham's Wellington squadrons operated on 15 nights in June, bombing targets in France and Germany. Sergeant Lionel Austin Morris and crew on 38 Squadron failed to return from the operation to Baden-Baden on the night of 14/15 June. Two crewmembers were killed and four survived to be taken prisoner. 214 Squadron at Stradishall flew its maiden Wellington operation when it was despatched to the Black Forest.

On 15 June two Wellingtons on 99 Squadron and six on 149 Squadron took off from Salon for a raid on Genoa. Violent thunderstorms en route prevented all but one of the Wellington crews from finding their targets and seven bombers were forced to return to Salon with their bomb loads intact. On 16 June another 38 Squadron Wellington was lost when New Zealand Pilot Officer Edward Walter Plumb's aircraft suffered an engine failure during a transit flight and went out of control at 200 feet before crashing at Marham Fen. Plumb was killed and two fitters on board were seriously injured. On the night of 16/17 June nine Wellingtons at Salon made another attempt to bomb Italy but only five crews were able to find and attack the Caproni works at Milan. This bombing attack by the Wellingtons was the last made by the RAF from any base in France. Crews returned to Salon to discover that the French had sued for an armistice and effectively, all future operations were brought to an end. The RAF force was evacuated from Marseilles on 18 June. On the night of 20 June Wellingtons on 99 Squadron were engaged in operations over the Rhine Valley south of Karlsruhe. Acting Flight Lieutenant Percy Pickard's Wellington IC was hit over Münster and he was forced to ditch about thirty miles off Great Yarmouth. Pickard and his crew were picked up by a high-speed launch thirteen hours later and landed at Gorleston.⁷¹ The bombers were out over Germany in force on every night between 17 June and 22 June. There was a pause of only one night on 22/23 June and that was because the weather was bad. But the battles of France and Flanders had cost Bomber Command, in about six weeks, two-fifths of its front-line strength.

During July 1940 the Wellingtons of 3 Group carried out attacks on west and northwest Germany, with the occasional raid on targets in Denmark. Unrestricted warfare now threatened from both sides of the Channel. During the mid-morning of 8 July New Zealand and Commonwealth crews stationed at Feltwell, home of 75 Squadron RNZAF knew there was a 'flap' on when they were commanded to air test their Wellingtons. Sergeant Robert Shepherd, a nineteen-year-old WOp/AG and front gunner in Flying Officer 'Joe' Larney's crew, recalls: 'We went out to dispersal to carry out our checks. In my case, I checked the radio and the front turret guns and changed the accumulators. Later on in the war radio and R/T checks were limited because the Germans were listening out on all frequencies. It would indicate to them what preparations for a raid were in the offing. Having completed the DI we flew a forty-minute NFT (Night Flying Test) for checks on engine and flaps etc. After lunch we went back to the squadron for lectures on aircraft recognition and radio and gunnery. At 1700 hours in the station HQ we were briefed that our target would be Mors in Denmark. Our station commander, Group Captain Modin, was respected by all ranks. He was posted to the Far East in 1941 and was unfortunately taken as a PoW in Singapore. Wing Commander Buckley, our squadron CO and Flight Commander, Squadron Leader Cyrus Kay, both of whom were Kiwis, were great commanders, highly respected and loved for the way they led the squadron on operations.

'After briefing we went back to the mess to pass the time away until after take-off, which in our case was scheduled for 2145 hours. Security was fairly lax. After briefing was over one could leave the station and quite unintentionally divulge the 'target for tonight'. Later, from the time briefing commenced, the main gate was closed and nobody allowed out until aircraft were over the target. Up to take-off one felt tense. We went out to our kite, P9206/L ('for Larney') and Joe, our Kiwi skipper and Pilot Officer Harry Goodwin, the navigator, inspected the bomb bays and flaps. Then it was all aboard. Larney ran up the engines. All OK. We got the green light from the control tower and soon were airborne. After take-off we were more relaxed; our minds occupied with our jobs. I put the 'J' switch over to intercom and radio to enable me to listen out on base frequency for any messages like 'BBA' (return to base) or change of target. There was none. We crossed the coast and our IFF was switched off. I test fired my guns with a short burst and reported to Larney by intercom that all was OK. I remained in my turret right up to the bombing, assisting the navigator by getting him fixes. The target loomed and I saw flak and searchlights for the first time. I thought, 'We won't get through that' but as we got nearer it seemed to disperse. We dropped six eighteen-hour delay bombs, together with incendiaries and 500lb bombs from about 10,000 feet.

'Crossing the enemy coast I got on the radio and checked in with base. The skipper was limited as regards communication by R/T. The equipment then was the TR9 with a range of only fifteen miles. Pilot Officer 'Hank' Hankins, our second dickie, took a brief spell at the controls. Nearing the base we were given permission to land. Joe turned and landed without incident. Malfunctions were reported to the ground crews. One cannot praise them highly enough. How could we operate without them? They were highly skilled in all trades. Our lives were indeed in their hands every time we took off. We headed for debriefing, anxious to get it over so we could go to the mess for egg, bacon and milk before bed.'

On 10 July a German aircraft dropped 18 bombs near Marham airfield and a simultaneous attack was made on a decoy site at South Pickenham near the airfield. On the night of 18/19 July Pilot Officer W. H. C. Hunkin and crew were shot down on the Bremen raid and taken prisoner. Marham's Wellington squadrons were operational on 11 nights in July with a raid by 24 Wellingtons on the night of the 27/28th being the biggest so far when Cologne, Hamm, Soest and Hamburg were attacked along with 19 Hampdens.

On the night of 2/3 August when 63 Hampdens, Wellingtons and Whitleys visited six targets in Germany, Canadian Pilot Officer Reginald Torrance Gerry's Wellington on 115 Squadron ditched in the North Sea off Wells returning from Germany. Two Wellingtons were sent out to look for the aircraft and the Wells lifeboat was also launched but no trace was found of the crew. On the night of 14/15 August another Wellington was lost when Sergeant Gregory crashed at Brancaster returning from the Lünen aluminium works with the loss of all the crew. On 22/23 August Sergeant N. C. Cook on 115 Squadron crash landed at Wood Dalling returning from Mannheim and Sergeant Henry Victor Watts the front-gunner, died of his injuries. Unrestricted warfare now threatened from both sides of the Channel. On the night of 23/24 August the Luftwaffe rained bombs on London, the first to fall on the capital since 1918. Bomber Command was quick to retaliate, for on the following night, 24/25 August, it despatched 81 Wellingtons, Hampdens and Whitleys to Berlin as a reprisal. The flight involved a round trip of eight hours and 1,200 miles. Seven aircraft aborted and of the remaining force, 29 bombers claimed to have bombed Berlin and a further 27 overflew the German capital but were unable to pinpoint their targets because of thick cloud. Five aircraft were lost to enemy action, including three, which ditched in the North Sea. Bombing results had been unimpressive but the RAF had scored a great victory for morale.

When Berlin was bombed again on the night of 28/29 August crews from Marham were among the 79 Blenheims, Hampdens, Wellingtons and Whitleys that took part in raids on the German capital and other targets. George Bury, Pilot Officer Barr's navigator on a 115 Squadron Wellington recalls.

'The target was Klingenberg Electric. Having been warned that the area was very heavily defended, we decided to fly at 15,000 feet. That was 5,000 feet higher than our normal height. At this height it was essential to use oxygen all the time, but after a few hours the masks became wet and uncomfortable to use. But, if taken off, frequent movement was very tiring. As it turned out the flight as far as we were concerned turned out to be fairly uneventful.

Searchlights were very active. Although one did pick us up, he failed to keep us within his beam long enough for the others in the group to join in. When just ahead we saw a Wellington caught by two at the same time and quick as a flash many others concentrated on the same target and he was caught in a cone of at least ten searchlights. The whole area around the aircraft was as bright as day and no matter which way he turned and twisted, they easily held on to him. The last we saw of him he was in a steep dive with shells bursting all around. This was our eighth flight and the first time that we had seen another aircraft. We were beginning to think that we were fighting the whole war on our own.'[72]

Berlin and Cologne and airfields were attacked again on the last night of the month, 30/31 August. By the end of 1940 the 'Big City' as it was to become known to bomber crews, would have been bombed on ten occasions.

In September Wellingtons of 3 Group made repeated night attacks on invasion barges massed in the Channel ports ready for Operation 'Sealion', the proposed German invasion of England. Other desperate measures were called for by Bomber Command. Unrestricted warfare manifested itself again on 4 September when the Intelligence Officers told crews they would be despatched to the Black Forest, where the Germans were massing heavy armament. They were to carry a new incendiary device called 'Razzle'. This consisted of a wad of wet phosphorous placed between two pieces of celluloid, which ignited to produce an eight-inch flame when the phosphorous dried.

Wellingtons of 149 Squadron had first tried an experiment on the night of 11/12 August, carrying fifty biscuit tins each filled with up to 500 examples but Churchill, fearing that such tactics could lead to German reprisal raids, had ordered the scheme to be postponed. Bob Shepherd of 75 Squadron RNZAF recalls. 'I took the lids off the tins and there were wads swimming about in a solution. I opened the flare chute and one by one, tossed out the contents of three tin loads from about 10,000 feet. We also dropped a full load of incendiaries and six 250 pounders. There was hardly any flak at all.'

The Marham Wellington squadrons were operational on eleven nights during the month and 248 sorties were flown for the loss of just one aircraft. This occurred on the night of 11/12 September when Flying Officer Richard Guy Allen on 38 Squadron failed to return from a raid on Germany when the aircraft crashed at Ostend in Belgium with the loss of all six crew. The RAF bombing directive of 21 September gave support to priority attacks on oil refineries, aircraft factories, railways, canals and U-boat construction yards while electric power stations and gas works in Berlin should also be bombed. On the night of 23/24 September Berlin was selected for a special retaliatory attack and was bombed by 119 Whitleys, Hampdens and Wellingtons. However, most of the objectives were missed and many bombs failed to explode. In September 1940 the Luftwaffe had been forced to abandon massed daylight bombing and the invasion fleet was dispersed. Bomber Command could again turn its attention to city targets. [73]

Sergeant 'Johnnie' Johnson recalls.[74] 'So 1940 progressed with operations and losses increasing. Down south, Fighter Command, quite remote from us, had fought and won the Battle of Britain. War had become to ground crew a routine, albeit a routine with no time or work boundaries that could be defined. Feelings had to be hardened - there was no time or opportunity to grieve over that missing crew with whom a few hours before you'd been drinking and chatting.' 'The Ship Inn' at Narborough had benefited from the influx of servicemen at Marham, becoming a favourite watering hole for the airmen. Robert Crisp had been landlord since the First World War, having served in the RFC as an aircraft mechanic. He and his wife had four children and Joan, the youngest daughter, later married Australian pilot Wing Commander Rodney Gibbes DFC.[75] Late in 1940 it was decided that all RAF aircrew were to be given NCO status. Overnight all the airmen flying on operations were made up to Sergeant - airman one day, Sergeant the next. Imagine the effect of this on the Sergeants' Mess!…overnight they were swamped with large number of youngsters, to whom mess tradition mattered a lot less than tomorrow's bombing target.'[76]

In October the Marham Wellington squadrons endured extensive cloud cover over German targets and bombs were dropped instead on alternate targets. On the night of 7/8 October Squadron Leader Rex Oliver Oxley Taylor and crew on 38 Squadron failed to return from the operation to Berlin when twelve individual targets were ordered to be bombed by over 40 Wellingtons and Whitleys. On 16/17 October 65 Hampdens and Wellingtons attacked Bremen, Kiel and Bordeaux while eight Marham Wellingtons were ordered to attack Merseburg. Some aircraft dropped incendiary devices into the Harz forests.[77] Only two of Marham's Wellingtons located the target at Merseburg. On 24/25 October Flight Lieutenant Eugene George F. Chivers and crew were lost on the operation to the Blohm & Voss shipyards in Hamburg. Returning from the attack on oil refineries at Gelsenkirchen in the early hours of 28 October Pilot Officer Harold Humphrey Rogers crashed at Booten, near Reepham in Norfolk and two of the crew were injured.

On the night of 30 September/1 October just over 100 aircraft bombed targets in Germany and the Channel ports. Three of Marham's Wellingtons were tasked with bombing the marshalling yards at Ehrang. Ten more were part of a formation of Wellingtons detailed to bomb the Reichsluftfahrt Ministerium (German Air Ministry) in Berlin. Seventeen crews, including seven from Marham, claimed to have attacked this single building in the Leipzigstrasse but just six bombs fell on the German capital and the Air Ministry was not hit. Pilot Officer Donald MacLean's aircraft on 38 Squadron was shot down attacking Leipzig. McLean was killed. His five crew survived to be taken prisoner. Two other Wellingtons on 115 Squadron, flown by Pilot Officer A. J. J. Steel and Sergeant Cyril Wessels, failed to return from the raid on the Osnabrück marshalling yards. Steel and Sergeant R. P. Mogg bailed out and survived to be taken prisoner. All six men on Wessels' crew, who may have been shot down by a night-fighter, were killed.

In the last week in October 1940 twelve crews on 75 and 149 Squadrons at Mildenhall and 38 and 115 at Marham received orders from 3 Group to leave for the Mediterranean to form the Malta Wellington Flight on the beleaguered island. Sergeant 'Johnnie' Johnson found himself on a list of fifty names from both flights of 38 Squadron and 115 Squadron and the Station

Commander, 'a remote figure rarely seen', arrived and informed them that they were going on detachment to an undisclosed destination for three weeks or more. The necessary airmen for servicing the aircraft left at once by sea and arrived in Malta after a week. Long-range fuel tanks were fitted in the bomb bays of the Wellingtons and the selected crews were given briefings on routing procedures. On 30 October three Wellingtons on 115 and three on 38 Squadron led by Squadron Leader Patrick Foss took off from Marham. Pilot Officer Alexander John Robert Pate DFC who was flying one of the 115 Squadron Wellingtons, flew into a balloon cable near Iver, Buckinghamshire and the aircraft crashed killing all the crew. A second Wellington on the squadron flown by Sergeant Forrester developed problems with the fuel feed from the long-range tank and returned to Marham. The four remaining Wellingtons arrived safely at Luqa early the following morning. They were joined later by more Wellingtons on 38 Squadron, led by Wing Commander Thomson. As soon as they arrived at Luqa after a long flight over enemy-occupied France, the aircrews were ordered to raid oil tanks in Naples harbour on the night of 31 October. Being the first bomber element on the island, the ad-hoc unit was obliged to make use of any and every person, whatever service they were in, to load, arm and refuel the Wellingtons, but the operation was a great success and a repeat was planned for the following night. Only three of the five aircraft took off safely, one crashing near Rabat and another in a quarry soon after take-off.

A return to the UK was delayed as raids were made on targets in Sicily, southern Italy and Yugoslavia and the Flight took part in the successful attack on the Italian fleet in Taranto harbour by dropping flares. A raid on a large number of Italian Air Force aircraft at Castel Benito in Libya was then mounted, and a PR reconnaissance next day indicated that over 100 of the enemy aircraft had been destroyed or damaged. Night raids on Naples continued, and attacks on concentrations of Ju 87 Stukas on Sicilian airfields were also made, with some losses to the Flight.[78] For a month thereafter the Wellingtons were joined by others which put in raids on the Italian 'boot' prior to completing their journey to Egypt. This arrangement was disastrous for morale and also, 38 Squadron never did return to England. Their place at Marham was taken by Wellington ICs on 218 Squadron, which arrived from Oakington in Cambridgeshire.

Marham's Wellington squadrons were operational on only seven nights in November 1940. The night of 14/15 November proved unlucky for Sergeant H. J. Morson on 115 Squadron, whose thirteenth operation it was. Morson's Wellington was hit by flak before reaching Berlin and on the return he ditched in the North Sea. Five of the crew got into the dinghy but Sergeant Edgar Albert Dean, the second pilot, emerged from the escape hatch over the cockpit and missed his landing on the wing. He fell between the fuselage and the engine and was not seen again. The rest of the crew were rescued and put ashore at Great Yarmouth by HMS *Pelton*. Morson and his wireless operator, Sergeant D. H. H. Cleverley were later awarded the DFM for their devotion to duty.

On the night of 16/17 November, 127 bombers, the largest number yet despatched, raided Hamburg. By the end of 1940 Berlin would have been bombed on ten occasions. Included in the force were eleven Wellingtons on 115 Squadron, which began taking off from Marham at 17.20 hours. Bad weather affected the operation and only 60 aircraft reported bombing Hamburg while 25 aircraft bombed alternative targets. Only four of the 115 Squadron Wellingtons found the primary target and the flak and German fighters caused havoc. Wellington P9286/K piloted by Sergeant Donald Ewart Larkman was shot down by Oberleutnant Egmont Prinz zur Lippe-Weissenfeld, Staffelkapitän, IV./NJG1. It was the Austrian prince's first victory. The aircraft crashed at Winkel, Holland with the loss of all the crew. Wellington R3213/S flown by Sergeant Denis Duncan English also failed to return to Marham when it crashed at Falkenburg with the loss of all six crew. Flight Lieutenant Van landed R1034 at Marham despite the aircraft being badly shot up. T2606 flown by Pilot Officer A. Tindall was attacked by four Bf 110s in the target area and the front-gunner, Sergeant E. Jarvis was badly wounded. Tindall got the badly damaged Wellington home but he was forced to crash land at Bircham Newton. Jarvis later died of his injuries. P9299 flown by Pilot Officer Roy crashed at Wittering but there were no injuries to the crew.

A trip to the German capital on 26 November proved to be Bob Shepherd's 30th and final op of his first tour.

'I flew with Pilot Officer Saxelby; 'Joe' Larney (later Squadron Leader Larney) having completed his tour on 29 September on our trip to the oil refineries at Magdeburg. We got through and I left for a long rest before returning, in 1942, to fly a second tour. Saxelby did not make it. He was shot down in 1942 and was made a PoW.'

Bob Shepherd had certainly led a charmed life in 75 Squadron. He was one of the last of the original pre-war air gunners stationed at RAF Feltwell to survive a first tour. Others were not so lucky and many of his pre-war contemporaries, like nineteen-year-old Bill Hitchmough, had been killed. Hitchmough was a gunner on Pilot Officer William John Finlayson's crew, which failed to return on Berlin on the night of 23/24 October 1940 when Bomber Command had despatched 79 Wellingtons to many targets including the German capital and Emden. Next morning Shepherd was airborne with Pilot Officer 'Spanky' McFarlane with orders to mount a search off the Danish coast. A dinghy was found but there was no trace of the crew.

Bad weather hampered operations throughout December and 115 Squadron were on operations on only eight nights while 218 Squadron did not fly its first operation from Marham until 20 December when two of its Wellingtons attacked Ostend. Three 115 Squadron Wellingtons were lost in December.[79] These continual high losses of crews could only be made good by young men passing out of the OTUs, even if they were not fully trained or as familiar with their aircraft as they would have liked.

Footnotes
68   Three Wellingtons had been dispatched from Feltwell on 4 April but had been recalled.
69   On 19 May a total of 132 serviceable aircraft was available to the Army Air Service but this total included 28 obsolescent Fokker C.V and C.X two-seat reconnaissance aircraft, the latter dating from the mid-thirties., 16 equally elderly Koolhoven F.K.51two seat advanced training biplanes and six

Lorraine Fokker D.XVII-4 single-seat fighter biplanes of 1933. The 1st and 2nd Fighter Groups were equipped with the lightly armed D.XXI, the AAS's standard single-seat fighter but its bulky Bristol Mercury 8 radial engined and fixed, spatted undercarriage resulted in a maximum speed of only 286 mph.

70   Canadian Pilot Officer Douglas William West Morris and R3152/J and Flight Sergeant Leonard George Moores and P9298/H on the 20th; Flying Officer D. F. Laslett and P9297/F on the 21st and Flying Officer Vivian Allen William Rosewarne and R3162 on the 30th.

71   Group Captain Percy Pickard DSO DFC and Wellington *'F for Freddie'* were later featured in a propaganda film, *Target for Tonight*. Pickard would lose his life on the legendary attack by Mosquitoes on Amiens prison on 18 February 1944.

72   *RAF Marham* by Ken Delve. (PSL 1995).

73   When Bomber Command took the decision in May 1940 to start strategic bombing of Germany by night, there was little the Luftwaffe could do to counter these early raids. The subject of night fighting was raised at a conference of German service chiefs just before the war and according to *Kommodore* Josef Kammhuber, who was present it was dismissed out of hand with the words, *'Night fighting! It will never come to that!'* Up until May 1940 the night air defence of the Reich was almost entirely the province of the *Flak* arm of the Luftwaffe. No specialised night fighting arm existed though one fighter *Gruppe* (IV./(N)JG2) was undertaking experimental *Helle Nachtjagd* (illuminated night fighting) sorties with the aid of searchlights in northern Germany and in the Rhineland. IV./(N)JG2 flew the Bf 109D with the cockpit hood removed as a precaution against the pilots being blinded by the glare of the searchlights.. The *Helle Nachtjagd* technique used in 1940 (and early 1941) was entirely dependent on weather conditions and radar-guided searchlights simply could not penetrate thick layers of cloud or industrial haze over the Ruhr and other industrial centres in the Reich. Kammhuber realised that *Helle Nachtjagd* was only a short-term solution and soon concentrated all his energies in developing an efficient radar-controlled air defence system. *Battles With the Nachtjagd: The Night Air War Over Europe 1939-1945* by Theo Boiten and Martin W. Bowman. (Schiffer Publishing. 2006).

74   *RAF Marham Transition To War* by E. C. 'Johnnie' Johnson. *West Norfolk Aviation Journal. No.2* (Summer 1994).

75   Flying Officer Rodney Gibbes had a lucky escape on 1 June 1940 when he was pilot of Wellington R3154 which crashed at Lastingham Hills, Yorkshire. Two of his crew were killed and Gibbes and the other members of his crew suffered shock and minor injuries. On 2/3 September 1941 a Wellington on 218 Squadron flown by Squadron Leader Gibbes DFC was hit by flak and crashed in the sea off Belgium. The crew came ashore three days later at Westgate near Margate in Kent. Gibbes was lost flying in the Mediterranean in August 1943. Peggy the second daughter married Sergeant Philip Wilks a 218 Squadron Wellington rear gunner, who survived the war and after a career with BOAC he became landlord of 'The Ship' and with Peggy as landlady, remained there from the 1960s to the early 1980s.

76   Narborough House, less than four miles from the airfield, was the ideal solution. Late in 1940 the Army moved out as the RAF moved in and the Rowley family transferred to the vicarage. The RAF used the whole of the house as a Sergeant's Mess, completely refurbished the property.

77   'Razzles' and 'Deckers' consisting of small phosphorous pellets in celluloid strips were dropped through flare chutes to start fires among crops and in forest areas. The incendiary devices had to be kept in tins of alcohol and water until dropped so that they would ignite when they dried out.

78   *Military Aviation in Malta G.C. 1915-1993* by John F. Hamlin (GMS Enterprises 1994). The Malta Wellington Flight was given new status on 1 December 1940 when sixteen Wellington ICs were used to re-form 148 Squadron, which had been absorbed by 15 OTU in May that year.

79   On 8/9 December Australian Pilot Officer Albert Tindall strayed off track on the return from the raid on Bordeaux and he crashed into a hillside at Cefn-y-Strad near Tredegar in Glamorgan. All the crew died. On the night of the 11/12th Sergeant Geoffrey William Hartland and crew on 115 Squadron were lost without trace on the operation to Mannheim and on 29/30 December Pilot Officer Peter Gordon H. Salmon and crew on 115 Squadron also failed to return.

Chapter 4

'How Deep Is The Night'

No one could ever find Gelsenkirchen because of the industrial haze. Kitely decided to bomb and shoot up an airfield in Holland on the homeward trip. It was very exciting and we dropped our bombs. He dived the Wimpy down to 300 feet and I fired about 1,000 rounds at chance lights and searchlights and the rear gunner had a go as well.'

Alfred Jenner

In 1940 the RAF was so desperately short of aircrew that training courses for new intakes were notoriously short. At 15 OTU at Harwell the gunnery course, which should have been one month was in fact two and a half weeks. Sergeant Alfred Jenner, a WOP-AG, did at least make one flight over enemy territory - a 'very scary' trip to Paris on a leaflet-dropping sortie before being posted in mid-November to 99 'Madras Presidency' Squadron in 3 Group at Newmarket Heath, as Alfred Jenner recalls.

'Incendiary bombs were exploding in 99 Squadron's sleeping quarters when I arrived on a cold, foggy November evening. They were going off in the open fireplace of the room under the Rowley Mile grandstand on Newmarket racecourse, which served as NCO aircrew billets. Fortunately, the bombs were British incendiaries, or pieces of them, which bored airmen, were throwing into the fire to enliven their lives after the previous night's raid on Gelsenkirchen. The talk was all of earlier raids, old comrades on other stations and those who had already 'gone for a Burton' (killed). 'I soon found out that every other aspect of life on an operational squadron was different from that at disciplined training establishments. You were not, for instance, expected to parade at 6 am, or to worry about kit inspections, nor even to be particular about dress, unless you were down in the town of Newmarket where Army Police could never understand the camaraderie of the air. 'You were expected to be meticulous in the performance of the job you had been trained to do and when in the air to obey commands without question. Discipline was vital we soon discovered, not the least because of the primitive conditions in which we had to live and fight. Newmarket was a racecourse, not a sophisticated permanent station like other squadrons enjoyed. The grandstand was always dirty and we could never keep our clothes clean. Our mess was just another room under the seating enclosure of the grandstand. Our ablutions were a makeshift building outside. We boiled our guns clean in the erstwhile harness room, which served as an armoury. Our aircraft were dispersed all over the racecourse, wherever there were trees to provide cover.

'Casualties were light for my first two months at Newmarket. Then it began, first with a loud bang while we were at lunch one day. We rushed outside and there at the racecourse winning post was the twisted remains of a Wellington. All inside were dead, including a young pilot who only the night before had been proudly displaying the small revolver given to him by his father 'in case he ever needed it in an emergency'. Worst of all was the loss of the so-called Broughton bomber, bought by the good citizens of the English town of that name. We knew every member in the crew of that machine and were therefore devastated when it crashed on take-off at the end of the runway and burst into flames. There were only two survivors, badly injured. The others burned to death as we watched helplessly. The rest of us then had to take off over the still burning funeral pyre of our comrades. Crews were very keen and the ground crews knew their job. Although bomb loads were small and we did not always hit our targets, we firmly believed we were very good for morale. It did people good to see and hear us going out.

'I made my first operational trip on the night of 16/17 December 1940 when I flew as front gunner in Sergeant Fletcher's crew. We were to scatter-bomb Mannheim in a 'town blitz' in retribution for the destruction of Coventry a month before. Operation 'Abigail', as it was code-named, would be in retaliation for the German bombing of Coventry and Southampton. A force of 200 bombers was planned under Operation 'Abigail Rachael' but in the event when it was forecast that weather conditions over the home airfields would deteriorate the numbers were reduced to 134 bombers, including 61 Wellingtons; the first 'area' bombing raid on a German industrial target. Aircraft were despatched to the target singly. At this time we could not afford crew losses from collision or bombs falling on each other's aircraft so this was the only practical way. It was cold and lonely in the front turret but my Brownings never froze up on any of the operations I would fly. However, if one carried an apple, we were warned not to eat it; it would break your teeth! From a safety point of view, the front turret was preferable to the rear, which could be an exhausting trek to reach in our flight gear. The rear gunner was protected by two slabs of armour plate, which could be joined together to protect his chest. However, in the front turret I could only rely on armour plate behind the pilots to stop bullets hitting me from the rear. The primary function of an air gunner at this time was to be a heavy flak spotter for the captain. He told us to keep our eyes peeled and report enemy aircraft and flak gun flashes immediately. We dropped our bombs on Mannheim from about 12,000 feet and although it was my first experience of flak, we came through all right. We landed back at Newmarket after being in the air for six hours and ten minutes.' Unfortunately, incendiaries carried as markers by eight leading Wellingtons were dropped in the wrong place and the subsequent bombing had been widely spread. Three aircraft were lost and four more crashed in England.

Wellington observer Albert E. Robinson on 115 Squadron recalls.

'Bombing by night presented a formidable barrier to the young crews of

Bomber Command in 1940-41. If groping blindly through the curtain of darkness that had descended over Europe was to be overcome, it was crystal clear that in the initial stages an awful lot was going to depend on the crews themselves. Trial and error mostly only resulted in a high casualty rate. Unfortunately, it was with little result for so great an effort, a potpourri of calculated risk, personal skills and circumstances that favoured the more successful crews. The 'X' factor, a quality difficult to define but one that enabled them to take advantage of more than a full share of luck lifted them high above average. Whatever the mixture, a fierce determination to succeed in spite of the numerous setbacks was a common denominator and it united the crews almost without exception. With such resolution, the crews attempted to face up to their task. It was not made any easier by briefing officers who spoke at length about the necessity for precision bombing. It would not be too critical to suggest that some of these briefings were out of touch with reality. Truthful crews considered it a reasonable effort if the city itself was found, let alone a specific aiming point.

'There were many reasons for this but the principal culprit was night navigation. This was based almost entirely on the age-old theory of dead reckoning. There was no problem if all the links in the chain were known but if not, it could turn out to be a hit-or-miss affair, especially with little or no radio assistance to help with the calculations. The basic requirement for success was to establish the wind speed and direction but in order to assess these it was necessary at various times during the flight to define the position of the aircraft in relation to the ground - obtain a 'fix', as it was known to the navigator. Under variable conditions this was not always possible. The flight could be blown well off course, sometimes miles away if there were adverse winds and with it went little chance of finding out the true position of the aircraft. This in turn usually added up to wasted effort, with bombs being brought back or jettisoned in the sea.

'Inexperienced crews could end up on the slopes of a mountain or in the gray wastes of the sea. The North Sea in particular was a big enemy to Bomber Command; a heaving predator, menacing in its vastness to any crippled bomber struggling to maintain height over its darkened wilderness. The enemy coast to the hoped-for landfall in England offered little hope if a crippled bomber had to force-land and most certainly so if contact had been lost with any listening post as a result of a damaged radio. A bomber aircraft then was a lonely and desolate figure, struggling against the odds and with the chilling thought that no matter how expertly the aircraft was set down on the sea - turbulent or calm - the bomber would sink within minutes. There was the rubber dinghy, of course. It could be paddled but when exhaustion came and effort faded it would just drift along with the wind and tide, aimlessly and without hope, to a tortured end, unless providence took a hand. God knows how long this would take. Perhaps better not to have taken the dinghy at all.

'That's how it went. Such possibilities could only be accepted by crews with a philosophical shrug of the shoulders. It came with a host of other things but even so most crews were optimistic and they set their sights on completing the mandatory, magical number of 30 operations before being taken off for a rest at some training squadron. In comparison to the numbers involved, very few managed to achieve this; the average could have been as low as five missions before the Grim Reaper called the tune. Given the conditions, the chances of survival on any one operation, whether it was the first or 30th were not good. Any discerning bookmaker would rate the betting odds low. All aircrew were volunteers to a man but in saying this they needed to be. Each raid was equivalent to 'going over the top' in the 1914-18 war. However, if one were to put the clock back to the briefing room in 1940-41 and peer through the haze of cigarette smoke that hung in swirling clouds no one would have guessed it. It was more like a gathering at any sports club. We were boisterous, outgoing and extrovert but underneath this cloak there was a quiet confidence and rugged determination. Such an outlook was essential. The effort needed to penetrate Germany, certainly with the out-dated aircraft at the crews' disposal in 1940-41, required a deep-seated motivation and a special quality.

'We were lucky to have the Wellington. The Wellington was probably the best of the bunch when compared to the other bombers. A good old war-horse, it was as loyal and forgiving as the crews were to the bomber. But the fact remains that it was outdated, unable to reach much height over the target, poorly armed, had no internal heat and when carrying a full bomb load of 4,000lb had a speed of less than half that of an enemy fighter. Freezing temperatures often coated surfaces with ice and frost, froze controls and radio sets and brought instant ice-burn should metal surfaces be touched without a glove. Engines were often suspect. (They invariably coughed and spluttered) and the dials on the instrument panel were constantly watched with anxious eyes, hoping that the readings would not give reasons for concern. Should one engine fail, as they often did, it was a heart-stopping moment with the certain knowledge that the Wellington would not be able to maintain height over a sustainable period. Its flying range would then be determined by irreversible factors such as the state of the aircraft, height at the time, angle and speed of descent and the skill of the pilot to nurse the aircraft along. They were always apprehensive lest the extra workload would cause the remaining engine to overheat - not the least of the problems was the possibility that it too could fail.

'If all this sounds gloomy, then add for good measure the fact that from take-off to return the Wellington would be flying in isolation. In many respects the raid would be one of individual effort and self-planning by the crews. Often the route to the target would be varied by crew preference. They normally took into account the known Flak areas but defences could alter their tactics or geographical position, so even the most carefully thought-out plans could go astray and bring the sting of the serpent at an unexpected moment. Strict radio silence did not help but this was essential because of the enemy's rapidly increasing radar detection. To break this silence was to invite trouble, the equivalent to sending a telegram to the Luftwaffe notifying them of intent!

'But all these shortcomings were shrugged off with an unflagging optimism. Metaphorically speaking we were all in the same boat and in any case anything bad happened to the other fellow - or at least so said the mind's defence mechanism. The more missions that were flown, the easier it became to believe this. It could also induce a state of mind dubbed by the crews as, 'flak happy'. This could loosely be interpreted as over-confidence, a mistake for which many usually paid dearly, joining the list of doomed aircraft. These unfortunate souls just took off and literally vanished, never to be seen again - just like a conjuror's rabbit. The toll under this category became harder to stomach as the casualty list mounted.

'Replacement crews to fill the gaps, proud of their newly won wings, keen and enthusiastic, came to the squadron like an endless belt at some factory complex. The crew room became a platform on which the passengers were ever-changing. There was barely time to get to know their names. Sadly, within a month, the fresh young faces who had been so eager to prove their worth would move along up the belt, often within days as crews were called upon to fly operations that were near impossible. Some were lucky, some not, but in all cases there was the same unpredictability as a name drawn at random from a hat. Not all were fresh faces either. The Grim Reaper was not choosy and some were veterans of many operations. They always came back and their demise sent an ice-cold shock through every level in the squadron. The sorrow of their passing gave everyone food for thought.

'With Bomber Command heavily committed, in principle any retrograde step was out of the question and Command was compelled to allow for these losses when planning. It was not a very happy thought for the squadron commanders to lose so many of their valuable, well-trained crews, but it is not possible to make an omelette without breaking eggs, a fait accompli that just about fitted in with a Wellington bomber squadron. Even so, Command intensified its efforts. There would be no respite, no letup and the battle, if Britain was to keep intact its position as the sole bastion in the struggle against a Nazi Germany, must continue to be fought.'

In January 1941 the weather worsened and snow fell. Marham's Wellingtons flew only six operations, all without loss, but on 15 January Flying Officer P. F. McLaren on 218 Squadron was killed on his first Wellington solo flight. The bad weather however seemed to work to the Luftwaffe's advantage and on 16 January ten small bombs were dropped on the airfield and some exploded near Lady's Wood and next to a barrack block. Damage was slight and there were no casualties. Despite more bad weather in February aircraft serviceability remained high and operational bomber raids continued on most nights with invasion ports at Le Havre, Boulogne, Brest and Rotterdam were frequent targets.

'In the New Year I was on ops again' recalled Alf Jenner. 'On 29 January we were told to bomb the *Tirpitz* at Wilhelmshaven. My pilot was Pilot Officer Coote, an ex-public school type who would stand no nonsense. All he wanted was to do a good job. He taught us that each man was reliant on the others. He was also a great 'jinker' (taking avoiding action against flak and fighters). Coote stayed over the target for three-quarters of an hour with German guns popping off at us. Our observer, who was in something of a panic, shouted, 'Why don't we drop the bloody bombs and get out?' Coote said in no uncertain terms, 'I'm the skipper of this ship and you'll drop the bombs when I tell you!' In fact we never did see the ship and we brought our bombs home.'

On the night of 7/8 February when 35 Wellingtons of Bomber Command attacked Boulogne, 115 Squadron provided ten of the attacking Wimpys. On the night of 10/11 February 1941 3 Group was able to put up more than a hundred

Wellingtons for the first time in the war when Hannover and Rotterdam were attacked 365 bombers. At Marham 115 Squadron contributed eleven aircraft and 218 Squadron, ten. Two Wellingtons failed to return from the raid on Hannover. One of them was a 115 Squadron Wellington flown by Sergeant Harold Rogers, who was returning from the raid and after almost colliding with another Wellington, decided to turn his navigation lights on. German intruders were over East Anglia and Rogers was attacked over the Swaffham beacon by Hauptmann Rolf Jung of 4./NJG2, who damaged his port engine. Rogers dropped down low to try to avoid further attacks but he was forced to crash land. The Wellington crash landed at Narborough and it was soon enveloped in flames. The crew managed to evacuate the Wimpy before it exploded.[80] The intruder was a specially modified Ju 88C of I./NJG2, which had begun flying offensive operations over England from Holland in early September 1940. German intruders returned to the area on the night of 25 February and a Wellington flown by Sergeant Hoos of 218 Squadron was shot down four miles from Marham. Three of the crew were injured. The front-gunner, Sergeant John Glynne Stanley, was trapped in the wreckage and he suffered severe burns and his leg had to be amputated later in hospital in King's Lynn. He subsequently died on 3 March.[81]

'On 11 February we brought our bombs home again' recalled Alf Jenner. 'Our target was Bremen but there was 10/10ths cloud and we got hopelessly lost. We flew back and saw a strip of coastline but we were not sure whether it was France, Germany, Wales or England. We flew up and down. I suddenly spotted two towers and realised it was the entrance to Lowestoft harbour (the town where I was born and had spent my childhood). We flew back to Newmarket and landed through a gap in the cloud with the bombs still aboard. We had not noticed they hadn't been dropped! We lost a lot of aircraft that night.'

Of a total force of 79 bombers, 22, including eleven Wellingtons, crash-landed in England on the night of 11/12 February when fog descended on most of the stations. Signals were sent out for aircraft to return as soon as possible and to use airfields in Lossiemouth and Kinloss if sufficient petrol allowed. At Marham visibility was down to just 500 yards and all the returning Wellingtons were advised to head for Wyton but then this airfield was became fogged in. Every available flare was lit at Marham but in the event none of the returning aircraft was able to land. Wing Commander Anthony Caron 'Tiny' Evans-Evans and his crew bailed out of their 115 Squadron Wellington, which then crashed at Wicken Bonhunt, four miles SSW of Saffron Walden.[82] Pilot Officer Clarke and his crew abandoned their Wimpy in the vicinity of Cambridge and it crashed on houses in Histon Road killing three elderly ladies. A fourth lady was badly injured. Three crews managed to put down safely at Wyton, two more at Alconbury while three more put down at Driffield, Newmarket and Bassingbourn. Sergeant W. S. Adam on 218 Squadron force-landed at Frampton on Severn near Stroud where it became stuck in the mud and the incoming tide. Flying Officer Anstey and his crew on 218 Squadron abandoned their Wellington over Tebay near Kendal in Westmoreland. Five other Wellingtons landed at Gravesend, Finningley, Tangmere, Withernsea and Lindholme. Altogether, 22 aircraft including eleven Wellingtons crashed in England and five men died.

There was more drama on 22/23 February when 29 Wellingtons were despatched to Brest to bomb warships there but only eleven aircraft bombed and four aircraft crashed in England on return. 115 Squadron contributed nine Wellingtons and Pilot Officer Clarke returned early with a technical problem but on landing he swung to starboard to avoid some buildings and ended up in trees to the west of the airfield. None of the crew was injured and the aircraft was repaired. At 0825 hours Sergeant Edwin Joseph Milton piloting 'F for Freddie' called for a bearing and this was acknowledged and orders given to divert to Feltwell but nothing more was heard. A few minutes later the Wimpy hit a tree and crashed at East Winch near King's Lynn. The aircraft caught fire and all six crew died. Aboard R1469/Q flown by Sergeant Bright, when about eight miles North of Morlaix his rear gunner, Pilot Officer Mills saw a Bf 110 flying about 500 feet below and astern. Mills opened fire with about 300 rounds from each gun into the 110's cockpit. The Messerschmitt was seen to shudder and dip its port wing as it turned to port. Mills asked Bright to turn quickly and a stall turn and dive brought his guns to bear again on the Bf 110's tail unit, which, after about 200 rounds from each gun, was seen to lose the port fin tail and rudder. The 110's nose came up and stalled into a spin disappearing through the clouds at about 4,000 feet.

On 23/24 February Canadian Pilot Officer Kenneth Norman Arthurs and crew on L7810/R, which was sent to attack Boulogne was heard calling for a fix from Hull at around 2145 hours. Nothing else was heard of the crew who were listed as missing. All were killed and the aircraft crashed near Pihen-les-Guines. On the night of 25/26 February Sergeant Hoos' Wellington on 218 Squadron was badly shot about by Feldwebel Ernst Ziebarth of 1./NJG2 and the Wellington IC crash landed in a field at Red Lodge two miles south of Swaffham. Three of the crew were injured.

The first bombing raid of March 1941 was flown on the night of the 2/3rd when 54 aircraft attacked warships at Brest. Wellington R3279 on 115 Squadron flown by Sergeant Geoffrey R. Pike dived into the sea off Teignmouth in Devon. Rescue craft were sent out and they found only the W/T operator alive. Two parachutes and the body of Sergeant Edward Fenwick were also found. A few days later, on the night of 12/13 March, when 86 aircraft including 54 Wellingtons attacked Bremen and other forces attacked Hamburg and Berlin, Flying Officer William Peter Crosse on 218 Squadron failed to return. His Wellington IC was shot down by Oberfeldwebel Hans Rasper of 4./NJG1. Three of the crew were killed while two men who survived were taken prisoner.[83] The night following, 13/14 March, 139 aircraft raided the Blohm & Voss shipyards at Hamburg and Sergeant John Abbott Donald returned badly shot up with the W/T operator Sergeant Jack Huffingley dead at his post. Donald crash-landed the badly damaged Wellington at Marham without further casualties. Three months' later Donald and his crew were lost on Kiel. Marham's Wellingtons flew ops on five more nights during March. On 30/31 March the Wellingtons began their campaign against the German battle cruisers *Scharnhorst* and *Gneisenau*, or 'Salmon and Gluckstein' (a famous London department store), as they were known, while the Halifaxes went after the cruiser *Prinz Eugen* at Brest. The warships were visited five times in April and the campaign was to last for more than ten months.

On 14 March Sergeant Alfred Jenner flew with Sergeant Kitely, a Canadian, on a trip to Gelsenkirchen. Jenner recalled:

'No one could ever find Gelsenkirchen because of the industrial haze. Kitely decided to bomb and shoot up an airfield in Holland on the homeward trip. It was very exciting and we dropped our bombs. He dived the Wimpy down to 300 feet and I fired about 1,000 rounds at chance lights and searchlights and the rear gunner had a go as well. Ten days later, on 24 March, 99 Squadron were briefed to attack the *Von Hipper* in Brest Harbour. Brest was very clear. From about two miles away I could see two ships when the Sergeant pilot ordered, 'Bomb bay doors open'. The bomb aimer, surprised, said, 'But we're too far away'. We dropped them anyway. Our pilot, who was only one short of his tour, was determined to survive. It was the only case of 'sugaring' I recall during my operations.'

Meanwhile, Eric Masters, a sergeant pilot who had recently arrived at Newmarket from OTU, waited impatiently to fly his first op with 99 Squadron. Squadron Leader Stanley Black, the CO, explained that Masters would captain a crew whose previous captain had been grounded. Black added that he would fly as an observer on the first two operations. In the first three weeks five operations were cancelled because of the weather. Masters recalls.

'I was becoming desperate to get the first op under my belt, to discover for myself whether I would make it - to find out just how scared one would be. Whilst I knew I had a super crew, I also knew they would be watching me very closely to see if I had any of the faults of their previous skipper. 'Finally, the day arrived and we set off to bomb Cologne. I was very nervous, not at the prospect of enemy action but having the CO along as my second pilot! It was in fact quite enjoyable and the ack-ack fire was nothing more than a nuisance. At times the Germans seemed keen on playing possum rather than give away the locality of a town by defending it too vigorously. One felt sorry for the crew of the other aircraft, coned in ten searchlights, weaving this way and that, trying to get away but we were glad they were taking the attention of the enemy. My landing back at Newmarket was my one 'black'. I dropped the Wimpy on the deck from about 25 feet instead of the normal five-ten feet and she bounced quite violently. I had to give her a quick burst on the throttles to keep her flying and let down again more gently. Squadron Leader Black suggested that it was because I had been used to concrete runways which reflected what little light there was and enabled one to judge 'hold-off' more accurately. Grass was comparatively non-reflective and one had to judge height entirely by the flares. I was feeling rather miserable about it myself. However, no harm was done. I did my second trip a night later, with the CO coming along, to Cologne again.'

By mid-March 1941 99 Squadron had moved ten miles distant to the newly completed station at Waterbeach six miles northeast of Cambridge. On the night of 31 March/1 April 4,000lb bombs were used operationally for the first time when modified Wellington IIs of 9 and 149 Squadrons dropped two on Emden. Four aircraft were detailed for this operation, two acting as cover for the two Wellingtons carrying the bombs. 149 Squadron's 'X-X-Ray', piloted by Pilot Officer John Henry Franks [84] successfully completed its mission but the second squadron Wellington failed to get airborne and slid to a halt in a barley field near the runway. The 'Wizard of Oz' painted on the aircraft had failed to work its magic. 'H-Harry' on 149 Squadron flown by Sergeant G. J. P. Morchen landed heavily on return, stalled and crashed. Sergeant Percival Ernest Butler one of the gunners, died of his injuries later. A second 'Cookie' was dropped by a 9 Squadron Wellington. These 'high capacity' bombs soon came to be called 'Luftminen' by the Germans.

During April Marham's Wellingtons flew 87 sorties for the loss of six aircraft, three of which crashed in England returning from ops. On the night of 3/4 April when the target was Brest, Wellington IC R1470/H on 115 Squadron flown by Sergeant C. M. Thompson was attacked by a Ju 88C of 3./NJG2 flown by Leutnant Heinz Völker. The Wimpy crashed into the mud banks at Ongar Hill near Terrington St. Clements five miles west of King's Lynn killing all the crew except Thompson. The rear gunner, Sergeant Russell, died later of exposure. It was on this night that 4,000lb bombs were used operationally for the first time when they were dropped on Emden. On the night of 8/9 April when Kiel was attacked by 160 aircraft, a Wellington on 218 Squadron was badly hit and flew home on one engine where it was landed at Horsham St. Faith near Norwich after all moveable equipment had been jettisoned over the North Sea. Also, all the maps were thrown out and the fixed aerial had been damaged by enemy action so the navigator and Sergeant H. Burke, the wireless operator, successfully navigated a course by a combination of guesswork and wireless bearings. Burke was later praised for his 'coolness and skill', which undoubtedly resulted in the safe return of the aircraft.

On 10/11 April 53 bombers comprising 36 Wellingtons, twelve Blenheims and five Manchesters headed for Brest to try and finish off the *Gneisenau* which had been recently damaged by a Coastal Command torpedo bomber. Meanwhile 29 Hampdens and 24 Whitleys went to bomb Düsseldorf and minor operations were flown to Bordeaux/Mérignac airfield and to Rotterdam. Four hits were claimed on the *Gneisenau*. The Wellington flown by Sergeant Arthur George Plumb on 218 Squadron failed to return, all six crew being lost. Five Hampdens were lost on the raid on Düsseldorf.

On the night of 9/10 April Alf Jenner flew his first operation from Waterbeach, with a new crew captained by Squadron Leader David C. Torrens.

'Torrens was our new Flight Commander. As he was new to Bomber Command it was decided to give him the most experienced crew. I was by now something of a veteran with twelve ops and I became Torrens' front gunner. First WOp was Arthur J. Smith; a splendid wireless operator who had served in the pre-war RAF in Iraq. The second pilot was Eric H. Berry, who came from a well-off Yorkshire family and who had flown private aircraft before the war. His wartime training had been short; converting straight from a Tiger Moth to a Wellington. Although he had only flown two or three ops he was well thought of and was about to skipper his own crew. Our rear gunner was Pilot Officer J.

F. Palmer and our observer, Pilot Officer P. A. Goodwyn, was from Ipswich.

'At Waterbeach we played a guessing game. If there was a 'breeze' that an op was on that night we would watch the petrol bowsers refuelling the Wimpys and note the number of gallons. If it was about 400 gallons that meant a trip to the Ruhr; if it was over 650, it must mean Berlin! Everyone was worried but did not show it. We had things to do to pass the rest of the afternoon. The wireless had to be checked and guns cleaned. At 5 o'clock on the afternoon of 9 April we entered the briefing room and sat down. At the end of the room was a large map, covered with a curtain. The Briefing Officer dramatically pulled the curtain aside and we were startled to see a red ribbon that seemed to go on forever! It meant a four and a half-hour trip to Berlin. The RAF hadn't been to the big city since the previous September. We all thought, 'Jesus Christ! Why me?'

'After briefing finished we ate our Flying Supper in the mess. It was rather poor fare; usually corned beef and chips, bread pudding and tea. Everyone was in a high state of nervousness and excited hysteria, although no one showed any sign of despondency. We were quite well trained and highly motivated.'

This was Jenner's 13th op and although he was not superstitious, he felt prompted to write to his wife. At 1900 hours the crew truck nicknamed 'Tumbril', took the crew to 'R for Robert' waiting at dispersal. Jenner recalls.

'It was really dark, cold and clear. A bombers' moon shone overhead. I climbed into the astrodome area of 'R for Robert' and stowed my parachute. Our pilots wore theirs in flight. As we taxied out and lined up on the new tarmac runway I gripped the astrodome hatch clips, in case I needed to get out quickly, as I always did. We were away first. Torrens thundered down the runway (our bomb load was small because of the need for extra fuel). With flaps full on we climbed slowly into the sky above Waterbeach. I climbed into the front turret immediately enemy fighters might already be about). Grinding away slowly we headed for Southwold; our point of departure. Nearing the coast of Holland I exclaimed, 'Enemy coast ahead!' There were a few shots then all was quiet again. The captain talked quietly to us, telling us to keep our eyes peeled. Then the fun began. A succession of searchlights picked us up and passed us on from one to another until we could see the multitude of coloured flak bursts over Berlin. We had been told that there were 1,000 guns at Berlin. They couldn't all fire at us but it felt like it. Down below, Lake Wannsee shone in the moonlight. Buildings, or imagined buildings, appeared in the Berlin suburbs below. We could actually smell flak. The Germans were very good gunners. A shell knocked out one of the engines. Fortunately, it did not catch fire. Torrens feathered the prop. We dropped our bombs and droned away. Nearing Brunswick Torrens came on the intercom. 'Sorry to tell you chaps but we will not make it back. You will each have to decide if you want to bail out or stay in the aircraft for a crash-landing.'

'I had previously decided that should such an occasion occur, then I would jump. I looked at the altimeter. It read 1,100 feet (300 feet less than recommended). The ruddy bulkhead at the front prevented me from turning the turret door handle. (To bail straight out of the turret would have taken me into the turning props.) To my relief, Eric Berry opened it from the other side. Flying Officer Goodwyn and I bailed out. The remaining four crew, including Pilot Officer Palmer, the rear gunner and Sergeant Albert Smith, the WOp/AG, stayed with the aircraft and crash-landed at Wolfenbuttel, near Hannover. They set fire to the aircraft before being captured and made PoWs. Goodwyn and I joined them in Stalag Luft III.⁸⁵

On 12/13 April 66 aircraft including 35 Wellingtons returned to Brest, which was visited again on the night of 22/23 April. On the second raid T2560/E on 115 Squadron flown by Sergeant Palmer crashed near Swindon on diversion to Wroughton. Sergeant Francis Elliott Shaw, the second pilot, was killed. A Wellington on 218 Squadron flown by Sergeant William Henry Swain RNZAF failed to return and another flown by Sergeant W. S. Adams crashed near Clenchwarton station two miles west of King's Lynn. On 24/25 April, when 69 aircraft including 39 Wellingtons attacked Kiel, another 218 Squadron Wellington, flown by Sergeant E. J. Chidgey crashed near Barton Bendish. All the crew survived. On 25/26 April when 62 aircraft including 32 Wellingtons were despatched to Kiel, Flying Officer George Brian S. Agar and his crew of 218 Squadron failed to return. Theirs was the only aircraft lost and none of the crew survived.

At Waterbeach, one day late in April 99 Squadron crews were awaiting the call to briefing when they were surprised to hear Merlin engines, as if two Spitfires were landing together. Sergeant Eric Masters recalls:

'We all rushed to the windows to see a very unusual Wellington landing. It had Merlin engines instead of Pegasus radials. I was told to report to Wing Commander Black, who told me it would be my aircraft and that I had better have a chat with the ferry-pilot who had brought her in to learn of any different handling features. He told me it handled very well except for being extremely nose heavy due to the in-line Merlins moving the c-of-g forward. He said the trimming wheel was right back with very little more adjustment and he hated to think how she would handle with 'the' bomb on board. He then told me this Mk.II Wellington was made to carry one 4,000lb bomb - the first of the blockbusters!

'Next day I took the new aircraft up for a test flight and found that the increased power from the Merlin engines was most noticeable, especially on take-off and climb. The usual bomb bay, with its opening and closing doors, was not big enough, so the doors had been dispensed with, leaving a large indentation along the bottom of the fuselage. It was not rigged for any other selection of bombs and had just the one release gear. This harming of the aerodynamics of the airframe made the aircraft somewhat 'lumpy' to handle but the smoothness of the in-line engine power with the increase in airspeed outweighed every possible criticism.

'I still had my standard Wellington Mk IA assigned to me and in fact did five more missions in the aircraft before my first in the modified Wellington. It was on 5 May that I first took a 4,000lb bomb on ops, to Mannheim. By then the squadron had received another Mk II Wellington and there were twelve others distributed amongst squadrons in the Group. There were plenty of spectators, including myself, at the bombing up to see the massive bomb being winched into the bomb bay'. It appeared to be a number of metal barrels welded together with a slightly pointed nose cap stuck on one end - merely, I thought to tell which was the forward end. It was quite a shock to see that quite a proportion of it was protruding and I wondered what effect this would have on the handling of the aircraft. I thought, too, that the bomb would not fall in the way a normal bomb would but would most likely tumble over and over. However, our flash photo later showed the bomb bursting; a real fluke.

'Following this we had a very busy period. We went to Brest on 7 May and to Hamburg (with the second 4,000lb bomb) on the night of 8/9 May 1941.[86] On the 10th we went to Berlin (with another), then one to Mannheim on 12 May and another, to Cologne on 17 May, before receiving my commission to Pilot Officer.'

During May the Marham Wellington crews divided their attacks with two raids on the warships in Brest harbour early in the month and raids on German cities in the Ruhr. They took part in three raids on Hamburg and on the second raid, on the night of the 10/11th, a 115 Squadron Wellington flown by Pilot Officer Saunderson dropped a 4,000lb Minol bomb, which went by the more familiar names of 'Cookie', 'Blockbuster' or 'Dustbin' bomb. In a Wimpy the bomb doors and floor were removed and the bomb attached by a 1-inch wire hawser and toggle to a metal beam introduced under the main spar. An axe was supplied to cut the hawser in case it hung up. That same night a 115 Squadron crew were shot down by a German night-fighter using the 'Helle Nachtjagd' (illuminated night fighting) interception method whereby German fighters with the aid of searchlights in northern Germany and in the Rhineland tried to intercept RAF bombers.[87] Don Bruce, Sergeant-observer on 115 Squadron in 1942, wrote the following account on the shooting down of the Wellington from his squadron.

'The weather in the British Isles on Saturday 10 May 1941 was fine with little or no cloud. Visibility was good and similar conditions obtained on the Continent with some high and medium cloud over northwest Germany. There would be a full moon that night. On the bomber squadrons the usual morning routine activities were taking place, Marham was reverberating with the noise of Wellington bombers bearing the code letters 'KO', as 115 Squadron crews lifted off on short cross country flights to air test machines, equipment and guns. Twenty-six-year-old Sergeant John Anderson touched down on the grass airfield around mid-day in Wellington R1379 KO-B having completed his air test. After taxiing to his dispersal point he and his five-man crew clambered down the ladder to wait for transport back to the Flights. John Anderson, an experienced operational pilot, had recently taken command of this new, combat inexperienced crew. He had flown three operational flights with them. The second pilot was a twenty-year-old Australian, Sergeant Alex Kerr. Sergeant David Fraser, also aged twenty, was the rear gunner. The observer, who carried out the dual role of navigator and bomb aimer, was Sergeant Bill Legg. Sergeants' Geoff Hogg and Bernard Morgan as wireless operator and front gunner respectively completed the crew. Back at the Flights John Anderson noted that instructions were chalked on the boards for the ground crew to fuel and bomb up his aircraft. It signified they would be on operations that night. In the late afternoon in the company of other participating aircrews he and his crew attended briefing and learned that orders had come through from Bomber Command HQ for an attack on Hamburg. 119 bombers were being dispatched to bomb the general city area, Altona power-station and the shipyards. Sixty of

Wellington I fuselages in the Weybridge erecting shop. (Vickers)

The immensely strong geodetic construction of the 'Wimpy'. (Vickers)

Wellington B.I (K4049) the Wellington prototype which flew for the first time on 23 December 1937. (Vickers)

Wellington I L4280 over the River Wey during its approach to Weybridge in 1938. It later served on 148 Squadron and on 19 August 1940, while serving on 15 OTU, was destroyed in an air raid at Harwell. (RAF Museum)

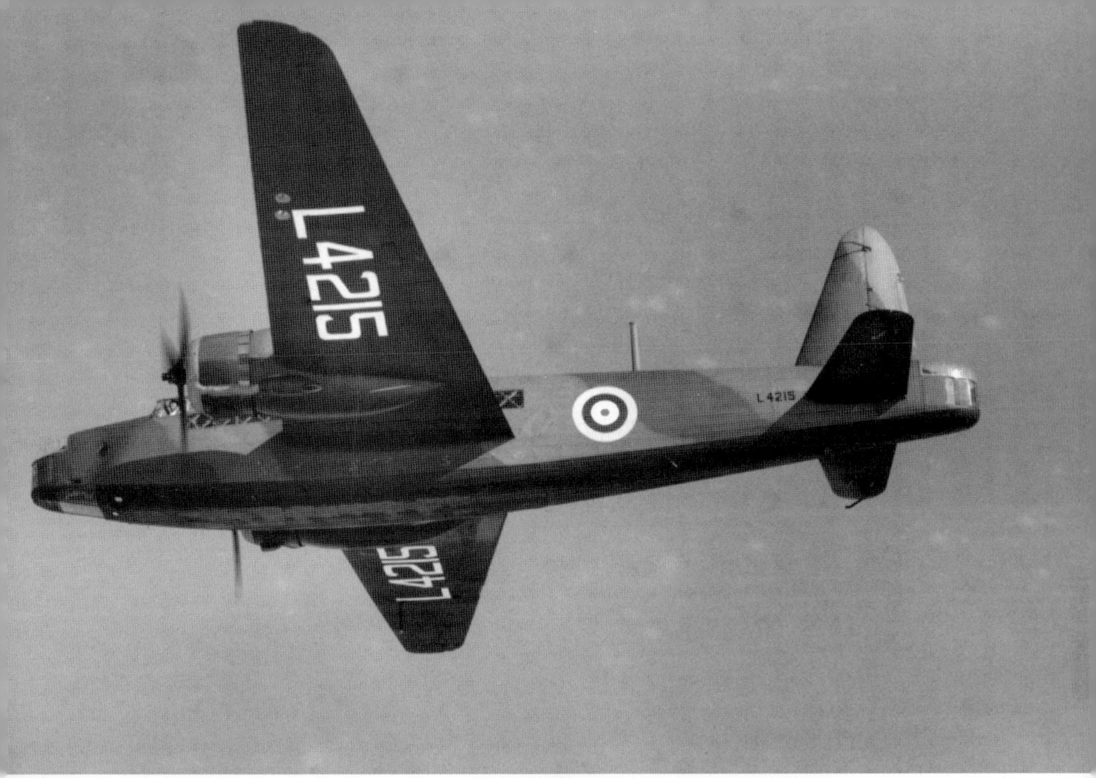

L4215, the first Wellington I to enter RAF service, seen here circling Mildenhall on 10 October 1938 for acceptance by 99 Squadron.

Engine fitters overhauling one of the Bristol Pegasus XVIII. Engines on a 37 Squadron Wellington at Feltwell in July 1940. (IWM)

Wellingtons on 149 Squadron overfly Paris on Bastille Day, 14 July 1939.

Wellingtons on 149 Squadron in formation with Hampdens on 7 Squadron over the French countryside on Bastille Day, 14 July 1939.

Wellington I L4212 production prototype in the display park at RAF Hendon with Short S.23 C Class Empire Flying Boat G-AETW *Calpurnia*, one of 28 ordered by Imperial Airways straight from the drawing board, passing overhead. On 27 November 1938 *Calpurnia* crashed, sank and was wrecked on Lake Habbaniya, Iraq.

Above: The prototype Mk.III L4251 was the 39th Mk.I airframe from the 1st Production Batch. It was converted to use the Hercules HEISM as an alternative to the Pegasus. It is here seen with DH 'bracket' type propellers and hydraulically powered Frazer Nash FN5 nose and FN10 tail turrets with .303 inch machine guns. In the ventral position just behind the bomb bay an FN9 turret was inserted in a retractable mount.

Above: Wellington I of the Royal Aircraft Establishment.

Left: Wellington IA crew on 149 Squadron at RAF Mildenhall on 21 December 1939 prepare for a North Sea shipping search operation when 24 Hampdens and 18 Wellingtons failed to locate any targets. Part of the Hampden force was mistakenly attacked by RAF Spitfires on 602 Squadron when returning to land in Scotland and two of the Hampdens were shot down in the sea.

9 Squadron Wellington Is in formation in spring 1939 when the unit took part in the 2nd International Salon of Aeronautics at Brussels in July. KA-A L4274 nearest the camera is being piloted by Squadron Leader Lennox S. Lamb a New Zealander. He was killed in a mid-air collision involving Flying Officer John Frank Chandler's aircraft (L4363) on 30 October 1939 when piloting L4288 WS-A. Lamb and South African Flying Officer Peter Edward Torkington-Leach's crew were killed. Chandler and his three crew also died. The squadron emblem of a green bat is derived from the official motto 'Per noctem volamus (Throughout the night we fly'). Behind is L4274 KA-K. (IWM)

Right: Navigator at his station. The crew of early Wimpys consisted of two pilots, observer (who was also responsible for aiming the bombs), wireless operator/air gunner and rear gunner. Another gunner might also be carried to man the front turret.

Wellington IA N2871, which, heavily-damaged managed to land at North Coates following the disastrous daylight raid on 18 December 1939.

Czechoslovak airmen, with a proud fighting record, arrived in England following the capitulation of France and formed in July 1940. On 8 August 1940 311 Czechoslovak Squadron was reviewed by Dr. Benes, President of the Czechoslovak Republic. The Czechs operated with 3 Group from September 1940 to April 1942, flying Wellingtons from Honington and East Wretham.

Flying Officer Gregory, the pilot (right) and rear gunner Sergeant Beckett, (left) on Wellington IC X9746 on 149 (East India) Squadron, safely back at Mildenhall, examine the damage caused to their aircraft by a German night fighter, during the raid on Duisburg on 18/19 August 1941. During the attack, the fabric covering the rear fuselage caught fire and Beckett had to use his hands and parachute pack to beat out the flames. Sergeant Reed and Pilot Officer Raffaelli were injured. Gregory was awarded an immediate DFC and Beckett a DFM. The unique geodetic construction enabled Wimpys to take such punishment in their stride.

Wellington II W5379 on 12 Squadron at Binbrook which was lost with Pilot Officer Douglas William Drummond Faint and crew on the raid on Cologne 10/11 October 1941. Faint and three of his crew were killed. Two others were taken into captivity.

Left: Sergeant James Ward on 75 Squadron RNZAF who was awarded the Victoria Cross for his actions on the night of 7/8 July 1941 when the target was Münster. (IWM)

Wellington crews on 75 Squadron RNZAF at Feltwell in early 1941. (British Official)

Above: Wellington N2912 on 215 Squadron at Bassingbourn in mid-1940. This aircraft was serving on 11 OTU at Bassingbourn when it was shot down on 24 April 1941 by a Ju 88C piloted by Feldwebel Gieszubel of I/NJG2. The Wellington crashed out of control directly onto another of the unit's aircraft, R1404 at dispersal. The 19-year old pilot, Sergeant Francis Norman Alstrom and 30-year old Sergeant Ronald Wilson were both killed. Sergeant Nicholls walked from the wreckage with only minor injuries.

Above: Sergeant Rupert 'Tiny' Cooling second pilot and Sergeant 'Duggie' Douglas' on 9 Squadron at Honington, Suffolk. (Cooling)

Left: The crew on 'Pinocchio' give their thumbs up after a raid.

A Wellington IC of 301 (Pomeranian) Squadron is refuelled at Hemswell in Lincolnshire, August 1941. This Polish unit had formed in July 1940 and, after a brief spell on Fairey Battles, operated Wellingtons until the squadron was disbanded in April 1943, due to a shortage of Polish crews. 301 Squadron flew 1,220 Wellington sorties, losing 29 aircraft and 203 aircrew killed or taken prisoner. (IWM)

A Czech bomber crew in February-March 1941. (IWM)

Wellington II W5461 EP-R on 104 Squadron at Driffield, which FTR from Berlin on the night of 12/13 August 1941. Squadron Leader H. Budden DFC and his crew were taken into captivity. (IWM)

Wellington Ia P2515 on 37 Squadron which was downed by flak during a Nickel (leaflet) raid near Eifel on the night of 23/24 March 1940. Sergeant Douglas Warren Wilson was killed and four other crew were taken into captivity. Canadian Flying Officer Philip Francis Templeman the pilot was seriously injured and died on 31 March.

Wellington IC of 311 Czechoslovak Squadron and Whitleys at dispersal at Talbenny on the coast of St Bride's Bay in 1943. (Bill Cameron)

A GR.XIV and crew on 304 (Polish) Squadron. (IWM)

Leigh Light Mk.XIV Wellington with underwing rockets. (IWM)

Above: Wellington Ic on 311 Czechoslovak Squadron late in 1942 at Talbenny. The Czechs were posted to Coastal Command in April 1942. (Zdeněk Hurt)

Right: 311 Czechoslovak Squadron crew beside their Coastal Command Wellington. (IWM)

Below: Wellington IC Z1111 KX-N on 311 Czechoslovak Squadron at Talbenny. (Zdeněk Hurt)

Above: Wellington XIII 'Stickleback' torpedo-bombers. (RAF Museum)

Crew on 'S-Sugar', 407 'Demon' Squadron RCAF at Wick in Scotland: standing left to right, Warrant Officer George Grandy, wireless operator; Flying Officer Gord A. Biddle, pilot; Pilot Officer Ken Graham; seated, Flight Lieutenant Maurice Neil and Flight Sergeant Harvey Firestone, one of the wireless-operator-air gunners. Flying Officer George Deeth, the second pilot, remained in England and is missing from this photo. (Firestone)

Wellington VIII of Coastal Command in the Middle East in November 1944. (IWM)

Blackpool-built Wellington XIII 'Stickleback' torpedo-bomber. (RAF Museum)

Wellington XIV 'H-Harry' on 458 Squadron RAAF takes off from Gibraltar in February 1945 on an anti-submarine patrol. 'X-X-Ray' is in the foreground. (Australian War Museum)

A GR.XIV and crew on 304 (Polish) Squadron. (IWM)

these aircraft would be Wellingtons. Hampdens and Whitleys, plus one Manchester, the forerunner of the Lancaster bomber, would make up the complement. The target for the crew of KO-B was the dock area at Hamburg.

'Swinging round to line up with the take off strip at 2217 hours the crewmembers of KO-B were very much preoccupied with thoughts of their immediate future. They could not know that the Luftwaffe had already begun a devastating fire-attack on the City of London. This attack, aided by good visibility from a full moon and an abnormally low tide in the River Thames leaving firemen short of water, would create a 'second' Great Fire of London. They could not know that a lone German fighter was within six minutes' flying time of the British Isles. Bf 110 coded VJ+OQ with Rudolf Hess the Deputy Führer of Germany at its controls was fast approaching its zero hour.

'An uneventful outward flight punctuated only with a flak burst from an isolated battery along the route brought them to the port of Hamburg. Homing in on the target at a height of 11,000 feet they began to make their bombing run, but fierce opposition from the defences in the form of close proximity flak threw them off course. Sergeant Anderson turned to make another run across the target and this time Sergeant Legg was able to release his bombs. Weaving out of the intense flak barrage they turned onto a predetermined course at full boost. Almost immediately they were picked up by three radar-controlled searchlights and coned in the beams of their attendant searchlight batteries.

'The heavy flak now located and started hitting them. Hydraulic pipes in the aircraft were ruptured, releasing hydraulic fluid, which caused the rear turret to jam at an awkward angle. David Fraser also reported over the intercom a fire in his turret. Further, his vision was obscured by hydraulic fluid and oil, which had spread over the perspex windows of the turret. His electric gun-sight had been put out of action. The observer, Bill Legg, made his way towards the rear turret with the cabin fire extinguisher. In the meantime David had stamped out the fire. As Bill made his way back to the cabin he could see Alex Kerr standing in the astrodome watching out for fighters. In the event of an attack Kerr would direct the pilot in his evasive action. Suddenly the flak batteries stopped firing. It signalled the immediate presence of a night-fighter.

'Twenty-two-year-old Leutnant Eckart-Wilhelm von Bonin of 6./NJG1 piloting a Bf l10 night-fighter had been vectored into the vicinity of the enemy aircraft. The searchlights outlining the Wellington bomber had eased his task. He was now manoeuvring into position for an attack from the rear starboard quarter. This was his first operational interception. He was keyed up and very apprehensive of the two guns in the bomber's rear turret. Von Bonin would eventually become a night-fighter ace with thirty-seven victories to his credit but he was now to be tested in battle for the very first time. Closing fast on the bomber he could not understand why the rear turret was not swinging in his direction. The enemy gunner must have seen him at this range. Tense, with the adrenaline pumping, he opened fire. As he did so he realized only his machine guns were firing. He had overlooked the firing button for the 20mm cannon. It was a blessing in disguise for the British crew.

'Back in the bomber Alex Kerr heard David Fraser's terse voice over the intercom, 'Night-fighter on our tail'. He swung round in the astrodome and saw a dark shape moving rapidly into position on the starboard quarter. As he shouted instructions over the intercom to the pilot he felt Bill Legg brush against him as he returned from the rear turret. The fighter's nose danced with pinpoints of flame as the German pilot opened up. Kerr felt a heavy blow as though he had been punched simultaneously all over his body. He was knocked backwards on to the canvas bed in the aircraft. Before he lost consciousness he noticed a fire had started in the reconnaissance flares which were amidships on the starboard side. They were close to the oxygen bottles. The machine gun bullets had wounded him in ten places including a bullet in his liver. Bill Legg was standing next to Alex Kerr when the fighter attacked. He was off the intercom and didn't know what was happening. A hammer-like blow hit him in the lower part of the back. He twisted involuntarily and received several other hits. With blood oozing from his back and stomach he crumpled and fell unconscious to the floor.

'John Anderson, aware of the bright yellow flame burning amidships, began to throw the Wellington about in an effort to blow out the fire. His efforts were unavailing. The bomber continued to burn fiercely. Fearing an explosion would blow the aircraft to pieces he gave the order to bail out. Although David Fraser's turret was jammed at an angle he managed to squeeze through the narrow aperture left by the partly obscured door and gained access to the fuselage where his parachute was stored. As he made his way to the emergency escape hatch aft of the beam machine gun on the starboard side he saw Alex sitting in front of the hatch. He was obviously badly wounded and very dazed. A quick examination of Bill Legg who was lying further up the fuselage convinced David that he was dead. He returned to Alex, who in the meantime had managed to remove the cover from the escape hatch and was sitting with his legs dangling through the hatch. David placed Alex's hand on the ripcord and pushed him out. He was relieved to see his parachute open. David followed. By now Bernard Morgan and Geoff Hogg had both made good their escape. Having set the automatic pilot John Anderson scrambled down to the escape hatch and bailed out. Unfortunately he landed in the River Elbe and drowned. The aircraft continued on course burning brightly, carrying the badly wounded, unconscious figure of its observer.

'The crumpled body of Bill Legg began to stir as he slowly regained his senses. He still wasn't sure what had happened and by an immense effort of will staggered to his feet and climbed over the main spar to get to the cockpit. He was amazed to find the pilot's seat empty. Slowly it dawned on him that he was alone in a burning aircraft 9,000 feet above Germany. He had to get out and get out quickly. His parachute was under his table. Having retrieved it he made his way forward to the main escape hatch. Carrying the parachute in his hand instead of immediately clipping it on his harness he stood over the escape hatch looking down into the night. At that moment his strength seemed to ebb. The chute slipped from his grasp. He watched with dismay as it fell through the escape hatch and into the darkness. His position was now desperate. He had never been officially trained as a pilot and had only taken over the controls of a Wellington briefly for a straight and level flight with one of his pilots.

'Weakness brought on by his wounds dulled his senses. He didn't panic. With great difficulty he climbed into the pilot's seat and took over the controls. He released the automatic pilot and switched to manual control. As there was no possibility of surviving he decided to stick the down and crash, taking something or someone that was German with him. Losing height rapidly he found he could pick out rivers, fields and buildings in the bright moonlight. He pulled back on the stick and levelled out at about 600 feet. One field appeared to be much larger than the rest. He decided to try to crash in it. Easing back on the throttles, unable to employ flap because of the damaged hydraulics, he approached at a speed of 100 knots to avoid stalling. At a height of around 100 feet he closed both throttles and braced himself for the crash. About three-quarters of the way along the field the Wellington touched down, bumped along on its belly and stopped. Having released the pilot's escape hatch Bill found he was too weak to pull himself through it. Two German soldiers from a nearby flak battery climbed onto the burning plane and lifted him to safety.'[88]

The station's only other loss during May was Wellington R1280 on 115 Squadron flown by Sergeant Sayers, which lost a propeller and unable to maintain height, had to be force-landed half a mile short of the runway at Oakington.

On the night of 12/13 June 1941 405 (Vancouver) Squadron RCAF at Driffield, Yorkshire, made its operational debut when the Canadian squadron despatched four Wellington IIs to Schwerte. With the better weather to come operations were flown from Marham on eleven nights in June with Kiel and Cologne being the most frequently visited targets. On the night of 12/13 June when 82 Wellingtons visited the railway yards at Hamm, Marham despatched a dozen Wellingtons of 115 Squadron. Shortly after take-off R1805/T flown by Sergeant Robson developed engine trouble and he was forced to jettison his bomb load over the Wash and return to Marham. As the Wimpy crossed the airfield boundary the second engine failed and the aircraft crashed, hitting a tree and seriously injuring two of the crew. Sergeant George Aikenhead died later of his injuries. A few days later, on 17 June another Wellington was written off when Pilot Officer Amery Yeo Evans crashed at Palgrove Farm near Sporle during an air test. Only one man survived. On 20/21 June two 218 Squadron Wellingtons were lost on the raid on Kiel when 115 aircraft, including 47 Wellingtons, were despatched to bomb the *Tirpitz*. Sergeant Gordon Grant Jillett RNZAF and Sergeant Mason John Fraser RNZAF were lost without any survivors. Theirs were the only Wellingtons lost on the raid, which failed to find the German ship and the aircraft unloaded their bombs on Kiel instead.

On the night of 23/24 June 44 Wellingtons and eighteen Whitleys made a heavy raid on Cologne. Pilot Officer Douglas Sharpe flew one of the Wellingtons despatched by 115 Squadron. His rear gunner, Sergeant R. F. 'Chan' Chandler, who had been involved in a 3 PRU Wellington prang' the previous month, recalls. 'Things seemed to go wrong after bombing Cologne. There was a lot of chatter on the intercom between the pilot and the navigator. There was no doubt whatsoever that we were lost. The crew were repeatedly instructed to keep constant watch for any sign of land through the cloud. Shortly we saw the coastline. There were repeated comments about 'Fuel State'. The aircraft was throttled back and a gradual descent was made. I was invited by Pilot Officer Sharpe to bail out over land. I declined, thinking it was best to stay with the aircraft and crew.'

Sharpe nursed the ailing bomber back to Suffolk, where almost out of fuel, he decided on a crash landing. Chandler recalls. 'It so happens that the area around Bredfield, Burgh and Pettistree is very flat and a suitable length of pastureland was selected. Sharpe made a gradual descent and approach. I jettisoned my turret doors and my back was to the starboard side as we dropped to a height of about fifty feet. I lowered my goggles and eased myself out on the edge of the turret. Looking out and down with the ground rushing past at an alarming rate of knots, I thought of rolling out of the turret. Looking along the fuselage I could see trees ahead and slid back into the turret. The next second there was the most tremendous crash and I lost consciousness.'

The Wellington had hit the trees and crashed into some council houses at Debach. Incredibly, a man with a child in his arms jumped to safety from the bedroom window of the smashed house. 'Chan' Chandler suffered serious leg, head and arm injuries but would recover. Sergeant Fred Tingley, the second pilot, died later as a result of his injuries. He was the only fatality. Sharpe was unhurt but was killed on his next trip.

Another Wellington was written off on 24 June when R1501 crashed on take-off but Sergeant Skillen and all the crew escaped before the aircraft burned out.

The air war was entering a new phase with the enemy night defences beginning to inflict heavy losses on Bomber Command. As one Wellington pilot said at the time, 'losses were running at approximately five per cent so one believed one was living on luck after the 20th trip. One was just as likely to 'buy it' on the first as on the last.' During June the German night-fighters destroyed 66 aircraft. On the night of 29/30 June two Wellingtons on 115 Squadron and one on 218 Squadron flown by Australian Pilot Officer Francis Egerton Bryant failed to return from the raid on Bremen. One of the 115 Squadron Wimpys was piloted by Flight Lieutenant Jack Alexander James Bailey DFC who was shot down by Hauptmann Walter Ehle of StII/NJG1.[89] The other was Wellington R1509/P on 115 Squadron, which was flown by Pilot Officer Alan McSweyn RAAF, who also encountered a night fighter. He recalls.

'Our first enemy action was heavy flak as we were en route for Bremen. Apparently, although we were not aware of it at the time, we had been hit, because some ten minutes before reaching the target the port engine overheated, the oil pressure dropped and I had to cut the engine just as we reached the target area. We went ahead and bombed the target, dropping from about 13,000 feet to 11,000 feet after the engine failure and there having difficulty in maintaining height on one engine after leaving the target. As usual we experienced searchlights and flak after leaving Bremen. I had to decide whether to try to stay at 9,000 feet, where we seemed able to maintain height, but would have to run the gauntlet of both light and heavy flak, or whether to take violent evasive action, losing even more height in the process, or dive for the ground to get out of danger at roof-top level. The latter two choices lessened the chance of getting home on one engine, so I elected to stay at 9,000 feet, warning the crew to watch for night fighters. Sure enough, the flak ceased while we were still coned by searchlights and then without warning I saw tracer fire passing us and felt the shudder of our rear guns firing. Some days later we were told by other crewmembers that Jimmy Gill, my rear gunner, had shot down a single-engined fighter, probably a Me 109. Almost simultaneously there was another burst of cannon and machine-gun fire, which came straight up the fuselage from rear to front, swathed the right side instrument panel, knocked off the navigator's left earpiece as Wilf Hetherington stood in the cockpit beside me. It hit Bill Wilde, the co-pilot, in the thigh as he stood looking out of the astrodome and seriously wounded Jimmy Gill in the shoulder and chest. Immediately the starboard motor caught fire and ahead and climbing right in front of us I saw the Me 110, which had caused the damage, but which could not be seen by Ted 'Laddy' Gibbs, the front-gunner. Within seconds the whole starboard wing and fuselage was alight; the fire extinguishers were ineffectual and I found the aircraft virtually uncontrollable, so I gave the order to bail out. Wilf Hetherington crawled forward to the front turret to release Teddy Gibbs, while Bill Wilde, though wounded, crawled to the rear escape hatch to warn Jimmy Gill to leave and bail out from there. I saw Laddy Gibbs, Wilf Hetherington and Frank Davidson, the WOp, leave by the forward hatch and looking back, I could see that Bill Wilde had gone out the rear hatch and Jimmy Gill had gone from the rear turret.[90]

'By now the starboard wing had disintegrated and the aircraft was spinning down out of control. With some difficulty I was able to reach the forward hatch and after some effort got it open and bailed out. My parachute descent was unsensational, although my flying boots blew off as I left the aircraft and landed in the rear of a farmyard in fairly long grass, landing so quietly among an unconcerned herd of thirty or so cows that I remained on my feet and didn't roll over. I was surprised by the quietness. I had no idea where my aircraft or crew had landed and realised that surrounding wooded areas probably concealed both. I was able to grab a bicycle from the farmhouse nearby and began riding and walking in a vain hope to reach Holland and perhaps help.'

Alan McSweyn reached a military aerodrome and managed to get in the cockpit of a Bf 110 but was apprehended while trying to start the engines. Apparently, he motioned from the cockpit to a Luftwaffe ground crewman to assist him with starting the engines. The German fell for it but when McSweyn pressed the starter button the prop nearly took the German's head off. He then spotted McSweyn's dark blue Australian uniform and the game was up! McSweyn concludes.

'The rest of the crew all landed in the same area. Jimmy Gill, apparently dazed but not fatally injured, landed in a tree, did not realise how high he was, released his parachute harness and dropped about forty feet to the ground, badly hurting his back. Bill Wilde meanwhile, could not walk so rather than leave the two wounded men, the other three alerted some Germans and asked for medical help. Although the wounded were given the best possible medical treatment in hospital, Jimmy Gill died, mainly from a broken back. Wilde fully recovered and the doctors told him that while they regretted being unable to save Gill, his death was really a blessing because had he lived he would have been a paraplegic for life.'[91]

In July RAF Bomber Command was operational over enemy targets on six nights, with three targets being hit on three of the nights and two targets being bombed on three other occasions. Wellingtons and to a lesser degree, Hampdens and Whitleys, still constituted the main bombing effort on German cities and the harbour at Brest. With the repeated attacks on German targets enemy night-fighters were everywhere.

On the morning of 1 July 115 Squadron despatched three Wellingtons on a sea search for a dinghy. Sergeant Smith on R1063 was attacked by three Bf 110s. Although the Wimpy was hit three times the aircraft escaped serious damage. None of the Wellington crews sighted the dinghy. On the night of 2/3 July when 52 Wellingtons of Bomber Command bombed Brest, Bf 110s appeared again when X9663 returned with cannon holes in the fuselage. On the night of 4/5 July when the target was Brest, Sergeant Parsons, the rear gunner on Wellington X9671 on 115 Squadron flown by Sergeant John Trevor Wallace RNZAF, claimed to have shot down a German night-fighter. The night following, 65 Wellingtons and 29 Whitleys attacked Münster for the loss of one Whitley. On 6/7 July 21 Wellingtons and 88 Hampdens visited Brest and 47 Wellingtons set out for Münster and 15 Wellingtons and 31 Whitleys were detailed to raid Dortmund just east-north-east of the Ruhr Valley - the hottest spot that had ever been entered in a flying crew's log. Sergeant Wallace's Wellington was attacked by Bf 110s again and in the ensuing eight-minute combat the crew co-operated superbly and only very minor damage was suffered.[92] Wellington X9672 flown by Sergeant Berney could not shake off the fighter and he had to jettison his bombs. During this combat the rear gunner, Sergeant Robert William Ronald Kerruish was killed. One crewmember was killed on a Wellington on 75 Squadron when it hit a tree during a night flying exercise while trying to land on one engine at Methwold. On the Münster raid Wellington R1063/D on 115 Squadron piloted by Sergeant Oswald Arthur Matthews RNZAF crashed in the North Sea with the loss of all the crew after being attacked by Oberleutnant Helmut Woltersdorf of 4./NJG1. Although a SOS was sent, the subsequent air and sea search failed to locate the crew.[93] A Wimpy and two Hampdens failed to return from the raid on Brest.

'D for Donald', a Wellington IC[94] on 405 Squadron piloted by Flying Officer Ronnie Fraas got into trouble returning to Pocklington from Dortmund. Sergeant M. G. A. McKenzie was the 27-year old Canadian navigator. A little over a year earlier, when an aircraft in which he was flying solo went out of control and necessitated a crash landing, wiping out the aircraft but resulting in no serious injury to himself, except to make him feel completely incapable of performing a successful landing again, with the effect that he gave up piloting and became a navigator. McKenzie recalled:

'The flight to the target was, in the main, uneventful - as far as these things go. Naturally, we flew quite close to Rotterdam, which put up its usual welcome in a slight barrage of lights and anti-aircraft shells - but we de- synchronized and took evasive action - and that incident was soon behind us - forgotten.

'What time are we due over the target?' The Captain spoke for the first time.
'At 1230: I answered.
'This was always arranged by the Wing Commander - so that all the Squadron - in conjunction with any others taking part - arrived over the target

at the same instant, in order to divide the ground defences among many - rather than anyone kite receiving the full blessing from the earth.

'The time now escapes me - but after checking our position by the stars - and re-checking by radio loop bearings, I was satisfied that we were well on track - the prevailing wind would hold good - by the appearance of atmospheric conditions - and a consultation with the met forecast form - so I settled down to munch on an orange.

'Of course, we were de-synchronizing and flying in an evasive manner all this time - in order to confuse the detectors - but the average course, air speed and height were all to a navigator's satisfaction.

'All this time countless ribbons of light were cutting the darkness all around us and now and then a burst would rock us ever so slightly - that was fine - it meant that locating our kite was proving to be a bit of a task to them - and they only fired when sure that your position was accurately plotted - so, as long as the bursts just rocked us - well, the detectors were picking up the wrong note. It must be understood that this takes longer to tell than it takes in the actual flight - and the navigator managed to get about two successive bites out of the orange - the rest of the time checking and re-checking position, air speed, course, height, track and ground speed; plotting star sights and fixes, radio loop bearings, fusing the bombs; setting the distributor arm in order to drop the stick in the most effective way.

'Our height is 12,500 feet,' I said to the captain 'and we should bomb from 10,000?'

'Got it,' said Ronnie Fraas. 'I will glide down now.'

'Hold back the speed as we are ahead of time, now,' I warned.

'Fine - but it is rather quiet tonight, isn't it - probably night fighters. Hello, front and rear gunners - keep a sharp eye. Take over Bill [Pilot Officer W. S. O'Brien the second pilot], I want some coffee.'

'So back he piled - clapped me on the back and we toasted the blitz of Dortmund in our thermos tops. And back he went. Up to the astro-hatch I went to have a look round - only to be completely dazzled by a perfect wall of light - which seemed to envelop us - and hold like the very devil - and then came that unmistakable sound of bursting ack-ack shells - a sound that is almost impossible to describe - I think if you magnified the cracking of a nut under water you'd have it.

'There was the one that was close - we pitched from it - and yet another after another - yes, they had us buttoned - those ground boys were sure on their toes tonight and each one came closer and closer - no doubt we were for it, unless, yes - to drop a parachute flare - that usually blinds them and gives us an escape.

'Going to drop a flare,' I fairly blasted the intercom.

'Good show,' the Captain had tense tone.

'So, seizing the bulky flare I staggered - yes, with the furious tossing and pitching about the sky of our kite - a crawl would describe my journey better.

'Opening the flare chute, I was startled to see a searchlight streaming right up into my face, nothing is more surprising than that - and unnerving - it makes one positive that it was meant for you alone - and although the impossibility of it is obvious, you are sure that the ground can see you clearly. However, to drop the flare and ease the situation - with a ring and a rasp it was gone and without waiting for any effect I tumbled back to my table - as I was a bit faint from lack of oxygen and a horrible suspicion came over me. Yes - Good God - we were smack over the Ruhr Valley and the time - 1230 - ten minutes to fifteen ahead of schedule - which meant that we were alone - terribly alone - just the right meat for that terrible barrage - no wonder it seemed worse than anything previous - we were getting all of it!

'Here I become slightly confused - the flare had its effect, but we all felt that 'Jerry' was too good tonight and we would soon be twisting and twitching about the sky very soon again. We were dead on track and would be over our particular target in eight minutes - all things allowed. Up to the bomb compartment I went and lay on the floor over the glass panel - to guide the kite to our point - only to be almost blinded by a battery of lights from the ground. Quickly I closed my eyes - for too much of that light could blind me to the target - Jerry's plan, of course.

'Let the bombs go,' the captain really shouted - if I had only listened.

'But we aren't over the target yet.' I took a quick look at my watch.

'Let the bombs go,' he repeated.

'And knowing full well he was remaining cool - I took no notice - as I could see the Dortmund-Ems Canal docks ahead - and the chance to get our target had too strong a hold on me - I honestly didn't know that the frightful barrage of lights and shells existed - two minutes would see our job done - and by the look of things - done well!

'For God's sake drop those damn bombs, boy.'

'Yes captain.' For now the target was coming down the drift wires of the bomb sight.

'The next few seconds were like hours. Could I hold off long enough? It never occurred to me that I was in no position to judge. The Captain should be obeyed on the spot and the argument dealt with in the safety of the Mess. But I do want to make it clear that the chance of 'doing the thing' was too overpowering - and who can criticize?

'I seemed to push that switch with my whole body and it seemed a great relief that I sang out, 'Bombs going, going, going - GONE!' Only to find - on peering out to see their work - myself thrown clear back under the pilot's feet, after what seemed an ear-splitting crack. And not a word was said by anybody. After all, even if it was the heaviest blast, we had been throwing about a great deal, but the starboard engine had packed up and the Captain sounded quite cool.

'The last burst had done its work and we now had one engine to travel six hundred miles.

'After giving the course home I sat down - or tried to - what with our twisting and turning - then jumped up and gave another course in order to fly us north of the Ruhr. Coming in had been too hot. Then a multitude of thoughts roared on me; we had arrived too early; why; whew! It was hell; had my navigation gone wrong; must check it; couldn't find anything wrong; had our speed been too much, on the glide; the log said no; should I have led the captain on; why were we ahead of schedule; should have dropped them when ordered; but I was the air bomber and I gave the orders on that; was my last fix incorrect - and on and on in the same channel.

'We were losing height steadily, but not quickly and we had plenty to spare. But it meant working like the devil on the navigation. We had to get home as quickly as possible - and our early arrival on the target had shaken my faith.

'After an age I could see the Zuider Zee coming up and a perfect hell of flak beyond it - that would be Rotterdam - and it was right on track. We must go round - our altitude was too risky and easy for the light flak. So I gave the Captain a large alteration to starboard - as the Jerry fighters were too thick south of the city.

'Over the Zee now - and then bright flashes of light came through the starboard windows and then 'The engine's on fire!' The second pilot speaking.

'Not badly - just a low, slow flame, more inside the cowling than out - but the wing petrol tanks.

'And now we were visible for miles - any fighter would be able to see us - I can almost see the gunner straining through the darkness for a dark, fast-moving shape.

'Now we were over the North Sea and this was the time really to work.

'Asking the wireless to get me a loop from X [wartime censor] - I went back to take a star sight - but the flames from the engine were now bright enough to interfere with the proper use of the sextant.

'How the devil was I to get a sure fix now - the wireless handed back the loop reading and it was duly plotted on the chart - but in too much of a fore and aft line to check ground speed - but wait - that loop station was not useless after all - it was only about ten miles north of our aerodrome - why not fly that bearing until the coast came up?

'No time was lost in giving the new course and my work was eased slightly. It had been impossible to work out an estimated time for the coast.

'Muffled explosions were coming from the engine and with each one the flames went higher and higher. Honestly, each explosion seemed to ask each one of those questions over and over again. I tried working faster and harder - making the wireless sweat giving me the same loop over again and again. At least we were making good the required track.

'Hello, boys,' the captain said in that same cool tone, 'we are losing height and may have a spot of rowing to do - I am doing my best.'

'God knows, he was flying like a genius.

'Better jettison everything.' The captain was a little worried now - the engine was a mess, 'flares, floats, ammunition, guns.'

'So the three of us went to work - we opened that chute and every loose thing we could put hands on went down to the sea. The fire had us badly worried - we had heard too much about charred remains being washed up - yes, we were three nervous lads. Two of us would never fly again.

'Nothing to do now, but sit and wait. We tried eating our chocolate and currants, but they were tasteless. I'll never forget those moments.

'The fire was bigger and much worse - the sea was close and relentlessly beneath us. Our track through the sky was like a comet - surely a fighter would see us and attack, let's hope they aren't patrolling the coast.

'Quickly checking the track again - I looked out and could see a long dark shadow. That must be the coast - and I really prayed. But we were losing height near those cliffs north of Flamborough.

'Alter course twenty feet port,' I shot at the captain. Quickly mentioning the cliffs, I added, 'there's a good chance of pin-pointing south of Flamborough.'

'Good lad.' And his words cheered me amazingly well.

'How we were losing height; how that fire was blazing; how did it all happen? Yes, it was, it was all my fault - I must clear by getting us home - right down on our own aerodrome.

'Coast ahead and a beacon flashing - where is that beacon, navigator?

'Checking with the list and the map - we were south of Flamborough all right and heading further south - into Hull - and a balloon barrage.

'My God - what is the matter with me - my navigation has gone right to hell.

'Working like the devil - everything seemed twice as heavy and difficult - I gave a course that would bring us over Driffield aerodrome, the nearest one to the coast just east of our station - then I started to laugh.

'Here I was - graduated from OTU in top place with a rating of 'About the Average' - here I was going absolutely haywire. Of course, all this was my fault, right from the start - 'Will be of immeasurable value to his squadron and crew' - Ye gods!

'What's that beacon?'

'Running up and looking I saw - with extreme relief that it was Driffield - but our height - dangerously low - and the engine fire was an inferno - spreading well out on the wing. How in the name of God were the flames avoiding that petrol? We had expected to blow up a long time ago - and what a suspense that had been.

'Land at Driffield.' Now the second pilot was excited, 'we'll never make back. Land at Driffield!'

'The skipper didn't answer and I automatically gave the course for base.

'My work was finished and try as hard as I could my head wouldn't settle. Our height was negligible - and the second pilot was pouring instructions out to the skipper - one right after the other.

'Should have landed at Driffield - we'll never make it.'

'There's the green light. You missed it.'

'Land down wind - off the runway - but land quickly.'

'The fire was now roaring and drowning the sound of our one engine. The wireless op. was pulling my arm.

'Lie down on the floor,' he actually shrieked in my ear - and he proceeded to do so.

'Shall I come up front?' asked the rear gunner.

'As I started to crouch - the kite seemed to turn right over - and there was a terrific tearing sound.

'Here I have to stop and wait - I know what happened in the next few moments, much thought has made it clear to me. But I want to record truly my mind as it worked in these moments - and what I physically felt.

'Hot, burning flames were all around. I screamed - the wireless op just disappeared - now there were screams all around me - dreadful screams -

searing, blasting, searing flames - and a dirty, filthy odour - strong of burning fabric, oil and wood, with a strong impression of burning hair. Still those screams - vaguely I knew my own voice was nowhere in that sound. My face seemed to be passing right through solid walls of fire - it couldn't have been - but the flames, that were everywhere, were deluding me - and still that vile smell. Even now its impression is quite strong.

'The crashing tumble was over and I just sat there - why, I don't know - but just sat there and knew that my left arm was hurting like the devil somewhere under and behind me. The stillness - such stillness - was broken only by the sound of the fire. I must get away and tried to - but something - cables, wires, I don't know what - was wound around my chest and legs preventing my moving. I tore at them with my right hand; tore like fury, over my head, stood up and tried to kick my legs free. Then an arm of fire shot at me - it seemed right through me and again I 'screamed and then as if my voice had been a signal, there came the most horrible screams I thought I would ever hear again.

'At last I was free and I stumbled to my right - the way was blocked - I turned again and threw myself clear and lay on the ground - no fire - just cool air and ground.

'How long I was there I don't know, but I got up and looked at the wreckage; it seemed to be spread over yards and the flames were white and high. Then I saw Tom Brown, the wireless op slowing moving up and down in what seemed to be the spot from where I had come. His face and hands were black and he seemed to be looking at me and I swore those two white eyes seemed to be accusing me - 'You did this!' and I felt guilty, dreadfully guilty. Coming in a little closer I wave my hand and yelled at him - 'This way, Tom'. My face and hands were now stinging intolerably and I turned away, went a few steps and turned back - Tom was just standing there - again I waved and yelled - surely he could see me - other screams prevented his hearing me. Then I heard voices and shrubs crashing - turning I saw the boys coming from the aerodrome - I ran to them calling for help and two of them took hold of me - one of them hurting my arm very much.

'Come along now.'

'But I wouldn't. I just stood there and looked at that inferno. 'Get the boys out, they're still in there.'

'All right, old man, somebody is taking care of them.'

'Looking, I could see figures running around and in that fire - when suddenly there was a series of smashing explosions and thousands of tiny flaming particles seemed to roar up into the sky - the spare petrol - now myriads of colours - the Very cartridges.

'Oh, you'll never get them out now - all of them are done.' My voice sounded miles away.

'During this time the two lads had been trying to get me on to the stretcher - and now, it was all done, so down I went. The arm and hand were hurting me fearfully.

'Next I remember we were in the sickbay and voices and people all around - who was moaning like that - turning my head I saw other stretchers around with somebody in each one - the boys had pulled them out - it was marvellous.

'I knew that black face next to me.
'Hello, you.'
'Hello, Mac - hear the skipper?'
'So it was the skipper moaning like that. Who had been screaming?
'Skipper - hello - I'm sorry.'
'And that's all I knew.'[95]

On the night of 7/8 July on the return flight at 13,000 feet over Ijsselmeer, Squadron Leader R. P. Widdowson's aircraft on 75 Squadron RNZAF was attacked by a Bf 110 night-fighter. The rear gunner was wounded in the foot but managed to drive off the enemy aircraft. Incendiary shells from the fighter started a fire near the starboard engine and fed by a fractured fuel pipe, soon threatened to engulf the whole wing. Sergeant James Ward RNZAF the second pilot climbed out of the astrodome into a 100-mph slipstream in pitch darkness a mile above the North Sea. By kicking holes in the fabric covering of the geodetics he inched his way to the starboard engine and smothered the fire, which threatened to engulf the aircraft. Ward's actions earned him the Victoria Cross. (He was killed two months later, shot down in a Wellington over Hamburg.)

That night, Eric Masters on 99 Squadron, was flying the 30th and final operation of his tour, a sortie to Cologne. Masters was philosophical about it.

'Our losses were running at approximately five per cent so one believed one was living on luck after the 20th trip. One was just as likely to 'buy it' on the first as on the thirtieth.' All went well until Masters' crew approached the Rhine. 'Pilot Officer Don Elliott, my Canadian navigator, came to stand beside me. There were two areas of AA activity ahead and I decided to head between them so that Elliott could pick out the river reflecting the moonlight from the south and from his map would be able to place us exactly. We discovered we were just south of Cologne. I wanted to get a really good run at the target and needed to get north of the city. There was no need for navigation now and having passed over the river I turned north and flew past Cologne on its eastern side watching the flak exploding, flares dropping, flash bombs illuminating huge areas and bombs bursting. I felt remote from it all. North of Cologne I turned over the river and headed south. Elliott was now in the prone bomb aiming position, just below and in front of me, getting a very clear view of the river and giving me course corrections to keep us in line with the target. The activity over the target had practically ceased and it became very peaceful. One of the gunners remarked, 'Everyone else seems to have gone home, skipper'. In these last minutes I had kept straight and level and at the same speed for much too long. The Germans must have wondered about this crazy lone raider. We were caught in the bluish-white beam of a master searchlight. Six more standard searchlights coned us. Now the whole fury of the Cologne defences concentrated on us. I increased speed, still heading for the target. The flak followed us expertly, throwing the aircraft about. Johnny Agrell, the second pilot, who was watching it all at the astrodome ready to deal with the flash-bomb, called out that we had been hit.

'I had felt a judder in the control column and then found it rigid in the fore and aft direction (elevator control). As I had been holding it in the dive I was now unable to bring the nose up.' In vain Masters tried to correct. 'The flak was still after us. I told Don to jettison the bombs (live) in a last hope to get the nose up but when this failed, I realised we were virtually out of control at 10,000 feet and losing height rapidly. I had no alternative but to give the order, 'Bail out!' I was thankful my chest parachute pack was in its storage position. At times I had been known to forget to take it on a trip and I had delegated Don Elliott to make sure it was always on the 'tumbril'. I was glad that on this occasion he had not let me down.' Eric Masters bailed out and was captured. He spent the remainder of the war as a 'guest of the German government'.

On the night of 8/9 July Wellingtons on 75 Squadron raided Münster again. When Bomber Command despatched 57 Wellingtons to Osnabrück on 9/10 July 115 Squadron contributed four Wimpys. On the return Squadron Leader Sindall had a double engine failure in X9673 and with the aircraft showing no inclination to recover, he ordered the crew to bail out. Almost as soon as they had done so and just before he was preparing to leave, the engine picked up again and Sindall landed the Wellington at Brackley.

In the summer of 1941 ground trials of the new radar navigational aid 'Gee'[96] were in progress at Marham, Norfolk.[97] Twelve pilots and 12 observers from 115 and 218 Squadrons were involved in the trials and had been informed they would not be undertaking operational flying until these were completed. Understandably they were surprised to be notified of briefing for an attack on Sunday 13 July 1941. It was to be a 'maximum' effort consisting of 69 Wellingtons, 47 of which were targeted on Bremen, 20 on Vegesack and two on Emden. All crews would encounter heavy cloud and icing. Sixteen aircraft would claim to have bombed Bremen. Two Wellingtons would fail to return from the Bremen attack.[98] In 115 Squadron the all-sergeant crew on Wellington IC R1502, W. J. Reid, pilot and captain, Geoff T. Buckingham, observer, M. B. Wallis, wireless operator, M. G. Dunne, front gunner and T. W. Oliver, rear gunner, were short of their regular second pilot. He had been sent to London to attend a Commission Board. 27-year-old Sergeant-pilot Frederick Birkett Tipper, who was regarded as a jinx on the Squadron, took his place. The crew that he had flown with on his first sortie had suffered a very shaky 'do'. On his second operation the aircraft had crashed on take-off, fortunately with no fatal result. Bremen would be his third operational flight.

The observer's chair in a Wellington moved backwards and forwards in tracks firmly fastened to the floor of the aircraft. When he boarded the aircraft Buckingham found to his intense annoyance that the tracks to his chair were broken leaving it free to slide all over the place in the event of violent evasive action. Furthermore, the chair cushion was missing. Instead of throwing his parachute pack on the bed as he usually did - he would have to sit on it in lieu of the cushion. Little did he realize that before the night was out the object of his annoyance would save his life.

The sky was clear in England but over the North Sea thick cloud was encountered. As they approached the enemy coastline there was a partial thinning of the cloud and Sergeant Tipper was able to pass a pinpoint on the Dutch Coast to his observer. Tipper then left the cockpit and made his way aft to the astrodome where he would keep a constant vigil for night fighters. The

Wellington was now at 9,000 feet. Buckingham had just spotted Texel Beacon and was returning to this station from the cockpit when Sergeant Oliver in the rear turret yelled over the intercom, 'Fighter'. Simultaneously he opened up with his guns racking the fuselage with vibration and filling it with the fumes of cordite. Oberleutnant Egmont Prinz zur Lippe-Weissenfeld, Staffelkapitän, IV./NJG1 had just made his initial strike setting the starboard engine of the bomber on fire. He was now somewhere out in the darkness manoeuvring for a second attack. Buckingham rushed forward to the cockpit and pressed the starboard engine fire extinguisher button. This put out the fire. Next he jettisoned the bombs and gave the pilot a reciprocal course to fly. He then returned to the cabin to check his log. At this moment the second attack occurred and it was far more devastating than the first. Cannon fire from beneath the bomber raked the whole length of the fuselage wounding all members of the crew, some more seriously than the others. Buckingham blacked out. When he came round he was lying across the step, adjacent to the forward escape hatch. As the aircraft had gone into a dive the loose seat, which he had cursed so roundly at the beginning of the flight, had slid to the nose and deposited him on the floor by the escape hatch. His parachute pack, which he had used as a cushion, was lying on top of him. He took stock of the situation. The bomber was on fire and he was wounded in face and arm with cannon shrapnel. There was a hole in the back of his leg, which was bleeding profusely. The door to the front turret was wide open. There was no sign of the pilot. Fastening his parachute pack to the harness he found that one J-clip had been smashed by the cannon fire. He used the remaining clip then heaved on the edge of the escape hatch. In an instant he was out and away into the night. Hanging awkwardly beneath his parachute, suspended at an angle by one clip only, he made a bad landing injuring his anklebone. Tipper's body was recovered from the wreckage.[99] It was assumed that Tipper had been killed by the second burst of fire from the night fighter. Later zur Lippe visited the crew in hospital and expressed his regret that a member of the crew had died. He said he was after the bomber not the crew.[100]

On 14/15 July 78 Wellingtons and 19 Whitleys were dispatched to Bremen where they were given three aiming points, the shipyards, the goods station and the Altstadt. Crews reported the 'whole town was ablaze'. Four Wellingtons were lost from the Bremen raid.[101] Sergeant Tony Gee on 149 Squadron brought 'N-Nuts' home to Mildenhall after being coned in searchlights at 8,000 feet over Bremen and fired on by accurate flak. Gee finally escaped but he was down to 2,000 feet. His navigator/bomb aimer, The Right Honourable Terence Mansfield, who was flying his 11th operation, recalls.

'No-one was wounded but as daylight came we found lots of it coming in everywhere. Our wireless was not working so we could not tell base that, although we were a long way behind schedule, we were still coming. By the time we got back to Mildenhall we were classed as overdue. Someone classified the damage to R1593 as not repairable and 'N-Nuts' was taken away in pieces.'

In the half light of dawn on 15 July Sergeant Jack Cyril Saich and the crew of a Wellington IC of 9 Squadron was returning to Honington with six 500lb bombs still in her bomb bay after a raid on Bremen. Three hours and forty minutes earlier, 'T-Tommy' had been caught in the glare of searchlights over Bremen at

11,000 feet, hit four times by flak and set on fire. Sergeant English, the rear gunner and Sergeant Telling, the second pilot were wounded by shell splinters. Flares stored in the port wing ignited and two large holes were blown in the starboard wing and rear fuselage. Much of the fabric covering the tail fin was burned away before the fires were finally extinguished. The bombs could not be jettisoned because of damage to the hydraulic and electrical systems. One main wheel refused to lower, the flaps were inoperative and the fuel gauges had read 'zero' for the last two hours of the flight. The area picked out for an emergency landing was a large field near Somerton, Norfolk. However, telegraph poles had been erected in all fields in the vicinity as an anti-invasion measure in 1940 and these could not easily be seen in the dim light. 'T-Tommy' touched down, went into a swing and slammed into one of the wooden poles, finishing with its fuselage broken in two. Incredibly, all six crew emerged from the wreckage with little more than a few bruises.[102]

On the night of 15/16 July the Wellington flown by Flight Sergeant Neil Caldwell Cook on 115 Squadron was shot down by Hauptmann Werner Streib of StI./NJG1 and the bomber was later reported to have crashed near Nederweert in Holland. None of the crew survived. Streib was also responsible for shooting down a 218 Squadron Wellington flown by Flight Lieutenant John Stokes with the loss of all the crew.[103] On the night of 21/22 July when 37 Wellingtons and 34 Hampdens visited Frankfurt and 36 Wellingtons and eight Halifaxes attacked Mannheim one Wellington (Z8788/H) failed to return. There were no survivors on the crew of Sergeant Norman Lachlan Johnston RCAF on 115 Squadron.

A daylight raid on 24 July certainly made the Wellington crews sit up and take notice. As one of the crewmembers recalls, 'we just couldn't believe our ears when the CO said that crews were to participate in a daylight operation against the German battleships *Scharnhorst* and *Gneisenau* lying at anchor in the French port of Brest.' A total of 150 aircraft were planned to make the attack in formation but at the last moment this had to be changed because of the departure of the *Scharnhorst* to La Pallice. The force to Brest was then to be composed of 100 aircraft of which three were to be Flying Fortresses flying at 30,000 feet in the hope of attracting German fighters prematurely. Then 18 Hampdens escorted by three squadrons of Spitfires with long-range fuel tanks were to attack in anticipation of drawing off more enemy fighters. Finally, the main force of 79 unescorted Wellingtons of 1 and 3 Groups were to attack in the final wave. The Wellingtons, Hampdens and Fortresses made daylight attacks on the *Gneisenau* and the *Prinz Eugen* while Halifaxes attacked the *Scharnhorst* at La Pallice. Marham sent a number of Wellingtons on the major attack at Brest. All three Wellingtons on 115 Squadron were engaged by Bf 109s. During the combats the Wimpys were not hit but their gunners claimed to have shot down three of the enemy fighters. Two of the Wellingtons were damaged by flak but all claimed to have hit the target. Six hits were reported on the *Gneisenau* - two of them by Sergeant Prior - but these could not be confirmed. Ten Wellingtons, including a 218 Squadron Wimpy flown by Pilot Officer Morrisson Jolly RNZAF and two Hampdens failed to return. Jolly and three of the New Zealander's crew were killed and two survived to be taken prisoner. Five Halifaxes were lost in the attack on the *Scharnhorst*.

Intensive operations continued into early August, seven being flown during the first 12 days. On the night of 3/4 August, when 34 Wellingtons were despatched to bomb Hannover, the Wellington flown by Pilot Officer John Arthur Maxwell RCAF of 218 Squadron took off from Marham at 22.28 hours. Cloudy conditions caused severe turbulence and Maxwell's Wellington also suffered a partial instrument failure and at 2300 hours seven miles north east of Norwich he ordered the crew to bail out. The Wellington crashed at Salhouse near Norwich and the Canadian pilot was killed. At Hannover the target was cloud covered and one aircraft, a Wellington IC of 218 Squadron flown by Wing Commander John Lionel Howe Fletcher, was lost. Fletcher and three of his crew were killed and two survived to become prisoners of war. On 5/6 August targets at Mannheim, Karlsruhe and Frankfurt were attacked for the loss of nine aircraft including four Wellingtons were lost. One of them was flown by Flight Lieutenant F. L. Litchfield on 115 Squadron and all the crew survived to be taken prisoner.

On the night of the 11/12th when 115 Squadron despatched ten Wellingtons to railway targets at Mönchengladbach none of the 29 Wellingtons that were despatched by Bomber Command was lost but the target area was completely cloud covered. The operation marked the first service trial over enemy territory of the 'Gee' navigational and identification device which was carried out successfully by two Wellingtons on 115 Squadron during the raid. On the night of 12/13 August nine crews, including 'Gee' trials aircraft, took off from Marham for Essen and Hannover. Wellington Z8835 one of the 'Gee' trials aircraft, flown by Sergeant John Wallace on 115 Squadron, was shot down by Feldwebel Ernst Kalinowski of 6./NJG1, crashing 1 kilometre southwest of Grafel with the loss of all on board. Another 70 aircraft meanwhile had set out for Berlin and a further 30 Wellingtons, three Stirlings and two Halifaxes went to Essen. Returning to Marham Pilot Officer Wood on 115 Squadron piloting T2563/D switched on his navigation lights and almost immediately he was attacked and shot down by Oberfeldwebel Peter Laufs of I./NJG2 flying a Ju 88C intruder. The Wellington caught fire and Wood force landed at Smith's Farm near Scottow near RAF Coltishall in Norfolk. All of the crew except for Sergeant Bernard George Evans RNZAF, who was killed, escaped without serious injury.

Only four operations were flown during the second half of August. On the night of 14/15 August when Bomber Command attacked Hannover, Brunswick and Magdeburg, two more of Marham's Wellingtons were lost when Sergeant Cecil George Alway on 115 Squadron and Pilot Officer Winston Claude Wilson of 218 Squadron failed to return. Alway's crew were all killed and only one man survived on Wilson's aircraft. On the night of 18/19 August two more 218 Squadron Wellington ICs were lost. Sergeant Kenneth Charles Shearing and his crew were shot down by Feldwebel Siegfried Ney of 4./NJG1 and the Wimpy flown by Sergeant H. G. Huckle was lost with one man killed and five becoming prisoners of war.

On the operation to Mannheim on the 27/28th 91 aircraft of Bomber Command set out for the city and good bombing and many fires were claimed without loss. However, on their return to England, seven Wellingtons and a

Whitley crashed. Two of the 115 Squadron crews bailed out over Norfolk and the third crashed at West Raynham. The month's operations ended with raids on Mannheim and Frankfurt on 29/30 August when 94 Wellingtons were despatched by Bomber Command. Two Wellingtons failed to return from the Mannheim operation. One of these was flown by Sergeant John Kemp Murdoch, which was believed to have been shot down by an intruder near Martlesham Heath. Five men were killed and a sixth died later of his injuries.

In September the high rate of bomber attrition continued as the Nachtjagd increased its capability and bombing operations increased. During the month 115 Squadron alone flew 81 sorties on nine operations for the loss of six Wellingtons.

Flight Lieutenant/Acting Squadron Leader Seymour Preston Barnard, known simply as 'Barney' to his friends was flying a Wellington on 214 Squadron in September 1941 '...heading for Holland to a familiar routine and along a route often traversed. The weather was good with light broken cloud - clearing. Over the Dutch coast the usual sparklers aided and abetted by pencils of searchlights. They gave no cause for alarm as we dodged through and over them before altering course.

'We were well on our way and began to notice that the ground defences were conspicuously absent. It was uncanny and not to our liking. We speculated that perhaps night fighter patrols had been increased with a wider range. My apprehension grew as John Harvey informed me that the radio seemed to have packed up. However, he was working on it. Snowy advised we were coming up to Munster. Naturally, we would avoid the place.

'Suddenly, the darkness ahead was split by a barrier of searchlights miles across and sweeping the sky. This was a new one to us, at least in this area, but I saw a gap and changed course slightly to take us through. Beams were wandering around on either side of us, but we appeared to have made it when snooker-wise, one second in the black; the next in the blue. The master searchlight had exposed directly beneath us and we were caught in its bluish light whilst all the others for miles around fastened on to us in a blinding cone of unreality. We were a moth suspended by an invisible thread. Ordering everyone to hang on tight I threw her about, twisting and turning like a demented rabbit with a god on its tail. Working with the master light the flak opened up. It was heavy calibre stuff and they had us accurately taped. Shrapnel thumped into the kite and the smoke from shells was illuminated into ghastly shades by the beams. I put the nose down in a near vertical dive, keeping my head down to avoid being blinded. We lost thousands of feet and the ASI was reading over 350 mph. Praying that the wings wouldn't part company, and using every ounce of brute force, I eased her out of this mad convulsion and put her into a tight turn with umpteen 'G'. Mercifully, we were out of the fiendish glare and once more back in to the stygian. Gaining some height I ordered Snowy to jettison the bomb-load and we felt their departure with gratitude.

'Everyone miraculously answered to my call and we seemed to be in one piece, although from the holes, gashes and flapping portions, we were lucky to be airborne. However, the possibility of structural damage and ruptured fuel lines existed. The engines were coughing and the temperature gauges showed a rise, therefore I throttled back and adjusted the mixture which seemed to calm them down a little. It then became a question of nursing her back, which raised the rather thorny question regarding the state of our hydraulics. It was bitterly cold because the heating had gone. But on the plus side we had radio contact again which brought the astounding news that due to fog over England the operation had been called-off. All the other aircraft had returned some time ago. Thus: single-handed, we had taken on the whole might of Germany Continuous fuel readings pointed to leaks in the system and I reduced speed to around 120, maintaining as much height as possible. But the cold was numbing and, when we could stand it no longer, we descended to 6000 feet where the chill was less severe. Both engines continued to cough and splutter still, and it was to my utter relief when Snowy announced the coast was 'coming up. As soon as possible I originated a Mayday call - our predicament being decidedly tricky. Back came the news 'completely fogbound: divert to Manston.' Height was now difficult and as we ploughed towards Manston I alerted everyone to the possibility of bailing out but, slowly, slowly we carried on until, at last, we came within R/T range of Manston tower. We had priority landing clearance and we began to let down through the yellowy murk. My eyes were glued on the altimeter until I eventually glimpsed the gooseneck flares.

'Now for the landing. According to the indicator lights the undercarriage was down and locked. But I discovered we had no flaps. Flares began to race past as I shut the throttles and we dropped on to the grass in a succession of bounces. A touch of brakes, but no response. Incredibly the undercart seemed to be holding notwithstanding the sheer pounding it was taking because of our speed over the uneven grass surface. The flares continued to flash past, but we were slowing down and we trundled into the darkness beyond. Then, with an awful crack, the undercart parted with us and we shot on to our belly - the props bending and twisting as they tore up great clods of turf. Onwards we slithered with a fearful rasping and tearing noise, through the barbed wire fence surrounding the perimeter until we came to a stop athwart the Ramsgate Road.'

That was the last Barney knew because his safety straps burst and he was knocked cold as his head was thrown against the panel. The crew scrambled out bruised and shaken and, missing Barney, went back inside the aircraft to find him slumped over the column. He was to spend months in hospital recovering from severe head injuries. It marked the end of Barney's operational flying. However, he later became involved in the development of FIDO and was subsequently transferred to Intelligence.[104]

On 3/4 September 140 aircraft set off for Brest and all aircraft of I, 4 and 5 Groups were recalled, probably because of worsening weather at bases but four aircraft did not hear the signal and with the 3 Group aircraft, proceeded to the target. Some 53 aircraft bombed the estimated position of the German warships through a smoke-screen. No aircraft were lost but two Wellingtons, including one flown by Pilot Officer Scholes, which was abandoned over Horrabridge near Tavistock, Devon and a Whitley crashed in England. On 7/8 September 197 bombers went to three aiming points in Berlin while another 51 bombers headed for Kiel. The Berlin force comprised 103 Wellingtons, 43 Hampdens, 31 Whitleys, six Halifaxes and four Manchesters. In all, 137 crews claimed to have bombed their allotted targets in Berlin. Fifteen bombers were missing in action and at least ten, including two Wellington ICs on 115 Squadron were believed shot down by night-fighters.[105] A Wellington II on 218 Squadron flown by Squadron Leader H. L. Price crashed in a wheat field at Hall Farm, Barton Bendish after flying from the Dutch coast with the starboard engine on fire. All the crew survived. On 26/27 September, when 104 aircraft set off for targets at Cologne, Emden, Mannheim and Genoa, all were recalled because of forecasts of fog at bases. The Wellington flown by Sergeant Marven Ernest Farnan on 115 Squadron crashed in the sea off the Friesians with an engine on fire after bombing Emden and all the crew perished. On the night of 29/30 September when 139 aircraft of Bomber Command were despatched to four aiming points at Stettin, 95 bombers claimed good bombing but eight aircraft were lost and two of them were 115 Squadron Wellingtons that fell victim to night-fighters. There were no survivors aboard X9673/B flown by Sergeant Leonard Harold Ellis who was shot down by Feldwebel Ernst Kalinowski of 6./NJG1. Only the rear gunner aboard Sergeant Arthur Robert Hulls' Wimpy that was shot down by Oberleutnant Ludwig Becker of 4./NJG1 near Groningen survived to be taken prisoner.[106] Five more aircraft of Bomber Command crashed in England on return.

Terence Mansfield on 149 Squadron, who on 26 September, while en route to Genoa, had been recalled over France due to forecast bad weather at base' recalls that 'three days later the Wellingtons went all the way. Mansfield continues. 'We had a lovely view of the Alps but Genoa was mostly covered by cloud so bombing was on estimated position using the coast. After leaving Genoa our wireless blew up and cloud developed solidly below 10,000 feet so navigation was solely on astro fixes. Fortunately, we hit the Mildenhall Lorenz beam almost on ETA. Duggie Fox, my pilot, turned on to it and descended in the low cloud. Honington had been alerted and they fired a massive assortment of pyrotechnics as we approached and we crawled in under a cloud base of, at most, 200 feet.'

On 30 September the Wellingtons carried a new weapon, as Terence Mansfield recalls. 'We carried a new 65lb incendiary for marking purposes. This horrid weapon was very light case, rather like a large oblong tin, the contents of which were spontaneously combustible on contact with air. The resulting fire was very visible but it was a menace, as a leak brought fire. On 12 October we again carried 65lb incendiaries, to Nurnberg. We had orders to drop only on visual. It was totally dark and although we flew around the area for forty minutes, we could see no ground detail. Then bombing started but it was not Nurnberg. Anyhow, we went over to investigate at just over 4,000 feet and I was confident that I could make out a small town. Since the fires were well established, we added to them and sent a signal back that we had bombed a secondary target. Further astro fixes on the return trip confirmed my calculated positions. On landing, we were told that we were the only crew not to find the target but our photograph proved that we were right and that almost the entire attack had been against the wrong place. We got our haloes back! On 7 November, my last [trip] with Duggie Fox and 149 we carried the 65lb incendiary again. The outward route was appalling, with high cloud, very bad icing and turbulence and rattling hail. Using the occasional breaks in the tops; I managed to get a series of astro fixes, so that at least we thought we were almost on track.

Total cloud cover at the target meant that we could not drop our bombs and we brought them all the way back! That we crossed the Suffolk coast almost on track and only five minutes late on ETA proved the value of my sextant. We saw no signs of any defensive action and felt sure that the high losses, 21 of 170, were due solely to the weather.'

In the closing days of 1941 149 Squadron at Mildenhall began exchanging its Wellington IIs for the Short Stirling. 3 Group, since it operated Bristol-engined bombers, had in August 1941, been selected for re-equipment with the Short Stirling. On 24 December there was a taste of things to come when the Avro Lancaster entered service with 44 Squadron at Waddington. Meanwhile, in the summer of 1941 some units like 10 Squadron were still expected to soldier on with the obsolete Whitley until the end of the year when conversion to the Halifax finally took place.

Footnotes

80 Rogers later gained a DFM and he was commissioned. He was KIA on 8/9 April 1943 flying as second pilot of a Halifax II on 76 Squadron.

81 Between January and October 1941 I./NJG2 claimed 125 aircraft destroyed for the loss of 55 aircraft and 74 aircrew. Dozens more aircraft were damaged in the intruder attacks. As a direct result of the *Fernnachtjäger* (long-range intruder) operations over England, the RAF was forced to end night flying training in East Anglia, Yorkshire and Lincolnshire. Moreover, I./NJG2's continuous presence over England had a huge psychological impact on RAF aircrews. In mid 1941 it was planned to use the Dornier Do 217J over Britain as this type had greater endurance than the Ju 88 but on 12 October 1941 Adolf Hitler ordered all night intruder operations over the UK and the North Sea. See *Nachtjagd; The Night Fighter versus Bomber War over the Third Reich 1939-45* by Theo Boiten. (Crowood Press. 1997)

82 43-year old Group Captain 'Tiny' Evans-Evans DFC was the Coningsby station commander when he was killed on 21/22 February 1945 flying a borrowed Lancaster on 83 Squadron.

83 Rasper had trained as a fighter pilot during 1939-40 and his Bordfunker Feldwebel Erich Schreiber (KIA in 1943) claimed a 'Wellington' (more probably a Whitley) off Egmond on 15 December 1940 as their first victory. After his 7th *Abschuss* (victory) on 12/13 June 1941 (Wellington T2996 on 103 Squadron flown by Flying Officer Chisholm, who was KIA along with his crew) Rasper was awarded the 'Bowl of Honour- for 'exceptional achievements in the Air War' by Reichsmarschall Göering. After his 8th victory on 21 January 1942 Rasper was posted to a night-fighter training unit where he was an instructor for three years until he became operational again in early 1945 in II./NJG101. On 16/17 March 1945 he claimed his 9th and last Abschuss, a Viermot over Nürnburg. Leutnant Rasper flew his last sortie, a ground attack mission on 26 April 1945, when his aircraft was caught in radar-directed American flak at low level. He bailed out and was taken prisoner but his *funker* was found dead near the wreckage of their aircraft. *Battles With the Nachtjagd: The Night Air War Over Europe 1939-1945* by Theo Boiten and Martin W. Bowman. (Schiffer Publishing. 2006).

84 Squadron Leader John Henry Franks DFC was pilot of a Wellington on 57 Squadron when he was KIA on 29/30 June 1942.

85 On April 9/10th 80 aircraft - 36 Wellingtons, 24 Hampdens, 17 Whitleys and 3 Stirlings - went to Berlin. 6 FTR.

86 360 aircraft (plus another three on mining operations), the largest number of aircraft so far dispatched, were sent to mainly Hamburg and Bremen.

87 In May German nightfighters claimed 41 bombers destroyed

88 In captivity Alex Kerr recovered from his wounds fairly rapidly and a year later on 11 May 1942 was recaptured after an attempted escape. With Bill Legg it was far more serious. A fellow prisoner Dr. Chatenay carried out several operations on him. Chatenay was a young French doctor who took a great interest in Bill's case. He carried out miraculous feats of surgery with limited

medical supplies under primitive conditions. The open hole in Bill's back never healed. He was repatriated in October 1943 under an exchange of PoWs with the Germans. In August 1944 he recommenced flying duties as an instructor. The other crew survivors were repatriated at the end of the war. Exactly fifty years after the original incident, on 10 May 1991, the three bomber crewmembers met Von Bonin at Hohn German Air Force base. It was a very emotional occasion. Von Bonin embraced them all. He said that in 1941 when he had attacked their bomber he had been very annoyed with himself because he had forgotten to arm his cannon. Meeting them now he was very pleased that he hadn't set the 20mm cannon button to 'Fire'. Eckart-Wilhelm von Bonin eventually reached the rank of Major and was decorated with the Ritterkreuz (Knight's Gross) on 5 February 1944 when he had gained 31 victories. At that time he was Kommandeur of II./NJG1. He ended the war working for the Luftwaffe Inspector of Jet Aircraft. Two of Von Bonin's brothers serving in the Luftwaffe were killed on the Eastern Front. The Russians captured their father, Oberst Bogislav von Bonin, a Luftwaffe officer, in March 1945 and since then he remains missing. Eckart-Wilhelm von Bonin died in January 1992.

89 All of Bailey's crew were killed. Major Walter Ehle, 35 night and 4 day victories in ZG1 and NJG1, Ritterkreuz, KIA 17/18 November 1943 in crash at Horpmoel near St. Trond airfield.

90 It is quite possible that Leutnant Russmann of St III/NJG3 who claimed a Wellington south of Papenburg at 0145 hours flew the Bf 110.

91 Although the surviving crew members were all confined to PoW camps, Alan McSweyn soon successfully made his escape, though his fellow escapee died from exposure while they were crossing the Pyrenees. Alan was back in England by Christmas 1942, nearly six months after he was shot down. Awarded the Military Cross, he then served with Transport Command until returning to his native Australia in January 1946.

92 On 12/13 August 1941 Sergeant John Wallace and crew were shot down on the operation on Essen. There were no survivors.

93 Woltersdorf was KIA on 1/2 June 1942 in crash at Twente airfield, shot down by a 3 Squadron Hurricane. He had 15 night and 8 day victories in ZG76 and NJG1.

94 W5490 LQ-D.

95 Adapted from AIR/49/357. Ronnie Fraas died two days' later. The other members of the crew were Sergeant Tom Brown; Sergeant T. J. Doyle and Flight Sergeant J. Luckhurst. A Medical Note at the end of the report stated; '...this officer has lost his confidence in flying as a result of his experience and will not be fit to fly from a psychological point of view for some months. He has quite considerable nervous predispositions. His background at home is not stable and his parents do not get on together. He is imaginative and intelligent, but before joining the RAF showed a tendency to over-conscientiousness and was inclined to overwork. He had considerable responsibility for one so young. He joined the RAF for various motives, partially to escape from his work and never really achieved complete confidence in himself as a navigator. He is inclined to blame himself for his aircraft being damaged as a result of this fact. This self-blame and lack of confidence persist. I am not at all sure whether one will ever get this man to fly again operationally although he may well fly in another capacity. He is improving and dreams less about the accident. I would agree to his being sent to Canada and suggest A4B category for three months. In his description of the accident he showed his nervous temperament and tendency to dramatisation to an abnormal degree. His physical injuries were moderately severe burns of both hands and arms, responding well to treatment with considerable use of both hands. Very mild burns of the face have produced no disfigurement. DISPOSAL: Sent to Canada.'

96 A navigational and blind-bombing device, which was introduced into RAF service during August 1941. It consisted of the reception by equipment in the aircraft of transmission from a 'master' ('A') and 2 'slave' stations ('B & C') situated on a base line about 200 miles long. The difference in the time taken by the 'A' & 'B' and 'A' & 'C' signals to reach the aircraft were measured and displayed on a CRT (Cathode Ray Tube) on the navigator's table in the aircraft. From then on the aircraft could be located on 2 position lines known as 'Gee' co-ordinates. Accuracy of a Gee fix varied from less than ½ a mile to about 5 miles, depending on the skill of the navigator and the strength of the signal. 'Gee' range varied with the conditions from 300-400 miles.

97 1418 Flight was formed at Marham with four Wellingtons in December 1941 to develop *Gee* before it went into widespread use. This Flight moved to Tempsford on 1 March 1942

98 The starboard engine of a Wellington IC of 75 Squadron flown by Sergeant F. T. Minikin cut as the bomber crossed the coast at 6,000ft and crashed in the sea near Corton, two miles North of Lowestoft. Both pilots, who were injured, were picked up. Rest KIA.
99 R1502 had crashed at 0028 on 14 July at Onderdijk, 5km South of Medemblik.
100 In total Major Egmont Prinz zur Lippe-Weissenfeld scored 51 victories in NJG1 and NJG5 and he was awarded the Ritterkreuz with Eichenlaub. He was KIA on 12 March 1944 in a flying accident near St. Hubert in the Ardennes.
101 Oberleutnant Helmut Lent (4./NJG1), Leutnant Eckart-Wilhelm von Bonin (6./NJG1) and Unteroffizier Benning of 1./NJG3 each destroyed a Wellington. Lent's victim has been identified as W5513 of 104 Squadron and von Bonin's as R1613 of 214 Squadron. Unteroffizier Benning's victory was either T2737 of 149 Squadron or W5726 of 305 Squadron.
102 Saich and Telling were each awarded the DFM for their exploits. Saich and five other crew, including Sergeant Eric Trott, who had been aboard 'T-Tommy', were killed when their Wellington was shot down in flames by a German night fighter near Terwispel in Holland during the costly raid on Berlin on 7/8 September 1941. Sergeant Telling was killed six months later when his Wellington broke up during a training flight near Thetford, Norfolk.
103 Oberst Werner Streib, 67 Nachtjagd victories (including 30 Viermots) in 150 sorties with NJG1, plus 1 as Zerstörer in I./ZG1. Ritterkreuz with Eichenlaub and Schwerter. Died 15 June 1986 in Munich.
104 Jack Mappin, writing in *Intercom*.
105 R1772 piloted by Sergeant R. B. D. Hill was shot down over Kiel Bay by a Bf 110. Hill was killed and was buried in Kiel War Cemetery. Five crew bailed out safely and they were taken prisoner. R1798 flown by Sergeant Ian Patrick McHaffie Gordon was shot down on its return from Berlin by Oberleutnant Helmut Lent of 4./NJG1 as his 23rd *Abschuss* (victory) at 04.58 hours near Drachtstercompagnie in Friesland province with the loss of all the crew.
106 Becker, born in Dortmund in August 1911, volunteered for the Luftwaffe in 1934 and became a Stuka pilot before joining the Bf 110 Zerstörer and becoming a night-fighter pilot in July 1940. In 1941-42 Becker - 'The Night Fighting Professor' - became one of the leading Experten in the Nachtjagd. Instrumental in introducing the Lichtenstein AI radar in 1941, though most night fighter aircrew liked to rely on the 'Mk I Eyeball', Becker had one of the still experimental sets installed in his Do 217Z night fighter at Leeuwarden. His and Nachtjagd's first AI victory was in the early hours of 9 August 1941 in a Do 215B-5 night fighter when 44 Wellingtons of Bomber Command attacked Hamburg. Becker shot down six RAF night bombers 8/9 August-29/30 September 1941. He shot down 40 bombers in 1942. At Leeuwarden on 26 February 1943 30-year-old Hauptmann Ludwig Becker, Staffelkapitän 12/NJG1 a great night fighting tactician with 44 night victories, waited to fly his very first daylight sortie. Shortly before taking off from Leeuwarden 1135 hours in a formation of 12 Bf 110s of IV./JGI led by Hauptmann Hans-Joachim Jabs, in pursuit of the American daylight raiders Becker was informed of the award of the Eichenlaub (Oak Leaves) to his Ritterkreuz (Knight's Cross), which had been bestowed on him on 1 July 1942 after his 25th night victory for his leading role in the development of the night fighter arm. They intercepted the B-17s and B-24s, returning with claims for two shot down but Becker's Bf 110 was lost without a trace. The 'Night Fighting Professor' and his Funker Feldwebel Josef Staub fell victim to the gunners of B-17s or B-24s. *Battles With the Nachtjagd: The Night Air War Over Europe 1939-1945* by Theo Boiten and Martin W. Bowman. (Schiffer Publishing. 2006).

Chapter 5

They Sowed The Wind

'Zero hour for the target was a quarter to eleven. We had a special mission to carry out and arrived a little before the main force of bombers. The Germans picked us up and for fifteen minutes we had twelve guns all to ourselves. The rear gunner counted them. Some of the shell-bursts were extremely close.

'At two minutes before zero hour the wireless operator said through the intercom, ' Hello, Skipper! Sparks are coming up through the floor. Standing by with a fire-extinguisher.'

'Well, I've been on sixty-three operations. My log-book shows 450 operational hours and I've seen trouble before. I wasn't unduly worried and circled again round the target. The guns were further away from us this time.

'Then the wireless operator came through and said, 'Hello, Skipper! It isn't sparks any more. It's flames.'

'Next moment the whole Wellington lit up and I was blinded. It was about half a minute before I could see anything but this painful yellow light and I could not tell where we were going. My eyes hurt badly and smoke and fumes caused violent coughing. I could not see my instruments. It was like trying to look straight into the sun, or like being in the centre of a continuous photographic flash. A flare, sufficient to light almost the whole target, had caught fire in the bomber.

'I have seen many aircraft burning in the air and I know how short is the time before they break up. I gave the order to bail out.

'The crew went out in correct order. I felt the rear gunner rotating his doors onto the beam and felt him dropping out. I saw the wireless operator come forward and jump and I was able to watch the bomb aimer and navigator fall into space.

'It was my turn now and I got out of my seat to find my parachute. It was not there.

'I groped my way back through the light and searched everywhere. Unable to find the parachute, I returned to my seat and thought. I decided to crash-land immediately. It seemed to me that at any moment the Wellington would crack. To try to put out the flames during my descent I slide-slipped.

'Slowly I became more used to the glare and down at 1,000 feet I peered at the ground for a suitable landing-place. To the Germans I must have seemed like a torch in the sky and I think they believed I was no longer worth their ammunition.

'Then suddenly it became as dark as it had previously been light. The jinking could not have extinguished the burning flare, but it must have broken it off.

'I kept the aircraft as level as I could, waiting for my night vision to return and trying to remember what was the last course the navigator had given me before he went. It seemed to me a very long chance that I would come through. Every member *of the crew of a Wellington has an essential job and it appeared impossible that I should be able to cope with all of them.*

'I set course for Dieppe because I knew the countryside around there very well. Several times I had to leave my seat for adjustments in the body of the aircraft. For these excursions I switched into the automatic pilot, but once the aircraft began to spin down and I scrambled back to my seat only just in time.

'I was flying at 4,500 feet over the sea when both engines cut. There had been no petrol showing on the clock for nearly an hour and I thought it possible that there was none left in any of the tanks. I went back again to change over to the remaining supply and one engine suddenly picked up, sending the aircraft down into a spiral dive. I was not far from the sea before I got back to the seat, straightened out and pulled up the balance-cock so that the other engine came on. The Wellington flew on and I made a good landing.

'The missing parachute was found under the bed.

'From now on anything can happen.'

The Squadron Leader added that, looking back on it the whole thing seemed so fantastic that he wondered if the Wellington wouldn't have got back without him, all on its own.

He thought he had seen the incident once in a film.

A Squadron Leader DSO, The Fire was Bright by Leslie Kark.

So far, Warrant Officer J. W. B. Snowden's crew on 115 Squadron had survived everything the enemy could throw at them but the constant preparations and flying ops was always a severe test, as Albert E. Robinson, his observer, recalls. 'Orders filtered down from high command to the squadrons and in smoke-filled rooms the crews were briefed in detail. If it were a tough target, an unrestrained groan would echo through the briefing room. On the other hand, an easier one would produce a mild cheer and if the squadron commander even as much as hinted that there was the smallest chance of cancellation, this was met by much stamping of feet and an enthusiastic round of applause. The CO would listen and a faint smile would cross his face. He had heard it all before. He had flown many operations and he understood the crews' outlook. To him this show of humour, usually expressed in an offbeat way best described perhaps as black humour, was quite normal. Whatever it was it covered up quite a lot. This was just as well, since in the few hours following the briefing the adjutant would be reaching for his telegram pad to write out the condolences to loved ones waiting at home. The sight of the telegram boy always caused a chilling premonition and a clutch at the heart.

'There was much to do before an op. There were maps and charts to prepare, target approach to consider, known fighter bases to ring round in red ink and a whole host of other things to do. It was a busy period, but preparation was vital. Much had to be examined in microscopic detail and the better the grasp of this, the more likely the success of the operation and in all probability the chances of survival too. Even so, with all the work and concentration required, somehow it always seemed to be completed with a good hour to spare before take-off time. That hour always took its toll. Irrespective of experience or how many operations had been completed, that hour became the waiting time. It passed with a dreadful slowness. A jumbled-up mass of crews muffled in their flying leathers watched the clock tick over and urged it on, for it gave them time to consider the possibilities that lay ahead and above all offered so much time to think. They were a cheerful, resourceful, happy-go-lucky bunch, mostly in their teens and in almost hourly touch with death, but on the surface at least, they had an apparent fatalistic acceptance of this role. The mess had an atmosphere of its own. People talked in hushed whispers or on a higher note than usual and there was an edgy tension. Some wrote letters to a loved one; others thumbed through magazines in a restless way. Some were fidgety, some composed, while others just sat, deep in their own thoughts. Yet, once in the air, with the onset of danger, such thoughts would evaporate completely. The operation would be all that mattered and it called for an authoritative grasp of the nettle. The game would be on.

'For the crews that came back, life on the squadron was almost a world on its own and not only in the world of bombing either. The close-knit relationships were evident in their off-duty times too and these were celebrated, perhaps not too wisely, at the 'Red Lion', an old-worldly hotel with a thatched roof and a wealth of oak beams already blackened by the smoke of ages. A much favoured meeting place for the crews, it saw many boisterous, heavy nights with endless frothy pints of beer and a piano banging out bawdy songs with an emphasis that threatened to lift the timbered ceiling that almost brushed our heads. Even when the casualty lists were running at a high level, these carefree times carried on as usual and the frothy pints continued to be hoisted high and drunk with perhaps even more appreciative relish. Callous? Uncaring? Not so. That way some sort of sanity was preserved. Each one had to take his chance. Who would be next? So, live for today, enjoy it while possible. Most crews did just that. Even so, very few left the hotel without a backward glance at its panelled walls and glittering brasses, always with the thought that it could quite likely be for the last time.

'That this comradeship, both on the scene of battle and during these relaxed off-duty periods, bore relationship to the atmosphere in which school games were played was no accident. In fact, many squadron commanders actively encouraged this attitude. In a sense, it was a convenient hat and coat hook fixed in some mythical pavilion on which to hang the trauma, a contrivance that also acted on carefully defined lines to help mould the team spirit with which these games were played. To cast this mould was easy. Most of the crews were barely out of school anyway. It was only the setting that was different.

'It was apparent right from the very moment on an operational day when the crews strolled over to the mess for breakfast. An early morning mist might be floating over the base in grey wispy patches, a hazy cloak settled over the runways. It became a familiar sight to the crews and almost a permanent feature of the flat, moisture-filled greenness of the open farmland that surrounded the base and stretched for miles.

At dispersal points the Wellingtons, stark and austere in their camouflage paint, stood waiting - a colossus in their own right with their six Browning machine-guns jutting from their turrets and ominous in their setting. A petrol bowser stood alongside some of the aircraft. Soon it would pump the high-octane fuel into the tanks and a tousled-haired mechanic would peer from the cockpit waiting for the signal. There was always a scene of great activity, as the ground staff fussed around, each to their own job and a lot would depend in their attention to detail.

'The aircrew by now had dispersed, each caught up with the technicalities of their own job. They would not meet again until briefing. As for the navigator, he had a recently introduced system of astro-navigation to study. In reality it was a basic affair, consisting of a sextant, a rather splendid watch for time keeping and a hooded projector set over the navigator's table. There was illuminated astronomical data on the chart, on which the sextant readings were plotted. It was a brave effort by the boffins to help offset the weakness in night navigation, but under operational conditions it had its limitations. One of the drawbacks was that it was necessary to fly a straight and level course at a constant speed for a protracted period - a gift-wrapped present for German radar. The bumpy, wallowing Wellington could not, by any stretch of the imagination, be described as the ideal platform from which to take hand-held sextant readings. Also there was the question of the stars' visibility themselves, for they were often blotted out by heavy cloud. On the nights when the Plough in Ursa Major could be seen, this was not only useful in the construction of a mental star map, but it was easy to pick out Polaris, the Pole Star. Poised several light years above the North Pole to an accuracy of one degree, it had guided travellers throughout the ages. Now, with its ancient origins and religious beliefs, it was to come ironically to the aid of bomber crews.

'However, crews at that time gave little significance to such significant or philosophical meanderings. Operations were not the Holy Grail, just a job, which in the interests of their nation they had been called upon to do and that was their sole object, nothing else. Any personal feelings could not be allowed to swerve or distract. With this in mind and the completion of briefing, it was time to go.

'At dispersal points, in the already darkened sky. The crews at their stations, the pilot made ready to start the two Pegasus radial engines. Starter buttons were pressed and there was a cough and a roar as they fired. A column of grey smoke with a sheet of flame shot out from the exhaust. The crews settled down in their positions. Engines were throttled back to tick-over position and with the pilot's thumb-up signal to the waiting ground staff the chocks were hauled away from the wheels. Throttles were pushed forward and the engines answered with a roar. Guided by twinkling lights, the Wellingtons, gorged with the bomb loads tucked in their bellies, trundled slowly to take-off position. It was all systems go.

'The training manual made it look so simple. Throttles were manipulated to gain full power The aircraft responded with gathering speed and if all else was carried out correctly, the Wellington took off But, sitting at the end of the runway, waiting for the green flashing light that was cleared for take-off, it did not seem so simple. In fact, there was a sense of disbelief that nagged at the stomach that the lumbering, heavy Wellington, laden to the maximum with bombs and petrol, would ever leave the ground at all. But it did - well, usually

- but if there was ice or frozen snow on the grass airstrip and this affected lift, or there was a significant splutter from either of the engines at the critical point of lift-off then either of these could threaten disaster. The normal load of 650 gallons of petrol for an average run, plus the 4,000lb bomb load usually carried, could make quite a hole in the ground. Tense moments these, broken only by a sense of relief when the bomber left the ground and began to make its circuit of the airfield ready to set course for far-off Germany.

'The Wellington gained height slowly, very slowly. High above on a clear night a myriad of stars pin-pricked the sky with their brilliance. The black nose of the Wellington tilted towards them and the defiant roar of the two engines filled the air with vibrating noise. A lot would depend on those engines. They would have to blast effortlessly away for a good many hours and more than one aircrew said a silent prayer as they listened to the roar. But there were many other items to consider and the list was compounded with problems that seemed endless. Weather could be problematical. Accurate forecasts, with the scant information available to the meteorology officers, were rare. It was more successful to wet a finger, hold it up and hope. Since all operations were dictated by requirements of war, often this meant flying in appalling conditions. High gusty winds, fog with thick cloud up to high levels and particularly ice, were common enemies. Ice could layer itself over the wings and create drag to the point of stalling as the Wellington lurched and sagged in a series of sickening movements. Adverse conditions could make themselves known in the space of a short time, sometimes before leaving the English coast. Then it became a lonely trek flying through the murk until the Dutch coast was reached.

'Flak, either from the coastal guns or the numerous flak ships anchored off the Friesian Islands, would come up. An umbrella barrage and dotted tracer like a giant firework display were joined by the probing searchlights spreading their light like some huge, luminous spider's web trying to lure the victim into its mesh. Ahead, blips bobbing and dancing on electronic screens indicated our position to the controller. Then the night fighter bases were alerted. We hoped with some measure of callousness that the blips would be caused by another aircraft. Since it was an invisible thread that connected the Wellington to the night fighter, the gunners in our aircraft did not know until the actual moment of interception. So we, the crew, sat, tensed, waiting for the sight of the Messerschmitt night fighter From now on the Wellington was in grave danger.

'This was never more true than on a moonlit, cloudless night. The art of crossing the Dutch coast was by concealment in the clouds. But this too had its drawbacks since it was necessary for navigational purposes to 'fix' the exact crossing point and naturally this meant emerging from the cloud cover This we hoped would be over the Friesian Islands or, to be more specific, the island of Schiermonnikoog. Mere hiccups on the chart maybe, but an area with which we had become familiar, especially Schiermonnikoog. If we were correct when we broke cloud cover, it boiled down to a quick movement, 'fix' the position as soon as possible, then head back to the concealment of the cloud with full boost and airspeed. It sounds reasonably simple, but even so it may have been just the moment for which the night fighter crew was waiting. Individual aircraft flying in isolation - and that's how it was for us in 1940-41 - were comparatively easy meat. German radar used the time that this early warning afforded to put the night fighter in a position to suit themselves, usually from astern and below and always it seemed when the Wellington broke cloud for the 'fix'. The Me 110 night fighters were only too pleased to take advantage of this and were quick to exploit these favourable circumstances. Then the bomber would break into a stomach-heaving routine of carefully rehearsed evasion - not so much to shoot down the fighter, but purely as an evasive tactic. A fighter claimed might be exciting news in the mess, but the successful completion of the operation took precedence. Anything else was a bonus.

'Of course, this assumes that the fighter had been spotted before the attack. If not, the first indication would come with a staccato crackle as the red tracer streaked across and the cannon fire of the Messerschmitt was vicious, both in range and effectiveness, far more than the .303 machine-gun fire of the Wellington. An unexpected attack usually spelled disaster, but it must be said that given an early sight of the enemy fighter, he did not have it all his own way. The Wellington, with alert gunners, could give a reasonable account of itself and facing aggressive, accurate fire the enemy fighter would often break away and seek easier meat. Even so, it was an apprehensive moment for the crews and as the gun turrets rotated in the sky, searching with an intensity for the fighter, it was essentially a moment of quick reaction. An off-guard, dreamy relaxation or a split-second delay would quickly decide the issue.

'Even with this risk of interception it was of paramount importance to get a 'fix' as the Dutch coast was crossed. This enabled the ground speed and track over the territory to be calculated and made it easier to pick out the landmarks as we flew over Holland. It was a strange, eerie feeling as we did so. To us, Holland was a territory of friendly people and there was a sense of outrage that the Nazis occupied it. We liked to think that when the Dutch people heard the drone of our Wellingtons they recognised it as a gesture of hope. This was confirmed on numerous occasions when flashing lights from down below spelled out a welcome in no uncertain terms. Such a sight made our flight more personal and acted as a strong fillip to morale.

'Naturally the German defences did not see it that way and the inevitable flak came up. If this flak was widespread and heavy, it sometimes made diversion necessary and this, in many instances, could take the Wellington far away from the calculated track. This caused a period of frustration, since it was not always easy in the darkness to refix the aircraft's position. At such moments of indecisiveness the poor navigation facilities came into question. As one crew member put it succinctly, as we strode out to our Wellington for take-off: 'Here we go again with a map, pencil and rubber Oh well, the target is only 600 miles away and as for the return, well, just forget it.' It was not quite like that of course, but in the early days of the bombing campaign it just seemed like that. Certainly the loss of compass course and a confused meander over hostile territory provoked high irritation when the search turned out to be fruitless. But it was not all failure. Success came along too and then the flush of achievement took on a positive and welcome role. It made all the effort and sacrifice worthwhile.

'At such times, Essen, Cologne and Bremen were not cities; they were targets - seething holocausts with a glowing spread of a spitting shambles down below. Skies were made colourful by different shades of flak - greens and red predominated - and they were filled with a blinding light that dazzled and compelled the pilot to bank steeply as the searchlights wavered and probed in their systematic search for the raider. Often a whole series of searchlights positioned in a wide circle would take their cue from a master searchlight set in the centre of this circle. This vertical shaft in the sky stood quite still, until the operators felt that they had accurately calculated the height and speed of a particular aircraft. Then it would switch from the vertical with the swiftness of a striking snake in its attempt to centre its beam on the unfortunate aircraft. If this happened, then the other searchlights would simultaneously and instantly converge at an apex above the Wellington and in effect form a giant cone with the bomber trapped in a flood of light. Slowly they would bring the nose of the cone down forcing the bomber lower and lower and then, at a given signal, massed guns would fire up the cone with a fierce intensity that lit up the sky with its menace. When coned it was an almost impossible situation for any aircraft and the only escape lay in violent evasion, sometimes to the point where it put the aircraft's structure at risk, threatened catastrophe and gave the unfortunate souls nightmares. Most such endeavours were fruitless. Like a flickering moth trapped by light, the bomber was rendered impotent as it was pounded by the guns.

'Often, other crews over the target saw a blinding flash in the sky as a coned aircraft was blown into fragmentary pieces by a direct hit. It was not a very pleasant sight, or indeed one to inspire confidence, but whatever the feeling it could not be allowed to distract. It made sense to take all necessary precautions of course. But the task to seek out the aiming point was mandatory and still an issue to be solved - not easy for the bomb-aimer as he strained his eyes through the perspex panel let in the floor near the front gun turret and looked down at the blazing inferno. Often blinded by the glare of searchlights and the target obscured by smoke, it was difficult for him to pick out detail. The panoramic display by the entire pyrotechnics in full view was not the most reassuring sight. It needed strong nerves and a calm disposition, since at that moment, having established the aiming point, the bomb-aimer was virtually in charge of the aircraft. He guided the pilot by calling out steering instructions over the intercom. It was a big responsibility and it decided the success or failure of the operation.

'All bomb-aimers hoped to get it right with the first run over the target. Any repeat performance that he deemed necessary did not go down well with the crew and it was an unhappy voice that came over the intercom when the bomb-aimer decided to abort the run-up for some particular reason and requested the pilot to go around again. To use a bomb sight effectively meant that a straight and level course had to be flown through the thick spread of flak, not a happy thought, especially since this usually meant fleeing through the centre of its seething core. It was an effort that stretched nerves to the full. It brought on a pulsating trepidation and caused butterflies in the stomach.

The stark reality was that the outcome would only rate as high as the chance spin at a roulette table, with always the disquiet that out of the hundreds of shells layered in the sky, just one hit in the right place would be enough. So, given all this, it was a welcome moment when the bomb aimer, satisfied with his sighting, pressed the bomb release button and yelled over the intercom 'Bombs gone!'

'This was the signal to get the hell out of it and the Wellington was dived, twisted and turned in its dash to break clear of the flak-infested area. Full boost, full airspeed, full everything was applied and the bomber shuddered and creaked under the strain. It was an apprehensive feeling for the crews, since the next few moments would be decisive and all eyes looked for some sort of opening in the fierce barrage set up by the guns. Anywhere would do. Direction was unimportant. Just an opening that could offer some sort of chance. The decision was made - the crew held their breath - and the bomber hurtled through the chosen path. The flak - vivid orange splotches and fragments of hot metal - burst around, rattling the fabric of the bomber. Then, as the Wellington screamed away, there was a numbed realisation that the sky had cleared as if by magic. The iron curtain had been breached. With composure gained and clear of the danger zone, there was a compelling fascination to bank the Wellington steeply and take a look at the holocaust as it receded. It was an awesome sight, truly a Dantean inferno, as the illuminated tracer streaked up forming an illusion of the wires of a giant birdcage covering the area. Set in its midst was the dull red glow of the stricken city. For the crews it was not the moment for reflection. The raid must be viewed in context and judged as a success.

'Now all efforts had to be centred on the struggle to get home. This was tempered by the thought that the long trip to base would be a virtual repeat of the perils that had loomed getting to the target. It was always a sobering thought, but not one without some advantage, with the comforting knowledge that radio locations in England would be listening out for any message, however faint, to give what help they could. This would include a QDM, a radio bearing for the aircraft to home base, a navigator's dream, but with one vital snag - the aircraft had to be within a short range of the English coast before the beam became effective. For the Wellington crew flying in the remote depths of Germany it had to remain a wistful dream for the time being. Even so, the feeling as the course was set for base was simplicity itself: 'We'd made it coming in and we'd make it going back.'

'Even the Wellington seemed to enter into the spirit of things. Shorn of its burden of bombs, all 4,000lb of them, it became buoyant again, easier to handle, much faster and able to reach greater heights. These factors gave the crew a feeling of superiority, as the light flak was unable to reach us. The heavy stuff was still there of course, but with some knowledge of their position and the evasive courses we flew, it was possible to avoid the brunt of their fire.

'The Wellington droned on, each minute bringing it nearer to home. Crew morale grew higher with every mile. Then at length the Dutch coast came up and so did the flak and searchlights. It was the usual reception, but down below there was the familiar sight of the Friesian Islands and from now on, if the night fighters left us alone, it was a straight run over the North Sea - a happy thought if all went well. There was the added reassurance that the radio people would be listening, ready to give the all-important heading that would bring us over the red flashing light - with its coded letter of the day and its proximity to base. That is if all did go well, but it would be unwise to rely on this. Often, with success within grasp, the roulette wheel could throw up the wrong numbers. If it did, the perils were by no means over. A pea-soup fog or densely packed mist - common enemies to the returning bomber - could shroud the home airfield, close down the base and make diversion necessary, sometimes quite a distance away. Often other areas had conditions almost as bad, so a weary aircrew, after many hours in the air, had an unwelcome trek as the aircraft flew on its long tiresome path through the murky half light of a breaking dawn. It was a journey with petrol gauges mostly running at danger level, which in the long run usually meant little alternative but to put down wherever possible. This was a risky business, especially on an airstrip ill-equipped to receive a heavy bomber.

'Even when the home base was fully operational, the dangers had not yet passed. An enemy aircraft, usually a Ju 88, could be prowling around the base ready to pick off the unwary - and their proficiency at this was never to be doubted. Sometimes, to achieve an easier kill, it was not unknown for the more audacious German pilots to enter the circuit, navigation lights full on, hoping that their bluff would work as they intermingled with the bombers circling the airfield. If this ploy did succeed, they would then wait until a bomber prepared to land and attack. This was when the Wellington was at its most vulnerable, with braking flaps down, landing speed adjusted and all attention being paid to touchdown. It was a hapless situation for the bomber, which had no chance at all of surviving this attack; a sad ending on the very last lap of a gruelling operation. Such a disaster was a stark reminder that with the hazards of operational flying nothing was finally settled until the Wellington was safely down, had taxied to dispersal and the exhausted crew had clambered out.

'Emotions ran high at this point. At de-briefing most crews were over-stimulated, excited and shaken up, but at least the kitchen staff on the squadron were down to earth and many bomber crews will recall the tempting smell of the bacon and egg breakfast served in the mess on return. With the crews reasonably calm now, it was a pleasant, relaxing moment. Not only did the food titillate the palate, but it was also an opportunity to reflect on the reprieve - temporary or not - swim with the sweetness of life and with the not unwelcome thought that the crew would be stood down for a possible two days. Not a lot in terms of time, but enough to prepare mentally for the next operation and psychologically this was important if the composure to face the future was to be achieved. Traumatic days, grave days and the responsibility that had been thrust upon Bomber Command in the years 1940-41 had become not so much a battle but a crusade to hold the fort until the nation gathered strength. This carried with it a vital significance, not only to Britain but also to the whole of Europe, perhaps even to the whole world.

'As for myself, a Me 110 [piloted by Oberleutnant Paul Gildner of 4./NJG1] operating from the German base at Leeuwarden, made a copybook attack from astern and below on our Wellington at 19.30 hours on the night of 31 October/1 November 1941 when the target was Bremen. We never saw him until it was too late. We were never in with the chance of a shot. He just loomed out of the murk with a startling suddenness and opened up with a prolonged and devastating burst of cannon fire. It was all over in a matter of seconds. No time to consider. One minute we were happily on course and the next we were plunging down and about to crash, ironically, on Schiermonnikoog itself. Fate decreed that I should survive this, plus some enlightening, even if somewhat dreary years in German prison camps before liberation by Russian troops in May 1945.'[107]

October 1941 had begun badly for 218 Squadron at Marham. On the night of the 10/11th when 22 Wellingtons were despatched to Bordeaux, the Wellington flown by Sergeant V. G. Haley failed to return. Haley evaded capture and four crew were taken prisoner while one man was killed. Sergeant McClean's Wellington meanwhile, came down in the sea off St Alban's Head on the Dorset coast. Two crew died despite an extensive search by the St. Ives lifeboat. On the 13/14th when 53 Wellingtons and seven Stirlings were despatched to bomb Düsseldorf, the one aircraft lost was the Wellington flown by Sergeant Frederick Harry Ewart Dearden on 115 Squadron. All the crew were lost. On the night following, 14/15 October, when 80 aircraft including 58 Wellingtons were sent to Nuremberg the Wellington flown by Sergeant K. G. Fisher took off from Marham at 2310 hours only for the port engine to fail and he made an early return. The aircraft collided with trees and Fisher was injured. For those aircraft that flew the operation conditions were very bad with icing and thick cloud and most of the bombers hit alternative targets. On 16/17 October 87 aircraft including 47 Wellingtons set out for Duisburg. The target was cloud covered and only estimated positions were bombed. The Wellington IC flown by Flight Lieutenant Dunham which was the first time a 218 Squadron Wellington had taken off with a 4,000lb bomb was abandoned after the port engine failed crossing the coast outbound and the aircraft crashed at Cantley ten miles southeast of Norwich.

If October had begun badly for 218 Squadron then November was to prove an equally tragic beginning for 115 Squadron. On 11 November the Wellington III piloted by Sergeant Gordon David Hankinson Dutton crashed at Carol House Farm near Swaffham during fuel consumption tests and a cross country flying practice. Dutton and his crew and Flight Lieutenant Harry Sidney Mellows, the Medical Officer, all died in the crash. Two weeks later, on 24 November the Wellington flown by Sergeant George Robert Bruce crashed two miles southwest of March in Cambridgeshire during a training flight and the six crew and three ground crew aboard for the ride were killed. It appears that during low flying Bruce collided with a line of railway trucks on the March to Spalding railway line.

Meanwhile, early in November Sir Richard Peirse, C-in-C RAF Bomber Command, decided to mount a major effort against Berlin. The operation went ahead on the night of 7/8 November despite a late weather forecast, which showed that there a large area of bad weather with storms, thick cloud, icing and hail would cover the North Sea routes to the German capital. 5 Group objected to the plan and they were allowed to attack Cologne instead but 169 bombers were sent to the Big City as ordered. Twenty-one aircraft including ten Wellingtons were lost. One of these was X3206 on 214 Squadron flown by Pilot Officer Lucian Ercolani, which ditched off Thorney Island, Sussex on the return. The son of an Italian furniture designer and manufacturer who had come to England in 1910, Lucian Brett Ercolani was born at High Wycombe on 9 August 1917 and educated at Oundle, where he excelled at sport. He left school in 1934 to work at his father's company, Ercol. When war broke out he joined the RAF and trained as a pilot in Canada, returning in May 1941 to join 214 Squadron. Ercolani had reached Berlin and he dropped his high explosive load successfully through a gap in the clouds but before the crew could release their incendiaries the gap closed as Lucien Ercolani recalled: 'It was our twenty-fifth trip as a crew, our third trip to Berlin. It was 10/10 cloud most of the way. We thought we were over target and it was obviously defended, but we couldn't identify it, so we didn't know if we were doing the right thing. We had a load of incendiaries. We dropped them all and just as we were coming back we were hit with ack-ack. What we didn't know was that one of the racks of incendiaries must have hung up inside the aircraft, and when the ack-ack hit they were set off and of course they burn for a long time. So we were virtually alight with these things, and they gradually burnt away all of the fabric. The belly of the plane was practically burnt out. The fabric round the mid-part of the fuselage was gone. The fabric on the starboard wing was all burnt away and both wings were badly holed and torn. The plane was nose heavy, although the trimming tabs were wound fully. My pals were marvellous, they put everything they could on the fires; when the extinguishers had run dry they threw the rest of our coffee over it and peed on it.

'There was smoke coming through into the cockpit and I opened the two lids over my head, which was the worst thing that I could have done, because that sucked all the acrid smoke past me. I got everybody to put their parachutes on and we were ready to jump out. I was about to tell them all to jump, but realised we were still flying. Where there's life there's hope and we kept on flying.

'We were burning all the time. We'd lost a lot of power, or rather we had a lot of increased drag; that was really the moment when we could have panicked and done all sorts of silly things. But we kept flying. It was quite difficult to hold the aircraft; all the centre section was badly gone. What made it worse was that it was difficult to find out where we'd actually got to.

'We were gradually losing height all the time. As we were approaching the coast I realised that petrol was being used up faster than normal; the question was whether to jump there, or take a chance of getting through. Everybody was very good about it. They were all getting ready to jump out, and I had my parachute handy, but you want to hang on if you can. So we hung on. There was a hell of a wind blowing. We crossed the coast and we still hung on. Our wireless op. had got some sort of message through, but we didn't know where we were.

'Then, of course, we were over the water, a couple of hundred feet up. There was a gadget on the Wimpy where you pulled a knob and it put both engines on to both petrol tanks. Normally, one engine ran on one, and the other engine on the other. The two engines didn't always use the same amount of petrol. So when you got right to the end, you pulled this plug and whatever petrol was left in either one, fed both engines. So I did that, and we knew that we didn't have very long to go. We weren't much above the waves. We could see searchlights about the place and were hoping that we'd cross our coast, but we didn't. We had been flying back for three hours and still the plane was ablaze. Then the engines went, and I think I remember saying good luck to everybody.

'When you know that you've come to face with the moment of truth there's almost a feeling of relief. I tried to make some sort of landing but the next thing I knew was that there was a terrific crash. Bang we came down nose first and as we went under the water I could hear the sound of things crumpling up and I saw the light of the moon shining down in the water. I felt like a spectator watching it all happen; it didn't seem to be happening to me at all. I tried desperately to get out, but the instrument panel had collapsed back on me, pinning me down. I definitely thought I'd had it then and that I was finished. Then the plane floated up again out of the water; that freed me and I was able to pull myself out through the escape hatch in the top of the pilot's cockpit.

'The first thing I saw was the rear turret and the tail of the Wellington twisted right round, facing towards the front. I could see the dinghy and I could hear the rest of the crew calling to each other. I swam for the dinghy but, before we were all in, the aircraft sank.

'There was an extraordinary sense of quiet, a sense of relief. We were rather glad to be alive. But at the same time sad. I felt what a pity it was for those waiting at home, particularly my dear wife [Cynthia Douglas, whom he had married in 1941].

'Then, of course, you begin to wonder where you are: do we just sit here, do we try to get back? If we're going to try and get back, what direction do we go in? Everybody was remarkably cheerful. In those days they had rum on the dinghies. We also had water flasks in the dinghy, but unfortunately the yellow stuff they had put in as a marker had got into the water. But the rum did us a bit of good.

'The flares didn't work. We could see searchlights, and we thought that we were in the middle of the Channel. We had some funny little paddles, we felt that the right thing would be to try to aim towards England. We did everything we could to paddle that way. People were in remarkable spirits, we didn't actually have to do anything to keep spirits up. Everybody did it quite naturally. We just paddled and slept, paddled and slept.

'We had come down at about three o'clock in the morning. It was very cold. The weather wasn't too bad at first. The next day it got quite rough. The chaps were very good, and we realised we were all in bloody trouble together. We couldn't blame each other for it or anything like that. We had a little miniature compass, an escape compass. We could see searchlights and we heard two or three aircraft, so again we tried to let our flares off, but none of them worked.

'I don't think any of us got to the stage of despair, or thought we weren't going to get out of it. That's the law of youth, of course, but I don't know how we thought we were going to get out of it. I suppose we weren't there long enough to get to the stage of desperation.

'On the third day I saw what I thought was a German submarine periscope, but in fact it must have been a lobster pot marker. It appeared to be moving very fast through the water, but that was just the tide sweeping past it. Then we saw land and I saw a bit of green and a football post and thought this is probably England. In fact it was the Isle of Wight. Then we gradually got closer, so we paddled harder with everything we had. We suddenly saw an Air Sea Rescue launch, but to our pride we got ourselves ashore, at Ventnor. By then some people had climbed down to help us in. I stood up to walk ashore, but fell down. My ankle had broken.

'I can't tell you what it was like to feel safe again. It was wonderful just to lie back in that ambulance and not have to worry about or think about anything. We were taken to the National Chest Hospital, where we were the only aircrew that they'd had, and they made a tremendous fuss of us. They sent in whisky, everything. In my room there was a wardrobe full of all the booze you could want, including lots of champagne. In the mornings, we sent out for Guinness and played cards drinking black velvet. None of the crew were badly injured. I had my broken ankle and they thought that I was badly injured because I had blood all over my face, but in fact it was only a small cut.'

Flying Officer Ercolani was awarded an immediate DSO, a very rare accolade for so junior an officer, 'for 'outstanding courage, initiative and devotion to duty.'108

A few nights later, on 15/16 November, 49 Wellingtons were sent to bomb Emden while another 47 aircraft attacked Kiel. On the Emden operation four Wellingtons including the one piloted by Sergeant Alan Christopher Homes on 115 Squadron were lost. All of Homes' crew were killed. Pilot Officer Stock on 115 Squadron ditched in the sea off Whitby and he and his crew were rescued by a destroyer crewed by Norwegian sailors. At Kiel, four Wellingtons including the one flown by Sergeant Alan Cook RAAF on 115 Squadron were lost. All of Cook's crew perished in the North Sea after the Wellington was ditched.

On the night of 26/27 November when 80 Wellingtons and twenty Hampdens went to Emden, only 55 aircraft bombed in cloudy conditions and three bombers were lost. One of the two Wimpys that were lost was the one flown by Sergeant Helfer, which had taken off at 1715 hours and was ditched in the sea off Wells at 2306 hours. Helfer had considered that the beach might be mined and the RAF ASR launch that rescued him and his crew told him that his assumption was correct! Helfer had suffered a series of mishaps. On 2/3 September on a raid on Ostend he and his crew had ditched off the Belgian coast and had been rescued. On 12/13 October their Wellington had been damaged after landing on return from Nürnburg.

By the end of November-December 1941 mainly because of the weather, Marham's Wellingtons had been operational on just eleven nights. There were only two losses and both the 218 Squadron Wellington ICs crashed over

England returning from sorties to Brest. One of them was put down at Upavon on 11/12 December and the other, on 16/17 December, was crash landed at Holme Farm near Powerstock, four miles northeast of Bridport, Dorset. The crew bailed out and one member suffered a broken leg on landing. At the end of the year Wing Commander Trevor Freeman, CO of 115 Squadron, was awarded the DSO. Mention was made in his citation for his many sorties over a long period. One of these was an attack on Cologne in September when in spite of fierce opposition, he descended to low level and flying over the sea for over an hour searching for the objective, he eventually found the target and he and his squadron bombed it. Also mentioned was the attack on Turin on 10/11 September when Freeman made a successful attack from low level despite heavy opposition. In December also Squadron Leader Foster and Pilot Officer Miller were awarded the DFC and Sergeants Berney and Gilpin received the DFM.

The year 1942 began badly for Britain and her allies. January could hardly have been less auspicious with extremely bad weather conditions and operations being curtailed by heavy falls of snow. At Holme-on-Spalding Moor, for instance, Wellingtons on 458 Squadron had to have their wing surfaces brushed clear of snow before they could take off. The operation, to Brest, then went ahead as planned shortly before midnight, but one aircraft, suffering from severe icing, crashed on take-off, killing two crew members.

Overseas, British and Commonwealth forces received bad reverses in both the Middle East and the Far East. On 11 January the forces of Japan invaded Java and paratroop attacks on Sumatra soon followed. On 19 January Burma was invaded. By 31 January all British units in Malaya had been forced to withdraw across the straits to Singapore and it was only days before the island fell. Meanwhile, on 21 January Erwin Rommel had begun his second counter-offensive in the Western Desert and British forces were falling back everywhere. Urgent steps were at once taken by the British Chiefs of Staff to bolster their flagging forces in both theatres of war. Although bomber squadrons were too valuable to be spared, in January 1942 99 Squadron at Waterbeach received the news that its Wellingtons and crews were to be transferred to India. Two Wellington bomber squadrons - 99 and 215 - also served in the Far East. The climate affected both airmen and aircraft alike as Charles Fox, a pilot on 215 Squadron based at Pandeveswar, a fair weather strip twenty miles from Asansol, recalls:

'The flying conditions were something we had never experienced before. Taking off with a bomb load in the heat of the day was sometimes frightening. Plus the storms day and night. Clouds rising to 20,000 feet had to be flown through. We just could not get above them and they covered such an area we hadn't time to go around. The air currents in these storms were such that even with the stick forward we were still climbing and vice versa. I was lucky in having such a great pilot. He didn't show any fear but I'm sure that he must have felt something. His comment was 'if this f------ aircraft flaps her wings any further, we won't need engines!'

'The squadron stayed at Pandeveswar from May 1942 to August 1942, when we were posted to south-east India. During those months, operations were carried out, both day and night, against the Japs. Our crew took part in two daylight raids on Akyab airfield within three days. Surprisingly, we had no opposition, although two twin-engined aircraft were sighted taking off and heading south towards Rangoon. We then went in and dropped our load in two runs. Although we had one 250lb bomb hang up we carried on and strafed everything in sight. There were some Blenheims on the ground and as we left I noticed one Hudson on fire. I presume these had been unserviceable when the Japs took the airfield. Some of the operations we flew were supply drops to both troops and civilians making their way to India from Burma. The most notable to me was trying to drop medical supplies to a group of civilians in the Naga Hills on the Indo-Burma border.'

In July 1943 a 310 FTU, Harwell crew received, direct from Vickers, a brand-new Wellington X, HE947, on which they carried out a 16-hours' acceptance test before flying it to Hurn, prior to taking it out to India. Eric Barclay, the navigator, recalled: 'The trip to India went by way of Hurn-Port Lyautey-Ras El Mar-Castel Benito - Tobruk - El Agheila - El Adem - Cairo - Ismailia - Lydda - Habbaniyah - Shaibah - Kuwait - Bharein - Sharjah - Jask Island - Karachi - Allahabad; though en route we changed aircraft to Wellington X HE957. In October 1943 the crew arrived in Jessore, north of Calcutta, where 99 and 215 Squadrons were then stationed, both operating Wimpy Xs, with 16 aircraft to each squadron.

'Both squadrons were flying operations against targets in Burma, from Mandalay to Rangoon, mostly against lines of communication but including various towns and centres. One aircraft on 215 was converted to take a 4,000lb cookie and was usually a lone raider. We were posted to this squadron. On one trip, on 24 December 1943, we loaded up for a trip to Mandalay and needed to clear at least 10,000 feet if we were to get over the Arakan hills. One hour after take-off the starboard engine had to be feathered and naturally, with a full load of bombs and petrol we lost 8,000 feet rapidly - we hadn't reached those hills yet. The pilot, Flight Sergeant Nixon, managed to get the aircraft under control after unloading all bombs safely and some petrol. However, he needed help to hold full opposite rudder and some rope was tied to the starboard rudder bar and two of the crew literally leaned on it to maintain straight and level flight. We had no radio (which was charged from the starboard engine) but finally landed at Chittagong at first attempt. Chittagong at that time was being used by fighters and on landing there a ground wallah came tearing out to us to order us off the runway in no uncertain terms. Apparently some fighters were due to land. After our dicey trip we were decidedly edgy and this bristling twit was informed strongly that if he could taxi a twin-engined aircraft on one engine he had better come and ******* well try it!

'The 14th Army then were surrounded by the Japanese inside the Imphal valley, where Hurricane-bombers were operating from Kangla, Palel and Imphal airstrips. 215 Squadron was given the task of supplying them with the necessary 250lb HE bombs and daily we ferried loads of these bombs to these airstrips inside the valley. Our crew flew a total of 25 such trips during May-June 1944, returning to our base each evening, taking with us up to two soldiers on leave to Calcutta. By the end of June 1944 I was tour-expired and 215 had begun re-equipping with Liberators. As for the Wimpy, I considered it a good all-round aircraft, a veritable workhorse for the RAF at that time and apart from the feathering incident always found it highly reliable.'

In England on 11 January 1942 419 Squadron at RAF Mildenhall made its operational debut in Bomber Command when the Canadian squadron despatched two Wellingtons to Brest where the German battle-cruisers *Scharnhorst* and *Gneisenau* were bottled up by the Royal Navy. Amid general speculation that the two German capital ships must soon leave the port, the bombers stood by. On the night of 28/29 January 1942, two Wellington IVs of 458 Squadron RAAF returned to their base at Holme-on-Spalding Moor from Boulogne amid rumours of their imminent move abroad. Any doubts were quickly removed with the arrival on the station of Wellington ICs fitted with tropicalised Bristol Pegasus engines which the squadron was to swap for their Pratt and Whitney twin-row Wasp-engined Wellington IVs, for operations under desert conditions. As early as December 1941 Wellington Mk.ICs were converted for mine laying and torpedo bombing operations in the Mediterranean. Wellingtons flew anti-submarine operations until the end of the war.

Another change in January-February 1942 saw 218 Squadron re-equip with the Short Stirling. On the night of 17/18 February, 156 Squadron, RAF Alconbury, flew its inaugural Wellington operation when three aircraft joined the Bomber Command stream attacking Essen.

When, on 12 February, the *Scharnhorst* and *Gneisenau* finally made their dash for their home ports the RAF and Royal Navy were found wanting. In the late afternoon, when all else had failed, three Wellingtons and two Stirlings from RAF Mildenhall were despatched to attack the German ships. However, they failed to find them in poor weather and two of the Wellingtons failed to return. Almost immediately, the squadron was declared non-operational again when its Wellington 1Cs were replaced with the Hercules-engined Wellington III.

From 1942 onward mass raids were the order of the day, or rather the night, with little attention paid to precision raids on military targets. On 22 February, having been recalled from the USA where he was head of the RAF Delegation, Air Chief Marshal Arthur Travers Harris CB OBE arrived at High Wycombe, Buckinghamshire, to take charge of RAF Bomber Command from Air Marshal Sir Richard Peirse KCB DSO AFC, who had been posted to India on 8 January. [109] From mid-1941 Harris had been head of the permanent RAF delegation in the United States in Washington DC and one evening in December during the first great Washington conference between the leaders of the British and US war efforts, Marshal of the RAF Sir Charles Portal, Chief of the Air Staff sought out Harris and asked him to take over RAF Bomber Command. Harris was directed by Portal to break the German spirit by the use of night area rather than precision bombing and the targets would be civilian, not just military. The Air Ministry decided that bombing the most densely built up areas would produce such dislocation and breakdown in civilian morale that the German home front would collapse. The famous 'area bombing' directive, which had gained support from the Air Ministry and Prime Minister Winston Churchill, had been sent to Bomber Command on St. Valentine's Day, 14 February, eight days before Harris assumed command.

Immediately upon taking over his post, Harris stated that the only international convention that he and his command would feel obliged to honour, was an agreement going back to the Franco-Prussian War of 1870-71 that prohibited the release of explosive devices from gas-filled airships.

Harris's concept was to break the German spirit by the use of area rather than precision bombing and the targets would be civilian, not just military. Such a concept two years before would have been unthinkable but Harris saw the need to deprive the German factories of its workers and therefore its ability to manufacture weapons for war. Mass raids would be the order of the day, or rather the night, with little attention paid to precision raids on military targets. However, Bomber Command did not possess the numbers of aircraft necessary for immediate mass raids. On taking up his position Harris found that only 380 aircraft were serviceable. More importantly, only 68 of these were heavy bombers while 257 were medium bombers. Undaunted, said, 'The Germans entered this war under the rather childish delusion that they were going to bomb everybody else and nobody was going to bomb them. At Rotterdam, London, Warsaw and half a hundred other places, they put that rather naive theory into operation. They sowed the wind and now they are going to reap the whirlwind...'

With the new directive bomber operations at night entered a new phase that was not restricted to one side of the divide. Harris saw the need to deprive the German factories of its workers and therefore its ability to manufacture weapons for war. To wage the all-out offensive Harris could call upon the Handley Page Halifax and Short Stirling and the new four-engined bomber, the Avro Lancaster. During 1942 eleven Wellington squadrons in Bomber Command re-equipped with four-engined bombers and one was transferred to Coastal Command. The first to re-equip was 218 Squadron, which began conversion to Stirlings, the fourth squadron in 3 Group to do so. 218 Conversion Flight was formed on 28 February and most of the unit's work was carried out at Barton Bendish. Although the available runway area at Marham had been extended since the original airfield had been built, it was still a grass airfield and not really suitable for bombers requiring a 900 yard take off run when fully loaded. As a consequence, 218 Squadron's sojourn would be short, with the unit moving to Marham's satellite station at Downham Market which had hardened runways, in July 1942. A few weeks later 115 Squadron would also leave Marham, for Mildenhall. 218 Conversion Flight joined 1657 Conversion Unit at Stradishall in October.

Meanwhile 3 Group bomber operations continued from Marham. The weather and the need to convert 218 Squadron largely reduced operations in January-February 1942. In March despite an increase in foggy nights, there was an upsurge in operations and on 3/4 March Harris selected the Renault factory at Billancourt near Paris, which had been earmarked for attack for some time, as his first target. A full moon was predicted so Harris decided to send a mixed force of 235 aircraft, led by the most experienced crews in Bomber Command to bomb the French factory. It was calculated that approximately 121 aircraft an hour were concentrated over the factory, which was devastated and all except twelve aircraft claimed to have bombed.

On the night of 8/9 March Pilot Officer Ronald Percy Runagall DFC and crew on 115 Squadron were lost on the raid on Essen. During March the first 'Gee' navigational and target identification sets were installed in operational bombers and these greatly assisted bombers in finding their targets on the nights of 8/9 and 9/10 March in attacks on Essen. On the latter, 187 bombers, including 136 Wellingtons, set out for the target. One of the Wellingtons, a Mk III on 9 Squadron, which took off from Honington, was piloted by Sergeant James Cartwright. Shortly after taking off from Honington a radio message was received stating that the Wellington was returning to base with engine trouble. It was not the first time Cartwright and his air gunner, Sergeant David Nicholas, had encountered trouble with a Wellington. Both were veterans in the squadron and on their sixth operation, on the night of 9 November 1941, they were involved in a dice with death while returning from a raid on Hamburg. Cartwright was flying as second pilot to Sergeant Pendleton when their Wellington developed engine failure in the vicinity of the target. They returned to East Anglia on one engine but stalled and crashed in a wood near RAF East Wretham. The aircraft was totally burnt out but none of the crew suffered any lasting injuries. Cartwright was later given his own crew and Nicholas went with him. On the occasion of the Essen operation Cartwright and Nicholas were not so fortunate. Near Harleston, Suffolk, an eye witness saw the bomber circle once with the engines spluttering then saw an engine on fire and flames streaming behind it. Cartwright went around for a second time. The note of the engines then rose to a high-pitched whine as the aircraft dived to earth. None of the six crew bailed out before the Wellington crashed in a ball of flame in a meadow, scattering a number of propaganda leaflets about the area. Among those who died was the WOp/AG, Sergeant Albert Edward Singerton whose brother Reg was a radio technician at RAF Honington. The two brothers often conversed on the radio on the Wellington's return flight to base and Reg had been best man at Albert's wedding in May 1941.

On the night of 12/13 March 460 Squadron RAAF at RAF Molesworth made its operational debut when five Wellington IVs joined the bomber stream, again attacking Emden. During March Essen was visited on no less than six nights. On the night of 25/26 March when 254 aircraft were despatched to the city, which was being attacked for the fourth time that month, it was the largest force sent to one target so far and Marham contributed 17 Stirlings and ten Wellingtons. On the night following, 26/27 March, 104 Wellingtons and 11 Stirlings returned to Essen and ten Wellingtons and a Stirling were lost. Two of the losses were Wellingtons on 115 Squadron.[110] Meanwhile, Harris had decided that the incendiary bomb was his best weapon in the war against German civilian centres and he had chosen Lübeck, a historic German town on the Baltic, with thousands of half timbered houses, as an ideal target for a mass raid by RAF bombers carrying incendiary bombs. On 28/29 March 234 bombers, mostly carrying incendiaries, set out for Lübeck. Eight bombers were lost but 191 aircraft claimed to have hit the target. A photo-reconnaissance a few days later revealed that about half the city, some 200 acres had been obliterated. On the night of 28/29 March, when 234 aircraft visited Lübeck, two more Marham aircraft failed to return. A Wellington III on 115 Squadron flown by Sergeant William Ballard was lost with all the crew. Flak defences were a constant thorn in the side of RAF Bomber Command operations. The increase in night bombing raids in the more favourable spring weather (in April 115 Squadron's Wellingtons flew 189 sorties on 16 nights) met with a rapid rise in German aerial victories.[111] On the night of 12/13 April Wellington X3596/B piloted by Sergeant Albert Ernest 'Jim' Holder was shot down by Oberleutnant Hans-Dieter Frank of 2.NJG1 near Maarheeze in Holland.

On 23 April Air Vice Marshal Edwards, Chief of the Air Staff of the RCAF, visited Mildenhall to inspect 419 Squadron, commanded by Wing Commander John 'Moose' Fulton DSO DFC AFC. This squadron was one of several which had perfected the technique of dropping bomb loads of 4lb incendiaries over Lübeck and Rostock. On the night of 25/26 April 1942 311 (Czechoslovakian) Squadron flew its last operation of the war before it was posted to Coastal Command, when five aircraft were despatched to Dunkirk. Also in April 214 Squadron began converting to the Stirling and 405 (Vancouver) Squadron RCAF, at Driffield, Yorks, began converting to the Halifax.

For three consecutive nights, beginning on the night of 23/24 April, it was the turn of the Baltic port of Rostock to feel the weight of incendiary bombs. The raids on Lübeck and Rostock prompted the Luftwaffe into reprisal, or 'Baedeker' raids (named after the German guide book to English cities) on Canterbury, Exeter, Norwich and York.

On 26/27 April, a starry, cold, clear night, with a full moon, yet another 115 Squadron Wellington fell victim to a night-fighter. At half past one in the morning of 27 April only the most inquisitive Danes living in southern Jutland felt able to brave the -3° temperature to look out to see the RAF bombers once again headed for Rostock on the Baltic coast. Just over a hundred aircraft were despatched and crews were in no doubt that the flak defences would have been strengthened considerably and enemy night fighters would be alerted once more to the possibilities of a 'kill'. Twelve Wellingtons of 115 Squadron took part in the raid. One of them was X3633 'Y-Yorker' piloted by 23-year- Sergeant Alfred Fone, a Yorkshireman from Leeds, whose ninth op this was. His rear gunner was Sergeant Albert Edward 'Sim' Simmans, who was flying his fifth operation. This was Sim's second crew. He had been forced to part company with the first, in 40 Squadron at Alconbury, when he developed problems with his ears. No doubt this was caused by the combined effect of a swimming accident as a youngster when he had hit his head on the bottom of the pool, exacerbated by the pressure changes associated with flying. After hospitalisation at Halton, 'Sim' was able to resume his flying career, despite a warning that flying could have an adverse effect on his hearing in later life. He crewed up with Fone and an all-Sergeant crew consisting of Irvine Rollinson, second pilot, Alexander Saint, observer from Bonavista, Newfoundland and two Scots, William Smith, wireless operator and James Small Grieve, front gunner. 'Sim' had also become engaged to Ann Wynn, a WAAF and they had made plans for a June wedding. On his last leave home to Barking, Essex on 2 April Sim's aunt had repaired his silk flying gloves, which he was wearing now to help protect his 'trigger' fingers from freezing at altitude over Jutland. On 13 April Fone's crew had flown a 'Gardening' sortie and on the 17th had taken part in a raid on Le Havre. On their third operation on 23/24 April they had been part of a bombing raid on Dunkirk.

Everything seemed to be going well. They had taken off in KO-Y at 2223 hours and had crossed Norfolk and the North Sea without incident. Any thoughts Sim might have had concerning lingering mess bills and a paltry pay-slip of only £2

10s [£2.50] had to be put to one side. As the bomber stream of incoming aircraft approached Sylt at around 0100 hours young and older Danes alike followed the sounds of the RAF bombers' engines and those of the German night fighters as they tried to seek them out. Bomber after bomber crossed from west to east. North-west of Toftlund at 0200 hours a searchlight suddenly coned Fone's Wellington and machine-gun fire could be heard as a Bf 110 of II./NJG3, which arrived from the south-west, made several passes at the aircraft, which caught fire. No one aboard the Wellington bomber stood a chance. Still carrying its bomb load, 'Y-Yorker' crashed and exploded at a crossroads west of Neder Jerstal, a tiny hamlet of 22 houses. Windows and doors of buildings nearby were blown out. The German Wehrmacht and Field Gendarmerie and the Danish civil police immediately blocked off the roads surrounding the crash site. Wreckage from the burning Wellington was scattered over a wide area and a large fire started and burned for hours despite attempts by firemen from Toftlund and Agerskov to put it out.

On 27/28 April Wellington III X3639/K on 115 Squadron piloted by Sergeant Leslie Godfrey Harris, was lost on the raid on Cologne when 97 aircraft were despatched by Bomber Command. Altogether, the raid cost six Wellingtons and a Halifax. In Cologne over 1,500 houses were hit or damaged and 19 other premises affected and over 1,680 people were bombed out. The following night, 88 aircraft of Bomber Command attacked Kiel in bright moonlight. The German defences shot down five Wellingtons and a Hampden. On the night of 29/30 April when 88 aircraft were despatched to the Gnome & Rhône factory at Gennevilliers in Paris, three Wellingtons failed to return. One of the losses was X3593/C on 115 Squadron piloted by Sergeant Walter Frank Reynolds, which was shot down near the French capital.

In a portend of things to come, on 3/4 May 1942, the 100th anniversary of a great fire, Hamburg was visited by 81 bombers. Hamburg was found to be completely cloud-covered but while only 54 aircraft bombed on to its estimated position 113 fires were started in the city of which 57 were classed as large and over 1,600 people were bombed out. On 4/5 May when 121 aircraft were dispatched to Stuttgart, A Wellington III on 115 Squadron flown by Flight Lieutenant John Arthur Sword DFC AFC was shot down. All six of the crew bailed out but Sword and Sergeant Harold William Batty died due to insecure parachute webbing and they fell to their deaths. A second Wellington III of 115 Squadron was lost at 1600 hours when it hit a 240 feet wooden radio mast in poor visibility during a training sortie over Norfolk and crashed at West Beckham, 3 miles southwest of Sheringham. All three sergeant pilots who were on board were killed.

On 17/18 May 32 Stirlings and 28 Wellingtons of 3 Group carried out mine-laying in the Friesians and the Heligoland areas. German night fighters were active and five Stirlings and two Wellingtons were shot down. A further 27 aircraft went to Boulogne and one Stirling flew a night leaflet raid to France. Wellington III X3644 'A-Apple' on 115 Squadron flown by Sergeant Francis Norman Butterworth failed to return from a 'Gardening' sortie and all five crew were killed. Two nights later, on 19/20 May when 197 aircraft set out for Mannheim, 11 aircraft including four Stirlings and three Wellingtons of Bomber Command failed to return. When 77 aircraft including 31 Wellingtons and nine Stirlings were sent to bomb the Gnome & Rhône factory at Gennevilliers near Paris on 29/30 May little or no damage was done to the factory. Four Wellingtons and a Stirling were lost.

Top level consultations between Air Marshal Sir Arthur Harris and his subordinate commanders had revealed that the raids on Rostock had achieved total disruption. Whole areas of the city had been wiped out and 100,000 people had been forced to evacuate the city. The capacity of its workers to produce war materials had therefore been severely diminished. Harris had for some time nurtured the desire to send 1,000 bombers to a German city and reproduce the same results with incendiaries. Although RAF losses would be on a large scale Churchill approved the plan. Harris gave the order 'Operation Plan Cologne' to his Group Commanders just after mid-day on 30 May so that 1,000 bombers would be unleashed on the 770,000 inhabitants. However, Harris could only accomplish this by using untried crews from the Operational Training Units (OTUs), many of them flying Wellingtons and even Blenheims and Hudsons.[112] All bomber bases throughout England were at a high state of readiness to get all available aircraft airborne for the raid. At Marham, 115 Squadron contributed 18 Wellingtons and 218 Squadron, 17 Stirlings. Five of the Wimpys carried a 4,000lb HC bomb. Two Wellingtons carried a single 1,000lb GP plus five 500lb GP bombs and eleven aircraft each carried nine SBCs.

All bomber stations throughout England were at a high state of readiness to get all available aircraft airborne for the raid. On paper the actual number of serviceable aircraft totalled 1,047 bombers - mostly Wellingtons (602) - almost 300 of which were clapped-out OTU aircraft. The raid was to be led by the 'Gee'-equipped Wellingtons and Stirlings of 1 and 3 Groups who were to operate in a fire-raising capacity.[113] They were allotted a time span of 15 minutes to set the centre of Cologne alight with loads of 4lb incendiary canisters.

At the end of the briefings at each station a message from Sir Arthur Harris, a last rallying cry to his crews, was read out. 'The force of which you form a part tonight is at least twice the size and has more than four times the carrying capacity of the largest air force ever before concentrated on one objective. You have an opportunity, therefore, to strike a blow at the enemy which will resound, not only throughout Germany but throughout the world. In your hands lie the means of destroying a major part of the resources by which the enemy's war effort is maintained. It depends, however, upon each individual crew whether full concentration is achieved. Press home your attack to your precise objective with the utmost determination and resolution in the foreknowledge that, if you individually succeed, the most shattering and devastating blow will have been delivered against the very vitals of the enemy. Let him have it - right on the chin.'

In all, 898 crews claimed to have hit Cologne and almost all of them bombed their aiming point as briefed. Fifteen aircraft bombed other targets. The total tonnage of bombs was 1,455, two-thirds of this tonnage being incendiaries. Post-bombing reconnaissance certainly showed that more than 600 acres of Cologne had been razed to the ground. The Air Ministry reported after reconnaissance had been made that 'In an area of seventeen acres between the Cathedral and the Hange Brücke forty or fifty buildings are gutted or severely damaged. Buildings immediately adjacent to the south-eastern wall of the Cathedral are gutted. There is no photographic evidence of damage to the

Cathedral, although the damage to the adjoining buildings suggests that some minor damage may have occurred. The Police Headquarters and between 200 and 300 houses have been destroyed in another area of 35 acres extending from the Law Courts and the Neumarkt westwards almost to the Hohenzollernring. An area of three and a half acres between St. Gereon's Church and the Hohenzollernring has been completely burned out.' The fires burned for days. In his report to Chief of Police Himmler, Gauleiter Grohé recorded that 486 people were killed, 5,027 injured and 59,100 rendered homeless, 18,432 houses, flats, workshops, public buildings and the like were completely destroyed, 9,516 heavily damaged and 31,070 damaged less severely. 'The immense number of incendiary bombs dropped' had caused 12,000 fires of which 2,500 had been major outbreaks. Albert Speer, Minister for Armaments and War Production, was with Goering at the Veldenstein castle in Franconia when the Reichmarschall was told of the reported weight of the attack. Speer said that Goering shouted: 'Impossible! That many bombs cannot be dropped in a single night!'

It was estimated that from 135,000 to 150,000 of Cologne's population of nearly 700,000 people fled the city after the raid. In the early hours of 31 May the roads to Cologne started to fill with lorries bring relief supplies - 34,000 items of clothing for adults, 50,000 items of clothing for children, 61,000 sheets, 90,000 boxes soap powder, 700,000 cakes of soap, ten million cigarettes and 100,000 metres of curtain material. A small army of 3,500 soldiers, 2,000 prisoners of war and 10,000 labourers arrived to assist the 5,200 workmen in Cologne detailed to clean up the city. As a result almost all routes, except in the city centre, were able to function under temporary repair within ten days of the raid. To help in this process of recovery the schoolchildren were immediately sent on holiday because all school buildings that had survived the bombing were needed as emergency centres. Some 370,000 claims were submitted for war damage. Dr. Josef Goebbels, Hitler's Propaganda Minister, shrugged off the implications of the raid and wrote in his diary, 'Naturally the effects of bomb warfare are horrible when one looks at individual cases but they must be put up with.'

Bomber Harris received messages of congratulation from Sir Archibald Sinclair the Secretary of State for Air and as far afield as Lieutenant-General Golovanov his Soviet opposite number. Harris responded in kind. 'We will not cease our efforts until Hitler's Germany cries, 'Enough'!'

In England squadrons repaired and patched their damaged bombers - no less than 116 aircraft suffered damage, twelve so badly that they were written off - and within 48 hours they were preparing for another 1,000-raid, against Essen. (The weather had proved unsuitable immediately after the raid on Cologne). At nightfall on 1 June 956 aircraft including 347 aircraft from the Operational Training Units took off and headed for Essen. Despite a reasonable weather forecast, crews experienced great difficulty in finding the target. The plan was similar to the recent raid on Cologne except that many more flares were dropped by the 'raid leaders' flying in Wellingtons of 3 Group. Seven of the 22 Halifaxes on 76 Squadron were briefed to attack the precise aiming point, a large shed in the centre of the Krupps Works. Twenty Wellingtons were to pinpoint their position and then release flares to illuminate the entire target area for the fire raisers of the marker force. The remaining 120 Halifaxes were to join the Main Force attack. But the target-marking force had great difficulty finding the aiming point because the ground was covered either by the industrial haze or a layer of low cloud and results were poor, with bombing scattered over Essen and at least eleven other towns, particularly Oberhausen and Mülheim, in or near the Ruhr.[114]

Essen itself escaped lightly and Krupps was once again almost untouched. Although seemingly lacking the concentration of the earlier raid on Cologne the bombing nevertheless was effective enough to saturate the defences. Of the 37 bombers lost on the second 1,000-bomber raid on Essen, twenty were claimed by night-fighters.

After Cologne and Essen Harris could not immediately mount another 1,000-bomber raid and he had to be content with smaller formations. On 2/3 June just 195 aircraft, 97 of them Wellingtons, carried out a follow-up raid on Essen. The story is told of how one morning at planning, after spending his usual quarter of an hour looking at the photographs of the previous night's raid and the Met charts, Harris glanced up and said, 'Essen'. Saundby coughed a little deprecatingly and murmured, 'Excuse me, sir but I think the boys are getting a little browned off going to Essen every night.' Harris summed up the situation in two words, 'So's Essen!'[115]

On the night of 3/4 June 170 bombers were dispatched on the first large raid to Bremen since October 1941. Crews reported only indifferent bombing results and eleven aircraft failed to return. On 5/6 June in the raid on Essen by 180 aircraft twelve aircraft - eight of them Wellingtons - failed to return and the bombing was scattered over a wide area.[116] On the night of 19/20 June the RAF raided Emden and 194 aircraft, including 112 Wellingtons took part. Of these 131 crews claimed to have bombed Emden but bombing photographs revealed that part of the flare force started a raid on Osnabrück, 80 miles from Emden, in which 29 aircraft eventually joined. Emden reported only five HE bombs and 200-300 incendiaries with no damage or casualties. The RAF lost nine bombers including six Wellingtons. On 20/21 June 185 RAF bombers made a return raid on Emden but only part of the bomber force identified the target and only about 100 houses were damaged. Eight aircraft, four of them Wellingtons ICs, failed to return. On the night of 22/23 June 144 Wellingtons, 38 Stirlings, 26 Halifaxes, 11 Lancasters and eight Hampdens attacked Emden again for the third night in a row. 'Good' bombing results were claimed by 196 of the crews but decoy fires are believed to have diverted many bombs from the intended target. Six aircraft - four Wellingtons, one Lancaster and a Stirling - were lost.[117] Emden reported that 50 houses were destroyed, 100 damaged and some damage caused to the harbour. Six civilians were killed and forty were injured.

A briefing called on 25 June had everybody buzzing with surprise. It was another 'Thousand Bomber Raid', the third and final 'thousand' effort in the series of five major saturation attacks on German cities and 1,067 aircraft would attack Bremen. Although only 960 aircraft including, from the OTUs, 272 aircraft, became available for Bomber Command use, every type of aircraft in Bomber Command was included, even the Bostons and Mosquitoes of 2 Group which, so far, had only been used for day operations.[118] Bomber Command never before, or after, dispatched such a mixed force. After Churchill had intervened and insisted that the Admiralty allow Coastal Command to participate in this raid, a further 102

Hudsons and Wellingtons of Coastal Command were sent to Bremen but official records class this effort as a separate raid, not under Bomber Command control.

The tactics for the Thousand Raid on Bremen were basically similar to the earlier 'Thousand' raids except that the bombing period was now cut from 98 minutes, which was a feature of the Cologne raid, to 65 minutes. Bremen, on the wide River Weser, should have been an easy target to find and the inland penetration of the German night-fighter belt was only a shallow one. There were doubts about a band of cloud which lay across the Bremen area during the day but this was being pushed steadily eastwards by a strong wind. Unfortunately the wind dropped in the evening and the bomber crews found the target completely covered for the whole period of the raid. The limited success which was gained was entirely due to the use of 'Gee', which enabled the leading crews to start fires, on to the glow of which many aircraft of later waves bombed. In all, 696 Bomber Command aircraft were able to claim attacks on Bremen. Generally the results were not as dramatic as at Cologne but much better, than the second 'Thousand' raid to Essen. Once again, as at Essen, a layer of cloud intervened between the force and its objective. Most aircraft in the first wave bombed blind on 'Gee' and the glow of the fires this caused, reflected in the cloud and aided identification for the succeeding waves. Bremen reported a strengthening wind at the time of the raid which fanned the many fires started throughout the town, increased the extent of the damage and left whole areas of houses in ruins. Twenty-seven acres of the business and residential area were completely destroyed. The RAF plan to destroy the Focke-Wulf factory and the shipyards was not successful, although an assembly shop at the Focke-Wulf factory was destroyed by a 4,000lb bomb dropped by a 5 Group Lancaster. A further six buildings at this factory were seriously damaged and eleven buildings lightly so. Damage was also experienced by the Atlas Werke and the Vulkan shipyard, the Norddeutsche Hiitte and the Korff refinery and by two large dockside warehouses.[119]

Although the raid was not as successful as the first 1,000-bomber raid on Cologne, large parts of Bremen, especially in the south and east districts were destroyed.[120] The German high command was shaken but 52 bombers were claimed destroyed by the flak and night fighter defences for the loss of just two Bf 110s and four NCO crewmembers killed or missing. No less than 48 aircraft were lost; the highest casualty rate in the war so far. A total of 1,123 sorties (including 102 Hudsons and Wellingtons from Coastal Command) had been dispatched and fifty Bomber Command aircraft and four from Coastal Command were lost. This time the heaviest casualties were suffered by the OTUs of 91 Group, which lost 23 of the 198 Whitleys and Wellingtons provided by that group. All but one was manned by pupil crews.

The decision to form a new Canadian command had been taken in 1942 and a headquarters was established at Allerton Park, Yorkshire, on 1 December 1942. 420, 424 and 425 Squadrons of the RCAF were selected in January 1943, along with other Canadian bomber squadrons, to form 6 Group RCAF, which officially became operational on 1 January 1943. At Leeming 408 (equipped with the Halifax) and 424 Squadrons took up residence and 419 (also equipped with the Halifax) and 420 took up station at Middleton St. George. Dishforth became home to 425 and 426 Squadrons, while Croft accommodated 427 Squadron. At Dalton 428 Squadron moved in. A sixth airfield at Skipton-on-Swale was still under construction.

On the night of 3/4 January 1943 6 Group flew its first operation when six Wellingtons of 427 Squadron were despatched to lay mines off the Frisian Islands. By March seven Canadian Wellington squadrons were operating within 4 and 6 Groups of Bomber Command. On 10 March Sergeant Alex Mitchell (a Scot) and his crew, most of whom were Canadian, were posted to 427 Squadron. At first the crew were given daily assignments to test the flight capabilities of their Mk.X and to install new equipment. Stuart Brown the navigator, from Brandon, Canada recalls.

'On 16 April we flew our first op; an uneventful trip to Mannheim with 3,500lb of bombs. On 28 April we flew a very dicey do, mine-laying near sea level on the Elbe estuary, from which only four out of ten aircraft from our squadron returned. Immediately following this trip 427 Squadron was reorganised to become 1664 Conversion Unit for the training of crews to fly the larger Halifax bombers. Senior crews were posted in from other Wellington squadrons and in May our crew was posted to 428 Squadron to continue operations from Dalton, Yorkshire. May 1943 saw the beginning of the Battle of the Ruhr and our crew flew five trips. Following the trip to Düsseldorf on 11 June we were posted back to 427 Squadron for conversion to the Halifax.'

On the night of 8/9 October 1943 the last bombing operation by Wellingtons of Bomber Command was made by the Poles on 300 (Masovian) Squadron, during a raid on Hannover. However, Wellingtons continued to serve with OTUs throughout 1944 and on occasion they were used directly against the enemy. Wellingtons also served until the end of the war with the 2nd Tactical Air Force in England and France. It says something for this remarkable aircraft that despite being designed before the war, it could still survive in combat conditions and against one of the most up-to-date fighters the Germans possessed.

Footnote

107 Warrant Officer Snowdon and crew in Wellington X9873 were the only a/c lost while four Whitleys FTR from the raid on Hamburg. It was Gildner's 20th victory and he added a 21st, a Whitley, later that same night.

108 In October 1942 Ercolani left for India, joining 99 Squadron near Calcutta. The squadron was one of two Wellington long-range bomber units used to attack enemy airfields and river, road and rail supply routes. Ercolani led many of these missions over the ensuing months before the squadron switched to night bombing. Inadequate maps, appalling weather and poor aircraft serviceability due to lack of spares added to the hazards of flying during the 'Forgotten War'. With the expansion of the strategic bomber force and the introduction of the long-range Liberator, in September 1943 Ercolani went to the newly-formed 355 Squadron. He flew many sorties deep into enemy territory, some involving a round trip of 2,000 miles, to destroy the supply networks used to reinforce and support the Burma battlefield. An important and frequent target was the Siam-Burma railway built by Allied PoWs. In September 1944 Ercolani returned as CO to 99 Squadron, where he won the respect and affection of his airmen, who affectionately dubbed him 'The Erk'. He led many of the most difficult raids himself, often taking his heavy four-engine bomber as low as 100 feet to drop his delay-fused bombs as his gunners strafed buildings or rolling stock. He attacked supply dumps and Japanese headquarters, and throughout the early months of 1945 regularly led forces of up to 24 Liberators against targets in Siam, southern Burma and on

the Kra Isthmus, often in the face of heavy anti-aircraft fire. He was the master bomber for an attack against the railway system at Bangkok and was mentioned in despatches. By the end of March 1945 the decisive battle for central Burma was won. He was awarded a Bar to his DSO. Ercolani was then put in command of 159 Squadron, part of the Path Finder Force, attacking targets in Malaya and flying a number of mining operations to distant ports, including Singapore - sorties of more than 20 hours duration. On 15 June he led a force of Liberators to attack a 10,000-ton tanker, the Tohu Maru, which had been located in the South China Sea. The mission involved a round trip of 2,500 miles. Flying in appalling weather, some of the Liberators were unable to find the target, while some were damaged by enemy fire. Ercolani attacked at low level and made three separate bombing runs, registering successful hits on the tanker, which caught fire. Subsequent reconnaissance reports confirmed that it had sunk, a devastating blow to the Japanese troops depending on its vital cargo of fuel. Ercolani was awarded an immediate DFC. He flew his last operation on 5 August when he attacked a target in Siam. Ercolani left the RAF in March 1946 and rejoined his father at Ercol. He formally retired in the mid-1990s but remained closely involved with the company until his death on 13 February 2010.

109 Sir Richard Peirse became AOC-in-C India on 6 March 1942. On 16 November 1943 Peirse was appointed Allied C-in-C, Air South-East Asia Command. While serving in this capacity he eloped with the wife of General Sir Claude Auchinleck, C-in-C India, an act which was universally condemned and effectively ended his career. Peirse died in 1970 aged 78. *The Right of the Line* by John Terraine (Hodder & Stoughton 1985).

110 KO-F flown by Sergeant Harry Taylor, and KO-Y flown by Pilot Officer Geoffrey Gordon Soames, which crashed NE of Arnhem. There were no survivors from either crew.

111 In March 1942 41 bombers and in April 46 bombers were brought down by German night fighters

112 599 were Wellingtons, including four of Flying Training Command and no fewer than 367 of the aircraft came from OTUs. The rest included 88 Stirlings, 131 Halifaxes and 73 Lancasters, the remainder being made up of Whitleys, Hampdens and Manchesters.

113 1 Group provided 156 Wellingtons and 3 Group, 88 Stirlings and 134 Wellingtons. A total of 131 Halifaxes were provided by 4 Group.

114 *The Bomber Command War Diaries: An Operational reference book 1939-1945*. Martin Middlebrook and Chris Everitt. (Midland 1985).

115 See *Pathfinders* by Wing Commander Bill Anderson OBE DFC AFC (Jarrolds London 1946). This attack was also widely scattered with just three HE bombs and 300 incendiary bombs falling in the city and 14 aircraft failed to return.

116 12 aircraft - 8 Wellingtons, 2 Stirlings, 1 Halifax, 1 Lancaster FTR. *Nachtjagd* was credited with 8 victories.

117 Two of which, were destroyed by Oberleutnant Rudolf Schoenert, St Kpt 4./NJG2.

118 472 Wellingtons, 124 Halifaxes, 96 Lancasters, 69 Stirlings, 51 Blenheims, 50 Hampdens, 50 Whitleys, 24 Bostons, 20 Manchesters and 4 Mosquitoes. Five further aircraft provided by Army Co-Operation Command were also added to the force. The final numbers dispatched, 1,067 aircraft, made this a larger raid than that on Cologne at the end of May. The entire 5 Group effort - 142 aircraft - were to bomb the Focke-Wulf factory. Twenty Blenheims were allocated the A.G. Weser shipyard; the Coastal Command aircraft were to bomb the Deschimag shipyard; all other aircraft except for 5 Group were to carry out an area attack on the town and docks. This raid was the last flown operationally by Manchesters, after which the type was withdrawn.

119 *The Bomber Command War Diaries: An Operational reference book 1939-1945*. Martin Middlebrook and Chris Everitt. (Midland 1985).

120 5 Group destroyed an assembly shop at the Focke-Wulf factory when a 4,000lb 'Cookie' scored a direct hit. 6 other buildings were seriously damaged.

Chapter 6

Desert War

'We took off early in the afternoon for the one hour forty minute flight to ALG 104 to refuel, then at take-off time we set course for Crete. When we arrived over the target it was well lit up. This was the first time I had seen flak at close quarters. George said over the intercom, 'Jesus Christ, look at that bloody lot!' The Skipper replied, 'This is light stuff tonight. Wait 'till you see Benghazi!'

'Wally' Gaul 29 October 1941 raid on German shipping in Suda Bay on Crete.

A raid by two Dorniers on Norwich during the afternoon of Tuesday, 9 July 1940 was enough to alter the course of destiny for at least one nineteen-year-old boy who witnessed the horror and destruction. Wallace Gaul always intended to volunteer for the Tank Corps. The German bombing raid on his home city changed all this. Despite his reserved occupation, Gaul volunteered for RAF aircrew. In September, while Gaul was taking the first faltering steps as an 'erk' at RAF Marham, 1,500 miles away a battle was raging in the Western Desert. When Mussolini had declared war on Britain and France on 10 June 1940, Air Marshal Sir Arthur Longmore in Cairo could call upon roughly 150 aircraft for the defence of Egypt and the Suez Canal, with about another 150 first-line aircraft scattered throughout Palestine, East Africa, Aden and Gibraltar. However, nine of the fourteen bomber squadrons were equipped with the Blenheim I. The rest were made up of biplane fighters and bombers and seaplanes. Only a few DWI Wellingtons were in place for minesweeping duties. Blenheims and Wellingtons, which were the only RAF aircraft with sufficient range to reinforce Egypt, had to cross the Bay of Biscay and then land at Gibraltar before making a night landing at Malta. This was clearly out of the question, so while the Wellington squadrons and OTUs kicked their heels in England, Blenheims and Hurricanes were shipped out via West Africa.

It was, perhaps, in the Middle East that the Wellington achieved its greatest fame, remaining a front-line bomber almost until the end of the war. When Italy entered the war in 1940 the RAF had no long-range bombers in the Middle East, but late that summer a small number of Wellingtons arrived from England. On 19/20 September Wellingtons on 70 Squadron made their first attack on the port of Benghazi and the so-called 'mail run' to that vital supply port for General Rommel's Afrika Korps continued almost nightly for several months.

For the remainder of 1940, throughout 1941 and for most of 1942, during the ebb and flow of the desert battles, the Wellingtons of 205 Group attacked targets of various types. Egypt was successfully defended against the invading Italian armies and on 24 October Mussolini turned his attentions to Greece. Four days later, the War Cabinet approved a plan for Wellingtons, temporarily stationed on Malta en route for Egypt, to be used in action against Italian supply ports in southern Italy.

'The Group had had a most distinguished history in the Desert from beginning to end' recalled Eric McLellan. He had entered the RAF after Oxford but defective eyesight prevented him from becoming a pilot. Nonetheless, he served the Technical Branch well throughout the war. 'It did as much as any unit to save the Delta and conquer North Africa by bombing Rommel's supply ports. The fine weather of the eastern Mediterranean and the sturdy simplicity of the Wellington made it ideal for the task, even when it was obsolete elsewhere. In particular, the weather made adequate for present purposes the robust methods of navigation immortalised in the 70 Squadron song [sung to the tune of *'Clementine'*]:

'Have you lost us, navigator?
Come up here and have a look;
Someone's shot our starboard wing off!'
'We're all right, then, that's Tobruk.'

'It was all heroic and it gathered as much myth as the Trojan War. If I may be allowed a personal note - they were the finest body of men I have ever had the honour of serving with and remained so after action from Mersa Matruh to Warsaw and back again to the Delta.'[121]

Meanwhile, following a period of night operations on European targets, on 8 November 1940 37 and 38 Squadrons were despatched to Egypt via Malta to help replace squadrons sent to Greece. 37 Squadron was detailed to move to Fayid in Egypt. Six Wellingtons had left on 8 November but one turned back. The others, fitted with extra fuel tanks, landed at Luqa on Malta during a raid soon after dawn next day after a nine-hour flight. The crews were instructed to rest and then to refuel the aircraft before continuing the journey to Fayid, but on returning to their Wimpys found that the fuel tanks had been removed and bombs loaded. The AOC Malta had decreed that any suitable aircraft passing through Malta were to be used for two operations from the island, regardless of how urgently its services were required elsewhere. In the event, the first such operation by 37 Squadron was abandoned, but on 13 November, an hour or so after the Fleet Air Arm had carried out their famous attack on Taranto Harbour with Swordfish aircraft, the Wellingtons were able to stir things up again with some 250lb bombs. While the five crews were away on this operation, another seven Wimpys, one flown by the CO, had arrived. He was most surprised to discover that 37 Squadron was still at Luqa! Eventually, on 21 November, 37 Squadron was allowed to continue its interrupted journey to Egypt.[122]

These two squadrons helped push back the Italians in the Western Desert and were ably assisted by 148 Squadron, which had re-formed at Luqa on 1 December 1940. On the day after reorganisation air tests were flown and a briefing was held for a raid on an oil refinery and railway yard at Naples. The outcome of this raid was uncertain due to poor weather, but three aircraft were able to bomb through gaps in the cloud, starting fires, while a fourth attacked an airfield at Catania in Sicily instead, claiming one aircraft destroyed on the ground. 148 Squadron's first notable success came on 7 December during a raid on Castel Benito airfield in

Libya by six aircraft. Achieving total surprise, although two of the Wellingtons were badly damaged, two hangars on the airfield were made unusable and an administrative building and a fuel dump were also hit. Many dozens of aircraft on the ground were destroyed with incendiary bullets. Next came a raid on Valona in Albania on 13 December by four aircraft, but ten-tenths cloud forced three to return with their bomb-loads. Following a raid by nine of 148 Squadron's aircraft on naval vessels in Naples harbour on 14 December came a message from the AOC Malta, Air Vice Marshal Hugh Pughe Lloyd - 'You have been born and also reached years of discretion at the same time. Your prenatal activities indicate a healthy child. Good luck to you all and may 148 Squadron and its association with Malta prove of ever-increasing benefit to the Empire'.[123]

By 16 December the last remnants of the Italian Army had been pushed back across the Egyptian frontier. Hitler now came to the aid of his fellow dictator. Late in December, while the Wehrmacht marched into Bulgaria with intentions on Greece, Fliegerkorps X began arriving in Sicily. Two more raids on Castel Benito airfield were made before Christmas. On 20 December nine aircraft attacked with great effect, hitting nineteen enemy aircraft, of which five were destroyed by fire, and severely damaging buildings. Two days later, only two of ten Wellingtons found Castel Benito, which was obscured by a sandstorm, so the others bombed the secondary target, Tripoli, where the power station and customs house were hit. After a brief respite at Christmas, further raids were mounted against Naples and Taranto and early in January 1941, three raids on Tripoli by all ten of 148 Squadron's Wellingtons. The arrival of Fliegerkorps X in the Mediterranean was a rude shock to the British, who hit back on 12/13 January when Wellingtons from Malta bombed Catania airfield on Sicily. One Wellington crashed into the sea alongside a trawler, HMS *Jade* and another failed to return to base. Ten enemy aircraft were claimed as destroyed on the ground and others damaged, while the HQ building and a hangar were also destroyed. On the night of 15/16 January in a follow-up raid on Catania another ten aircraft were claimed destroyed and a further hangar damaged. Still more raids on this vital target were made before January was out and the AOC once again signalled his congratulations.

During February 1941 raids on Castel Benito and Tripoli continued, notwithstanding the Luftwaffe's intense attack on Malta which had begun on 17 January. Three replacement Wellingtons arrived from England on 5 February, but one overshot on landing. To give the hard-pressed crews a rest, five aircraft took off for Heliopolis and two for Ismailia in Egypt, these two not being due to return as their crews had been posted. Fliegerkorps X could not prevent the rout of the Italian Army in Cyrenaica and early in February 1941 the last of the Italian troops surrendered. The Wellingtons had played their part with the continual bombing of the enemy but a greater test was to follow. On 12 February Rommel arrived in Cyrenaica and six days later Hitler named the General's forces the Afrika Korps. Once the Germans' intentions in Greece became obvious Wellingtons on 37, 38 and 70 Squadrons in the Canal Zone and 148 Squadron on Malta quickly struck at the main German airfields and the port of Tripoli. 148 Squadron's Wellingtons carried out raids on Catania, Tripoli and Comiso under ever-increasing difficulties caused by the German attacks on Malta. A particularly heavy raid on 25 February reduced the number of serviceable Wellingtons on 148 Squadron to two, six having been destroyed by fire, another one struck off charge and four needing several weeks' work to make them fit for further service.

On 13 March 148 Squadron received a signal ordering an immediate move to Egypt, although some personnel were to be left behind as a detachment for refuelling and rearming the squadron's aircraft which would use Luqa as an advanced landing ground. Two days later the Wellingtons were ferried to their new base at Kabrit and on 23 March 79 airmen left for Alexandria aboard HMS *Bonaventure*. At 1600 that day Ju 87s and 88s dive-bombed the ship, without causing any casualties and thirteen of them were shot down by 261 Squadron Hurricanes from Hal Far. The ship arrived safely at Alexandria on 25 March.[124] On 31 March Rommel's forces began mounting a counter-offensive and the meagre RAF forces were thrown headlong into the fight. Wellingtons on 37, 38 and 70 Squadrons, 'reinforced' by 148 Squadron, which after repeated air attacks had been forced to withdraw from Malta earlier in the month, made raids on Axis targets. By refuelling at Tobruk the Wellingtons were able to hit Tripoli in a bid to stem the flow of enemy material.

It was at Luqa that Pilot Officer Bill Astell joined 148 Squadron. He had reported at a RAF recruiting office in April 1939 and started his training at Mere aerodrome, Staffordshire, two months later. Bill's home was Spire Hollins, a rambling country house on a wooded hillside at Combs near Chapel-en-le-Frith in Derbyshire. His father was the chairman of a Manchester textile company and Bill spent most of his teenage years at a public school in Berkshire. A spell in Germany at Leipzig University and climbing in the Dolomites was followed by a short period working for his father at the company's mill in Staffordshire. Bill Astell had completed flying training at Salisbury, Southern Rhodesia in 1940 before arriving in Malta. He wrote home telling his parents that 'There are thousands of stone walls and not one field bigger than the lawn at home.' When 148 Squadron had moved to Kabrit in Egypt, there, close to the Suez Canal, Bill found 'sand everywhere'. Several advanced landing grounds were prepared in the desert to increase the range of the Wellingtons. Fuel dumps were hidden near the rough runways and the men stationed there lived in tents which had sand and sump oil thrown over them as camouflage. In November Bill Astell flew to a landing ground at Sidi Abd el Rahman, two miles from the sea and only 15 miles from El Alamein. There were frequent sand storms and the air crews' tents - some sunk into the sand, their poles cemented into 40-gallon oil drums - were often visited by scorpions and beetles. Night flying presented particular problems, the Wellingtons being guided to earth along a 1,300-yard strip of flickering goose-neck flares and glim lamps. When Bill turned his Wellington towards the distant flarepath of an advanced airfield at 2 am on 30 November 1941 he adjusted the throttles on receiving a green light and came in low, only to find another Wellington blocking the runway. Bill had almost lost flying speed. He pulled on the stick but knew he could not avoid a sickening collision.

'As I stepped out of the wreckage a tongue of flame caught me on the posterior,' he told friends later. The crew were luckier, scrambling clear without serious injury, but Bill spent two months in No. 19 General Hospital suffering from a nasty scalp wound and second-degree burns on his back. After a brief leave in Kenya, staying with old family friends who gave him two ponies to ride and he even shot a leopard in the garden, he resumed flying - this time with a new crew. 'They are completely new to the game,' he wrote home early in 1942. 'My second pilot is an Argentinean and the navigator a former parson.'

In January 1942 Kabrit became 236 Medium Bomber Wing and 104 and 148 Squadrons were based there. By now the air crews' main targets were the port of Benghazi and harbours in Crete and Greece, raids on enemy convoys carrying supplies from Italy to Rommel's army in Libya and attacks on landing grounds used by German fighters and Stuka bombers. One of 148 Squadron's Wimpys, piloted by Sergeant Hamilton, vanished during an attack on a German convoy in bad weather on 23 February and, after a short but heavy enemy raid on the Kabrit station on 3 March, Squadron Leader Baird finished his landing run on top of an unexploded bomb, fortunately without harm. In April Bill Astell dived for cover in a slit trench when several Ju 88s swooped over Kabrit at a height of 2,000 feet, dropping bombs that destroyed a hangar and four Wellingtons, killing one man and injuring ten others. A few days' later he wrote his parents that: *'We are in a big camp at the side of the Bitter Lake. The dining room is in one building but we live in wooden huts and there is an Egyptian servant for each room. We sleep under a big muslin net and we are lucky - the other ranks sleep in tents'* but he made no mention of the attack. On 13 May Bill Astell and his crew in 'R for Robert' were scheduled to fly on exercise from LG 106 and invited along two intelligence officers. 'Bill really put us through it,' recalled Pilot Officer Roy Chappell of 104 Squadron later. 'He did all sorts of stunt flying over the edge of the Qattara Depression. It was wild territory to crash in and we seemed near it at times.'

On 6 June 1942, however, Bill's parents received a telegram from the Air Ministry reporting that he was missing. While bombing the particularly well-defended enemy airfield at Derna, Bill Astell's aircraft had been attacked by a German fighter. Cannon fire hit the Wellington's rear gun turret and smashed the rudder. Fire broke out in the fuselage and starboard wing and the rear gunner and radio operator were seriously wounded. The machine rapidly lost height and Bill ordered his crew to bail out. Four managed to do so but Bill, with his navigator - the former parson, Pilot Officer 'Bishop' Dodds - at his side, had insufficient time and crash-landed the Wimpy in the desert, both men crawling from the blazing wreckage with burns. For five days the two surviving airmen fought to stay alive and avoid being captured by the enemy. They had nothing to eat for three days and at one stage almost stumbled into a German army camp. The men laid low by day and walked eastwards across the desert at night. 'Strange things happen to you when you feel you are dying of thirst,' said Bill later. 'Your tongue swells up, you can't see properly and you get a confused sense of time'. One night Bill cunningly used his knowledge of the German language that he had gained at Leipzig University to persuade a sentry to give him two pints of water from an enemy vehicle. 'Bishop' Dodds' condition deteriorated and Bill was relieved when he caught sight of a British long-range patrol. He scrambled over scrubland to contact them but failed and, to his horror, could not find the navigator when he returned. It was two more days before Bill was picked up by friendly Arabs and was able to walk into a British post. Subsequently he was awarded the Distinguished Flying Cross for 'displaying great courage and fortitude.' His friends at Kabrit immediately celebrated his return by enrolling him into the Late

Arrivals' Club, permitting him to wear the emblem of the winged boot on his flying suit. Astell's return to Britain for a well-earned leave was via Canada and the United States. His first attempt to return home from Canada was a failure - his ship colliding with a US Navy torpedo boat escorting the convoy and being forced to return to Halifax. A few weeks later, however, he crossed the Atlantic in style, on the *Queen Mary*.

In late October 1942 [125] Bill - now a flying officer - completed a conversion course on Manchester and Lancaster bombers and in early 1943 he was selected to join 617 Squadron and prepare for the famous Dam Busters' raid that coming May, on the night of the 15/16th. On 27 March he flew over to his native Peak District to make a low-level daylight over the waters of the narrow Derwent Dam and when, the following night, Wing Commander Guy Gibson did the same he nearly flew his Lancaster into the stone towers. On 6 May a flight of six Lancasters made several dummy night attacks on the Derwent Dam, much to the consternation of villagers in the valley below.

Late on the afternoon of 17 May 1943 a messenger cycled to Spire Hollins in Combs with an ominous telegram from the Air Ministry. 'We deeply regret...' Bill Astell and all his crew were killed. Astell was 23.[126]

The target was Tobruk. Flying Officer John King, an observer on board a Wellington of 104 Squadron, watched the town appear on the horizon with mixed feelings. This, at the end of 1941 was his thirteenth operational flight. He wasn't superstitious - but thirteen did have an unfortunate reputation. King was a conscientious officer, even to the extent of leaving his personal valuables behind when on 'ops.' Just before take-off he had handed his watch to the Station Adjutant with his usual cheerful smile. 'Just in case Adj' he had said. The Adjutant had laughed. 'I'll be here in the morning to hand it back,' he had replied. But when morning came, the Adjutant was there and King was not. Over Tobruk his Wellington had run into heavy and accurate flak. The port engine was hit and stopped. The pilot made several desperate attempts to feather the propeller, but in vain. The blades wind-milled around creating a terrific drag which the remaining engine found it difficult to counteract. There was nothing left but to turn for home and hope.

For a while it looked as if the good engine might win. But then, slowly but surely, drag and gravity overcame lift and thrust and the Wellington crept lower and lower. There was now nothing for it but a forced landing in the inhospitable desert. Three hundred miles from Alamein, the Wellington crash-landed in a smother of flying sand, and King and the other five crew members found themselves, luckily unhurt, in the middle of nowhere. They did not know it, but they were also on the threshold of a series of adventures which were to last many a long and painful day. Their morale was high, but at that time they did not know how reluctant the desert could be to give up its victims. It was not long before the aircrew had hit upon a plan. Their only chance, they decided, would be to sight a solitary German or Italian vehicle. One member would pretend to be a bailed-out German while the other five, revolvers at the ready, would hide and then kidnap the enemy.

For a day and a night they waited and saw nothing. Then King and one other set out to try to find a water-hole. On their return to the wrecked Wellington they were shocked to find that their comrades had disappeared. Had they been captured or rescued? There was then no answer to these questions. As King and his friend stood wondering, they heard the sound of a car engine. Across the sand a German Volkswagen was approaching the wreck. Quickly the two men crept into the Wimpy's tail and hid, until they heard, with amazed delight, the voices of their crew. Rushing out they saw the incredible sight of a German officer and two soldiers under orders from the four RAF aircrew. The four had managed to carry out 'Operation Hitch-Hike' without assistance from King and his comrade.

Deciding that the Germans would only be an encumbrance to them on their journeyings, the RAF left them sitting in the shade of the Wimpy, after having removed their boots and drove off with their newly acquired and well-laden Volkswagen, towards Allied lines. Fortune seemed to have smiled on them. But there remained one very knotty problem. They were, at the moment, well behind enemy lines. They ran little danger while in that area, but to get to their own lines they would have to cross the front, or outflank the enemy forces. They decided to drive until they were within walking distance of Alamein and then ditch the car and infiltrate through some thinly patrolled part of the German lines on foot. Full of confidence they drove on. Even the discovery, at one point, that they were crossing a minefield, did not dampen their spirits.

Soon they spotted an Arab encampment. Deciding that help from experienced desert navigators would be valuable, they drove over to them. As they drew near they noticed that not one of the men had a left hand; only a stump! One of the crew recalled the Arab custom of lopping off the left hand of a murderer or robber. These were not the best types to help them, they decided, and by-passed the sinister group of Arabs. As they drove on through the heat and the dust, the light began playing its usual tricks. Time and again there would be a joyous shout of 'Civilisation!' Only to be followed by disappointment as the blur on the horizon proved to be a mirage. Only once did the cry prove correct. And then they discovered that they were approaching the Luftwaffe airfield near Mersa Matruh. The detour around this stumbling block took the Volkswagen over rough ground and the tyres gave out. More delay as outer covers were stuffed with parachutes to replace the air which the inner tubes would not hold.

The small party pressed on. The Volkswagen had carried them 280 miles through enemy territory when the front springs broke. This was followed almost immediately by a sickening lurch as the rear axle snapped in two. The Wellington crew reckoned that they were, by this time, some twenty miles from Alamein and that twenty miles they would have to walk. They still had some food, their water-bottles and John King's trusty compass. Every few miles they had to stop, take off their cumbersome flying boots, shake out the sand and start again. Then they saw the German troops and minefield signs and knew they were within reach of the Allies; if only they could negotiate the last hurdle of the German front line. They decided to bluff; no German would believe that Allied men would be in their lines, so they waited until night and then marched boldly through the lines of tents.

But they were caught. It was a terrible blow and after a few hours driving they were placed in a PoW cage along with twenty soldiers. Italian guards gave them tins of meat but refused them water. Fortunately for the airmen an Army officer distributed the soldiers' water ration between all concerned, when the guards' backs were turned.

Next day the officer prisoners with an Army sergeant were bundled into a lorry with four Italian guards, bound for a permanent PoW camp. The RAF crew soon had the Army pair enthusiastic for an 'escape'; at dusk, when they had covered some 200 miles, the lorry was halted and two guards covered the prisoners with rifles whilst the other guards placed their rifles down and helped the lorry crew to prepare a petrol fire. The prisoners looked tired and dejected, so much so that one guard slung his rifle over his shoulder, and the other soon followed his example.

The Army sergeant edged closer to the guards, and as one put a cigarette into his mouth whilst offering another to his companion, the sergeant yelled 'NOW!' and grabbed at the shoulders of one guard. John King dived for the other as the Army officer threw himself on to the pile of guns. The other aircrew went for the drivers and the two unarmed guards, soon silencing them. In a few seconds they had turned the tables; not a shot had been fired and yet two of the Italians were moaning and all members of the enemy 'escort' were lying on the floor, terrified that they were about to be shot. The British decided to take the drivers and guards along with them and just as they were ordering one driver into the seat, two German vehicles appeared. Fortunately they took no notice of the mixed party.

That night they slept in the open, taking turns to watch the 'prisoners.' Next morning, with only half a can of water, one tin of meat and a small hunk of bread, the rations situation seemed desperate. The going was extremely hard and, again and again, the lorry bogged down and steam hissed from the radiator cap. No water could be spared for the vehicle until, on the second day, a derelict lorry provided rusty water for their lorry with a little to spare for the men.

On the third day the finding of a water-hole caused their flagging spirits to rise, until they saw that the hole was full of oil! Cheers died in their parched throats and they felt that this was probably their last day alive, now waterless and without food. King rode on top of the lorry, saying that if there was a water-hole he would see it first; in fact he produced more mirages than the others until, at last, he cried, 'Water ahead!' and, jumping down, he ran stumblingly over the burning desert. Believing they would find he'd gone crazy, the others approached warily, only to see that he was, indeed, lying beside a pool of milky liquid - water in a shallow saucer of desert. It was a miracle, as the water was ice-cold and must have percolated beneath the sands in some rock formation. The party bathed, filled their jerry cans and now felt certain of freedom, despite lack of any foodstuffs.

They were about ninety miles from the front lines again when the lorry packed up and, notwithstanding all their efforts to repair the engine, they failed to re-start it. Lying under the lorry they prepared for the inevitable slow death after the water petered out, but, in the distance, heard sounds of transport. Only too thankful to be prisoners again and receive food, they rushed out to give themselves up, only to find a British lorry of the Long Range Desert Group approaching. They were saved! Leaving the frightened Italians with what food they could spare, they drove off to the secret hideout of this desert patrol. After a few days of recuperation, the Desert Group contacted the HQ of the Special Air Services and an aircraft was sent to take them to safety.[127]

'War is not all danger and daring and decorations' recalled William Coote, a pilot on 70 Squadron. 'Fortunately, when large numbers of men are thrown together in the services there are always the wags, wits and practical jokers. On reflection, one tends to feel thankful for them since they contributed so much at times to making long, monotonous days bearable. One regular 'leg-pull' practised among aircrews flying on Nos. 70 and 37 Wellington Squadrons of 231 Wing, 205 Group in North Africa, was to suggest to new or replacement crews that they might like to freshen up with a shower after the long trip out from England. After deciding that a shower would be just what the doctor ordered, the unsuspecting pilot and crew were directed towards the far side of the airfield. Inquiries where the showers were brought the inevitable and serious response: 'You've been misinformed! The only showers hereabouts are where you've just come from!'

'As pranks were adapted to the situation and location so was 'lingo'. A rich air force vocabulary arose, far more varied than that within the home commands, due to the influx of personnel steeped in the language and expressions of many nations where they had previously trained or served.'

'In Italy and North Africa' adds John Heap 'we used a lot of Arabic and 'gypo' expressions in everyday conversation. As many service people had come out of India to the Middle East when things were bad, several Indian expressions were in use too. We had an exclusive squadron war-cry. It started off as something the Arab drivers used to shout to their horses on the streets of Cairo - 'Hod hod!' It became our catch-phrase. If you wanted someone to get a move on you'd say 'Hod, hod! you so-and-so.' We even used it in the air as identification. You'd hear people call up Control and just say 'Hod hod!' Control knew immediately it was a 70 Squadron aircraft.'

During the final advance of 1942-43 the Wellington squadrons moved to bases near Tripoli, remaining there until the end of the African Campaign. In the summer of 1943 the Wellingtons were grouped near Kairouan, Tunisia and were operated extensively by 330 Wing in support of the assaults on Sicily and Italy. During this phase they made a number of remarkably successful attacks on railway bridges in Italy, using 4,000lb delayed-action bombs dropped from very low level.

Living conditions in the desert wastes were always primitive but Harry Kidney, an armourer on 38 Squadron, who suddenly found he was in the front line, was, for once, thankful for the harsh desert elements:

'Circa March 1941, a small detachment on 38 Squadron was based at Gambut, a grim desolate place in the Libyan desert, once occupied by the Italian Air Force. I was one of the privileged few selected to be sent there. Gambut is approximately halfway between Tobruk and Bardia, inland from the sea, with the landing-ground sited on an escarpment with wadies running down from it. Our Wimpys were operating from here subsequent to the land forces' offensive which had come to a halt at El Agheila - some miles west of Benghazi. History shows Erwin Rommel appearing on the scene about this time and commencing to push our forces rapidly back towards Egypt. Orders came for the abandonment of Gambut and retirement eastwards to Sidi Assiz - a landing-ground near Bardia. Four armourers were instructed to remain behind after all other personnel departed to deal with armament stores. We were assured that transport would return later to collect us. It was with more than a little apprehension that we watched our colleagues depart in the early morning.

'We completed our assignment swiftly and returned to a derelict corrugated-iron shed located at the base of the escarpment in a wadi. This was a flea-ridden Italian relic. That day our transport failed to materialize and we knew the Afrika Korps was advancing rapidly; visions of Stalags loomed. Nightfall came and our imaginations ran riot as with every slight sound we expected massive blond Aryan types to burst into our shed firing their Mausers. Our thoughts were not entirely without substance as we learned later that enemy armour did traverse the landing-ground while we were hiding in the wadi. Two factors saved us: one was the element we hated and cursed most in the desert, the Khamsin, a scorching hot, soul-destroying sandstorm which blanketed everything out of sight within a few feet. Thus obscured, the Germans had not seen our shed in the wadi. The other factor was that Rommel chose to pursue his offensive deeper in the desert leaving the coastal area for the time being which enabled our belated lorry to reach us the next day, much to our relief. We set off at speed and reached Sidi Assiz, thankful for escape; but this relief was short-lived as enemy elements were reported approaching this vicinity.

'Once again we quickly boarded our lorry and went helter-skelter for the Egyptian border, reaching Fort Capuzzo extremely fatigued. Nightfall came so we decided to rest awhile but no; as soon as we were putting our groundsheets down, again it was panic stations when we learned the enemy was close on our tail. With alacrity we boarded our lorry and continued the fight eastwards, passing the border at Sollum, by which time it was dawn. Having reached a point somewhere near Sidi Barrani, exhausted, particularly the driver, we decided to rest whatever the consequences. Happily the Axis advance was halted at the Libya/Egypt border. So, after a few hours' rest we pressed on until reaching 38 Squadron's base at Shallufa, safe, thankful and in a bedraggled state, to learn that we had been listed 'missing'. Lady Luck had certainly been on our side.'

Many of the Wellingtons urgently required for bombing operations in the Middle East were flown out from England, staging through Gibraltar and Malta. The refuelling stop in Malta was fraught with danger as Joe Pugh a member of one of the crews ferrying a batch of Wellingtons out to the Middle East in 1941 recalls: 'At Gibraltar we were told that the trip to Malta was more dangerous than operations as the enemy usually knew when aircraft were going to land there and had fighters up from nearby Pantelleria to intercept. We took off in darkness and landed at Luqa airfield to learn that the Wellington that had left 'Gib' before us had been shot down. As we were carrying a Wing Commander and an Air Commodore we were given priority on refuelling and took off again after only a brief stay. Our destination in Egypt was reached without any problems, but we later learned that many of the other Wellingtons were bombed at Luqa and their crews spent the next two or three weeks filling bomb holes in the runway before they could get out of Malta.'

On 1 October 1941 Wally Gaul, now a Sergeant rear gunner in Sergeant Jim 'Cranky' Crank-Benson's crew, left 15 OTU at Harwell for the Middle East. Dave Clark was the second pilot, Jeff Jefferies the navigator, 'Brownie' Brown the WOp/AG and a Canadian, George Wetherhead, completed the crew as front gunner. Gaul recalls: 'The Met men predicted 10/10ths cloud over the sea. We were told, 'Keep away from Brest. If you have an engine failure, make for the white beaches of Portugal. You will see them even on the darkest night.' The CO added, 'Take off time is 0315. Crank-Benson will be the last of three aircraft to take off as his aircraft is faster. Good luck chaps and a safe landing.'

'We taxied to the perimeter track as the first Wellington was taking off. The second followed a few minutes later. We taxied onto the runway, a final engine test and waited for the green. Wireless transmission was out for obvious reasons. We got the green from the tower and it was 'OK chaps, here we go!' Engines roared to life and we began to move, slowly at first, along the flare path. There was a hell of a swing to port, a loud thud and several gooseneck flares were blown about by our slipstream. Jim was having a hell of a job getting the kite airborne. It crossed my mind that a Wellington had recently crashed and exploded at the end of the runway but with one more 'bump' we were airborne. My altimeter read 500 feet and still climbing.

'Jeff gave 'Cranky' a course to set for Redruth in Cornwall. We were flying at 4,000 feet and through the break in the clouds I could see a beacon on the Cornish coast flashing the letter of the day. 'Goodbye, England.' I thought of those at home in Norwich tucked up in their nice warm beds, so I opened my flask of coffee and had a sip of Johnnie Walker to keep out the cold.

'When we were over the Atlantic George reported, 'Flak on the port bow!'

'That's Brest,' said Jeff. We were flying at 9,000 feet now and the weather was improving. At last we were above the clouds and we could see the stars. Jeff took a fix and gave Jim a new course. The sky was gradually changing colour. Dawn was near.

'We landed at Gibraltar before taking off again, for Malta, on 8 October. The Briefing Officer told us to maintain radio silence: 'The Italians are red hot at three things: Singing, ice-cream and RADIO.' He also told us to keep low near the heavily defended island of Pantelleria, eighty miles south-west of Sicily and about fifty miles north of the east coast of Tunisia. At 0800 hours the weather report was good. It was warm with a cool breeze blowing from the sea. We taxied out and I could see Spaniards crowding around the closed gates waving to us as we turned to the end of the strip. Jim said, 'OK, everyone! Here we go.' The 1,700 horsepower Merlin engines roared into life. Gathering speed, I felt the tail rise. Jim said, 'Come on, old girl. Get up'. The sea was getting close. At the last moment the nose lifted and we were airborne. We were climbing steadily when Jim asked me if I could see the other kite. 'F for Freddie' is just behind', I said, 'and he's catching up.' We kept the coast of Spain in sight. I had a good view of the snow-covered peaks of the Sierra Nevada Mountains. As we turned away from the coast the white face of the Rock was jutting out from the blue sea. We set course for North Africa. Jeff said we should keep well out to sea off Bizerta because we would be fired at by Vichy French. 'F for Freddie' got too close and was lucky to get away with it. George spotted Pantelleria and we descended. We were so low our props made whitecaps on the sea. It was like sitting in the back of a speedboat in my rear turret. We got through undetected but ran into some really bad weather. 'F for Freddie' was bashing out with the Aldis lamp asking our position before we entered 10/10ths cloud and lost him. Jim tried to climb above the storm but it seemed to go to 25,000 feet. He said, 'I'm going down'. We descended at a fair rate and as we pulled out at 500 feet, George yelled out, 'Weave, Jim. We're on top of a convoy!

Jesus, that was close!' We were lucky. It was nearly always fatal to fly above our own ships as they would fire first and ask questions afterwards. Jim did a tight turn and climbed back into the clouds.

'Brownie picked up Malta asking for our position. Jeff gave it to Brownie, who transmitted it. Soon Malta was in sight. As we turned on finals I had a good view of the Grand Harbour at Valletta and the cities of Singlea, Cospicua and Vittoriosa and the airfield at Luqa. Black tarmac roads stood out in contrast to the white rock of the island. Jim made his usual good landing and we taxied to the dispersal. Eight hours had passed since we had left Gib. Even though it was late afternoon the temperature was well up into the high seventies. We asked if 'F for Freddie' had made it. There was no sign. I thought of Mac, their rear gunner, who was rather old at 31 and of Mansell, the pilot, a dry stick; and the rest of the crew. We had trained together and had had several good 'booze ups' in the 'Jockey' pub near Harwell. 'Well, that's how it goes,' we thought. As we were about to board the coach a Corporal from the radio room shouted, 'F for Freddie' has just sent out his 'indent' and is fifteen minutes from base'. We prayed that he had enough fuel to get in. Then we saw the Wimpy in the distance. Mansell made an emergency landing. He only just made it for, as they were taxiing to the dispersal, both engines cut, out of fuel.'

On Friday, 10 October, Crank-Benson's crew finally set off for Egypt. Wally Gaul continues: 'Midnight came and out we went to the aircraft for final checks. The engines roared to life and we started to taxi along Saffi Strip to the peri track to wait for the green. I saw black clouds, lit up by a large flash of lightning which went right down to the sea. I had never seen anything like this before. The Met boys had said it was harmless! It was all right for them. They didn't have to fly through it! We taxied out to the end of the flare path. One more check on the engines and we got the green. I felt the tail lift and after a couple of slight bumps we were airborne. Soon the flare path was out of sight and we were in the 'harmless' electrical storm. Jim and Dave had a hell of a job controlling the aircraft. We were tossed about like a feather in the breeze; down 500 feet and then up 500 feet. Jim tried first to get below it and then above it but the storm reached from sea level to 25,000 feet; a height we didn't have a cat in hell's chance of reaching. The escape hatch was blown off. Most of the instruments were U/S; it was cold and nobody spoke. The only sound was the hum of the two Merlin engines. I prayed we wouldn't lose those, like the hatch.

'After an hour we finally got into fine weather again. Jim asked for a flask of coffee up front but when I looked in the rear of the kite I saw that they had all been broken. The sun was beginning to creep over the horizon. George Weatherhead reported the coast coming up and as we turned east I had my first view of the desert. It was not as I had expected. No soft sand and swaying palm trees; just barren, rocky sand. Jim followed the railway line to El Daba where we were to drop a passenger. A lorry met us. 'Where's this place?' we asked the driver. 'Ninety miles from Alexandria and 185 miles from Cairo. Why, are you lost?' Jim took off in a cloud of dust and said he would 'shoot up' the comic of a lorry driver. Jim buzzed the strip at zero height and if this didn't put the fear of Christ up him, it did me. Soon we were flying over the Nile Delta. Children looked up to us and waved. They were not used to Wellington bombers flying low over the Delta. 1

could see Cairo on the starboard side. Jim flew on to El Fayum, our final destination. The airfield was chock full with every type of aircraft imaginable awaiting transfer to squadrons. We landed, took out our gear and waited to be picked up. A breeze got up and within seconds it was blowing gale force. It was like thousands of needles cutting into the exposed parts of the body. We hurried back into the Wellington. When the sandstorm finished our gear was buried under a load of sand.' Early in the morning of Monday, 13 October, the crew entrained for Shallufa. Wally Gaul continues:

'We reported to the Middle East Pool where aircrew waited for a posting to a squadron. A lorry took us to RAF Shallufa which was HQ 205 Group. In September 1941, 257 Wing in the Egyptian Canal Zone had been re-designated 205 Group. Nos 37 and 38 Squadrons were based here while 108 Squadron was based at El Fayid. Nos 70 and 148 Squadrons, both flying Wellingtons, were based at Kabrit. We spent the next few days learning about conditions in the desert at the Ground Training Unit. Flight Lieutenant Stanley, who had completed a number of ops, replaced Jim and we made a flight up to the 'blue', as the desert was known. We landed at El Daba ALG (Advanced Landing Ground) 104 and ALG 106 Fuka Satellite. The flight lasted almost five hours and we slept in the aircraft at night. On the return we landed at a couple more ALGs before returning to Shallufa. This trip was a real eye-opener for things to come and good experience for us. On Thursday, 23 October, we were posted to 148 Squadron at Kabrit. Kabrit was a permanent station with tarmac runways, sand-coloured hangars and buildings. Wellingtons were dispersed around the 'drome. 148 were a 'mobile' squadron and our living quarters were tents on the shore of the Suez Canal, near the Great Bitter Lake.'

By now, old hands like Canadian Sergeant Steve Challen, a veteran air gunner on 108 Squadron were used to flying regular raids on Libyan ports used by Axis shipping to supply their forces. They had also grown accustomed to the flak defences which were regarded by many as worse than at many German cities. Challen, who along with the rest of the crew answered the call for volunteers for the Middle East, recalls: 'On 24 September we were briefed for the 'milk run', Benghazi. Flight Lieutenant K. F. Vare a New Zealander, was rather keen to make a good show of our first op in the Middle East so we stooged straight over the town. Our target was supply ships against the harbour moles and quays. There had been a few before us so all kinds of flak was coming up, the lights making it difficult as usual to pinpoint anything. Around again. Vare decided to alter height and approach from a different direction in a shallow dive, hoping the increased speed would baffle predictors. No chance! The lights clamped on us, the multi-coloured flak seemed draped around us. I had fired some short bursts on the first run, knowing there wasn't much chance of putting out those lights, but perhaps the bits of spent lead raining down might possibly disrupt their accuracy. This time round even lower, I fired longer, calculated squirts until my port gun jammed. The .303 calibre ammo we were using was First World War vintage. Again 'No bombs gone'. I stripped my Browning to find out what the stoppage was, putting the parts with names like 'rear seat retainer keeper and pin' (who thought that name up?) on the ledge where the sides and dome of the turret joined. Third time around lower and slower from a different direction which must have been right for the aiming-point because the chant began: 'right, right, left a little, steady, steady, bombs gone'.

'The same instant there was a bang, a rattle against the turret and a burnt smell. I put out my hand to feel for the breech-block bits, but felt only breeze. Then a sensation in my throat; I wanted to cough but couldn't. Putting my hand-to my throat it was warm, sticky and wet. Switching on my mike I tried to report that I had been hit, but could tell there wasn't much noise coming out of me. Sergeant Gord Murray the Canadian 2nd pilot said 'Okay, Steve. Coming back'. We were out over the Med by now, in no danger from that 'hot spot'. The turret wouldn't move with the hydraulics so I engaged the hand gear, which needed two hands to wind the handle to centralize the turret so that I could open the doors and climb out. There was quite a breeze and light shining in on the port side where fabric had been stripped off. The hydraulic pipes supplying the turret had been punctured and oil sprayed everywhere, no mistaking the smell. I thought that maybe the rudder or elevator controls might be damaged, but was unable to see as I continued along the catwalk until meeting Gord on his way back. I sat on the fold-down cot while Gord shone his torch on my damage. Not much to be done other than place a field dressing over the wound holding it in place with my hand as I lay on the cot. 'Chuck' [Charles Ingram, a Londoner] came back for a look as did 'Gibbo' [Harry Gibbons, from Wales]. Paul Morey the navigator/bomb aimer and Vare were busy up front as the controls were not quite right.

'With dawn coming it was light enough for me to write some questions in a little diary, like: 'How big is the hole in my bloody neck?' and 'Where are you dropping me?' Wireless inquiry to base had advised landing at Fuka Main where an ambulance would be waiting. A soft touch-down at 7am. I crawled out of the mid under hatch where at one time in the design there was to have been a 'dustbin' turret. While people became a little impatient I produced my little camera and insisted the occasion be recorded as I stood near the damage for snaps to be taken. Taken to 21st Medical Receiving Centre, a tented hospital in the desert, I was operated upon at about 10am by Squadron Leader Wallace, assisted by his medical orderlies. He removed a piece of flak from my larynx. Unbeknown to him and me, there were bits embedded in my scalp which some time later were raked out as I combed my hair.'

On 25 October Wally Gaul flew his first operation.

'Dave Clark flew as second pilot while an experienced pilot took Jim Crank-Benson's seat. The target was Benghazi, the main port used by Jerry for supplying the Afrika Korps. We took off at 1500 hours for a two-hour flight to one of the ALGs in the desert. We were all keyed up when, after 45 minutes' flying, one engine packed up. We had to return to base. 'Four days later Dave and Jeff were allocated to other crews. The rest of us complained to the flight commander, but to no avail. (This move decided the lives of four of the original crew and the death of two of them.) Pilot Officer Owen took over as first pilot and Flying Officer Church, a Canadian, became the crew's Navigator. Crank-Benson was relegated to second pilot.'

'On Thursday, 6 November, we were lazing around outside the ops room waiting for the gen when the flight commander yelled for a volunteer to air test 'H for Harry'. Mackenzie, a pilot, said he would go. They wanted one more for the rear turret. I said, 'Sorry 'Mac', I haven't got my helmet'. (Gaul had also left his 'lucky' white and green spotted silk scarf and his mascots behind. Like almost all airmen, he was very superstitious and never ever flew without it.) One of the ground crew volunteered. We watched 'Mac' put 'H-for-Harry' through the test. Suddenly, he lost an engine (the Wimpy could fly on one engine safely). For some reason he turned into the 'duff' engine ('Mac' was an experienced pilot who had completed a tour of ops and was waiting for the boat home to 'Blighty'). He lost control and nose-dived into the edge of the Great Bitter Lake. There was just one big explosion followed by a cloud of black smoke. We all ran to the crash but we knew there was nothing we could do.

'On 12 November I flew my eighth operation, to Benghazi. Dave Clark was not 'on', not having crewed up yet. Jeff was on with his new crew. This was his second. As usual we flew up to the ALG and after we had refuelled, took off again for Benghazi. We bombed the target and were the first aircraft to land. This meant we had the pick of the 'grub'. The first few crews always got canned skinless sausages that were very tasty. The last to land got 'bully beef'. Soon, all the aircraft, except for one, had landed back at the ALG. We were used to this. It happened on every operation. We finished our meal and were about to turn in for the rest of the night (we slept in the kite at the ALG) when 'Brownie', running towards us, said, 'Jeff's crew is overdue'. Sleep was impossible. 'We were told much later that the missing aircraft had been shot down over the target and several crews reported that no parachutes were seen. We were used to losing crews, all of them our mates, but when Jeff went it was different. We had lived, trained and drank together. I could see his mum and dad when the telegram arrived at his home; the same home I had stayed in for one weekend during training.'

On the night of Monday, 17 November the Wellingtons struck at Derna. Wally Gaul's crew did not fly because their aircraft was having an engine change. On stand-down days Sergeant-aircrew were assigned other duties and Gaul was put in charge of some Italian PoWs. At 1630 hours the prisoners were transported back to their PoW camp. On the way back to Kabrit, Wally Gaul asked the driver if 148 Squadron 'had lost any kites last night?' The driver indicated that they had lost two, including one pilot who was a Flight Lieutenant with a DFC. Gaul was startled. 'We only had one pilot with the DFC and that was Dave Clark's pilot!'

'As soon as I got back I hurried over to our tent. The rest of the crew were there. As I entered, 'Brownie' said, 'Dave's gone. Some clot dropped a 4.5-inch flare above them as they were on a low-level bombing run. They were a sitting duck for the Jerry ack-ack. Several crews saw it happen. They had no chance of getting out or to drop their bombs. The kite exploded as it hit the deck.' Jeff's bed had been taken out and all of Dave's belongings were packed on his bed. Two of the original crew had not gone. Two nights later the target was Derna; the place where Dave and his crew were shot down. After the briefing we took off for ALG 104; an hour's flying time from base. As usual the first thing was a meal, then time to refuel and wait for take-off. Soon we were airborne and heading for Derna where we were to bomb the airfield. When we reached the target it was fairly quiet. The ack-ack was light, so it looked like this was going to be 'a piece of cake'. Our skipper knew what we wanted. He said he would go in at low level and told Ron, the navigator, to drop a single stick of bombs on each run in. We made half a dozen runs over the target and when the last bomb had been released, the Skipper gave us the OK to machine-gun what was left of the airfield. With George in the front turret, 'Brownie' on the beam guns and me in the rear turret, we let them have it. Above the noise of six Browning guns I could hear 'Brownie' on the intercom shouting out, 'You bastards. Take that you bastards! Go round again, Skipper; one more for Dave.' As we left the target there were six very hot Browning guns! We saw two Bf 109 fighters turning to attack us. As we turned violently to port I lost sight of them. I could hear George firing from the front and then I saw tracers going away from us.

'Two nights later, on Friday, 21 November, we waited at ALG 104 for the midnight take-off time. We went over to the aircraft for a few hours' kip. All the aircraft were parked in line. Our kite was not. We were in position near the flare path as we were to be first away. I was standing in the Second Pilot's position when I noticed flak in the El Daba area. Jerry was having a 'go'. We could hear bombs bursting. An aircraft flew low and headed toward us. He started to machine-gun from some distance away. We were out of our kite and heading for the underground air raid shelter. George was running in front of me and even though we were under attack, I had to smile as both his desert boots 'took off'. Not stopping to pick them up George dived into a slit trench with me right behind. Jerry had made his first run machine-gunning the aircraft that were in line, missing ours. On his next run he dropped a stick of bombs. Fires were started and the fire tender could not cope with so many kites burning. One aircraft was well alight. First the petrol tanks, then the bombs exploded, setting fire to Wimpys on the either side. Our Skipper was soon in the aircraft to taxi out of the area. Other kites were being towed to a safe distance. Two aircraft had been destroyed and six badly damaged. The remainder were slightly damaged but were un-flyable. One man was killed by machine-gun fire and another broke his neck when he jumped head-first into a slit trench. Several others were injured by shrapnel. Jerry had made a good job of it. November was an unlucky month for our squadron. We lost more aircraft and crews than any other month. I wondered how long my luck would last.

'On 18 December there was yet another change to the crew. Pilot Officer Owens was replaced by Flight Lieutenant (later Squadron Leader) The Honourable R. A. G. Baird. 'Brownie' was replaced by Flight Sergeant 'Drag' Parkin DFM. Jim was still our second pilot. George had a road accident and was not replaced on the crew. This meant we could carry an extra bomb if we did not have a front-gunner.

'On 26 February the early morning sun was creeping over the horizon. As I dressed I wondered what was on today? After breakfast we reported to Ops and waited for the 'gen'. A voice from the Ops room said, 'Ops on tonight, briefing at 12 o'clock. The target tonight is Benghazi.' The 'mail run' as it was called, was warming up its defences. 'Navigators have a slightly different course for the run in and you may find that Jerry has brought in extra ack-ack.' The Met officer added, 'Right, chaps. The weather should be clear over the target ...' (cheers and laughter from the crews - we had heard it all before). 'As I was saying, the target should be clear. You may run into 10/10ths cloud on the way.' The CO added, 'Well, chaps, I hope you all have a good trip. The best of luck' (cries of 'we need it') 'and hope to see you all safely back tomorrow.'

'Briefing over, I collected two Browning .303s from the armoury and took them out to the kite where I harmonised them with the gun sight. The armourers were

Wellington IIIs at 30 OTU Hixon, Staffs on 11 September 1943. (IWM)

In June 1943 Leconfield in Yorkshire was home to two 4 Group squadrons: 196 and 466 RAAF both equipped with the Wellington X. *YOUNG/ERS* receives some attention to its engines. The aircraft's name was chosen by its pilot, Pilot Officer R. Young and navigator, Sergeant R. Young! Foaming tankards replace the more usual bomb symbols to indicate 14 successfully completed operations. (IWM)

419 Squadron crew in the snow at Mildenhall on 9 February 1942. Left to right: Squadron Leader F. W. S. Turner; Pilot Officer Kenneth Edward Hobson; Flight Sergeants G. P. Fowler, C. A. Robson and Neil Greg Arthur RCAF; Sergeant Harley James Dell RCAF. A month later Pilot Officer Hobson was piloting Wellington III X347 on 419 Squadron when he and another member of their crew died of their wounds on the 28/29 March raid on Lübeck. After completing his tour with this crew, Arthur and Dell volunteered for one more op with the CO, Wing Commander 'Moose' Fulton DSO DFC AFC RCAF and were KIA with his CO on Hamburg on the night of 28/29 July 1942.

PR.XIII *Ritchie's Wonder* on 69 Squadron, 2nd TAF at Melsbroek, Belgium in October 1944. (RAF Museum)

Wellingtons on 300 (Masovian) Squadron at Hemswell, 17 June 1943. (IWM)

Wellington Ic T2996 PM-C *Sierra-Leone II* on 103 Squadron which crashed at Zwaagdijk Wervershoof on 12/13 June 1941. New Zealander, Flying Officer Robert Stanley Chisholm and his crew were all killed.

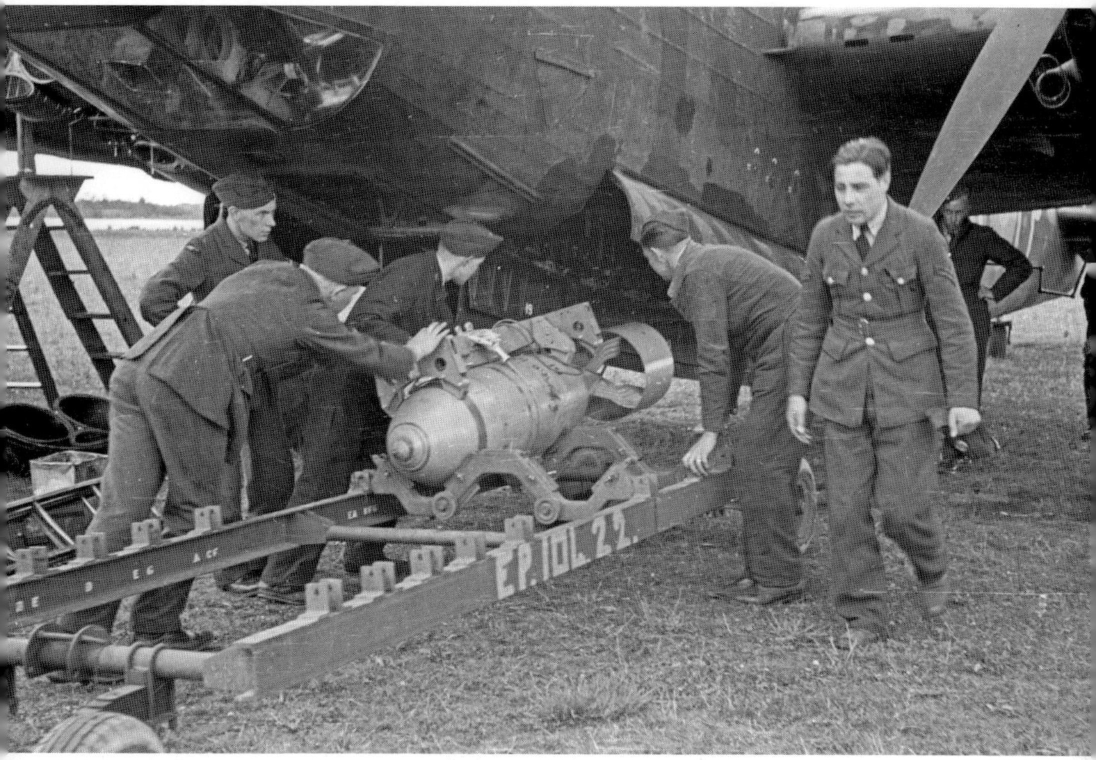

Armourers on 104 Squadron at Driffield loading up the bomb bay of a Wimpy with 500 pounders.

Wellington X HF598 on 300 'Masovian' Squadron which crashed at Hackthorn, Lincolnshire on an air test on the morning of 19 December 1943. Flying officer Jan Andzej Ochedzan and Sergeant Feliks Antoni Bluj were killed.

Wellington on 149 East India Squadron at Mildenhall.

A Polish crew in front of Wellington II Z8343 of 305 Squadron. Note the bomb log painted above the fin flash. (RAF Museum)

Wellington III X3763 KW-E of 425 'Alouette' Squadron RCAF which FTR with Flying Officer Joseph Alexander Theodore Doucette DFC RCAF and his crew (all KIA) from the raid on Stuttgart on 14/15 April 1943. Leutnant Franz Draude of 4./NJG4 shot X3763 down at 0146 hours and it crashed at Mussey-Sur-Marne (Haute-Marne) on the west bank of the Marne 8km S of Joinville. (IWM)

An Australian crew on 466 Squadron RAAF who completed their tour on 30/31 August 1943, the penultimate operation before the squadron was stood down to convert from Wellingtons to Halifaxes. Wellington HE984 *Snifter* has its insignia of Hitler, Mussolini, Goring and Goebbels confronted by a canine puddle. Nose armament had been discarded at this stage in the war and the turret sealed. (IWM)

Wellington B.III PH-B W5358 on 12 Squadron, which crashed at Binbrook on 25 July 1941 was repaired and served later on 158 Squadron at Driffield as 'T-Tommy', being lost on the night of 12/13 April 1942 when it crashed near Cologne on the operation to Essen. Pilot Officer P. D. McMillan RNZAF and crew were taken prisoner. (IWM)

Wellington II Z8345 EP-S on 104 Squadron in flight.

Sergeant Wally Gaul.

Sergeant pilot Henry Fawcett.

Lining up the two-torpedo load for a ship-hunter Wellington in the Middle East. (IWM)

DWI (Directional Wireless Installation) Wellington on 1 GRU in Egypt in 1944. (IWM)

On 19 April 1943 Group Captain John Alexander 'Speedy' Powell DSO OBE, the Wing Commander briefing officer to Pilot Officer Percy 'Pick' Pickard, in the wartime film of *Target for Tonight*, arrived from England to co-ordinate 142 and 150 Squadrons' efforts. He had earned his nickname because of his obsession to get to grips with a problem as quickly as possible and soon after his arrival at Blida, area bombing was replaced by precision bombing. The squadrons were uprooted from relative luxury and moved to Fontaine Chaude, 15 miles from Batna to take up station as part of 330 Wing. Fontaine Chaude was closer to the enemy, but very far out in 'the bundoo'. His briefing stance became his trademark. Arms akimbo, he would use his famous flyswatter as a 'swagger stick' and pointer at the same time. After leaving 330 Wing, 'Speedy' Powell went to HQ 15th Air Force where he became the RAF Liaison Officer. He and General Jimmy Doolittle developed a strong mutual admiration and respect for each other. Doolittle allowed 'Speedy' to go on a B-24 daylight raid. After bombing the target the Liberator was crippled by a direct flak hit which damaged the tail and part of the

wing and knocked out two engines as well as killing the pilot and navigator and seriously wounding the co-pilot. Powell lifted the pilot out of his seat and flew the bomber towards North Africa. He was able to gain some altitude before the third engine packed up and then, the last engine gave up the ghost. 'Speedy' glided the stricken plane onto a beach, pulled the wounded co-pilot out of the cockpit and then went off in search of help. An American DFC arrived two days after 'Speedy' had failed to return on 8 August 1944 - some say flying a P-38 and others, his personal Hurricane IIc over Yugoslavia.

Wellington XIIIs in Egypt in 1942. The nearest aircraft is MP707. (IWM)

On 22 February 1943 Major General James H. Doolittle, newly commander the North West African Strategic Air Force flew with Flying Officer Roberts and the crew of Wellington 'A-Apple' on 150 Squadron at Blida on a raid on the docks at Bizerte by night. The General was able to witness a well executed attack, with the majority of bombs going down in the space of two minutes. The goods station was hit and oil tanks were left burning. The fire could be seen for up to fifty miles away. The art work is of J P Reilly Foul, a British newspaper cartoon character. (IWM)

Budapest under attack during the raid on the night of 3/4 April 1944. (via Nigel McTeer)

Below left: Sergeant Anthony P. McTeer, rear gunner on Sergeant Gordon G. Pemberton's crew on 150 Squadron. (Nigel McTeer) Below right: Oberleutnant Hans Krause of 6./NJG101 who shot down Wellington LN858 on 150 Squadron in 205 Group, flown by Sergeant Gordon G. Pemberton, during the raid on Budapest on 3/4 April 1944 and crashed in Lake Balaton. (Nigel McTeer)

Sergeant Gordon G. Pemberton, pilot; Flight Sergeant Harry C. Redpath RAAF, WOp/AG; Sergeant W. R. Bennett, air bomber; Sergeant Anthony P. McTeer, rear gunner who were shot down on the night of 3/4 April 1944 on Wellington LN858 on 150 Squadron. (Nigel McTeer).

Watery grave for LN858 which was shot down during the raid on Budapest and crashed into Lake Balaton (or the 'Plattensee', as the Germans called it) the largest lake in Continental Europe. (George Puuka via Hans-Heiri Stapfer).

The Backbone of the RCAF Bully Beef on 424 'Tiger' Squadron RCAF at Kairouan-Zina in July 1943. (Harold Hamnett)

Wellington 'W' *Madame X* and Pilot Officer Walker RNZAF's crew on 150 Squadron on 20 August 1944 just prior to the crew's final op on their first tour, to the AFV Works at St. Valentin, France. Left to right: Ives, R-AG; Flying Officer Hindle, navigator; Pilot Officer Walker RNZAF, skipper; Flight Sergeant Les Hallam, air bomber; Sergeant Henderson, WOp. (Les Hallam)

Wellington VIII, a victim of unwelcome attention by the Luftwaffe during a bombing raid on Malta. (RAF Museum)

Wellington II of 104 Squadron under attack on Malta. (RAF Museum)

Squadron Leader Jones and Sergeant Dichiel of 99 'Madras Presidency' Squadron at Digri, India in 1942. (IWM)

Wellington with a Bengal tiger on the nose in India in about 1944. (IWM)

loading belts of ammo into the cans. Soon, everything was ready. The aircraft was towed to the end of the runway. (The Merlin was a good engine but was prone to over-heating and several crews had failed to get airborne when the engines were running before take-off.)

'The engines started and we took off without any checks. Apart from myself and the two pilots the crew were in the 'rest positions' on two suspended beds (this was the norm for all take-offs and landings). The inside of the Wellington was like an oven. I was stripped down to my shorts, flying boots and helmet. I had to keep my arms well away from the metal parts of the turret; otherwise it would burn my skin.

'Just as we were climbing it started to cool off. We opened windows and hatches to let in a nice cool breeze. A few hours later we would have to dress in flying clothing as it got very cold out in the desert at night. On the way up to the ALG the pilot went aft to ride in the rear turret. It amused him to operate the controls and to test the guns. When it was my turn to fly the aircraft I told him to stop buggering about as it upset my flying! (After all, I was the Sergeant Skipper and he was only the Squadron Leader rear gunner!) All through this the second pilot was in his seat ready to take over in an emergency. This was unlikely as we were out of range of enemy fighters.

'After one and a half hour's flying it was back to our normal positions for the landing at the ALG. Then there was the usual mad rush to the beer tent followed by a walk to the Mess tent for a meal. Take-off time was still a few hours away so we kipped in the aircraft until we were awakened by the Skipper. 'Fingers out, chaps; take-off in half an hour.' We changed into our flying clothes and Mae Wests by the light from the downward ident lamp. One last drag on the cigarette, then it was all aboard for another visit to 'Ben'. 'M for Mother' was the first to take off. We were carrying extra 4-5 flares as we had to light the target for the following kites. The flight commander always got the 'sticky' jobs and as we turned on to the target all hell let loose. It seemed that there were more searchlights and flak than ever. 'Drag' dropped a couple of flares. (It was the Wireless Operator's job to push the flares out through the flare chute.) 'Flares gone,' he yelled. I watched the flares slowly drifting down, lighting up the target like day. Ships in the harbour were belting away at us. We were getting the lot and we still had to make another run to drop the bombs.

'Now the main stream was going in. Each aircraft aimed at their given target. As we turned I saw one of the kites coned in the searchlights. It looked like a silver fish as he weaved to evade the lights. All the guns below were having a go at him. Then there was one big explosion. Burning pieces of aircraft began to drift slowly earthwards. 'Bloody hell!' I thought. 'Yet another kite and six boys lost.'

'We started the bombing run. 'Steady...left...steady...hold it...steady. BOMBS GONE!' After a straight and level run lasting several minutes we started to weave and dive. A searchlight held us for a few seconds. I was blinded by the light. Someone shouted over the intercom, 'They've got us! Get to hell out of here.' The Skipper quietly and calmly said, 'OK chaps, we're going round again...' This time we dropped the remaining bombs and then got the hell out of it. As we left the target it was well alight. Ron said we had scored a direct hit on one of the ships on the last run in. Well, the camera would confirm it when we got back. After a beer and a meal I forgot about Benghazi and was soon dreaming about the boat home. 31 ops - time to come off. How much longer was my luck going to hold out? I had another go at the Flight Commander about coming off. He said, 'We have a big job coming off and I know you won't want to miss it.'

'On 14 April the squadron changed from Merlin-engined Wimpys to Pegasus radial-engined Wellingtons. Next day we flew an altitude test with a full bomb load to see how high the Wimpy could fly with Pegasus engines. We climbed to 15,000 feet in just over half an hour. Next day we were at it again. We reached 15,000 feet but could not get above it. This was the highest I had flown in the desert. Our normal height was about 10,000 feet. Two days later we were told what the 'big job' was. Air Vice Marshal Hugh Pughe Lloyd AOC Malta had ordered eight Wellington bombers to Malta. I was picked as the rear gunner in the Wing Commander's crew. Each aircraft would also carry a spare crew.

'On Monday, 20 April, we took off from Kabrit for ALG 106. Eight Wimpys, sixteen crews, 96 aircrew and a few ground crews. We flew in formation as there had been an increase in enemy fighter activity in the area. A sandstorm was blowing at the ALG and made landing difficult. We stalled and hit the deck with one almighty crash. Although the aircraft was 'bent up' a bit, there were no injuries. We took off again at 2000 hours and after an uneventful flight, lasting six hours twenty minutes, we were on the circuit at Luqa. We were billeted at the Palace in Naxxar and told to stay out of sight when the raids were on. I woke up next morning to the sound of air raid sirens. No one bothered to get up. Then we heard the guns opening up. Although the bombs were some distance away, the palace began to shake. There were slit trenches at the rear of the building so we made a dive for them. Naxxar is on high ground so we had a good view of the bombing. The month of April 1942 will be remembered by the people of Malta. This was the month His Majesty the King awarded them the George Cross.

'On 22 April ops were on. We were taken out to the aircraft to get ready for the 'big one'. At last we were going to get our revenge on Jerry. Our aircraft had survived the first raid of the day. I was busy in the turret when the yellow flare went up from Luqa. Soon the sirens were wailing and I could see the first wave heading for the island. Our kite was in a sandbagged enclosure. As I wondered whether to run for the slit trench, the first bombs were falling on the airfield at Takali five miles away. Hal Far airfield was only two miles away. A lorry arrived and I was whisked away to Luqa. We made a dash to the underground shelter. The next wave was bombing the airfield at Luqa and Saffi Strip. On the way to the airfield another raid, on Luqa had started. We had to scatter. Our kite was OK but the runway had to be repaired. We had lost quite a lot of kites in the bombing and the ferry crews bound for Egypt were diverted to Malta so that our squadron could take them on ops that night. (Most of the new kites were bombed the next day and the same thing would happen again.) A lorry took us out to our kite. A final check by the ground crew for any shrapnel damage. Everything seemed OK. The engines were started and we taxied along Saffi Strip to wait for the green. Crank-Benson, who was flying on ops for the first time as captain, made a final check on the engines. We got the green and at last we were on our way. Sicily is only sixty miles from Malta and the target, the airfield at Comiso, was about the same distance inland. As we crossed the coast we were greeted with heavy flak.

We were flying at 8,000 feet so most of the 'stuff' was bursting above us. We ran into several of these heavy ack-ack sites on the way to the target and I could see other aircraft bombing airfields.

'Searchlights probed the sky. Flares drifted down to light up the target. Light flak spiralled up and bombs exploded on the airfield. The last of the aircraft in front of us had completed their bombing. Jim elected to go in over the mountains and make a low-level run over the target. The searchlights began to fade and the flak stopped. We had the target to ourselves. Jim said, 'Going in now. Here we go.' Over the mountain, a steep dive and we were running up to the airfield. Then the defences came to life again. The navigator was having a hell of a job seeing the target. Then, 'Hold it steady, Jim. I can see the target now. Steady... bombs gone!' Ack-ack guns on the side of the mountain were having a go at us. I fired my guns in that direction but I knew it was useless. It took my mind off things down below. Our bombs were forty-pounders with a 'mushroom' on the nose so that they scattered shrapnel across the airfield on impact. We left quite a few aircraft burning. I could still see the fires from several miles away. We ran into more flak but this was nothing compared to the target area. As we crossed the coast a hell of an explosion tossed the kite on its side. I told Jim there was a bloody great hole in the port side. Jim went back to take a look. He exclaimed, 'Jesus Bloody Christ!' Was he praying? I don't think so.

'Soon the beacon at Malta was in sight. We landed and began the long taxi to the dispersal at Saffi Strip. As usual I was the first to light up. Never had I enjoyed a fag so much before. A ground staff bod saw the damage and asked Jim, 'How the hell did you get home?' 'I didn't,' said Jim. 'The flak blew us back!' Our aircraft was U/S; two were shot down over the target; one was shot up and damaged. Total aircraft at daybreak ... four!

'On 24 April Malta suffered a very heavy raid and our kite was hit. Two more kites were missing from the previous night's raid. The squadron was in a bad way. On 25 April we were told we were returning to Egypt. I was not sorry to hear this. I had completed 34 ops and the 'old ring was beginning to twitter'.

'At 1700 hours on Sunday, 27 April we left the Palace at Naxxar dressed in full flying kit to the cheers of the locals in the square. The Maltese Times gave us a big write-up about our bombing of enemy airfields in Sicily. This had raised morale no end. After briefing we had to wait for aircraft to arrive from Gibraltar. Soon, our kite arrived. It was refuelled and the gear stowed inside. The ferry crews, who would be shipped back to Blighty by sea later, were not pleased to lose their aircraft. We touched down at Kabrit at 0830 hours. As we left the aircraft we were greeted with, 'Cor, you should have been here last night. We got raided by Jerry... one 'angar wos 'it.' The Cockney driver prattled on and on. 'How many kites?' we asked. 'About 'arf a dozen He 111s,' he said. We did not tell him that on the last raid on Malta 150 had taken part. This was the first time Kabrit had been bombed. Rommel was pushing the 8th Army back towards the Canal area, so he could bring his bombers down from the desert.'

On 6 May Wally Gaul flew his 35th op; an abortive single supply drop on Crete. Two days later he was dismayed to learn that his 36th operation was a dive-bombing raid on enemy shipping in Benghazi harbour. On an earlier raid one crew had turned off its engines as they had dived on the harbour, in an effort to fool the Italian sound locators and had then turned them on again as they climbed dangerously away. Although they would not attempt this manoeuvre on the 8 May trip there was another disconcerting aspect of the operation. Wally Gaul and the skipper were at the end of their tours but the rest of the crew were on only their second trip. Gaul recalls: 'We started our dive from .about 8,000 feet. Wheels down, 15° of flap, engines throttled back to idling, nose down, then into a steep dive... bombs gone... pull out at 300 feet, both engines on full power. Then I opened up my two Brownings. We were the only kite over the target. At this height I stood a good chance of hitting something.

'We ran into trouble on the way back to the ALG. The Skipper asked the navigator for our position. 'No idea at the moment,' he said. That's all I wanted to happen. To make matters worse one engine began to play up. The WOp/AG tried in vain to get a fix. It was daylight now and just to pile it on we ran into a ground mist. These mists occurred frequently over the desert at dawn, rising to about fifty feet. I said we could be over the salt marshes near Alexandria. I had seen these mists on several occasions. The navigator chose to ignore me. The Skipper called me up front. The front gunner was beginning to panic. We told him to get in the rear turret. It was the safest place if we crash-landed. I saw what looked like the coast. 'Over on the port, Skip,' I said. We followed the coastline to El Daba and flew on to ALG 106. We had been two hours adrift in the 'blue'.

'I met my ex-Skipper at Kabrit and told him I would not fly with the crew again. 'You won't have to,' he said. 'That was your last op; you're on the boat list.' The next day, 11 May, was my birthday!'

Footnote
121 Quoted in *Unforgettable characters in Air Warfare 1939-45* by Laddie Lucas (Stanley Paul and Co Ltd 1989). Post-war Eric McLellan became a member of the judiciary and was one of the prosecuting counsel in the celebrated case of The Great Train Robery. Ironically, the notorious Leatherslade Farm House, hideout of the robbers, had been a haven on the airfield perimeter where McLellan was a signals volunteer on the OTU at Oakley.
122 See *Military Aviation in Malta G.C. 1915-1993* by John F. Hamlin (GMS Enterprises 1994).
123 See *Military Aviation in Malta G.C. 1915-1993* by John F. Hamlin (GMS Enterprises 1994).
124 See *Military Aviation in Malta G.C. 1915-1993* by John F. Hamlin (GMS Enterprises 1994).
125 148 Squadron returned to Luqa from LG.167 on 7 December 1942 to be disbanded on 14 December.
126 *The 'Quiet Life' of a Bomber Pilot* by Peter Clowes writing in Wingspan magazine, February 1995.
127 John King's first operational tour ended in July 1942 without further incident. After his rest period he was posted as a bomb-aimer to 78 Squadron on Halifaxes. The number thirteen seemed to dog him, for on his thirteenth 'op' of his second tour he was shot down over Holland. By bad luck he chose to seek help at a lonely farmhouse which was the home of a collaborator, and John King saw the war out as a prisoner-of-war. For a few years after the war he returned to civilian life, but the lure of the Service was too strong. In 1949 he joined the RAFVR and a short time later was accepted as a regular once again with a short-service commission. It was his ambition to be accepted for a permanent commission, and, although at thirty years, he was rather old for this, his keenness won the day. He was granted a permanent commission as from 1 April 1952. Then fate stepped in with King's third crash-landing. On 22 May, a few weeks after his commission, a Lancaster in which he was a passenger crashed while landing at West Malling. Thirteen had twice proved unlucky for John King. 'Three,' it seemed, was doubly unlucky. Flight Lieutenant King, Adjutant to 25 Squadron, was killed in his third crash-landing. *Desert Flight* by Leslie Hunt, writing in *RAF Flying Review*, August 1958.

Chapter 7

Mad Dogs and Englishmen

'In the moonlight we found the flak very accurate as we did our first turn. We could see many shell bursts and we smelt the cordite smoke. Eric's first stick hit warehouses and his second fell across the railway marshalling yards.'

Flight Lieutenant Reg Thackeray

While Wally Gaul departed the Middle East for a well-deserved leave before a second tour on Halifaxes, others, like Flight Lieutenant Reg Thackeray, arrived in the Canal Zone to carry on the fight against Rommel's Afrika Korps. Thackeray, a second pilot, joined 40 Squadron at Kabrit on Saturday, 3 October 1942 from 2 Middle East Training School at Aqir, Palestine. The following Wednesday, 7 October, he was sitting in the right-hand seat next to Flight Lieutenant Morton, a New Zealander who was on his second tour, in Wellington IC K which, with seven others, made a night raid on Tobruk. Thackeray recalls:

'It was quite a shaker after 2 METS. The bomb load consisted of four 500lb and one 250lb GP bombs and we had a full load of fuel (750 gallons) for the expected nine-hour trip. We got the green light from the duty pilot at 2240 hours and thundered off the runway - a single line of 'gooseneck' flares to the left. Off the end of the runway at fifty feet we flew out over the Great Bitter Lake into considerable turbulence but the wheels came up and the take-off flap was retracted as we climbed over the brightly lit German-Italian PoW camp near Fayid. At 4,000 feet the Captain and I changed seats and we headed due west fifty miles south of the coastline in clear sky. There were massive cloud banks over the coast and sea and almost constant lightning. On ETA (0245 hours) the Captain took over the controls and we turned due north - the target area was clearly denoted by the barrage of shell bursts at our height of 13,000 feet and we soon felt the 'bumps' and smelt the cordite as we flew through the black puffs. The flashes of the guns could be seen through breaks in the cloud and the Captain agreed with Bill Ball, the observer, that these should be the target. We went in straight and level at 0315 hours but found ourselves closely engaged by predicted flak and had to lose height in evasive action. We finally dropped our bombs at 9,000 feet and left the target area at 6,000 feet at 0355 hours. Morton handed over the controls to me almost immediately - ETA Kabrit was 0730 hours and I was already feeling tired! We shared the workload. I had a 'wakey-wakey' tablet and saw dawn break before we reached Cairo. The captain made a good daylight landing and we all went off to interrogation in the Intelligence tent, followed by a breakfast of sausage and eggs. I slept all that day and the following night. One aircraft had returned early with elevator trouble and another, unable to locate the target, brought its bombs home. A Wellington which had sent an SOS failed to return. The crew walked back to our lines and rejoined the squadron early in November.

'By the end of October I had been to Tobruk four times and had been four times to attack aerodromes and the battle area in connection with Montgomery's advance from El Alamein. At this time the Wellington tour of operations was 200 hours or forty trips. I continued to fly as second pilot with a regular crew captained by Sergeant Mortimer. I did ten of my first twelve trips with him in six different aircraft. On the twelfth trip we had a full load for Tobruk of 250lb GP bombs equipped with steel rods on the nose fuses, about twenty inches long, designed to ensure that the bombs burst above the ground, thus causing maximum sideways blast effect. We had carried the rodded bombs on battle area trips at the time of Alamein and to attack airfields, but this was the first time to Tobruk. We were briefed to aim for the harbour buildings and dock installations, rather than shipping. The fitting of these rods necessitated the removal of the safety device from the nose fuse and no-one enjoyed carrying the bombs; a prang on take-off could be survivable if bombs were 'safe' but not with rods!

'Sergeant Mortimer took off fully loaded that night as No 2 aircraft. As we climbed away we saw a flash on the airfield behind us. On our return we learned that No 3 aircraft had burst a tyre and had exploded; the pilot was on his first trip as captain. We had a very good, clear sight of Tobruk harbour and our navigator started a big fire. This proved to be our Captain's final trip. I took over for the next one. Between the start of the 8th Army's advance from El Alamein and the middle of November 40 Squadron had moved twice to see how 'mobile' we could be in following the troops up the desert. In the past, the 'heavies' had stayed on the Suez Canal and along the Ismailia to Cairo road, while the main battle area had shuttled back and forth along the coast between Benghazi and El Alamein. Now, 40 Squadron made a first move to ALG 222A to the west of Cairo, followed by another move to ALG 104 near El Daba via ALG 237 (otherwise known as Kilo 40 - forty kilometres north of Cairo on the main road to Alexandria). We all came safely together at ALG 104, close to the coast, on 12 November. The landing ground was littered with wrecked German aircraft, including many '109s. We remembered that we had put ten rodded 250lb GP bombs and the contents of two containers of 40 lb fragmentation bombs in two sticks across the dispersal areas from 8,000 feet by the light of flares dropped for us by Fleet Air Arm Albacores, only three weeks before.

'During the following eight days we had rain showers and a sandstorm lasting 48 hours. Ops were scrubbed. On the night of 23 November I went as Skipper of my own crew to Kastelli airfield on the western end of Crete - some 400 miles north-west across the open sea from ALG 104. We were airborne at 1955 hours and set course on the forecast wind at a steady climb. There was 6/10ths high cloud giving a halo round the full moon. ETA was 2220 and we crossed the coast on track at 13,000 feet. One or two heavy gun batteries were operating and we saw two or three searchlights which were ineffective.

Circling the target area, we decided to bomb on a southerly heading across the airfield dispersals. The navigator had an excellent sight in the moonlight and our five 250lb bombs and two containers of 40lb fragmentation bombs went down in one short stick. There was no flak so the bombing run until 'bombs gone - jettison bars across' was straight and level. Then the nose went down, the height decreased, the speed increased and course for base was set. Our rear gunner, Sergeant Hammond, reported all bombs burst on the airfield and we settled down with fingers crossed to cover the 400 miles of open sea again at 5,000 feet. Outside, the air temperature was just above freezing. Sergeant Stewart, my second pilot, took the controls and I went back to pump oil to the two engines - which never missed a beat! We crossed the coast at El Daba and landed at 0115 hours. Interrogation was quickly over and we went off to an excellent breakfast of bacon and soya sausages, after we had learned that all nine squadron aircraft had attacked the target successfully and had returned safely.

'It was all good experience for our next flight three days later to Malta. Eleven aircraft were briefed for the trip and eleven reached Luqa safely. We had 'L for Leather', a full crew, our kit, full tanks and an over-load tank in the bomb bay, four mechanics with their kit and tool boxes. Somebody must have checked the all-up weight, I suppose. All I know was that the run on take-off was very long and we flew west along the coast at 1,000 feet in rain. After passing Tobruk we made our final landfall at Ras el Tin and there started our run of over 500 miles to Malta. We climbed through 10/10ths cloud and came into the clear at 9,000 feet. Navigation was by D/F loop on the Malta radio beacon, supplemented by star sights using the bubble sextant and the Astrograph, a sort of overhead projector in the navigator's compartment. ETA approached, we let down through the cloud and soon spotted the beacon at Luqa and the brilliant lights in the harbour at Valetta. Our approach to the runway was over the dockyards and we were glad to touch down at 0710 hours on Thursday 26 November, just as dawn was breaking. We landed with 400 gallons of fuel left - a useful addition to the island's reserves. About half the squadron aircraft and crews had flown to Luqa at the beginning of November. We were shocked at the thin, haggard appearance of our friends after only three weeks on 'the island. Although the blockade was virtually lifted by the arrival of the 'Stonehenge' convoy from Alexandria, rationing was very strict and severe.

'On Friday morning we were on the detail for a double sortie to Bizerta in Tunisia. Take-off was set for 1930 hours. The straight line distance to the target was about 280 miles so we had a full load of 520 gallons and a bomb load of four 500lb and eight 250lb GP bombs, with dockside buildings the aiming point. The Met forecast was poor and the weather turned out to be very similar! The cloud base was around 1,000 feet when we went out to 'L for Leather' and we were unable to start the engines owing to flat batteries on the starter trolley. It was 2100 hours before we were airborne and we were very much the last aircraft. We stayed below cloud at 800 feet and skirted the well-defended island of Pantelleria, heading for the coast south of Tunis. We were climbing on track and passed over Tunis at 10,000 feet. Bizerta was under a terrific bank of cloud and the heavy flak was spasmodic and inaccurate. Searchlights were ineffective in the cloud. Just before midnight there was a break in the cloud and Jeff Reddell, our New Zealand navigator, got a sight of the harbour. The break lasted long enough for him to bring me on to a straight and level heading at 10,000 feet and he set the 'Mickey Mouse' for a single short stick. After 'Bombs gone' I closed the bomb doors and turned onto a reciprocal course. Almost immediately a large fire was seen and Wally Hammond, our English rear gunner, reported a large explosion. The fire remained visible for fifteen minutes as we lost height to 'improve' the temperature. The oil in the constant speed units had frozen solid and it was quite some time before I was able to bring the revs under control. For long range economical cruising, it was our habit to run the supercharged Pegasus XVIII engines on the highest available boost pressures but the lowest possible revolutions per minute. We were back over the Gozo radio beacon before 02:00 hours but Malta was under cloud and Luqa took some finding. By the time we had landed, it was too late to bomb up and refuel for our second sortie so we turned in for interrogation.

'Our next sorties were to Sicily - two trips on the night of 30 November/1 December to Trapani aerodrome and two trips on the night of 3/4 December to the aerodromes at Catania and Comiso. We made two more trips on the night of 6/7 December to the docks at Bizerta and La Goulette, the deep sea port of Tunis. Then we had a fruitless trip to Tunis. There was 10/10ths cloud over the target. We had flown in cloud all the way and had had a wonderful display of St Elmo's fire on the way up to 10,000 feet where we came out into a clear starlit sky. Static electricity discharged itself round the propeller tips, between the machine guns in the turrets and on the windscreen as the raindrops hit the glass! There was no sign of the target on ETA so we turned back and made a very gentle landing with our full load of bombs!

'Next morning we were told that the main port engine bearing had failed so we had to say 'goodbye' to 'L for Leather' which had served us so well. She had taken me to Crete, brought me to Malta and we'd been out to Sicily and Tunis on eight occasions. Our next aircraft was DV566P. She took us to Palermo in Sicily early on the morning of 12 December following a report of bad weather over Tunis which we had been due to visit the night before. 'We again took 'P' to Tunis and La Goulette early on Sunday, 13 December. We were third off the runway at 1820 hours and set course as usual over the tiny island of Filfla off the south-west coast of Malta. There was little cloud and we pinpointed accurately on the coast south of Cap Bon. We could see flak bursting over Tunis and a good fire at La Goulette partly obscured by light cloud. There was no flak over the port so we stooged around and the cloud cleared by 20:50 hours. There was a quarter-moon giving good illumination of the target and we were able to go in to attack at 9,000 feet. We had four 500lb and seven 250lb GP bombs and decided on three sticks. Eric Laithwaite put the first stick near the electricity generating station, the second stick on the oil refinery and the third stick on two ships moored near the canal, just off the oil jetty. One ship was estimated at 8,000 tons and a fire was seen to start on this one. The fire, punctuated by explosions, was visible up to forty miles away!

We were safely back at Luqa for interrogation at 2255 hours. It was later confirmed that we had fired the ship and the report figured in the citation for my DFM - being a Pilot's Air Force, my navigator has always complained that he hit the ship but I got the gong!

'We were due for a return trip to La Goulette with take-off at 0030 hours on 14 December but we had to switch to DV647N as P had been grounded due to excessive oil consumption. All our Pegasus engines used a lot of oil - worn out by use and the sand in the atmosphere despite the Volkes air filters on the carburettor air intakes. Additional regular hours supplies had to be pumped by hand from a reserve tank carried in the fuselage. This was one of the second pilot's jobs and was jolly hard work at high altitude and low temperatures, which also caused high viscosity. As an example: in January 1943 HE115N used two gallons of oil per hour, say 145 miles! Ten gallons of oil was hand pumped - 550 strokes on a 'wobble pump' - on a sortie to Tripoli.

'On take-off at 0055 hours, the cockpit panel lighting failed and there was a terrific juddering on the control column. It was still possible to climb very gently. There was no improvement in the situation when the undercarriage and flaps had been cleared up, so I continued, straight ahead, up to 1,000 feet and made a wide circuit and long, powered approach, leaving the flaps up until the last minute. With 3,750lb of bombs and about the same weight of fuel I took great care to do a gentle 'wheel' landing. Back at the dispersal it was found that the cooling gills on the starboard engine were jammed in the fully open (ground running) position and this had disturbed the airflow over the tail plane and elevator causing the 'judder'. I was only in the air 25 minutes! The problem was fixed quickly but the OC Night Flying cancelled our take-off since we should have returned to the island in daylight! (The Times of Malta reported this 'Blitz' on North African docks as the biggest bombing raid ever launched from Malta and the weight of bombs the heaviest ever to have been dropped in a single night by bombers operating from this island'.)

'A double sortie to Tunis and La Goulette was made on the night of 15/16 December. Tunis was reached at 20:45 hours and in the moonlight we found the flak very accurate as we did our first turn. We could see many shell bursts and we smelt the cordite smoke. Eric's first stick hit warehouses and his second fell across the railway marshalling yards. We were back at Luqa by 2300 hours and airborne again at 0050 hours, after sandwiches. The moon had set by the time we got back to La Goulette but there was a blazing ship in the canal entrance to light the target area. The first stick fell on the harbour works and the second stick caused an explosion in the generating station. We were 'home' again at 05:00 hours and found some flak damage to the starboard wing and flap.

'On Friday, 18 December, these double sorties came to an abrupt halt. We were briefed for Tunis and took off at 1820 hours but as we passed between the islands of Linosa and Lampedusa, Bert Ward, our Yorkshire Wireless Operator, reported that our engine-driven generator had failed and he couldn't promise that we would have sufficient voltage in the batteries to drop the bombs if we continued to Tunis. I turned back but it was evident that the voltage would 'hold' for some time and the navigator gave me a course for

Comiso in southern Sicily. We delivered our bomb load there before returning to Luqa and landing at 2100 hours.

'Between the double sorties, the aircraft were marshalled in a line alongside the runway for refuelling and bombing up, whilst all the crews took a breather and had a snack. Because of our generator failure in HX382/M, we had switched our kit, bombsight etc, to DV512/J and were preparing for take-off at 2330 hours. At 2300 the sirens sounded and shortly afterwards a concentrated dive bomber attack was made on Luqa. The squadron lost seven aircraft destroyed and three damaged. After this, every aircraft was put away in protected dispersals along the Saafi Strip which ran across the island to Hal Far, the fighter aerodrome. The second pilot performed this arduous taxiing chore after the trip, whilst the captain, navigator, wireless operator and gunners proceeded to the Intelligence Section for interrogation. There were no casualties to air or ground crew during the raid. Most of us literally went to ground in slit trenches and shelters on the airfield. We were all very scared to be so directly on the receiving end and very lucky to survive.

'On 21 December five aircraft were available to operate against Tunis and ten aircraft took off for Tunis (or Sousse as the alternative) at 1810 hours on 25 December. The weather forecast was dreadful - heavy cloud up to 12,000 feet. We had 'N for Nuts' HE115 and didn't see anything on ETA at Sousse or Tunis so we brought our bombs back, as did most others. We felt relieved that we had not had to bomb on Christmas Day. (One crew ditched but were picked up by Malta ASR at dawn.) We had a tasty meal in the Officers' Mess on Luqa main camp before turning in at 0030 hours on Boxing Day.

'Attacks on Sousse, Sfax, Comiso, Palermo and Tripoli followed during January 1943 and became almost routine. Some were more difficult than others. One night our bombs fell out, due to an electrical fault, when the bomb doors opened and undershot the target (Sfax harbour) and fell in the town. Another night we lost an engine over Tripoli but managed to limp back to Malta (200 miles) losing oil from the 'good' engine. Then, on 22 January, we flew back to Egypt for leave and did not return to Malta. On 7 February I was told to muster my crew, organise transport to Fayid and find an aeroplane and fly it to ALG 1 where we should find 40 Squadron and other squadrons of 205 Group. I was given Wellington BB478, straight out of a major inspection and with no identification letter. She later became 'C' and we took her to Trapani and Palermo later that month. ALG 1 was at Magrun, thirty nautical miles south of Benghazi. It accommodated parts of 37, 40, 104 and 108 Squadrons in a large tented camp, with 70 Squadron away to one side. Within a couple of days 40 and 70 were on their own, the other squadrons having moved up to a complex of airfields at Gardabia, near Misurata, 100 nautical miles east of Tripoli, which had just been occupied by the Eighth Army. ALG 1 became waterlogged and after the sand had settled 40 Squadron joined them at Gardabia. The first few days there were spent air-testing aircraft, swinging compasses and making other general preparations for the resumption of operations. The Wellington squadrons in Algeria were using the Hercules-engined Mks III and X, whilst 37, 70 and 108 were re-equipped with these versions. All their Mk ICs (with the Pegasus XVIII) went to 40 Squadron. 104 Squadron had always used the

Mk II with Merlins and to ease the maintenance problems, had always operated from the same airfield as 462 Squadron RAAF, which flew some elderly Halifax Mk Is. Thus, we had plenty of aeroplanes and I was fortunate to be given the new Mk IC I had brought from Fayid. On 20 February she took us to Sicily. We were briefed to attack port installations at Palermo and had a load of six 500lb 'rodded' bombs. This trip turned out to be one of our more interesting ones. Visibility on take-off was poor and we did not see the flashing beacon at Horns to get a good pinpoint on the coast. Soon afterwards, we found ourselves sandwiched between two layers of cloud, so our Australian navigator could not calculate the course by reading the drift from flame floats dropped into the sea, nor could he use his bubble-sextant to get position lines from the stars. On top of this, we had a generator failure, so I ordered the radios and lighting to be used for essentials only.

'We pressed on across Sicily, seeing nothing, until we should have been over Palermo. Still nothing. So we turned south and within minutes we were engaged by a heavy flak battery. Coming down to 9,000 feet we found a break in the cloud and recognised Trapani harbour below us - our first pinpoint for four and a half hours and some sixty nautical miles from our primary target! We had a clear sight of the docks, so our bomb load was put down in one stick. We were well in range of the light flak by now and evasive action took us down to 6,000 feet before we were clear of the defended area. I saw an indicated airspeed of 280 mph at one time and we were not a little shaken up by the time we were back on the straight and level. Our navigator now had a good and accurate pinpoint and was able to estimate a new value for wind speed and direction and re-starting his air plot, he got us back to the North African coast (east of Tripoli, via Malta) very accurately. The whole trip had taken us eight hours and we learned when we went to interrogation that all aircraft had been recalled about the time that we were at Trapani because of weather conditions - our radio was dead by that time. Several of 37 Squadron's aircraft landed in Malta and two aircraft crashed on landing. Quite a night, one way and another!

'Two nights later we were again briefed for Palermo and had a completely successful trip, bombing the oil tanks from 12,000 feet by the light of a nearly full moon. Other crews were less lucky though and no fewer than thirteen aircraft diverted to Malta with flak damage. Warrant Officer Massey's crew on 40 Squadron was lost. Two nights later 'C' was ditched by Flying Officer Smith on his way back to base from an attack on Gabes. The port engine failed while the aircraft was over the sea east of the isle of Djerba and the captain made a successful landing in the area. All the crew took to the 'J-type' dinghy; land was reached in four days and they all got back to base with the help of friendly Arabs.

'When my name appeared on the detail on 25 February for my 40th trip, I was down to fly 'D-Dog' (HF904). The target was to be Gabes West Landing Ground, in an effort to reduce Luftwaffe support for the Afrika Korps, dug in on the Mareth Line. Four aircraft were due to take off but only three made it: 'O', 'X' and 'B'; 'Q' was unserviceable. Our load was 4,500lb, the maximum, made up of eighteen 250lb GP bombs with nose rods. I had signed Form 700 for a fuel load of 320 gallons - heavy load/short distance to the target - but the gauges showed 520 gallons. Assuming this to be because of sticking floats in the tanks the position was accepted and we started to run down the runway just after midnight. It was not long before the first and second pilots knew that 'O' was overloaded but since the desert runway was, more or less, unlimited in length and obstacles of any height were virtually non-existent, I just got the tail well up and watched the airspeed build up to 95 mph, hoping the tyres would stand the load. Eventually, she 'bounced' into the air and stayed there, so it was 'up undercart' and climb straight ahead. About four miles south of the airfield we had reached 150 feet and a slow turn brought us back over base to set course at 400 feet. Not a very good start, but we were up to 5,000 feet in 75 minutes and at 11,000 feet on ETA target. The landing ground was not visible through the haze so we pinpointed the town on the coast and did a timed run. We knew we had found the target when we were engaged by heavy flak - the first run was not straight and level and the second was made at 9,000 feet. Sergeant Williams, our Australian observer, had a good sight of the airfield and the eighteen bombs went down in one long stick.

'Further heavy and accurate flak caused us to abandon 'straight and level' for the camera and photoflash and we were all glad to be clear of the target area and on course for base at 7,000 feet. Oil was visible behind the starboard engine nacelle, so we realised the flak had been really close. A direct course back to base was plotted and since this took us close to Tripoli, which was crammed with Eighth Army Staff and supplies, we put the IFF set on to 'distress' and hoped the engine would keep running. I thought we could always divert ourselves to Tripoli airport if a real emergency developed. It did not, but we were diverted by radio to Gardabia Main and found that we were being treated as 'hostile' since our IFF was not functioning. As a result of this we had caused an air raid alarm in Tripoli. We had been in the air over six hours on our assumed fuel load, so we were officially' overdue' as well as 'hostile'. However, since we got back safely no action was taken in respect of the overloading. 'This proved to be my last operational trip. I was declared 'tour expired', took leave of my crew and a few days later flew back to Cairo. My forty operations had totalled 206 hours of night flying. Six weeks later I was back in the UK, later converting to Hercules-engined Mks III and X. These marks were just arriving at Gardabia when I left and 40 Squadron was given all the Mk ICs whilst the other squadrons got the Hercules, so 40 Squadron was the last to operate the IC.'

Chapter 8

African Adventure

Meet the boys of one fifty,
A real good crowd, believe you me,
Every night we've a date down Bizerta docks way.
We cruise along our Wimpey III
Just a couple of thousand above the sea.

Every night we've a date down Bizerta docks way.
And when we get there we know,
That we'll meet a bit of flak;
And so we stick down the nose
And it all goes round the back.

Zero boost and revs galore,
We turn our noses for home once more,
Every night we've a date down Bizerta docks way.

Words by Swain - tune *Down Forget-me-not Lane.*

There was nothing little-by-little about this 'Eric.' He was a big, snarling brute who roared and thundered and spewed destruction and often - too often - death. I came in contact with this unpleasant character early in 1942 when I was flying as a pilot with a Royal Australian Air Force squadron of Bomber Command. We were flying Wellingtons then; the good, faithful old 'Wimpy' that could stand endless punishment and still come up, or rather stay up, for more. Night after night we flew on what came to be known as the 'Mail run' to Tobruk; at that time a German stronghold. And it was there that I met up with 'Eric,' a heavy-calibre anti-aircraft gun embedded in concrete right in the centre of Tobruk harbour.

I first saw the result of 'Eric's' workmanship in conjunction with the searchlights about three weeks after Johnny, a fellow pilot, had been reported missing. Johnny was a good pilot - really good - and by his skill and the grace of God he had dodged and twisted his way out of the blinding lights that made him a sitting target for 'Eric.' But Johnny's plane, 'U-for-Uncle', was crippled. And there were miles of enemy-held desert between him and friendly territory.

But let me tell it as Johnny told me, sitting bolt upright in a Cairo hospital bed, encased from the waist to the top of his head in plaster with only his lips, nose and dark, pain-filled eyes showing. For Johnny had a broken neck

- a legacy of his encounter with 'Eric.' And this is his story:

'We were more or less a dead duck when we got clear of the target area. Harry the navigator had caught a packet of flak splinters in the stomach and was bleeding badly. The rest of the crew; Len the second pilot, Mo and Bluey the two gunners and Doug the wireless operator, were unhurt. But U-for-Uncle was in a bad way with the port engine labouring badly and the radio and intercom, out of action. We were losing precious height every minute. Then the port engine seized up and the starboard engine was already badly overheated. Len said he thought Harry was dead; he had been unconscious from the moment of being hit and did not seem to be breathing now. I was now facing the agony of indecision that comes to most bomber pilots at some time. Should I order the boys to bail out? Bail out to what? And perhaps Harry was still alive... A forced landing then? And simultaneously, a burst of inspiration and hope. The Germans held the coast road, but not to any depth inland. Turn a few degrees south and we would land in the desert, with a chance of Arabs finding us.

'One thousand feet. I ordered: 'Prepare for crash landing!' Four hundred feet...three hundred...two hundred...one hundred... zero: I saw Len's body hurtle forward and then blackness! From somewhere a thousand miles away I heard a voice - Mo's voice - saying: 'Skipper, Skipper, come on, Skip, you're all right.' Mo was kneeling at my side. It was broad daylight. The aircraft was a torn, crumpled wreck. 'The boys; how are the boys?' I asked. Quietly Mo told me. Harry was dead and so was Doug. Bluey's face was smashed and his ribs caved in. Len was bad, with his legs and pelvis twisted out of shape. 'And you?' I asked. Mo, the fiery little Jewish rear-gunner, Mo, who had hauled two men from the wreck, said: 'Oh, I guess I was lucky. Just my legs!' Then I saw that both his knees, raw and bleeding, were protruding from his battledress. For both his legs were broken and he had crawled over rocks and sand on his hands and knees to pull the others from the plane...

And what of Johnny? Simply he told me that he knew his neck was broken because of the way his head hung forward on his chest and the agony of trying to lift it. But he was the only one who could walk so he started walking, walking toward the east where their only chance of salvation lay. His simple words could never tell the real story of that journey; the stumbling and falling among the rocks with head lolling like a broken doll's; the agony of every step, not being able to see where he was going because he could not lift his head. Falling again and again until hands and knees were raw and bleeding, until pain was bearable through repetition as though it were something one had lived with all one's life. And then...'I saw it!' Johnny told me. 'An armoured car of the Long-range Desert Group was coming straight toward me. I pointed back to my tracks and the patrol soon found the aircraft. We were saved!' Johnny and his boys, their wounds healed, are back in Australia now. I like to think that if 'Eric' could have followed their story to the end their heroism would have broken his steely heart.'

Johnny Came Limping Home Philip Mather DFC.

Two Wellington Squadrons - 142 and 150 - played an important part in the night bomber operations during the Tunisian Campaign. These two Squadrons left England on the first day of the war and equipped with Fairey Battles operated during the German advance through the Low Countries and France, right up to the time of the latter's capitulation. Late in 1942 at the shortest possible notice, they left England once again. This time they were bound for North Africa, where they were destined to win fresh laurels. Field Marshal Erwin Rommel's lines of communication both in Tunisia and Sicily came in for continuous attention, convoys were afforded protection by the bombing of the Sardinian airfields and the 1st and 8th Armies were helped to success by the pounding of enemy aerodromes and transport. In addition, an anti-submarine standby was maintained, food was dropped on beleaguered French troops and fighter and searchlight co-operation was frequently carried out and millions of leaflets showered on Axis troops throughout the campaign. Each one of these activities played no inconsiderable part in helping to drive the Axis off the Continent of Africa and take the fight into enemy territory.

On 8 November 1942 the Allies landed American and British troops ashore on the coast of French Morocco and all objectives were quickly taken. Once Air Marshal Sir W. Welsh KCB had established a permanent headquarters for Eastern Air Command at Maison Carree outside Algiers, he realised that night bombers should be despatched from England without further delay. On 26 November, just as the bombing of Germany was gaining momentum, an urgent request was received from North Africa for two squadrons of Wellington night bombers to be urgently sent to Algeria. As a result, both 142 and 150 Squadrons were ordered, at short notice, to each prepare thirteen crews and a ground echelon, 100 strong, for shipment to North Africa. The understanding was that they would be on detachment for only three months. Thirteen specially 'tropicalised' Wellingtons arrived at 142 Squadron's base at Waltham, near Grimsby. Similarly, another thirteen arrived at 150 Squadron's base at Kirmington in Lincolnshire. On 9 December 142 and 150 Squadrons, ill-equipped and with no provision for replenishment, flew to Portreath, their advance base, leaving those who were left behind to merge with the home echelon of 142 Squadron to form 166 Squadron. At Portreath bad weather delayed the Wellingtons' departure. They finally left England on 19 December. All the crews were experienced; some were on their second tour. The universal thought was that operations in Africa would be 'a piece of cake' compared to flying night bombing raids over the Ruhr.

The Wellingtons refuelled at Gibraltar before carrying on to Blida, 35 miles south-west of Algiers. Blida is located under a fir and evergreen covered range of the Atlas Mountains which rise to a height of 6,000 feet. Situated in the centre of an intensively cultivated plain, its streets thronged with an assortment of every shade of people from jet-black to pure white. The novelty of their new environment never waned with the crews, who always found new fields to explore. For three months oranges and oeufs, tangerines and grape fruit formed their staple diet. Later, loquats and peaches, grapes, figs and almonds became the order of the day. Dates were also enjoyed, but only after undergoing careful scrutiny. The climate during the winter months, in spite or copious rains, was invigorating and those aircrews who went home from Blida took with them skins tanned by the winter sun. These and those who remained, would always carry with them happy memories of their first base in North Africa. The airfield had been built during French colonial days and boasted several large hangars, barrack buildings and workshops, which had once accommodated up to 8,000 British and Americans. Although it had a fairly well drained terrain the airstrip was very muddy and two of the Wellingtons crashed on landing.

Two squadrons of Wellingtons would only make a small impact on the land battle but any bombers were welcome at this time. The Wellingtons carried out a diversity of operations, ranging from the flying of supply drops to beleaguered French troops, anti-submarine patrols, leaflet raids and fighter and searchlight co-operation duties. The Tunisian campaign was a severe test for Allied forces. It would drag on from January until May 1943, largely due to the very effective generalship of Field Marshal Rommel and his highly trained Afrika Korps. Another factor in the campaign was the weather. Heavy rain prevented the first operation being flown until the night of 28/29 December when eight Wellington IIIs were despatched to bomb Bizerta docks.

Flight Lieutenant Ronnie Brooks DFC had a hang-up with his 4,000lb 'cookie' over the target while flying at 11,000 feet. Arthur Johnson, the bomb aimer-front gunner, recalls: 'I had just got the target beautifully into my bomb sight when 1 found the release gear had packed up. 1 tried three times to get the bomb away but it wouldn't drop. When I went to the bomb bay I found the couplings underneath the bomb had iced up.'

Johnson and the navigator, Flight Sergeant Jim Oldham, tried to unscrew the couplings but the ice was too thick. Oldham then got an axe and made a hole in the bottom of the fuselage big enough for him to put his head and shoulders through. With Johnson holding his legs, Oldham then hung through the fuselage and chipped away at the ice until he tired. Johnson then took his place. Flight Sergeant Chuck Delaney, the Canadian rear gunner, also had a try. The Wellington cruised around the target for about twenty minutes while the three men hacked at the ice. Fairly heavy flak was coming up all the time the airmen were chipping at the ice. Once the bomb was free of ice Johnson went back to his bomb sight and at the right moment, shouted to the other two airmen to let the bomb go. Delaney and Oldham gave a lusty push with their feet and the 4,000-pounder hurtled down onto Bizerta, exploding near a barracks.

During January 1943 bad weather continued to dog operations but 231 sorties were flown. Bizerta came in for heavy punishment, being bombed on no less than 22 occasions that month. The Wellingtons often used the concrete runway at Maison Blanche as an advanced base and landing ground when their airstrip at Blida was put out of commission by the weather. On 1 January Wellingtons on 142 Squadron, each carrying a 4,000lb 'cookie', mounted an operation on the docks and oil storage tanks at Bizerta. At briefing, crews were informed that the port, which was the main supply facility for the Afrika Korps, was heavily defended. The Met report was as follows: 'Light NE wind. 10/10ths cloud throughout, cloud base 2,500 feet - variable height. Icing index high in cloud.'

One of the crews who took part was Pilot Officer Alan Gill's crew on 'B' Flight. Norman Child recalls the operation:

'We took off at 0229 hours, set course for the Maison Blanche beacon and then time ran to the turning point thirty miles off the coast. We turned on course for Bizerta and checked our position with back bearing. We climbed to 6,000 feet for minimum 'cookie' height and flying in cloud. Radio navigational aids were very poor so we relied on dead reckoning. Through a small break in the cloud the rear gunner reported surf below and we were crossing the coast and drifting inland. The winds had obviously strengthened from the north and we were close to Philippeville. There was much turbulence. The Atlas Mountain range was only twenty miles inland. We changed course to port and climbed rapidly to try and break cloud for a star shot. We climbed to 13,000 feet and still we were in cloud. The aircraft was beginning to ice up rapidly. The position was serious. We could not climb above cloud and the weight of the ice was too much. The airspeed fell off. The target was only twenty miles to starboard. We decided to make a shallow descent to the target area. Searchlights ahead were shining through the cloud. The aircraft was vibrating badly and the flying speed was just above stalling. We selected a dropping position in the centre of the searchlight ring and released the 'cookie'. With a lightened load the aircraft was climbed another 1,000 feet and we broke cloud at 14,000 feet. The ice crystallized and broke up, great chunks being flung off the props. We got a good astro fix and set course for base, maintaining our height. We homed onto Maison Blanche beacon and descended rapidly through the cloud, icing up again. The cloud base descended to 1,500 feet and the warmer air broke up the ice. With a sigh of relief we crossed the coast and flew up the valley on the Blida beacon. We had been airborne for six hours 15 minutes.'

On the night of 14 January the weather was instrumental in the loss of two Wellingtons. Twelve aircraft were detailed to attack Bizerta docks and the Met report indicated (wrongly as it turned out) that conditions would be perfect. At the target conditions were indeed ideal and three blockbuster bombs burst successfully in the dock area. However, half way back to Blida the formation ran into a violent thunderstorm with 10/10ths cloud at all heights. Returning aircraft were forced to circle Blida and Maison Blanche hoping for a break in the clouds to enable them to land. Six eventually managed to put down at Maison Blanche and four more touched down at Blida. Flight Lieutenant Vincent DFC was forced to beach his Wellington near Djidjelli and he and his crew, including Squadron Leader Carmichael of Coastal Command, managed to clamber to safety. The seas were running so high that the Wellington broke up within minutes before any items of equipment could be saved.

Wing Commander J. D. Kirwan DFC the CO of 150 Squadron, carrying Flight Lieutenant Eric M. Summers, the Intelligence/Operations Officer to report on the flak at Bizerta arrived over Blida on ETA only to find the cloud down on the deck. To avoid hitting the mountains, the pilot turned out to sea again. For upwards of an hour he skimmed along the line of breakers. Once, he caught a fleeting glimpse of Maison Blanche, only to lose it when over the aerodrome. After eight hours in the air the petrol gave out and at one o'clock in the morning the crew bailed out over the Atlas Mountains. All landed comparatively undamaged in wild mountainous country. Summers, who came down gently in a muddy stream, stumbled up and down boulder-strewn mountain torrents for three hours until he reached a native village. The inhabitants, Kabyls, proved very friendly and search was at once made the length of the mountainside for other members of the crew. The Wing Commander was found in a gully with leg injuries. Pilot Officer Cavanaugh DFC the caustic Canadian wireless operator had a broken ankle, Pilot Officer J. H. Byles DFC the navigator, slight concussion, but the two sergeant gunners were uninjured. The relief of the crew at finding themselves all safe was only exceeded by the excitement of the local populace, headed by their Caid, Aitali Mohamed, in receiving such distinguished visitors 'straight from Heaven'.

Four nights later, on 18 January, Squadron Leader J. F. H. Booth and crew were among those detailed to attack the docks at Bizerta. Dropping two sticks of bombs, they circled offshore to observe the effect of the main attack. Then, in bright moonlight and with no cloud cover, they were attacked very determinedly by a Ju 88 night fighter. On the first attack the starboard engine was set on fire making the Wellington easy prey for the Ju 88 crew, anxious to finish off their quarry. The night fighter made three further attacks, knocking out the hydraulic system, rear turret, air speed indicator and flaps and setting a portable oxygen tank on fire. After delivering a fourth attack the fighter formated several hundred yards to starboard. An attack was then made from the front turret of the Wellington, which resulted in the fighter breaking off the engagement. When the fighter had broken off the engagement, Squadron Leader Booth ordered the crew to come forward to prepare to bail out. LAC J. Skingsley, acting as Flight Engineer, with great gallantry and complete disregard for his personal safety, ignored his parachute pack and attacked the blazing oxygen bottle. Being unable to put the fire out, Skingsley picked up the blazing bottle in his bare hands, carried it to the escape hatch and threw it out. He then proceeded to assist in lightening the machine by jettisoning all the equipment that was not screwed down. Squadron Leader Booth managed to bring the Wellington home for a crash landing and he was later awarded the DFC. By his actions, Skingsley undoubtedly saved the aircraft and lives of the crew. He was awarded the DFM.

The night of 21/22 January proved quite eventful too. Three distinct operations were undertaken. Bizerta Sidi Ahmed aerodrome was attacked by five Wellingtons of 142 Squadron and they registered two hits on the hangars and three on the runway. Meanwhile, five Wellingtons of 150 Squadron attacked a torpedo bomber base at Elmas aerodrome in Sardinia. The Wellingtons were obviously not expected because the airfield lights and those at three satellites nearby were blazing brightly. Flight Lieutenant

Donald Dunn could not believe his luck and he and his four crews put the airfield out of action for 48 hours. Two Wellingtons, flown by Pilot Officer R. I. L. Chisholm DFC on 142 and Flying Officer J. G. Roberts DFC DFM on 150 Squadron took off with full containers of food, to be dropped on beleaguered French Troops in the Ousseltia Pass. Some last-minute preparation was called for and a number of the elite of the station, including the CO turned out to help. Taking with him two of his ground crew, LAC's Eyles and Clark to assist in handling the containers, Chisholm was successful in dropping his load on the prearranged spot. Roberts, however, was forced to turn back owing to a mechanical defect, but not before he had jettisoned his load in the area. The following day the Wellingtons were called upon to assist the Eighth Army's advance into Tunisia with a bombing raid on enemy aircraft at Medenine, 500 miles distant. Later reconnaissance photos revealed that a number of aircraft had been destroyed on the desert air strip.

On the night of 31 January the Wellingtons attacked Sicily for the first time. Trapani, on the western end of the island, a port much used by the Axis to tranship war material to Rommel's forces in Tunisia, had been reconnoitred and found with a considerable amount of shipping along the quays and four skulking destroyers in the harbour. The night proved exceptionally dark and made bombing results difficult. However, three large fires were started and photos later revealed that the docks and adjoining warehouses had been well hit.

February opened with a second raid on Cagliari Elmas aerodrome. The weather, which had been bad, now deteriorated considerably. In spite of every effort, including daily briefings and bombing up, operations were possible on only eleven nights during the month. Bizerta was attacked on seven occasions. These constant raids on the Tunisian port helped stem the flow of supplies getting through to the Afrika Korps. About this time recognition was received from home in a message from The Chief of Air Staff, Air Chief Marshal Sir Charles Portal GCB DSO MC:

'My appreciation and congratulations to the air crews and other personnel concerned with 142 and 150 Squadrons on the most creditable performance the two Squadrons have put up since their arrival in the theatre. You have certainly shown us all what bombers can do'. Recognition from the CAS and an occasional reference on the BBC's Home News helped to make each and every one of the ground crews proud to realise that he was in the picture, doing something constructive to help win the war. In addition to their nightly bombing operations, the Squadrons, during the first three months at Blida, provided an aircraft each day, armed with 16 x 250lb bombs, for anti-submarine patrol. On two occasions only were they brought into service. No dividend was, however, declared on either occasion, though Sergeant M. Penman DFM claimed some near misses on what might have been a submerged submarine.

On 22 February the Wellingtons suffered their first casualties. Sergeant A. M. Jensen and crew on 142 Squadron failed to return from a raid on Bizerta. Three nights later, in bad weather, 150 Squadron lost Pilot Officer J. G. Swain DFC and crew while returning from another operation to Bizerta. The aircraft flew into the cloud-covered mountainside about ten miles east of Blida aerodrome. Swain was probably the most experienced pilot on the two Squadrons and certainly their most popular member. His sterling 'qualities were an inspiration to his companions and his bonhomie a source of unfailing delight. At the piano and the bar he led the community and choral singing, which helped to pass the rainy evenings. His simple nature and cheerful companionship made him everyone's friend. In the middle of February Wing Commander Kirwan returned to England suffering from the effects of an injury sustained while bailing out of his aircraft on the night of 15 January. He was succeeded by Wing Commander A. A. 'Sailor' Malan who had previously commanded a Blenheim V squadron in North Africa. Other changes, at top level, were also made. With the continued advance of the Eighth Army, a change in command and disposition of Allied Air Forces in North Africa was made. Mediterranean Air Command under Air Chief Marshal Sir Arthur W. Tedder GCB came into being and under him; General Carl 'Tooey' Spaatz took command of the North-West African Air Force, comprising all the Allied air units from Tunisia to Morocco. On 19 February the Wellington squadrons came into the North-West African Strategic Air Force (NASAF) under the command of Major-General James H. Doolittle USAAF, famous for his air racing days before the war and his leadership on the B-25 Mitchell raid on Tokyo from the deck of the carrier *Hornet* on 18 April 1942, for which he was awarded the Medal of Honor.

Doolittle wasted no time getting to know the units in his new command. On 22 February he flew down to Blida and went with Flying Officer Roberts and the crew of 'A-Apple' to see for himself the bombing of Bizerta docks by night. The General was able to witness a well executed attack, with the majority of bombs going down in the space of two minutes. The goods station was hit and oil tanks were left burning. The fire could be seen for up to fifty miles away. On the night of 12 March Prince Bernhard of the Netherlands and other high ranking officers attended the briefing for a raid on marshalling yards at Tunis. On 24 March Air Marshal Tedder visited Blida and addressed the crews. Morale began to soar with the arrival of badly needed replacement crews. Reinforcement crews were now beginning to arrive fairly regularly. The competition between the rival Wing Commanders to obtain the services of each crew as it arrived, together with the next three possible, provided almost daily entertainment for the Squadrons. Aircraft straight from UK were met at their dispersal by a wing commander and an 'erk' complete with paint and brush, ready to decorate its side with the appropriate squadron letters. About this time some American tanks pulled in for a night's shelter. A wag on 142 chalked his squadron letters on one; and it is an indisputable fact that, as soon as 150's CO heard this, he rushed out of the office to put his squadron letters on another.

Each squadron gave a party during March and on the 27th the station gave its first official party. This proved a phenomenal success. English nurses from Blida were much in evidence, both inside and outside the building. Many French Air Force Officers and their ladies were also present. The former, after three years of comparative abstinence, found the spirit willing but the spirits too strong. Undoubtedly a good time was had by one and all and Angle-French relations were firmly cemented. For the first three weeks of the month sorties were more social than operational. Air and ground crews had by now become sufficiently acclimatised to enable them to enter more fully into the life of the locality. The atmosphere had always been friendly and slowly but surely the language difficulty was overcome. With confidence increasing, keener enjoyment was derived from the days of well-earned rest, spent either up in the mountains or on the shores of the Mediterranean. With the Eighth Army now in Tunisia, the Wimpys were detailed to give direct assistance to the advancing troops. In spite of the weather, attacks were made on enemy landing grounds hidden away in olive groves for two nights in succession. Attacks were invariably scheduled to last as short a time as possible. Only the last man over ever reported the flak as anything other than slight or moderate. Despite the weather the Wellingtons managed to fly 115 sorties in March, ending as it started, with a trip on the 'mail run' to Bizerta and back.

The Squadrons now began to lose their old hands; Old in experience but still young in years, they returned' to the Old Country, on the completion of their tour - Pilot Officer 'Paddy' L. Grant DFM had completed 140 operational sorties - without doubt tour-expired. Flying Officer 'Kiwi' White DFC departed with the knowledge that he probably held the world's record with four consecutive night operational sorties. Squadron Leader R. 'Lyne-Shute' Pinkham DFC had to return in order to be provided with a fresh audience to listen to the nightly antics of his demoniacal Gremlins. Pilot Officer J. May DFC and Pilot Officer W. J. Whitewood DFC - 'Tweedledum and Tweedledee' - returned to England to brief aspiring navigators on the pitfalls of darkest Africa. During the first three months of the campaign no Wellington spares were received at Blida. Maintenance was kept up by robbing unserviceable and crashed aircraft. An average serviceability of 85% was however maintained, which in itself was a high and fitting tribute to the work of the ground staff. 200 men continuously kept an average of 20/25 aircraft serviceable. Armourers, fitters, riggers and electricians, each pulled his weight. A full-time job was made more difficult. By the tropical rains, which fell almost incessantly during February and March, but their unflinching determination to have all aircraft serviceable never failed. Much of the success in operating was due to the ground staff's honesty of purpose and cheerful willingness to carry on, sometimes well into the hours of darkness. Theirs, no less than, the aircrews', was the pride of achievement. A splendid job well and successfully accomplished.

On 17 April twenty Wellingtons were detailed to attack Tunis docks and marshalling yards. During the raid a burst of flak under Sergeant Chandler's aircraft pierced the petrol tank. With difficulty, Chandler succeeded in reaching the neighbourhood of Algiers Bay, where both engines cut. With the intercom failing the aircraft had to be ditched without warning to the crew. They were thrown in all directions. With the aircraft rapidly filling with water, Chandler scrambled through his escape hatch. The bomb aimer was thrown over the main spar and went out through the astrodome. The rear gunner, standing near the flare chute at the moment of impact, was knocked down and picked himself up to find water up to his shoulders: he went through the astrodome closely followed by the navigator, who had no recollection of what happened. The W/Op hit the door of the cabin and was shot out in front of the aircraft. They all then helped each other into the dinghy, where they lay completely exhausted. For 36 hours they drifted, always within sight of land. A C-47 and five vessels, which all came close, failed to have their attention attracted by the firing of Very cartridges. Eventually, they were picked up by the Polish destroyer Blyskowila, returning to Gibraltar after a few days for repairs. Flown back from Gibraltar, after a few days spent in recuperation, the crew were soon back on operations.

On 19 April Group Captain John Alexander 'Speedy' Powell DSO OBE of *Target for Tonight* fame arrived from England to co-ordinate 142 and 150 Squadrons' efforts and to form them into a Wing. Area bombing was to be replaced by precision bombing and a move nearer the front lines was imminent. The squadrons moved to Fontaine Chaude, fifteen miles from Batna to take up station as part of 330 Wing. On 6 May twenty Wellingtons were detailed to take off for a raid on Trapani. However, malfunctions and the inability of some crews to find their aircraft in the dark meant that only thirteen actually managed to take off. It was hardly an auspicious debut. Worse was to follow. En-route thick cloud and violent thunderstorms forced the remaining aircraft to abort. Ten Wellingtons landed back at Fontaine Chaude, one put down at Biskra, 'the Garden of Allah' and another landed near Guelma. Sergeant H. Venning DFM in the remaining aircraft ran out of petrol and crash-landed on a desolate stretch of the coast. None of the crew suffered any lasting injuries from their adventure. Tunis fell on 7 May and the Axis Powers were finally cleared from Africa on the 13th. With no targets in the desert left to bomb, the Wellington crews turned their attentions to Sicilian and Sardinian ports. In the course of a single week Palermo was attacked twice and Naples, Alghero, Cagliari, Marsala and Trapani were each visited once. On the first raid on Palermo the railway station and the docks received direct hits and several fires were left burning. On the second visit it was the power station that came in for particular attention. On 16 May crews made the long-awaited visit to Rome. However, the Wellingtons dropped nothing more sinister on the eternal city than a million leaflets, while the heavy stuff was used on the Lido di Roma seaplane base at the mouth of the Tiber, eighteen miles away. Leaflets or 'Nickels' had proved relatively successful in the desert. On one occasion, 7,000 Italians, each bearing a laissez-passer, had given themselves up in one day. On the night of 17/18 May 1943 Major-General James H. Doolittle flew with 142 Squadron to see for himself the results of a raid on Alghero in Sardinia.[128] In the middle of May Wing Commander Bamford handed over command of 142 Squadron to Wing Commander A. R. Gibbes DFC RAAF.

In December 1942 the Wellingtons of 142 and 150 Squadrons had flown to Algiers to become 330 Wing, North West African Strategic Air Force. Initially based at Blida, 40 kilometres south of Algiers, they had attacked Axis positions and airfields in Tunisia. Bizerta became something of a milk run; Tunis docks were not neglected. Rupert 'Tiny' Cooling, who had been posted to 142 from 9 Squadron in March 1943 and was now pilot of 'Y-Yorker', recalls:

'A lot can happen in a year. Eighth Army was pushed back and even the Suez Canal was threatened. By June 1943 the pendulum had swung back. Axis forces had been expelled from Africa: German resistance ceased on 12 May. In early May the squadrons moved forward to Fontaine Chaude; no more than a name on a map - a place where a spring of warm water rose beside the main road, the only road, linking Constantine and Batna. The little rivulet was much in demand for the laundering of clothes. Perhaps 'laundering' is too refined a phrase. The airfield and surrounding terrain had, in prehistoric times, been the bed of a soda lake. The water was brackish and in no way could soap be induced to lather. A railway lay to the east and on the southern edge of the landing area a mini-mountain rose some 600 feet above and barely 500 yards from the baked earth runway. The ground was hard and level, the parallel runways long, a useful attribute when taking off at full load in high temperatures with a pressure altitude of 2,800 feet. Two high hills four to five miles away had space between them, reassuring in case of engine failure on take-off. At the foot of the hill were the bell-tented quarters, mess tents. Bomber Ops, Stores and Sick Quarters. Scorpions, ants and a multitude of various beetles were already in residence and the latrine trenches were dug in open ground on the upslope within 400 metres of the cookhouse. Later sackcloth screens were erected so that those taking nourishment did not have to watch the eventual completion of the digestive process. 'Gippy Tummy' or 'The Trots' were endemic. It was not the nicest of places. Briefings took place in a shallow swimming pool like pit which shelved away from ground level. Boards propped against boxes and drums carried the maps and other data.'

The Allies now turned their attention northwards. A small but significant operation was launched, overshadowed a month later by Operation 'Husky', the landings in Sicily. The islands of Pantelleria and Lampedusa in the narrow waters between Tunisia and Sicily were crudely the Italian equivalents of Malta and were proving a stumbling block to the invasion of Sicily from North Africa. Both the largest and more important, Pantelleria was well fortified with a sizeable airfield; underground hangars provided shelter for bombers and torpedo carrying aircraft and was teeming with 11,000 Italians who had sufficient food and water to withstand a long siege. A small harbour was suitable for fast motor torpedo boats and even mini-submarines. Pantelleria lay astride any short sea route to the Sicilian coast and the Italians had already demonstrated an uncomfortable ability to use such offensive weapons effectively. Mountainous with steep cliffs to the water's edge its only possible landing beaches were well covered by defensive fortifications. Yet it had to be taken out and its garrison rendered incapable of effective interference. That task would be given to the air forces and Pantellaria was to be reduced by round the clock bombing. Fortresses, Mitchells, Bisleys by day, Wellingtons by night in a semi-continuous stream were to deliver a steady succession of attacks, frequent showers of bombs. After suitable softening up the Navy would throw in a final pounding before the troops went ashore.'

On 23 May, when Pantellaria first appeared as a target, crews assembled at 1400 hours: take-off 1900 hours. No. 142 Squadron would attack the airfield while 150 Squadron's target was the harbour. 'Tiny' Cooling recalled:

As 'S for Sugar' was back in Blida for a major it would be the Mark X, 'Z-Zebra' again tonight with eight five hundreds and a 250lb makeweight. Group Captain Powell, Officer Commanding 330 Wing did not believe in wasting space. Darkness fell as the aircraft crossed the coast at Hammemat. On a pitch dark night Pantellaria was not the easiest place to find on first acquaintance - an island eight miles by three became the proverbial dark black shadow against a pale black sea. But, ever helpful, the Italians threw up some heavy flak away to port. The target airfield lay at the foot of the main mountain two miles from the town and harbour. From 6,000 feet one could scarcely miss. Then it was back to base just as the moon rose at 2340 hours to touch down, debrief and bed by one o'clock. These were gentleman's hours.'

On 25th and 26th May 330 Wing moved forward yet again, to Kairouan - the holy city with the unholy smell, in the centre of a vast sandy plain. It ranks fourth in the holy cities of the Mohammedan World, only Mecca, Medina and Jerusalem taking precedence. Seven pilgrimages to Kairouan equal one to Mecca and entitle you to wear a green fez. Shortly after their arrival, the Luftwaffe dropped three bombs, all of which missed the airfield by a wide margin. 'Tiny' Cooling observed that the airfield was 'another baked earth runway within a broad plain of coarse grass and stunted bushes. This time there were no scorpions; the latrines were mostly enclosed with sackcloth screens about a wooden pole on which to perch above the pit. A few luxury models stood in isolation. Twenty miles away lay the coast. Crews could enjoy a swim once mines and wire had been cleared from the beaches. Altogether a much superior place even if the holy city of Kairouan itself, a couple of miles distant, carried the daunting notices 'Out of Bounds. Typhus' at each of its imposing gates within the surrounding wall. And Pantelleria was little more than an hour away.

'Group Captain 'Speedy' Powell jumped at the chance to bomb Pantellaria' recalled 'Tiny' Cooling. 'Bomb loads went up to 5,250lb, a pair of thousand pounders, five at five hundred and three two fifties. Fuel was cut by twenty per cent and aircraft would do three sorties a night. One crew would fly the first and last; a different crew the middle one. On the next night they would change places. It was a shuttle service; first take-off just before last light; the last return crossed the coast homeward bound at dawn. Each Wellington ferried almost 16,000lb of bombs to Pantellaria nightly and there were two squadrons of them. From 29 May to 10 June, the programme continued. The crews were delighted. If only the Italians held out long enough they could complete a tour of 40 ops in barely a month.

'It was a two and a half hour round trip; the first wave took off at sunset, the second somewhat before midnight, while the last was timed to cross the

Tunisian coast, homeward bound, at first light. It was an easy target to find; one would scarcely overlook an island of sixty square miles however dark the night, particularly with a peak topping 2,000 feet in the centre. The Italians helped too. Approaching, one was aware of a darker mass against the reflective blackness of the sea. Then a searchlight or two would spring up and grope uncertainly in the darkness. A thin hosepipe of light flak, pink, apple-green and white, might rise like a charmed snake and then vanish. The harbour was easily identified. The coast was distinctive and a course over the headland towards the peak ensured passing over the port, the town and the airfield. A right turn through ninety degrees put the aircraft on course for base. There might be a few thumps of heavy flak, a scatter of brief embers flowering against the sable coverlet of darkness; but in general, the crews were all happy. If only the Italians would hold out long enough, they might get their tour of forty ops completed in record time. Compared with Palermo, Messina, Catania, Naples, it was a doddle; in the vernacular, 'a piece of piss'.'

The scale of operations was gradually stepped up until the aircraft were doing three sorties nightly; the crews two on one night and one the next. From 29 May to 11 June Pantelleria was visited every night by the Wellingtons, 225 sorties being flown in twelve nights. As a fitting climax NASAF staged 1,000 day sorties, to which 330 Wing added 45 at night, some of the 21 serviceable aircraft making two and even three flights.

'At briefing at 1800 hours on Thursday, 10 June' recalls 'Tiny' Cooling 'we were on the mid detail. The Wellingtons of 330 Wing and of 205 Group would be mounting some 150 sorties - 300 tonnes of bombs on an area the size of a large village. The Navy had put in another bombardment, its fourth. Even Fontaine Chaude sounded a healthier place. 'The culminating point of an interesting experiment,' as Group Captain Powell put it. Crews were to watch out for specific signals from the ground in case the garrison chose to surrender. The navigator asked, in mock seriousness, if we should land to take formal possession!

And if the show was almost over it seemed a good time to take Dave the engine fitter who cosseted 'S for Sugar' and now looked after 'Y-Yorker'. He saw us off; he met us in. He called at the tent when we awoke with news of petrol and oil consumption, of minor snags he had found and what he had done to ensure his kite, our kite, was absolutely on top line. He seemed to lend us 'Y-Yorker' for ops provided that we took care of her. Whenever one of the crew went out to the aircraft Dave was there, his mop of fair hair oil stained his sunburned torso smeared with grease. Next to looking after 'Y-Yorker' he wanted to fly, to go on ops. He wanted to know what happened between the time he waved us off until the time 'Y-Yorker' rumbled back to dispersal and the engines whistled to a stop. We decided to take him to Pantellaria. 'Not a real op', we explained. A few coloured streamers of light flak far beneath, he might just hear the odd thump of heavy stuff, no searchlights, nothing like that.

'At dispersal 'Y-Yorker' squealed to a stop after her first foray. The bowsers chugged away, the armourers winched the load into the bomb bay. Just after midnight, 'Y-Yorker', refuelled, with another 6,000lb of bombs winched into her belly, was ready. We climbed aboard. 'Beanie' (Sergeant Harold Bean, the wireless operator) had smuggled an extra parachute and Mae West aboard. Dave stood beside me in the well beside the pilot's seat as I started up the two Hercules engines and then ran them up. As ever the run-up was a formality. There was not a tremor on the tachometers as we tested each magneto in turn. Revs and boost were spot on. Chiefy Sword disappeared towards the adjacent dispersal: Smudge, the rigger who was in the plot, handed up the ladder; the door thudded shut. Dave slipped into the back to don his harness. Smudge heaved away the chocks and with a brief burst of power, 'Y-Yorker' rumbled towards the flare path. A green Aldis flickered in the darkness; we lined up with the flares on our left, stretching away into a wall of darkness. Fifteen degrees of flap, cowling gills closed, brakes held on. Steadily the throttle levers advance; the Hercules raise their rumble to a roar then to an impatient howl. The Wellington trembled, eager to be airborne. Brakes off, control column pushed towards the instrument panel and with a plangeant paean of power 'Y-Yorker' surged forward, lifting her tail into the plume of dust behind us, surging eagerly forward. The flares accelerated to pass beyond the wing tip, there was a brief bump; the wheels touched once again; the last flare sped by as the altimeter slowly started to unwind and we were up into the blackness beyond. Bill, standing beside me, snapped down the detente and lifted the stubby undercarriage lever. Green lights on the instrument panel went out and were replaced by red as the wheels folded back into the engine nacelles. We were on our way.

'It was almost an hour later that Bill went down into the nose to set up the bombing panel. Dave stood beside me, peering into the darkness. Then the flicker of bursting bombs and the brilliant blaze of a photoflash threw the rugged outline of the island into sudden silhouette. Instead of following the normal approach we decided to give Dave a Cook's tour of the target, passing south and then turning towards the north-west for the bombing run. If this was to be an experience, we might as well show Dave something of the country. I turned slightly to starboard to pass south of the island for a run up the east coast before swinging left over the target. As we crossed the coast there appeared on our port side what looked at first like a flare but which grew suddenly larger, then larger still, emitting coloured stars as it fell slowly towards the surface of the sea. Suddenly, it was recognisable. The golden filigree of a Wellington's geodetic wings and fuselage, gyrating like a sycamore seed, slid slowly towards extinction in the water beneath. This was definitely not part of the programme. Somewhat shocked, we turned to line up on the harbour. There were flashes in the night sky, sudden white sparks against the darkness. We went in. as usual, at 6,000 feet but this time on a heading close to the course for home. Bill's voice came up over the intercom, 'Bomb doors open. Left-Left-Steady-Right-Bombs gone!' There was a sharp jolt as 'Y-Yorker' shed her load. 'Photo flash away', Beanie called out over the intercom as he launched the flash through' the flare chute. We held steady, awaiting the bright burst of light which would give us our picture. Then it was hell-bent for home. The compass needle had barely settled between the grid wires when the voice of the rear gunner sounded in our earphones. 'There's another kite going down in flames behind us.'

'We landed and taxied to dispersal. Dave slipped out of the aft escape hatch as planned. He was at the nose to meet us, as usual, as we climbed out. 'Shag' Sword had his doubts as to where he had been, but said nothing. Once more refuelled, re-armed, 'Y-Yorker' was off again to return with the dawn. Dave, as ever, was there to meet her in. He must have slept sometime.

'Four crew from one of the Wellingtons bailed out and landed on the island. The others were lost. Five men were on their last trip before screening, tour expired. We learned later that a fighter had been waiting in the darkness at the beginning of what had become a wholly predictable bombing run. It was the one we would have used had Dave not been with us and to show him something more interesting we came in the other way. It was the kite ahead and the kite behind us which copped it.'[129]

Pantellaria surrendered to the British 1st Infantry Division next day, 11 June. Lampedusa capitulated unconditionally after one raid by the Wellingtons! The way was now clear, once the last of the landing craft had arrived, for Operation 'Husky', the Allied invasion of Sicily, to begin.

Meanwhile, 330 Wing had been reinforced by four squadrons of Wellingtons from the Middle East and the arrival at Kairouan/Zina in Tunisia of 420 'Snowy Owl', 428 'Tiger' and 425 'Alouette' Squadrons of the RCAF from England. Fred Wingham, pilot of Wellington 'V-Victor' (later re-christened 'V-Virgin') on 420 Squadron, recalls:

'On 26 June we flew our first raid. We took off and headed for Kelibia Point, on the eastern tip of Tunisia and crossed the Sicilian Channel for Sciacca, on the west coast of Sicily. It was not a very good trip, as seven of our 500-pounders failed to release. We made several runs over the target but despite all our efforts we could not get rid of them. Nevertheless, we did manage to land safely at base. Beacons always helped guide us home but at 2,000 feet on a warm night one could literally smell Kairouan! Three nights later, on 29 June, we carried a mixed load to Messina; they all went in one stick on the docks and quayside. All our raids now seemed to be tactical. We bombed docks and airfields and railways. On one occasion we bombed a village to fill the streets with rubble to delay the German transport. The climax came on the night of 9 July. We were given another Wellington which was fitted with 'Mandrel' radar jamming equipment. I was also given an additional gunner because we would be on a long stint. We were sent to a point between Malta and Sicily. It was daylight in the early hours of 10 July when we got there. We set up and flew to and fro, using Mandrel to jam enemy radar. At this point the invasion of Sicily started. Other Wimpys were on other beats and we covered the whole south coast of Sicily. As darkness fell I could see Malta lit up like day with the action of the ships moving out. In the dim light of the night sky we could see the gliders being towed away to the dropping points and we saw some coming back. We were airborne for eight hours and ten minutes; rather a long stint.' Wingham's original Wellington was returned to him and further operations were flown in it, to Corsica, Sardinia and Italy. 'V-Virgin' caused many a raised eyebrow as Fred Wingham recalls:

'The squadron padre was a jolly soul and one day he looked at the beautiful, voluptuous female painted on the side and declared, 'She's far too broad in the hips for a virgin!'

In June 373 sorties were flown and 1½ million lbs of bombs dropped. The sweltering noonday heat reduced the possibility of working between 11 and 4 o'clock to a minimum. Nevertheless the ground crews, now brought up to full strength, stuck to their jobs and kept aircraft serviceability at a high standard. Some of the original Wimpys were now being sent back to Blida for 'majors', having completed up to 60 sorties. With the Axis out of Africa, all eyes were turned towards Italy. Pantelleria, Lampedusa and Sicily, the outlying islands had first to be taken. From 29 May to 11 June, when it capitulated, Pantelleria was visited every night by the Wimpys, 225 sorties being flown in 12 nights. As fitting climax, NASAF staged 1,000 day sorties, to which 330 Wing added 45 at night; some of the 21 serviceable aircraft making two and even three flights. One attack by the Wimpys and Lampedusa capitulated unconditionally! Attention then became focussed on Sicily. During the briefing for an attack on Castelvetrano aerodrome, the GC emphasised the importance of accurate bombing. Little Sergeant 'Mickey' Mortimer DFM asked for his aircraft to be loaded with long delays so that he could taxi in and lay an egg in each dispersal. The bombing of Catania and Syracuse, combined with frequent visits to each end of the train-ferry, linking the mainland and Messina, paved the way for the invasion of Sicily. By the end of June, 330 Wing had been joined by four Squadrons of Wellingtons from the Middle East and three, of the RCAF from England. The night bomber force now assumed quite formidable proportions and 100-Wellington raids began to come into operation. In September all three Canadian squadrons moved to Hani East ALG for further operations before flying home to the UK at the end of October.[130]

The establishment of airfields in Italy in December enabled Nos. 37, 40, 70, 104, 142 and 150 Wellington squadrons of 205 Group to move to airfields in the Cerignola area of southern Italy and a wider selection of European targets came within their range. The night bomber force had assumed quite formidable proportions and the tide in the Mediterranean Theatre was now turning in the Allies' favour. Crews were pleased to exchange the dust and heat of the North African desert for what they thought would be better conditions in the lush green vine groves of southern Italy. This did not prove to be the case. Camp comforts were more or less non-existent and weather conditions were often poor. Over northern Italy they could be fatal, as Roy Gristwood, a navigator on 142 Squadron, which shared Cerignola III with the 15th Air Force, recalls:

'On 24 November, during an attack on a ball-bearing factory in Turin, we were preparing to descend through 'cloud' when 'Mac' McNab, the gunner, shouted a warning to our Australian pilot, Flying Officer Lyn Clarke, that the 'cloud' was the snow-capped Alps! The Group sustained heavy losses with many aircraft running into the Ligurian Alps south east of the target area.'

During the Anzio landings in February 1944 205 Group harassed enemy troop movements behind the German lines, sometimes twice nightly. Roy Gristwood recalls:

'On the nights of 15/16 and 16/17 February we attacked troops and motor transport seen on the move in the [Grottoferrato-Manno-Albano-Velletri] area. Bombing was made visually from 4,000 feet. The operations were short - only just over three hours at the most - and no opposition was ever met, although some crews reported seeing fighters. They were probably other Wimpys stooging around. On 24/25 February we attacked the Steyr-Daimler-Puch aircraft factory in Austria. We were unable to make a landfall on the north Adriatic coast because of cloud. Crews were further frustrated because a lake, which was an inland turning point, was frozen and snow-covered which made it indistinguishable from land! The winds in the Alps are totally different from the Adriatic, so as far as we were concerned we could not positively identify the target. We saw some bombing fifty miles west, so we 'joined in'. Intelligence subsequently identified this as a minor railway town many miles west of Steyr. Some crews assumed that they were bombing Steyr, so they set off on homeward courses from their false position. Sergeant Armstrong's crew mistook the coast of north-west Italy for the coast of north Yugoslavia. When fuel ran low they bailed out over Corsica. Believing this to be northern Italy, they hid in the hills for several days until they were winkled out by the Free French. Some aircraft even landed in Sardinia. Many aircraft [four] were lost.'

On the night of 15/16 March Gristwood flew the 27th operation of his tour when 142 Squadron were part of the force of 67 aircraft that visited the marshalling yards at Sofia. One aircraft failed to return and ten crashed on their return. This trip was the first of three that Gristwood made to the Bulgarian capital.

'We carried 54 flares to illuminate drops for bombing aircraft. We had to stooge around the target providing illumination by periodic flare drops and this meant a longer flight time than normal bombing drops. Sofia was still lit up as we arrived over the city but they soon went out. They were replaced by about fifteen searchlights with light and heavy flak moving into action. Conditions over the target were perfect, but on our return the cloud base was down to 400 feet at Cerignola. After we landed and had been debriefed, we were breakfasting in the tent lines, about 1½-miles from the actual airfield, when we heard an aircraft very low overhead and coming in to land. A Wellington from a neighbouring squadron flew in out of the low cloud (now lower than ever) and landed between the lines of tents. The crew climbed out with their hands up - believing they had landed on an island off Yugoslavia! It was another example of how the dangers were not always flak or the Luftwaffe but the weather and lack of effective navigational aids.

'On the next night [when 21 aircraft were dispatched by 205 Group and all returned safely] it was Sofia again with the situation reversed. We carried nine SBCs (small bomb containers) totalling 800 four-pound incendiaries. This time there was 10/10ths cloud over the city but we had been told that 'authority from the highest source' had been given to bomb through cloud if necessary. Apparently Churchill had not forgotten the Bulgars for some misdemeanours during the First World War! A week later, on 24/25 March [when 77 aircraft were dispatched by 205 Group and three aircraft were lost, plus a fourth was written off when it crashed] we went to Sofia again with another cargo of 54 flares. Sofia was again under 10/10ths cloud so we could not identify the marshalling yards. The flak was the heaviest to date. They were learning.'

On 29 March Flight Sergeant Walker's crew arrived at Foggia to join 150 Squadron. Les Hallam, the air bomber, recalls:

'We were told that MF238 would be the aircraft we would be using on operations, but this did not turn out to be the case. Our Wimpy went into a pool for replacements required by the squadrons. Amendola airfield was used by American B-17s, flying daytime missions and by 150 and 142 Squadrons; both of whom were equipped with the Wellington X. From our tented camp site we had about a half-hour ride on the transport trucks to the airfield. Officers were quartered in a farmhouse and other farm buildings. Our Skipper did two trips with other crews before we did our first op as a crew on 15/16 April to marshalling yards at Turnul/Severin. Even at this stage of the war things were a bit 'Fred Carno' with regards to direction of attack. A lot of aircraft were victims of collisions over the target rather than to enemy action.[131] We were not at a very great height for our first op and the place was a blazing inferno when we bombed. We could feel the heat from the fires as we went over the target.'

Footnotes

128 The 47 year old, 5 foot 4 inch famed air racer was given command of the Eighth Air Force in England on 6 January.

129 Squadron Leader Roy Chappell, Intelligence Officer on 104 Squadron, wrote in his book, *Wellington Wings* of the night of 10 June: 'Several of our crews reported encounters with 'single-engined fighters, probably FW 190s, over the Pantelleria area. Single-engined fighters are unusual at night. Two of our aircraft are missing: 'X-X-Ray'... and 'W-William' (Sergeant Eason and crew) who were on their last operation before completing their tour. What cruel luck! Three of 'X-X-Ray's crew landed safely by parachute on Pantelleria: the other seven were lost.

130 In December they all converted to the Halifax.

131 In fact two Wellingtons collided at base on return. Both crews were killed. 92 aircraft were dispatched, of which one failed to return.

Chapter 9

Mediterranean Missions

'Suddenly Otto shouted that he had something on his radar. Orbiting, the blip appeared to the left, threatening to disappear to that side and I had to do a steep turn to port, then to starboard and again a little to port. Slowly the course settled down. It was to the west, therefore a returning bomber which unfortunately had already deposited its deadly cargo. The distance was about 3,500 metres at the same height. No mistakes now. Slowly but steadily Otto guided us to the foe. We dropped a little lower in order to see him better against the starry sky later on. At about 500 metres we matched his speed. Now all instruments were dimmed as far as possible. Otto was again at his post with his night glasses. Now began the phase of remoteness from worldly things, the rising of the adrenalin with the nerves exposed to the tips of our hair. One is no longer human, but a robot, ready for his final leap upon his prey. All movements are done as in a trance. Slowly we closed in on the enemy. Again, at about 300 metres, Otto noticed something and a little later I too was able to see the enemy. It was a Vickers Wellington. The guns were armed and without further ado I began my attack. All my frustration and anger at my late mishap went into my burst. The concentrated fire was so great that the Wellington exploded in the air and fell in many burning fragments to the ground. As I sheered off to port immediately after the attack, I avoided colliding with the falling bits. Finally the burning parts struck the ground...'

Leutnant Hans Krause

Leutnant Hans Krause had joined I./NJG3 as Technical Officer in November 1941. During the ensuing few months, the twenty-one-year-old pilot flew the Bf 110 on Himmelbett sorties, but in June 1942 he completed a conversion course at Gilze-Rijen on the Dornier Do 217, with which his Staffel at Rheine airfield was subsequently equipped. In his capacity as TO, he and his Funker Unteroffizier Otto Zinn spent July 1942 at Berlin-Diepensee airfield, test-flying and calibrating the 'Lichtenstein'-equipped Do 217 night fighter version. Shortly after returning to his Staffel on 10 September Nachtjagd proudly announced its 1,000th Abschuss (victory) of the war. To celebrate this special event, General Kammhuber[132] organised a 'kill-feast' on an airfield in Holland, which took place on the evening of 6 October and for which every Nachtjagd pilot with one or more victories was invited. As the only pilot in his Staffel without any kills, Krause had to remain behind at Rheine and although adverse weather prevailed, he and his crew had come to readiness late in the afternoon of 6 October. He returned with claims for two Wellingtons destroyed.[133]

By the beginning of April 1944 Hans Krause had doubled his score to four, all except one of his victories achieved while flying the Do 217-N2, a SN-2 radar-equipped night-fighter variant of the Dornier bomber armed with four cannon and four machine guns in the nose. Krause had become Staffelkapitän of 6./NJG101 in the summer of 1943 and was now stationed at Parnsdorf in Austria. 'The English bombers' job' recalled Hans Krause 'was to go over southern Europe and engage other bombers to fight. They did it as far as I know with good results. Also their targets were the industrial areas of Debrecen in Germany and steel and ball bearing works near the Slovak border and many railway stations used for the night push into Russia.'

By now the powerful Mediterranean Allied Strategic Air Force was playing a vital role in the conduct of the war. While the vast aerial fleets of 15th Air Force bombers and fighters pounded targets by day, the RAF Wellingtons and Liberators struck under the cover of darkness, stoking up the night fires.

'When I arrived on 150 Squadron in April 1944' recalled pilot Denys White, 'we operated from Amendola airfield, with a runway of wire mesh. We used this strip in conjunction with Fortresses and Lightnings of the American 15th Air Force; they bombed by day and we took the night shift.'

At Amendola 25-year old Sergeant Gordon G. Pemberton's crew on 150 Squadron were among the crews that went to briefing on 3 April to learn that this time it was a big one: Budapest, the capital of Hungary. This was the first night raid on Budapest and followed a daylight raid on the Ferencvaros railway station and the Dunai Repülögépgyár RT by the USAAF. The American bombers hit the Fanto oil refinery, which was SW from the Ferencvaros railway station. The target for the 87 bombers in 205 Group was the Manfred Works in the city itself. It was a long way, about seven hours' flying time and over enemy territory most of the way. Rumour had it that it was a raid to give moral support for the Russians because Churchill had promised that the RAF would do what it could to help them. Sergeant W. R. Bennett the air bomber who was from Lambeth in London studied the Target Information sheet. It was highly detailed:

'The target comprises a complex of four individual targets: The steelworks and aircraft factory of Manfred Weiss RT; the inland port; the oil refinery of Shell Koolaj RT and the Budapest/Osepel airfield situated on the island of Osepel in the southern suburbs of Budapest. The centre of the target complex is about four miles' south of the central built up area of Pest. The western side of the target area is bounded by the main stream of the River Danube and to the east, the branch stream known as the Soroksari Dunaag. The target is adjacent to the closely built-up area of Osepel to the south-east and across the Soroksari Dunaag to the built-up industrial and residential area of Pesterzsebet. Across the Danube to the west is the more sparsely built-up area of Budafok to the north and south of the target there is open country.

'The Manfred Weiss works are the largest and most important industrial concern in Hungary and their activities include heavy engineering in iron and steel, aluminium production, tanks, machine tools, shells, artillery, aero-engines or engine components and probably some castings for aircraft components. The aero-engine department is closely connected with the Dunai

Repulo factory at Szigetszentmiklos, seven miles to the SSW. The steelworks is the third largest in Hungary and includes a battery of Siemens-Martin open-hearth furnaces and a number of rolling-mills with an estimated annual production of 150,000 tons of semi-finished products. The aluminium plant has an annual capacity of 4,000 tons of ingot and produces semi-finished sheets, castings, forgings etc for the aircraft and aeroplane engine departments. The works are reported to employ 20,000 workers.

'The Oil Refinery is the largest and most important in Hungary and has an annual capacity of 150,000 tons. This figure represents about 37.5 % of Hungarian refining capacity and 1.24 % of total Axis capacity. There is storage for about 30,000 tons...' It went on to detail the inland port and the small airfield and gave facts and figures on the total target complex.

Sergeant Laurence London Taylor, the tall, bald 35-year old navigator on Pemberton's crew was especially interested in the route details. 205 Group were to attack at midnight from 13,000 feet. Being one of the first night attacks on Budapest, Intelligence had limited knowledge of what the defences would be. All they knew was that the AA artillery was mainly Hungarian with 4 and 8cm Bofors and 8.8cm German guns. Several German batteries also were stationed in Budapest. The air crews were warned to take care and not to stray off course and in particular to avoid the flak batteries situated at Zagreb on the way. They were to fly first on to the eastern end of Lake Balaton, which was to be their landfall position and from that point they were to commence their bombing run in to the target itself. Here they were to meet up with the other aircraft in a group at 15,000 feet and fly in together on the bombing run in order to blitz the target.

Taylor, a former London bank clerk, had put down the name of his sister in Southport, Lancashire as next of kin. Gordon Pemberton, who had worked in a hospital in Swindon before joining up at the age of 19, had put down the name of his wife, who was living in Cheltenham, and his father, Captain J. D. Pemberton, at the PoW camp at the Hartwell dog track near Aylesbury. Flight Sergeant Harry Redpath, the Australian WOp/AG had put down the name of his father who was living in Brighton, Victoria. Sergeant Anthony McTeer, the 19-year old rear gunner, who had been a steelworker at Delta in Newcastle before joining up, had put down his mother's name in Scotswood, as next of kin. Miss N. Rolph in Scarborough Road was also to be informed in the event of his death. On his first leave the young Geordie had shown his mother his air gunner brevet and asked her if she was proud of him. When she saw his uniform and realised that he had volunteered for air crew she smacked him across the mouth. His father decided it was best that they visit the 'Ord Arms'. When the young airman got up and sang *'How Deep Is The Night'* he received a standing ovation. The locals appreciated his devotion to the cause even if his mother didn't.

Budapest was Roy Gristwood's 32nd operation of his tour on 142 Squadron. Once again Flying Officer Lyn Clarke's crew was used for target illumination and the long trip to Hungary meant a reduced load of 36 flares to accommodate an overload fuel tank in the bomb bay. Needless to say, the weather was foul over Yugoslavia. Midnight came and the weather had cleared up and visibility over the plains below, except for a slight ground haze, was quite good. One crew was reminded of one of the verses of the desert version of *'Lili Marlene'*: *'Couldn't find the target, too much blooming sand'*. Gristwood recalls:

'We were the leading crew of illuminators and LN503 was the first aircraft over the city. We and other flare carriers lit it up for the bombers leaving fires raging below. There was flak and plenty of searchlights. 'Red' Fisher, our New Zealander bomb aimer, fell sick and we flew with 'odd' bomb aimers for a few sorties. When 'Red' came out of sick bay he flew some extra sorties with different crews to 'catch up' with us. He wanted to finish his tour at the same time as us, naturally. On a further attack on Budapest - one we did not go on - he flew and did not return. We assumed he was lost over the target but his crew may not have been very experienced and it could easily have been a navigational error (all our sorties were flown without any radar aids). We were probably the last of the dead reckoning dinosaurs in the European Theatre. 'Gee' was installed at Foggia during March-April 1944 but only the replacement aircraft and crews coming out from the UK were equipped and trained to use it.'

'At debriefing, two of the squadron aircraft had failed to return, believed shot down by night fighters. The remaining aircraft had identified the target in good weather conditions and under good illumination, dropping their bombs from 10,500 to 13,000 feet. Bombing appeared to be well concentrated in the target area; particularly the incendiaries and crews reported the target was well alight. Detailed observations of the results were difficult to assess because of the fires, smoke and dust from the many explosions caused by the bombing. Fires were seen for up to fifty miles away on the return journey. The target had been well defended both from the ground and in the air, with moderate to intense heavy anti-aircraft and intense light anti-aircraft guns with 'flaming onions'. Several enemy fighters were seen in the area. One enemy aircraft, a Focke-Wulf FW 190, was shot down by an attacking Wimpy over the target.

One of the two missing Wellingtons was LN858 on 150 Squadron flown by Gordon Pemberton. They had been intercepted by the *Staffelkapitän* of 6./NJG101, Hans Krause. 'The bombers' flights were always in groups of 30 or 40 and always at night' he recalled. 'On this night 3/4 of April it was only a single flight whose goal we don't know. There was no bomb dropping or any other noise and it was a bit of a mystery as to their objective. We had to respond to this. We started at 2214 at Parnsdorf and we went to the position that our intelligence gave us. We used our own radar at 4000 metres that could reach to the border. At 2340 my funker, Otto Fritz, notified that he had a contact at 3,300 metres. By 300 metres my co-pilot could see with his binoculars the enemy machine as a dark shadow. [Redpath would later claim that their attacker homed in on the glow from the navigator's angle-poise lamp, which Taylor had left on].

'When we were 100 metres below the shadow (which we identified as a Vickers Wellington) I attacked with my Do 217 and aimed my nose guns at the left engine and landing gear. I usually did this as the fuel was carried in the wings and I knew it would be disabled if I didn't shoot it down. Generally I used to shoot on the left wing engine and tanks until they had caught fire so that the crew always had a certain amount of time to jump. In this very case I got into the propeller whirl of the Wellington, creating a scattered fire that made hitting the targets exactly impossible. I scored the highest use of ammunition in all my shoot-downs. The Vickers pilot made desperate attempts to get a way and lost a lot of height but the motor started to burn and I thought the fire would bring it down so I stopped the attack. Because I did not want to get hit, I had to stay outside the angle that the rear gunner could sweep with his quadruplet machine guns. After my first burst of fire the rear-gunner shot back at certain intervals to avoid a second attack by me. As long as the left engine was burning there was no need to start a second attack. I hoped that the flames would spread as usual but this Vickers was different. The fire almost went out and only by a light glowing I could suspect the position of the Wellington.

'When I decided to take a second attack the Wellington had already - desired or not - lost so much height that it was too risky for me to continue flying in that hilly terrain. We were expecting the impact fire. I waited for the crash but it didn't come. But much to our surprise it didn't happen. It was impossible but the fire had gone out. Without an impact fire no recognition of a shoot down by the Air Force authorities - in this case they were hard as nails. We were very disappointed that we didn't hear the crash and because it was pitch black we were unable to see what happened. So we flew back to our base and landed at 0121. We were in the air for approximately three hours. We wanted to see in daylight if we could find anything so we left at 1525 and only then did we realize that we were in the district of Balaton. Because of the bad directions we were given the night before we didn't know. We looked everywhere for the crash site but we gave up and on the way back we decided to fly over north-west Balaton. My co-pilot saw the whole side and back part of the plane jutting out of the water on the lakeside. The pilot of the Vickers Wellington had made a masterful landing by very bad light and the loss of his machine. He picked the best place to try to land. We now believed that all five crew were safe thanks to an outstanding forced landing by the pilot near the shore and were probably captured as prisoners. After two hours flying we landed back at 1719.'

Sadly, a few days' later Mrs F. A. Pemberton in Cheltenham and Captain Pemberton at the PoW camp near Aylesbury received the distressing news that Gordon Pemberton had been killed. He had bled death but his sacrifice had not been in vain. The other members of his crew were taken into captivity. Harry Redpath lost an eye in the attack. Sergeant McTeer had his left ear shot off, the bullet lodged in his head and it would remain there for the rest of his life.

A German war correspondent in Keszthely, Hungary reported that 'for weeks there is hardly any day or night without air-raid alarm. No light at all comes out from behind the darkened-out windows of houses. Everywhere in the homes, even in the smallest houses, there are tubs full with water, bins with sand, all at the ready. The emergency packages for the shelters are ready and in many gardens there are protective ditches. Although the Hungarian people mostly know the aerial warfare only from hearsay, despite that, they will not neglect the air defence measures because they know that the American or British terror today or tomorrow, or on any day, may target their homes. The explanation for the seriousness and calmness with which the Hungarian people at every occasion apply the rules of caution is not their fear of the consequences, but the determination rather, to face the air raids whenever they occur.

'Sirens are wailing in the evening. The picture of the pleasant and famous little Spa-town that is in the southern corner of Lake Balaton changes inside of a few moments. The street lights go out. In the inn, the musicians stop their playing in midst their song. They turn off the chandeliers of the grand hall. Only some of the wall lamps remain lit. Their light is not shining far, so that the customers settle their bills with the head waiter at the lights of small pocket torches and leave quickly. Our soldiers and their Hungarian comrades and local civilians, who all sit together, disperse. They hurry home and the soldiers go to their designated places for the raid alert. In a few minutes, on the streets that otherwise have lively traffic on them, not a single soul can be seen. In the quiet it is only the base from which the steps of the air defence guards can be heard. The Hungarian people's air defence discipline is admirable. It remained calm and determined, unchanged.

'Crashed Germans?'

'No! British!'

'It is now already for two hours since the alarm has lasted, when suddenly a motor bicycle turns into the main square, at great speed. The young rider, a boy-soldier paladin, stops in front of the first German soldier and excitedly addresses him. As they do not understand each other's language, they go in the nearest house together. For there is no house around here where there is not a Hungarian who could not understand German. Mihály Kziilfiil, an economics student is the interpreter. A plane crashed into Lake Balaton, four kilometres away but several hundred metres from the shore. The crew of the aircraft are calling for help with whistle and light signals. The first question of the German soldier is that whether it is a German plane. There was not even any need to interpret this. Every Hungarian knows the word 'Deutsche'. The young soldier immediately answered: No! British! And this, in turn, was a word that the German understood well.

'The boy soldier had no proof that it was indeed a British plane, but the faith in victory in the Hungarian youth that spoke from his mouth. That belief made him speak with conviction, that the downed plane in the air fight can only be an enemy plane.

'The amphibian lorry in the waves of Lake Balaton. 'Alarm!' shrieks the German into the telephone handset. 'Alarm!' passes on the guard the report to the nearest German command centre. Our men with the iron crosses knew well the immediate emergency that was escalated to a higher state. It was within minutes in which time they occupied their seats of their land and water capable amphibious vehicles with combat helmets and machine guns. No one knew yet what would follow next. Their commander issued the order to the deputy commanders who, in turn, instructed their men. Immediately after this, the noise of their setting out roared up in the streets of the village. Soon they turned onto the country road that led to the lake. The rough North-eastern wind penetrated down to the bones and swept the waves onto the shores.

'One part of the vehicles fell back and these secured the site with machine guns from the shore. After this, the remaining vehicles carried on in the water in combat formation. From under the wheels soon disappeared the ground and the lorry that runs on the ground at once became a power boat. Just as these floating vehicles went through the reeds of the shore that reaches the pier, the water splashed over the windscreens. The noses of the lorry-boats dug deeply into the waves. In the illumination of reflectors the moss green water of the lake foamed up on the sides of the vehicles that sprayed from both sides the men sitting in it. The windscreen wiper could not cope with wiping for a long time now, and the driver can only see over them, by standing up. The shores disappear in the darkness of the night. Only the signals from the aircraft give directions at times on the rough waters. But the floating crafts carry on securely.

'They shot at us like devils.'

'Ahead, suddenly out of the darkness, the low silhouette of the long-stretched dark grey fuselage of the airplane loomed - they found the searched for craft, a twin engined Wellington bomber. Only some part of the waist and the right wing are out of the water, with a shot-out propeller on the engine. The Blue-red mark gives certainty: It's a British plane. Its crew is huddled on the fuselage in straddling position, shivering, and a civilian power boat that in the meantime already arrived there takes them on board. Four men, two of them injured. The fifth, the pilot, was pulled out dead from among the waves. They crouch in the warm inside of the power boat. For the onlooker neither seems to be a soldier. As they shiver from the cold and moan and groan, it does not seem a manly manner with which they huddle in the small warm place, completely drenched. In their eyes, which not long ago over Budapest sought targets out in the populace and family homes, there is the fear from death.

'Everything went well until we suddenly got into a hail of bullets and shrapnel. They shot at us like devils. Oh, it was over', they said. A resigning hand gesture told the rest...

'There among the papers that were found on them was a postcard-like print with British imperial arms, with English and Arabic text on it as follows:

'To every Arab nation! Greetings and peace be with you. The owner of this document is a British officer and friend of every Arab. Treat him well, give him food and drink, give safe haven from enemies. Help him reach the nearest British military station and you will get a generous reward. Peace and the grace of God be with you.'

'It was a warm evening, just before dusk, in the early spring of 1944' recalled William Coote. 'The aircraft on 70 Squadron were lined up for take-off on Tortorella airfield while the crews relaxed on the grass, waiting instructions. Presently the R/T sets left 'tuned to Control' crackled into life with orders to start engines. Immediately, everyone began making for the nose ladders to enter the Wellingtons. Next in line ahead of my aircraft was Flight Sergeant Harry Pollard's and I happened to glance in that direction. Harry's rear-gunner was entering his turret from the outside, as gunners sometimes did, and he began whistling. As I mounted the ladder there came to my hearing the first few bars of the verse to Stardust, Hoagy Carmichael's famous composition. The piece that runs: 'And now the purple shades of twilight time, steals across the meadows...' Just that: then I was inside the aircraft. Five or six hours later, after de-briefing, we sat in the mess tent having our flying breakfast. The places that Harry Pollard and his crew would have occupied were vacant. As far as I am aware they were never heard from again. Strange how particular associations persist: from then on, whenever I heard the strains of that melody, the memory of Pollard's rear-gunner climbing into his turret always seems to come to mind.'

Flying Officer Lyn Clarke's crew completed the 36th operation of their tour on the night of 3/4 May with a trip to the marshalling yards at Bucharest, which was visited by 62 aircraft. Gristwood recalls:

'It was an easy one! There was only light flak over the target but we got holed over Nis in Yugoslavia on the way home. Nothing vital was hit - an engine out would have been serious with the mountains still to be crossed but we got back safely. Thirty-six trips and only hit once within hours of finishing - a lucky tour for us all, except 'Red'.'[134]

The night following seventy aircraft attacked the Budapest-Rakos rail yards. On the night of Saturday 6 May 55 Wellingtons, eight Liberators and seven Path Finder Halifaxes were detailed to attack the Bucharest industrial area. Three Wellingtons and a Liberator failed to return. Les Hallam on Flight Sergeant Walker's crew on 150 Squadron recalls: 'This was one of our great moments. On our way back, the wireless operator spotted an enemy fighter, coming in to attack from the rear. The rear gunner let him have it and down the fighter went in flames. Its destruction was later confirmed. This was the first such success recorded for 150 Squadron. Flight Sergeant Walker got the DFC and the rear gunner was awarded the DFM.'

For three successive nights, starting on 25/26 May, 205 Group attacked the Germans in retreat at the Viterbo road junction in northern Italy. Les Hallam on Flight Sergeant Walker's crew on 150 Squadron recalls:

'On 27/28 May being only a short trip, only three to four aircraft took part at a time, but there were three or four take-off times through the night so, as far as the Germans were concerned, it amounted to an all-night attack. On 1/2 July we laid mines in the River Danube near Belgrade. This was a very scary experience! At 200 feet the river banks rose above us on either side and one slip by the Skipper and we would have been goners. On the second mining operation, on 30/31 July, there was action from the guns from one side of the Danube. As I was down in the bomb hatch in the nose of the Wellington there were red tracer bullets flashing past. We got away safely.'

Enemy night fighters and the risk of collision were other dangers faced on night operations. On the night of 23/24 May when twenty aircraft raided Ferrantino and another 27 hit Valmontone, two Wellingtons on 70 Squadron are believed to have collided. On the night of 6/7 July, when 61 aircraft of 205

Group attacked Feuersbrunn airfield and thirteen bombers were lost, a Wellington and a FW 190 were seen to collide over the target. A Ju 88 was claimed shot down by a 40 Squadron Wellington crew.

'Operating Wimpys in Italy in 1944 was something akin to Burma's 'Forgotten Army' recalled 'Denys White. 'We had no navigational aids at all and incendiaries were dropped to obtain our drifts over land and flame floats etc by night. The most experienced crews usually got to the target area first and dropped flares and then we had to bomb visually by the light of the flares. It wasn't until about July that we received 'Gee' and even then it was of limited range. A squadron of Halifaxes started to act as our pathfinders in late July, equipped with H2S[135] but their early efforts were a disastrous failure. We were supposed to drop our bombs on their target indicators (TIs), but these were usually miles from the target. Our crew became very demoralised until the Hallies finally began dropping their TIs properly on target.

'In addition to bombs we were expected to take along a load of propaganda leaflets - 'Nickels' as they were termed. When dropping 'Nickels' our instructions were to go upwind of the target area to release them. As can be imagined, having dropped our bombs no one wanted to hang about the target with mere leaflets. We devised a very good system to solve this nuisance. On dispersal prior to a sortie, we'd almost close the bomb doors after bombing up and then placed the packets of 'Nickels' along the inside edge of the doors, opened the packets and then fully closed the bomb doors. Thus, over the target, we dropped the whole issue in one go. This system worked remarkably well until one night when the sortie was scrubbed at the last minute. Next morning the armourers had to change the bomb load, opened the bomb doors and the leaflets scattered from Foggia to Naples...at least we weren't short of bog paper for the next few weeks!

'From a pilot's point of view, the Wimpy was a very strong aircraft and would take any amount of punishment from flak. However, it had its awkward characteristics too. On take-off one always had to throttle back sharply in order to work the accelerator pump, otherwise the engines were likely to cut out when opening up to full power. The Hercules engine was very good, though it suffered from trouble with the magneto occasionally. On landing one had to engage a sort of automatic trim, which meant having to push hard on the control column during the approach run. Then, on levelling out, one took great care otherwise the nose came well up. The automatic pilot was also a dicey affair, sometimes causing the Wimpy to dive steeply. For such emergencies a fire axe was kept handy to sever the hydraulics pipeline if the automatic pilot couldn't be disengaged smartly. One other disquieting habit was for the escape hatch over the pilot to fly off on occasion. In early July 142 and 150 Squadrons moved to Regina airfield north of Foggia and there we were on our own. Regina was just a dirt runway and caused many problems for our aircraft tyres; the stones, etc cutting the rubber. I always had to check the tyres prior to take-off of other aircraft whenever I wasn't flying ops - it was a dusty, filthy job but very necessary.'

Les Hallam on 150 Squadron recalls:
'The runway was a mud track through the field and the control tower was

a wooden building on stilts. By this time some Halifaxes had joined us as target Indicators. They dropped the red or green flares onto the target and if we dropped our load on these, then as far as the squadron was concerned, the raid was a success. On 21 July we raided the oil refinery at Pardubice. It was a success, as far as we were concerned, but all we had done was to more or less wipe out the population. The American B-17s had to destroy the oil refinery by daylight bombing.'

One of the new arrivals in Italy in the summer of 1944 was Jack Weekley, a navigator, who had completed an OTU tour on Wellingtons at Quastima, Palestine, before being posted to 150 Squadron at Regina. Weekley flew his first operation on 16/17 July when the squadron were part of a force of ninety aircraft that raided the Smederevo oil refinery in Yugoslavia. Each Wellington carried nine 500lb bombs and the main aiming points were the boiler house and cracking plant. Three nights' later, 150 Squadron were part of a formation of 109 aircraft that bombed another oil refinery, at Fiume Romanio in northern Italy. Both targets put up an intense barrage of light and heavy flak respectively. Two aircraft failed to return from the raid on Smederevo and one crashed at the end of the trip to Fiume. On the night of 19/20 July, when 94 aircraft attacked the Pardubice oil refinery, five bombers were lost. On 24/25 July, when 29 aircraft attacked Valence/La Trasorerie airfield Weekley's Wellington made a solo six-hour leaflet, or 'Nickel' raid on Piacenza near Milan. Weekley recalls:

'The idea was to drop the leaflets about seven miles away and allow the prevailing wind to scatter them over Milan. The bomb bays and the interior of the aircraft were stuffed with leaflets. Some were printed in German and others in Italian. One of the stories was about D-Day and the invasion. On target, we opened the bomb doors and let half of the leaflets go. Then we circled round, throwing leaflets out of the astrodome, while one crew member pushed leaflets out of the flare chute. It was estimated that we carried about half a million leaflets and so we circled tor some time but saw no fighters or guns.'

The diversity of operations continued. On 26/27 July three aircraft on 150 Squadron, each with nine containers in their bomb bays, made a supply dropping trip, code-named 'Lambley' to partisans in northern Italy. The crews dropped on a light which replied to their downward coded signal. Jack Weekley saw a flare from an enemy aircraft nearby but the Wellington crews encountered no opposition. On 3/4 August 85 aircraft including Wellingtons on 150 Squadron visited marshalling yards at Portes-les-Valences in southern France. It was a long flight - eight hours - and a bomb load of only six 500lb and two 250lb bombs could be carried. The remaining bays were taken up with an overload petrol tank because of the length of the trip. All the aircraft returned safely. Four nights' later, on 7/8 August, 150 Squadron loaded up each of its available Wellingtons with eighteen 250lb bombs when 74 aircraft made a five and a half hour round trip to the Szombatheley fighter aerodrome 150 miles west of Budapest. Jack Weekley explains:

'The object of the raid was to neutralise the 'drome to help a daylight raid next day by the American 15th Air Force. Some of our bombs were set for instantaneous detonation; others carried a six to 24 hours' delay. This was a typical mixed load for aerodromes. It was a bright moonlit night and a squadron of night fighters seemed to be airborne, waiting for us. We were one of the first to bomb. As we came out of the target another Wellington was only a few yards on our starboard side. Suddenly, it burst into flames and fell in three pieces. In the flames of the burning aircraft we saw a Ju 88 break away underneath us, so close we could see the aircraft markings. As we flew on we saw a number of aircraft going down.'

Four aircraft failed to return. It was a bright moonlit night and as the last aircraft in the main bomber stream Flying Officer H. W. James, the pilot of a Wellington on 70 Squadron, all too aware of the target the slow flying Wimpy presented to the enemy night fighters, felt particularly vulnerable. He dived away from the airfield after dropping his 4,000lb bomb to get clear of the area as quickly as possible before heading south-westwards across the Hungarian plain on the long journey back across Yugoslavia to Foggia. Their luck ran out a few miles from the target when the Wimpy was attacked by enemy fighters. The rear gunner, 37-year-old Sergeant Henry Whittaker, who had been a policeman in Birmingham before joining up, claimed one shot down but another fighter came up from underneath and poured a stream of cannon shells into the Wellington and set it on fire. The underside of the fuselage was soon well alight and James ordered the crew to prepare to abandon the aircraft.

Whittaker climbed out of his turret, crawled back into the fuselage to collect his parachute, clipped it on and waited for the command to bail out. He sat there for perhaps half a minute feeling the heat of the fire behind him, his turret filling with bitter-smelling smoke. If he didn't jump soon, he thought, it would be pointless because they were below 200 feet. Finally, he flicked on his microphone switch and called, 'Rear gunner calling skipper'. Immediately James' voice snapped back - 'Haven't you gone Henry? Get out, get out!' Whittaker asked, 'Have the others gone?' James said, 'Yes - get out!' Whittaker knew then that he must have missed the order when he had taken his helmet off to collect his chute. He swung the turret round. Through the smoke he saw trees zipping by almost it seemed as high as the aircraft. For a second he hesitated and then a wave of terrible heat hit him and backwards, he fell clear of the turret. As he somersaulted both hands went to the parachute on his chest: with his right he pulled the ripcord and as the silk burst out he seized a handful with his left and flung it over his shoulders in a desperate attempt to speed the process of opening. But the chute had only begun to stream when he hit the trees.

Fifteen seconds at the most after he had left the Wellington Luckily, the branches of a tall pine tree broke his fall. Whittaker then heard the explosion of the crashed Wimpy. He undid his harness and tried in vain to pull the parachute down from the branch on which it had hooked but the chute was too firmly caught up and in the end he had to climb down to the ground without it. Standing there in the pine wood his right arm seemed to have lost all its strength but otherwise he was unhurt. 'I had a feeling of elation not unmixed with awe that I had come through so miraculously,' he says. 'Although I knew I was in the heart of enemy territory, at least 200 miles from Marshal Tito's forces in Yugoslavia, I was not afraid because I felt, so strongly that the Power that had brought me down against a million-to-one chance would not desert me now.'

Whittaker made his way out of the pine wood to a road from where he could see the flames from the burning Wellington, leaping above the pines about half a mile away. He looked at it for a moment, knowing that James could not have survived and then walked down the road in the direction which he judged must lead to Yugoslavia. Presently he came to a village. 'It looked so beautiful and enchanting in the moonlight,' he says, 'that hungry and tired as I was, I felt for one brief moment like going down there and giving myself up, as I reasoned that people living in such a beautiful place could not fail to be kind and decent.' But the temptation did not last and he took to the woods again to bypass the village. It was daylight when a Hungarian policeman stepped from behind a tree and prodded him with a bayoneted rifle and Whittaker was taken into custody. Of the other four members of the crew who bailed out at 500 feet, only two came down safely. James stayed with the aircraft to give the others a chance and he was killed in the crash. The bomb aimer got out with more height to spare than Whittaker but he was killed as he fell into the same pinewood.[136]

On the night of 9/10 August 81 aircraft of 205 Group attacked the Ploesti Romana Americana oil refinery. Eleven bombers failed to return. The night following, 56 aircraft attacked the Kraljevo rail yards and thirteen other bombers dropped mines in the Danube. On the night of 12/13 August 61 aircraft of 205 Group bombed the Hadju Boszorrneny landing ground. On 13/14 August Genoa was the target for 59 aircraft, all of which returned safely. The following night 56 aircraft returned to France loaded with six 500lb and two 250lb bombs in their bomb-bays and fitted with overload petrol tanks for the seven-hour round trip. Other aircraft carried incendiaries. Their target was the port installations at Marseilles. Jack Weekley recalls: 'En route to France we flew over a large convoy. This was the invasion of southern France. As we neared the target we could see the fires of Toulon, bombed in the afternoon by the 15th Air Force. We were met with heavy and light flak.' One aircraft failed to return.

On 17 August the Wellingtons bombed the submarine pens and harbour installations at Marseilles, as the American 7th Army were to make their landing in southern France the next day. On 18 August the Wellingtons raided an aerodrome at Vanence/La Tresoreria. Most aircraft bombed individually with the aid of ground markers. Unfortunately, the markers were dropped in the wrong place and most bombs fell miles from the target. It was scant reward for a long, eight and half hour trip, requiring two over-load petrol tanks in each Wellington. Les Hallam flew the 38th and final sortie of his tour on 20 August 1944 when 205 Group raided the Hermann Goring AFV works at St Valentin in Austria. Their route took them on a track between Linz and Steyr, a heavily defended zone. The crews were met by a barrage of searchlights and intense flak. On 22 August, Wellingtons on 150 Squadron attacked the Miskolk marshalling yards in Hungary to hinder German supplies reaching the Russian front. Two nights later the marshalling yards at Bologna in northern Italy were bombed. Jack Weekley recalls:

'There was a change of time on target following the briefing but for some reason we were not told and so we were flying in the Po Valley in the target area for about half an hour all on our own. When the markers did go down we bombed successfully.'

On the night of 25 August it was Italy again as the Wellingtons struck at marshalling yards; this time at Ravenna. 'It was another disaster for us,' reflected Jack Weekley. 'There was an electrical fault on the aircraft. As soon as the pilot operated the bomb door switch, which was also the master switch, the whole bomb-load of nine 500 pounders fell. As the bomb doors had not had sufficient time to open fully, the bombs smashed through them. For a moment we thought we had been hit. The bombs fell well short of the target and we had a draughty journey home.'

On the night of 26/27 August 66 aircraft of 205 Group went in search of troop concentrations in the Pesaro area of northern Italy, each armed with a mixed load of 500-pounders and 250-pounders. The large bomb load meant that each Wellington had to carry a reduced fuel load so flight planning for the three hour forty minute round trip was critical. The Wimpys crossed the target area three to four at a time to prolong the raid. Next day, light bombers pounded the area and that night, 28/29 August, 40 aircraft returned to carry out the same procedure as the night before. This time the bombing took place only about half a mile in front of the Allied lines where the Polish Army was about to advance. In all, this night and day bombing was kept up continuously for 72 hours.

When 205 Group resumed raids on marshalling yards the Wellingtons were part of the force of 74 aircraft that bombed Ferrara on 31 August/1 September and 74 aircraft that attacked Bologna North in northern Italy on 1/2 September. The Hungarian and Rumanian railway system was especially important to the Germans and came under constant Allied aerial bombardment, while the Russians effectively deprived the Germans of the use of the Lwow-Cernauti railway. The only alternative route linking Germany with the grain lands of Hungary and the oilfields of Rumania was the River Danube, capable of carrying 10,000 tons of war material daily. By mid-March 1944 the Danube was carrying more than double the amount carried by rail. Even a temporary halt would seriously hamper the German war effort and in April 1944 205 Group began 'Gardening' operations, 'sowing' the waterways with mines. At first the 'Gardening' sorties were only flown when there was a full moon as the aircraft had to fly no higher than 200 feet and even heights of forty and fifty feet were reported. On the night of 8 April nineteen Wellingtons on 178 Squadron and three Liberators dropped forty mines near Belgrade. Over the next nine days 137 more mines were dropped and in May the total number dropped had risen to over 500. The effect on the supply route was catastrophic. Several ships were sunk and blocked parts of the waterway. By May coal traffic had virtually ceased. Canals and ports were choked with barges. No 'Gardening' sorties were flown during June, but on the night of 1/2 July 53 Wellingtons and sixteen Liberators dropped 192 mines in the biggest operation of the mining campaign. Four aircraft failed to return. The following night, when ten aircraft were dispatched, another sixty mines were dropped. By August 1944 the volume of material transported along the Danube had been reduced by seventy per cent. 'Gardening' sorties continued throughout September and October. Jack Weekley's mining operation took place on the night of 6 September and involved a round trip of five hours forty minutes.

'We mined the Danube about thirty miles south of Budapest. About four aircraft would be detailed to do the mining operation. There would be a raid on at the same time and the mining aircraft would fly some of the way in the main stream and then break away. Mining operations could only take place on about three nights a month when the moon was full because it was a low level night attack. The aircraft carried two 1,000lb Mark V parachute mines. These had to be dropped at a height of about 180 feet, or less. As it was moonlight and the height was so low the aircraft were targets for every ground weapon imaginable. The area chosen was a long narrow island in the middle of the Danube, which divided the river into two narrow channels. The aircraft concerned were briefed to mine a particular channel. As mining was done regularly, the enemy knew more or less when the operation would take place. Generally crews only did one such trip - one they did not look forward to.'

In mid-September 1944 heavy rainfall stopped operations as the earth and grass strips soon became heavily waterlogged. When conditions improved, on 26/27 September, the target selected for 86 aircraft was the Borovnica railway viaduct in northern Yugoslavia, which the enemy were using for troop and supply trains to Greece. Jack Weekley recalls:

'We bombed with eighteen 250 pounders. There was some heavy flak but a 4,000lb 'cookie' bomb was seen to hit the centre span of the viaduct. At this time 150 Squadron was broken up. The air and ground crews were posted to 40 and 104 Squadrons, the other Wellington squadrons at Foggia Main. Two other squadrons, 37 and 70, were based at Tortorella. So, 150 Squadron 'came home on paper' and was re-formed at Hemswell on Lancasters. My crew was posted to 104 Squadron at Foggia in October.'

On the night of 4/5 October, eighteen Wellingtons and four Liberators flew the final mining operation and dropped 58 mines in to the Danube in Hungary, west of Budapest, north of Gyor and east of Esztergom. Two others mined Khalkis. In six months of operations, 1,382 mines were laid by Wellingtons and Liberators of 205 Group in eighteen attacks.

Alan Ackerman reached 40 Squadron at Foggia Main in October 1944.

'The first thing we asked was where do we sleep and one of the chaps took us over to a tent. There were a couple of beds that were occupied and a couple of spaces. Our guide pointed to the spaces and was about to leave as we asked where our beds were. 'They become available,' he said, and left. So my first few nights were spent on the tent floor. But a bed did become available quite quickly. A Flight Sergeant in one of them didn't come back from a trip and I took over.'

In October Sergeant 'Tubby' Gaunt's crew were posted from 77 OTU Palestine to 37 Squadron at Foggia. Their first four operations were almost uneventful. Each time, they were scheduled to drop supplies to Tito's partisans in Yugoslavia. Normally, the canisters were dropped in daylight from 3-4,000 feet without parachutes. Sergeant Maurice 'Scats' Sandell, the air bomber, recalls: 'It was a strange experience to be shot at horizontally by small arms fire from sides of valleys. One time we had a freeze-up and we couldn't release the containers in the bomb bay. Eventually, the mechs had to chop them out with axes. 'Tubby' didn't like going round a target again. On another occasion, we dropped supplies to Italian partisans at Pecorra in northern Italy. It was like a Hollywood movie. They lit fires for us to go in. We had been briefed to avoid Udine where German jet aircraft were based. Another place to avoid was Pola (now Pula) on the Istrian coast of Yugoslavia which was one of the main sites for anti-aircraft batteries. It was a funny sort of war. We supplied pockets of partisans on one side of a mountain range and bombed the enemy on the other.'

During November 1944 operations were predominantly aimed at dropping bombs on targets in Yugoslavia, involving a dozen Wellingtons at a time. On 23 November when 40 aircraft attacked Rogatica and 33 aircraft bombed German troop concentrations at Uzice, each Wellington on 37 Squadron carried six 500lb bombs and a dozen 250 pounders. Gaunt's Wellington received five flak holes at Uzice but returned safely to Foggia. One other Wellington did not. The Wellingtons did not carry a front-gunner. This task was carried out when needed by the air bomber, as Maurice Sandell recalls:

'I would sit or stand beside 'Tubby' most of the time and only went into the front if asked. Flying in the front turret was so remote it was like flying with no wings. The front turret was so small I had to be helped out. Flying in the tail turret was much better. The bomb aimer's job in a Wimpy was the best job in the Air Force. On return trips I occasionally used to fly the aircraft. Then 'Geordie' Hazleden, our 'rough tough' tail gunner, who would tear down German night fighters with his bare hands if all else failed, would have a spell. I also helped out with map reading. One day 'Jock' Scanlon got lost. According to his reckoning, a cross-road would soon show up and give us an opportunity to get a 'fix'. It came and we flew over it. The Germans peppered us with 88mm shells. 'Jock' got his 'fix' all right!

'My main task, of course, was bomb aiming. Although the bombsight at OTU was an early type with manual drift wires, on the squadron we used an electric bomb sight. I fed the wind speed, height and various information into it from data provided at briefing and by 'Mac' McMememy, our wireless operator and 'Jock' Scanlon, the navigator. This would alter the angle on the glass plate with an illuminated cross for bombing. I would then select the sticks of bombs to be dropped using my bomb selector box, or Mickey Mouse as it was called. Normally, there were four or five bombs in a stick. The 500 pounders would be dropped first and then the 250 pounders.'

On 4 December 1944 Gaunt's crew flew the last of ten operations on 37 Squadronn when 54 aircraft dropped supplies over Yugoslavia. The squadron then re-equipped with Liberators, or 'Spam Cans', as the RAF called them and Gaunt's crew was among those transferred to 70 Squadron, where they continued to operate the Wellington. On 19 December they flew the first operation on their new squadron, when Matesevo bridge in Yugoslavia was attacked by four aircraft and 37 more attacked enemy road transport Matesevo/Kolasin. Two days' later they took off at 1335 hours for a three-hour round trip to bomb another bridge, at Mojkovac in Croatia. Another 28 aircraft attacked enemy road transport at Matesevo/Bijelo Polje. 'Scats' Sandell admitted to a 'hairy' feeling on take-off for they were carrying a 4,000lb 'cookie'. Sandell felt they were not flying a Wellington but rather a 'cookie with wings'. The object of the operation was to prevent German troops reaching the partisans' area. Unfortunately, both Gaunt's Wellington and a second which also carried a 'cookie', missed the bridge. However, Gaunt's crew were relieved to see the massive bomb go. As Maurice Sandell pointed out: 'At least when a 'cookie' was gone, it was gone; there was no question of it hanging up.'

The war did not stop for Christmas. On Christmas Day 1944 fifty aircraft were dispatched on a daylight supply dropping operation, code-named 'Crnomelj' to the partisans in Yugoslavia. 'Scats' Sandell Tubby on Gaunt's crew recalls: 'We strung along in a bomber stream in broad daylight just as if it was in the middle of the night. Good job there was no opposition. Supply dropping by daylight was a colourful sight. Supplies of guns, medicines, ammunition, clothes etc, were dropped using a different coloured parachute. This enabled the partisans, who could be seen quite clearly on the outskirts of the drop site, to grab some of each kind of supply and get away as quickly as possible. The next night we made another supply drop, code-named 'Cazrna' in Yugoslavia. This time we flew with the Flight Commander as pilot.'

On Boxing Day night, 26/27 December, 43 aircraft including those on 70 Squadron were dispatched to Casarsa in northern Italy to bomb a railway bridge. Pathfinders went in first and lit up the bridge with target indicators. When the Wellingtons arrived over the target, in moonlight, they could see quite clearly red flares at one end of the bridge and green flares at the other. Each aircraft carried a mixed bomb load of nine 500 pounders and four 250 pounders which were to be dropped in 'Blitz time' along the length of the bridge. Each Wellington flew singly over the target in trail and released its bombs but without success. 'At least,' thought Maurice Sandell, 'we will not run into each other this way.' As each stick of bombs dropped a photo flash, timed to go off when the bombs exploded, lit up the area like day while a camera, activated when the bomb release was pressed, snapped the scene below. The photo flash brought back bad memories for Maurice Sandell. Wellington fabric and fire were partners in death and at OTU more crews had been lost from accidents with photo flashes than anything else.

On 8 January 1945 'Tubby' Gaunt's crew awoke in their primitive tents pitched among the wine groves and set off for the Mess hut for breakfast. At briefing, the Wellington crews learned that the day's operation would be a supply drop to partisans in the Ljubljana region in Yugoslavia. Although this did not present the same dangers as a trip to Ploesti or some other oil target, there were other dangers, mostly from the elements.

'The briefing officer warned that bad weather could be expected over Yugoslavia. The ceiling would be about 16,000 feet and the safety height over the mountains only 10,000 feet.'

70 Squadron's crews began taking off around 1125 hours. 'Tubby' Gaunt's crew pressed on across the Adriatic, which was covered in thick cloud. 'Scats' Sandell recalls:

'We went into storm clouds and got tossed around like a 'pea in a drum'.

The instruments went haywire. At one time our Wellington stood on her tail and then went nose down. Everything hit the ceiling. Mud, which was always trudged into the aircraft, splattered everywhere. We were icing up. It got so bad that the flapping motion of the wings stopped with the weight of ice. There was a 'twang' as bits of ice spun off the prop blades and hit the fuselage. We never found the target and our supplies had to be brought back. Eventually, we broke cloud. Through the small clear gap on the windscreen 'Tubby' and I could see the 'white horses' of the wave tops on the sea. 'Tubby' exclaimed, 'We've made it, 'Scats'!' However, it was not the sea. The 'whitecaps' were in fact snow drifts of fir trees clinging to the sides of mountains. We were still over Yugoslavia! We took up our crash positions. 'Tubby' flew right up a valley, losing height rapidly. Suddenly, we hit. A tree took the starboard wingtip off and we went through a line of hedgerows. 'Tubby' had made a lovely crash landing and this was the only time I had seen a Wimpy crash not end in flames. This is probably because our Wellington had broken her belly and snow had poured in until it was knee deep. I was sitting on a little flap seat next to 'Tubby' who was strapped in. I blacked out. When I came too, I could see 'Tubby's' forehead denting the windscreen. I could hear the 'drip, drip' of petrol spilling onto the snow. I opened the escape hatch and said, 'After you, Tubby!'

'Geordie' had his legs jammed under the servo-feed in his rear turret. We got him out and jumped into the waist high snow. For the first time we noticed armed men and women dressed in green uniforms with little red stars on their forage caps. Luckily, we had landed among partisans. Immediately, some women came over and began collecting the dripping petrol in tins. They wanted to go inside the aircraft but we told them it was too dangerous. The partisans wanted the machine guns and they were stripped from the turrets. The supply canisters probably contained explosives but they took them anyway. They took everything they could get their hands on. A Yugoslavian who had worked as a lumberjack in Canada told us that this side of the valley was controlled by the partisans. The other side was controlled by Chetniks! The partisans set us on our way. We passed through various groups and British missions. Eventually, on 7 February, we reached the British military mission at Zara (now Zada) on the coast and were put aboard HMS *Calumba*, a depot ship, for the night. Next day, we sailed for the Allied repatriation centre at Bari aboard HMS *Wiltan*. As 70 Squadron members, our war was over. We were repatriated home from Naples by ship.'

In January 1945 70 Squadron at Tortorella had begun re-equipping with Liberator VIs, as had 104 Squadron at Foggia Main. On 21 February 205 Group 73 aircraft attacked Pola naval ordnance depot, as Jack Weekley recalls:

'We attacked in daylight. As usual, we flew night bomber stream tactics with no effort to formate. There was fighter escort in the target area, which was heavily defended. We were about the second or third aircraft to go in. The Wellington in front of us was hit and went down. Behind us a Liberator was hit. It went down on fire and broke up. We saw three parachutes go down right to the target area. One of our bombs hit the ammunition dump and in seconds there was a huge pall of smoke up to hundreds of feet (later the film in our camera proved it was ours). We were so fascinated that we went round again for another look. It was stupid in view of the opposition and more so when we got back and the CO told us we had finished our tour.'

While Jack Weekley was going home, others, like Les Hallam, returned to Italy and 150 Squadron in March 1945, for a second tour on the ever faithful Wellington X.

'I have often wondered whether 205 Group helped us beat the Germans or did a better job of putting the Iron Curtain countries in worse trouble by helping the Russian advance and their eventual take-over of those countries. Perhaps ops were easier, compared with the home-based 'big boys', but the air and ground crews had to endure much more primitive living conditions and lower food standards.'

The Wellingtons' last operation took place on the night of 13/14 March 1945 when six Wimpys accompanied a force of 63 Liberators in an attack on the Treviso North-East rail yards in northern Italy. Wellingtons were also used on a smaller scale in the Far Eastern campaign until replacement by Liberators at the end of 1944.

Footnotes

132 Up until May 1940 the night air defence of the *Reich* was almost entirely the province of the flak arm of the Luftwaffe. No specialised night fighting arm existed though one fighter *Gruppe* was undertaking experimental 'Helle Nachtjagd' (illuminated night fighting) sorties with the aid of searchlights in northern Germany and in the Rhineland. The Helle Nachtjagd technique used in 1940 and early 1941 was entirely dependent on weather conditions and radar-guided searchlights simply could not penetrate thick layers of cloud or industrial haze over the Ruhr and other industrial centres in the Reich. Kammhuber realised that Helle Nachtjagd was only a short-term solution and soon concentrated all his energies in developing an efficient radar-controlled air defence system. On 22 June 1940 Hauptmann Wolfgang Falck, Kommandeur, I./ZG1 who had some experience with radar-directed night-fighting sorties in the Bf 110 flying from Aalborg, Denmark during April 1940, was ordered to form the basis of a Nachtjagd, or night fighting arm, by establishing the first defence of the Ruhr with the aid of one flak searchlight regiment. In July Göring ordered Kammhuber to set up of a full-scale night fighting arm. Within three months, Kammhuber's organisation was remodelled into Fliegerkorps XII and by the end of 1940 the infant *Nachtjagd* had evolved into three searchlight batallions and five night fighter Gruppen.

133 Krause's first Abschuss was Wellington III BK313 KO-B on 115 Squadron on its way home to Mildenhall. Twenty-two-year-old Flying Officer Leonard I. Smith RCAF and his crew perished and were laid to rest in the Reichswald Forest War Cemetery. The second Wellington that Krause shot down was DF639 on 75 Squadron RNZAF captained by Sergeant George William Rhodes. Again, there were no survivors when the aircraft crashed in flames at 2330 near Hardenberg in Holland. *Night Airwar: Personal Recollections of the conflict over Europe, 1939-45* by Theo Boiten (The Crowood Press 1999).

134 On 8 April 1944, for one special operation, Wellingtons attacked concentrations of German troops in the Yugoslav town of Niksic.

135 H2S was a 10cm experimental airborne radar navigational and target location aid developed by Dr. Lovell at the TRE (Telecommunications Research Establishment) at Malvern, Worcestershire, which produced a 'map' on a CRT display of a 360° arc of the ground below the equipped aircraft. It was first used in January 1943.

136 *See Into the Silk* by Ian Mackersey (Granada Publishing 1978).

Chapter 10

Maritime Operations

'How the hell we were supposed to know what fifty feet was at night is beyond comprehension. We lost one crew with the exception of the tail gunner when a pilot misjudged the prescribed fifty feet and dug in. Also, when a torpedo is incorrectly dropped it can come up out of the water looking for the joker that dropped it. Guess that could be called a self-inflicted wound. Twice, I saw a captain of a destroyer wait until he saw our dummy torpedo drop and then haul his ship over so hard that our torpedo missed by a country mile.'

Stephen A. Oliphant, an American pilot serving in the RCAF who did his torpedo training on the Wellington at Abbotsinch. He never saw action on torpedo-dropping Wellingtons, joining the USAAF shortly after completing training.

Apart from service with Coastal Command, Wellingtons also served in the maritime role throughout the Mediterranean, Middle East and Far East Theatres. It will be remembered that 458 Squadron RAAF, left England at the end of January 1942 to take up a torpedo-bomber role in the Middle East. Wing Commander Mulholland led three Wellington ICs, which had been fitted with 'tropicalised' Bristol Pegasus engines, off from Stanton Harcourt. The flight to Malta via Le Havre, a distance of some 1,460 miles, was made without mishap until the formation reached Malta. Mulholland overshot the island and he and his crew perished when they were brought down by enemy night fighters. The other three Wellingtons touched down at Luqa safely.

On 27 February 1942 the second formation of Wellingtons left England for the Middle East, flying the first stage of their journey from Portreath to Gibraltar before continuing to Malta. The first 458 Squadron Wellington to land in Egypt touched down at Kilo 26, a landing ground halfway between Cairo and Alexandria, on 1 March. The rest of the squadron flew in over the next few weeks and ground personnel arrived from their previous base at Holme-on-Spalding Moor, mostly by sea. Training in the new role of a torpedo-bomber unit followed, but it was a 'conventional' load of 250 pounders and armour-piercing bombs that were dropped when the first operation was flown, on the night of July 25/26. A single Wellington, piloted by Sergeant Ian Cameron, took off from Abu Sueir and dropped its bombs on enemy positions in the Qutefryca area. By September 1942 the full complement on 458 Squadron had arrived in the Canal Zone and the unit was now based at Shallufa, flying torpedo bombing operations. The squadron, together with two other Wellington squadrons, 38 and 221, formed 248 Wing of 201 Group. 221 Squadron had arrived in Egypt in January 1942 with a brief to use their ASV sets to locate enemy convoys for torpedo-armed 'Fishingtons' of 38 and 458 Squadrons to carry out the actual attacks.

38 Squadron had served in the Middle East since November 1940. At Shallufa during the latter part of 1941, the squadron had added minelaying sorties to its list of activities. Charles Booth, a 38 Squadron Wellington radio operator, recalls:

'On minelaying runs to Benghazi we did an afternoon take-off from Shallufa with full weapons plus maximum fuel, no overload tanks, and flew the two-hour flight to an advance desert landing strip, usually LG09, to top-up the tanks. It was always a dodgy landing on near-virgin desert with a Wellington and a large load. 38 Squadron was the only squadron on minelaying duties. When there was a shortage of mines we used tailfin cartons filled with sand. We would make raids with these, interspersed with real mines. Our magnetic mines could be set in any of 16 polarity positions. Enemy shipping movements, therefore, could not take place until their minesweepers had made 16 sweeps over all the approaches to Benghazi. Dropping mines required three or four runs. Mine-laying involved two crews working every second night, but it was usually very busy with bombers overhead because the attack would involve other squadrons bombing the town and harbour heavily. All aircraft, therefore, were timed precisely at half a minute each at heights between 10-12,000 feet. Minelayers were to go in at 200 feet during melee to drop close-in, either inside the harbour or up to half a mile on deep approaches.

'We had a meal at LG09 at about 6 o'clock and had a detailed last briefing. Take-off for Benghazi was 22:00 hrs. Engines run up on 'U-Uncle' revealed port engine gills adjustment were faulty. Switch off. Called engine mechanic. On examination he said he could set gills at an optimum position then he'd have to adjust. The delay meant we would have to 'drop' an hour after main attack and without other supporting bombers: i.e., alone! Also, we were ordered to drop one mile out from the harbour entrance. It was thought to be less fraught!

'We took off from LG09. Using aircraft letter 'D' we telegraphed in Morse 'DI, DI, DI'. (On the way back we'd telegraph 'DO, DO, DO'.) No other transmission as enemy could fix our position. Next aircraft in sequence listening followed on. We crossed the coast from the south. Bright moon to eastward. No cloud. Shore silhouetted. Flew close in under cliffs. On sighting harbour approach, banked out to position one mile out 200 feet altitude. No lights of any description to be seen ashore. Enemy did not suspect a 'lone one'. We made our drop run north. Could have got away with it but the 'Mickey Mouse' selector did not let the mines go. Flight Sergeant Roger Mannel, the pilot, said on intercom: 'We'll turn and run back with same track to drop'. Once I flew with a captain who made 13 runs because he wasn't satisfied! The crew played absolute hell with him.

'Round we came, levelled; nothing from the shore! The enemy, too late, realised our north run and that we had not dropped! Blue and white searchlights and all guns were ready to engage. We would have been better close-in because all heavy 40mm flak cannon up and down the harbour and adjacent coasts could not depress their guns sufficiently and reach us. We had only just felt the two mines go when everything happened! A radar directed blue master searchlight came on. There was no searching around the sky. We were in the beam. Our only recourse was violent diving and weaving and hopefully be elsewhere when the shells started arriving. The Germans are indomitable fighters. Nothing seemed to shake them. White searchlights everywhere tracked the blue. Guns flashed like striking matches. The next instant, shells were bursting everywhere. All hell around and bright red light from flashing shells. Shattering impacts close to the aircraft, with debris titter-tattering all over, through the aircraft skin. A piece of shrapnel entered the tail turret above Jock McCombie's head and lodged in his starboard ammunition pan. At 200 feet we could not 'evade' but simply bank out to sea and out of range. Checking for damage, there were holes and rips everywhere, and three large areas of geodetic, perhaps a metre across, were completely wide open and the IFF [identification friend or foe] blown away. We got back but 'U-Uncle' was in the hangar for repairs for three months.'

In December 1941 a pressing need for torpedo-carrying aircraft with sufficient range and the ability to carry more than one weapon at a time, led to trials being conducted using modified Wellingtons as torpedo-bombers. The nose turret was removed to improve pilots' vision forward, the bomb bay was modified to hold two torpedoes and later, long-range fuel tanks were fitted.

On 20 December 1941 Wing Commander John Chaplin, the CO, made the first practice drop of two torpedoes and his success was followed by a series of dummy torpedo drops by Chaplin's crews. In February 1942 the whole squadron ceased to become a purely bomber unit and the 'Fishingtons' were transferred to 247 Wing, 201 Naval Co-operation Group. There began a period of operations exclusively against Axis shipping. Chaplin found that the best method of attack was to approach the target at eighty feet and drop their two tin fish from 1,000 yards distance. Mostly, attacks were carried out at dusk or by moonlight to minimise the threat of flak and detection by enemy fighters. In March, with the installation of long-range fuel tanks, attacks were made on shipping as far afield as Patras (Patrai) in Greece. In May, the first successful torpedo attacks were made on an enemy convoy, resulting in two hits and one ship beached. The squadron now had detachments based in Malta, Palestine and along the Western Desert.

On the eve of the Battle of El Alamein on the night of 1 November 1942, the 'Fishingtons' on 38 and 458 Squadrons were used against enemy shipping north-west of Tobruk. The next day a German destroyer was bombed by two of 458 Squadron's Wellingtons. Anti-submarine patrols and mine-laying operations in the Gulf of Sirte were carried out during the remainder of the month. Some of the squadron's Wellingtons were sent on detachment to outlying bases in the desert and even further afield. On 17 January Wing Commander Johnson, the CO and twelve Wellingtons flew to Malta and landed at Luqa to begin torpedo strikes on Axis shipping. The 'Fishingtons' flew in all kinds of weather, including severe electrical storms, which caused losses of men and machines. During two months, February and March 1943, the squadron flew over 1,250 operational hours. May 1943 saw the start of several moves for Wellington torpedo-bomber units. 458 Squadron moved to LG91, Amiriya, with further moves to Benghazi, Misurata and Tripolitania. Meanwhile, at the eastern end of the Mediterranean, 36 Squadron, equipped with Wellington VIIIs, flew into Blida from India, where it had been engaged in maritime duties, to begin anti-submarine duties in the Mediterranean. During June 1943 458 Squadron was largely based at Protville, near Tunis and together with 38 Squadron, joined in the offensive against enemy shipping in the Mediterranean. During the summer of 1943 Wellington Mk VIIIs with ASV radar entered service on 38 Squadron. The 'Goofingtons' as they were known, proved very effective hunter/killer aircraft; the squadron's first success in this role occurring on 26 August when an enemy tanker was torpedoed and sunk. By September Wellingtons on 458 Squadron were attacking targets in Corsica and Italy. Maritime reconnaissance operations were operations were exceptionally long and tiring, involving searches throughout the vastness of the Mediterranean. On 13 September a 458 Squadron Wellington, with a single 18-inch torpedo aboard, logged a total of ten hours twenty minutes' night flying time on instruments during a search in the area Sardinia-Genoa-La Spezia-La Rocca. On 26 September one of its crew discovered and depth-charged a U-boat, forcing it to surface and leaving it in a damaged condition. Two days earlier 294 Squadron had been formed at Berka equipped with a mixture of Wellington ICs and XIs and a few Walrus II amphibians for ASR duties.

Despite successes, losses were high and in the UK volunteers were called upon to train in the dangerous art of torpedo bombing. In July 1943 Ernie Payne was posted to 7 OTU at Limavady. 'I joined Flying Officer 'Mac' McGaw's crew flying in Wellington Is and IIs. McGaw volunteered us for torpedo work and in September 1943 we were posted to 1 TTU at Turnbury for a seven-week intensive course. We started with low flying over the sea by day and night (with the assistance of flares). The object was to keep the plane at fifty feet above the water. We then did simulated attacks on designated ships, using first a camera that operated when the bomb doors opened and later, a torpedo with a dummy warhead. 'At night the method was to first find the ship using ASV then, if it was a moonlit night, the skipper would lose height and make his attack, using the moon to silhouette the target. If there was no moon, two sticks of 4,100 candlepower flares were dropped at right angles to each other so that whichever way the ship turned it would still be silhouetted.

'There were many incidents; the fifty feet above the sea at night being one of the main problems. Too high, the torpedo bounced (as one of the ships found out), too low usually resulted in prop damage, or, as happened on more than one occasion, the Wellington hit the sea. When we were lumbering down the short runway at Turnbury in a Wellington I with a 2,000lb torpedo on board we wondered more than once if we were going to make it.'[137]

Meanwhile, Wellingtons were carrying out maritime operations in the Gulf of Oman and Indian Ocean. On 12 September 1943 621 Squadron had formed at Port Reitz, Kenya and personnel were sent out from England. One of the pilots was Sergeant Henry Fawcett. A constable in the Sheffield City Police Force when war broke out, Fawcett had wanted to join the RAF since his first flight in an Avro Avian from York racecourse at the age of thirteen. In 1941 the Home Office decreed that any police officer who wanted to become a pilot or navigator could join the RAF. Fawcett enrolled and subsequently passed out as a pilot. After training in the UK and Rhodesia, Fawcett was posted to 3 OTU at Cranwell. At this time Ju 88 night fighters were shooting down Wellingtons in the area. After one week Henry Fawcett was sent to 78 OTU at Haverfordwest. Squadron Leader West, a regular since 1937, who had completed two operational tours and a third tour as an instructor, became the pilot. The new crew completed Ferry Training at

Talbenny and in August 1943 made operational sweeps out over the Bay of Biscay in brand new Wellington XIIIs. West's crew received their overseas posting to 621 Squadron on 6 September 1943. They left Hum and flew their Wellington XIII, grossly overloaded with fuel and spares, to Cairo via Fez and Castle Benito. Then they flew west, to Khartoum, Djouba, Nairobi and on to their final destination at Mombasa; a total flight time of some 35 hours fifteen minutes. At Mombasa, West's crew flew anti-submarine patrols over the Indian Ocean. On one ten-hour search they looked for an aircraft which had gone down in the sea. They also dropped supplies to survivors from a shipwreck who had managed to swim ashore on the African coast. They were picked up the next day by another aircraft. The September anti-submarine patrols and convoy escort duties gave way to reconnaissance of a different kind on 21 November. Inland of Mogadishu, Somalia, the Wellington crews carried out a 'Tribal Recce'. Fawcett recalls:

'A group of marauding tribesmen had been pillaging and raping and we were sent out to find them. It was fantastically hot and bumpy. We found the tribe and dropped signals to the Army. Next day an Aussie crew went out in their Wellington and against orders, strafed them from their gun turrets.'

In December 1943 621 Squadron moved to Khormaksar, Aden. West's crew were one of several sent on detachment to Bendiskassim, south of Aden, where the Wellingtons continued flying anti-submarine patrols over the Indian Ocean for some months. By February 1944 its sister unit at Khormaksar, 8 Squadron and 244 Squadron at Sharjah, had begun conversion to the Wellington XIII. Both squadrons were engaged in anti-shipping and maritime reconnaissance over the Indian Ocean and the Gulf of Oman respectively. 8 Squadron had been in Aden since May 1942 and 244 Squadron had been at Sharjah since 1943, with a detachment at Masira.

Not all operations were anti-shipping, as Alan Smith, a WOp/AG on 8 Squadron, recalls. 'On one occasion we transported the Sultan of Muscat, with his bodyguards, from Ras al Hadd to Salala on our way back to Aden. The Sultan sat at the Nav table and I looked after the two near-naked bodyguards aft of the bomb bay. After we had been flying for an hour my Canadian skipper, 'Red' St Henri, shouted 'What the hell is going on back there?' The aircraft was starting to weave about. I found the problem. One of the bodyguards was winding his toes around the wires leading back to the twin tabs. I gently persuaded him to untangle himself! Accidents were not uncommon at Aden. One night Flight Sergeant Mac McGiveney was landing at Khormaksar and taxied over a 'goose neck' flare. He set the tyre alight and in a few minutes all that was left was a Wimpy skeleton - the quickest crew evacuation on record.'

Meanwhile, on 4 October 1943, in the Mediterranean Theatre with the Allied campaign in Corsica reaching a successful conclusion, the Wellingtons of 38, 221 and 458 Squadrons bombed the last remaining evacuation port at Bastia. Two days later the Australians were posted to Bone to begin anti-submarine operations. Although orders stated that their torpedo gear must go with them to Algeria, the squadron would in future be armed only with depth charges. A number of anti-submarine and air-sea rescue operations were carried out during November-December. in November 1943 203 Squadron in North Africa exchanged its Martin Baltimores for Wellington Mk IIIs and moved to Santa Cruz for maritime operations in the Indian Ocean. On the night of 11/12 December Wellingtons of 36 and 458 Squadrons, each armed with eight depth charges, together with Venturas on 500 Squadron, flew cover for an Allied convoy of 53 ships. A U-boat was attacked and kept submerged north of Cape Bugaruni until early afternoon on the 13th when it was the recipient of more depth charges, this time from a destroyer of the Royal Navy. With batteries running low and foul air making breathing difficult, the German Commander was forced to scuttle his craft.

During December 1943 new Mark XIV Wellingtons, fitted with Leigh Lights, began equipping the maritime squadrons in North Africa. Training was badly hampered by torrential rainstorms which turned airfields into muddy swamps. By now detachments had been sent further afield. A 458 Squadron detachment was based at Grottaglie, Italy, while detachments on 14, 500 and 458 Squadrons were stationed at Ghisonaccia on the eastern side of Corsica. Anti-U-boat operations were carried out from the island until mid-April 1944, several aircraft having been lost through ditchings. Other detachments were sent to Malta. The U-boat had now become the main threat to Allied forces in the expanse of the Mediterranean. Accordingly, 38 Squadron had dropped its torpedo role and had reverted to a normal maritime reconnaissance unit, although on occasion, its crews still carried torpedoes. On the night of 2 February 1944 the 4,300-ton MV *Leopardi*, with four destroyers in escort, was located by six Wellingtons. The Wellingtons attacked, amid intense anti-aircraft fire, with bombs from 5,000 feet and torpedoes from fifty feet. The Leopardi exploded and sunk, but two aircraft, including the one which launched the final torpedo, were shot down. Seven days later a Ju 52 was shot down from the rear turret of a Wellington engaged on offensive operations in the Aegean. During April two Ju 52s were shot down during a return flight from minelaying operations in the harbour at Rhodes. The difficulties the enemy faced in supplying its forces in the Aegean were reaching impossible proportions and the maritime Wellingtons added to them by moving ever closer.

On the morning of 2 May 1944 Wellington 'T-Tommy' on 621 Squadron skippered by Flight Lieutenant H. Roy Mitchell was carrying out an anti-submarine patrol just south of the Gulf of Aden when south of Cape Guardafui near Ras Hafun, Somaliland, the crew suddenly came upon a U-boat, fully surfaced and steaming along at about 12 knots. It was the U-852, which had been active in South Atlantic waters for several weeks.[138] On the night of 13 March Heinz Eck, the commander, had sunk the 4,700 ton *Peleus*, a Greek freighter under charter to Britain. Next day, Eck had ordered his crew to open fire on the helpless survivors wallowing in the sea on life rafts with machine guns and hand-grenades and fire from the twin 20mm and the 37mm flak guns on the U-boat. As Mitchell made his attack run Eck gave immediate orders for a crash-dive. At 800 yards' range Sergeant W. R. Stevenson, 'T-Tommy's front gunner opened fire, hitting around the conning tower and at 50 feet a stick of six shallow-set depth charges was dropped with deadly accuracy. At least two of the explosions damaged Eck's main induction and his batteries and caused flooding, forcing him back to the surface. 'T-Tommy' radioed for assistance and for twelve hours six aircraft on 621 and 8 Squadrons carried out six attacks on the crippled U-boat, whose gunners nevertheless put up a spirited but futile defence. Meanwhile HMS *Falmouth*, at the time of 'T-Tommy's' initial attack escorting a convoy from Mombasa to Aden, was ordered to leave the convoy and proceed to the scene. Early next morning, U-852 was sighted. Before the sloop could reach her, Eck ordered his U-boat to be scuttled and set on fire, while surviving crew members made for the nearby shore in Somaliland where Eck and 58 crew later surrendered to a Royal Navy landing party assisted by the Somaliland Camel Corps. Flight Lieutenant Mitchell was awarded the DFC and Sergeant W. R. Stevenson received the DFM. After the war, on 17 October 1945, Eck and two of his senior officers were found guilty by a military court in Hamburg for the murder of British and Allied seamen from the Peleus and were shot by firing squad on 30 November.[139]

On 23 May 458 Squadron moved from its North African base at Bone to Alghero on Sardinia. The first operation was carried out on the night of 13/14 June when ten Wellingtons were sent on a search west of the island for U-boats, but without success. By now the Leigh Light Wellingtons not only provided illumination for the Beaufighters on 272 Squadron, RAF, but were fitted with Mk.IX bomb-sights for bombing strikes on targets in northern Italy.

Although shipping targets were getting rarer, on occasions the enemy appeared in relatively large numbers. On an earlier raid, on 1 June, Wellingtons on 38 Squadron spotted a convoy of three merchantmen escorted by three destroyers and four corvettes. They shadowed the force until, low on fuel; they were forced to return to base after dropping their bombs in vain. The next day a strike force sank two of the merchantmen, one destroyer and two corvettes. Five enemy aircraft were also shot down during the action. That night the squadron was out in force, bombing and torpedoing in Candia harbour where the remnants of the convoy had sought refuge. One Wellington was shot down. The failure of this convoy to reach its destination with the bulk of its supplies marked the beginning of the end for the Germans in the Aegean. On the night of 29/30 July Flight Lieutenant Rubidge, a South African pilot on 458 Squadron, searched in vain for shipping targets near La Spezia and Nice, so he turned his attentions to the shipyards and factories at Pietra. No hits were made and the Wellington crew had to ward off light flak and attacks by two night fighters. They landed safely back at Alghero after five hours forty minutes in the air.

In August 1944 Henry Fawcett, late of 621 Squadron, was posted to 38 Squadron at Benghazi as a Wellington Skipper. His Second Pilot was 'Alex' Alexander while the navigator was a Scot, Sergeant 'Jock' Nimmo. His WOp/AG was Ernie Brown, an ex-professional footballer with Newcastle United, while Jack Dougary, his brilliant nineteen-year-old radar operator, had been a cub reporter in Fife. The final member of the crew was Bill McLeod, the rear gunner. Fawcett's crew operated from a forward base at En Shemir where they flew anti-submarine patrols and convoy escorts by day and night. In addition, the maritime Wellingtons flew mine-laying and leaflet dropping operations and even dropped spikes onto airfields in Crete to hamper Ju 52 operations.

On the night of 12 September the Wellingtons on 38 Squadron struck at Maleme airfield on Crete. The German defences assisted the RAF crews by inadvertently turning on the lights; mistaking the Wellingtons for Junkers Ju 52s. Each Wimpy dropped twelve 200lb bombs straight across the runway from 8,000 feet. The bombs were fitted with timed delay fuses which caused the bombs to explode at half-hour intervals to deny the Germans the use of the airfield for 24 hours. The

Wellingtons came under heavy fire as Henry Fawcett recalls: 'One piece of flak as big as a turnip went through one side of the front turret and out the other. Another piece went through the fuselage making a pencil hole through the 'king post' on the empennage. Fortunately, it did not drop off. The air stream peeled off about thirty feet of fabric. Dougary, who was a bit of a comic, took the hot-air tube and stuck it down the front of his flying suit. He still complained of cold in the 140-knot wind. Seven nights later, on 19 September, 38 Squadron mounted a maximum effort against the *SS Corona*, which lay at anchor in Porto Lagos in the Aegean. Each Wellington carried eleven 200 lb bombs but the raid was not entirely successful. Henry Fawcett recalls: 'my bombs missed by half a mile but they set a naval barracks on fire.'

In September 1944 458 Squadron had also moved to Italy. They alighted at Foggia, with the main elements moving north to Falconara where they shared the airfield with 454 Squadron RAAF, with 450 Squadron RAAF, based nearby. On 14/15 September 458 Squadron flew its first operation from Falconara when Warrant Officer Priest sank a 2,000-ton ship. On 15 September 36 Squadron flew its last maritime operation. Three days later the squadron completed the first leg of the journey to the UK to join Coastal Command, finally arriving at Chivenor on 26 September.

On 4 October 38 Squadron dropped leaflets on Crete and Rhodes. Henry Fawcett recalls: 'The whole fuselage was filled with leaflets. We circled right around Crete pushing out these bundles. It was on flights like this that we used to get torchlight signals from freedom fighters in the hills. Even if we could read Morse they were in a foreign language.' On raids like this opposition from Ju 52s could be expected. Normally, this three-engined transport provided little danger but they were capable of firing a very heavy gun from a side door. Fawcett recalls: 'On one occasion three Ju 52s formated on our tail. McCleod spotted them. He shouted, 'The aircraft with three engines!' Then he opened up and away they went.'

The Aegean conflict drew gradually to a close and at the end of September an advance party from 38 Squadron had left Berka III for the Delta, where they boarded a ship for Piraeus. The party was ultimately based at Hassani airfield near Athens which had recently been vacated by the Luftwaffe. By 14 November the whole of 38 Squadron had installed their Wellingtons on the airfield. Greece proved a welcome change of climate after 23 months in the desert, but on 28 November part of the squadron was posted to Grottaglie, near Taranto and the . Italian Theatre of Operations, while the remainder of the squadron found itself confined to base as civil war broke out in the recently liberated country.

By December 1944 38 Squadron was stationed at Kalamaki. The Greek Civil War was beginning to get into full swing, so on 6 December the remaining Wellingtons, packed with tents and supplies, took off and made the three-hour flight to Grottaglie amid small arms fire and artillery. The squadron spent Christmas 1944 in tents and billets situated on muddy fields. In addition to bombing operations, its tasks, as part of the Balkan Air Force, included dropping supplies in Greece and Yugoslavia.

On January 1945 the Wellingtons made the thirty-minute flight to Bari where they loaded up with supplies to drop to the partisans in Yugoslavia. At Bari, Henry Fawcett broke the tail wheel. 'Taxiing in what I thought was deep rutted mud turned out to be baked hard. An oleo went through the turret. The throttle on the replacement Wellington had become disconnected and the pilot who brought her in did a very worthy single-engined landing.'

In the New Year the snows receded and operations began again with renewed vigour. On the night of 3/4 January four of 458 Squadron's Wellingtons and six Beaufighters of 272 Squadron mounted an armed reconnaissance off Pola. One of the Wellington pilots spotted a 2,000-ton oil tanker and dropping a mercury flare, called in the 'Rockbeaus' to attack. The fighters badly damaged the ship and stopped it in her tracks.

On 25 January 1945 458 Squadron flew to Gibraltar to resume anti-U-boat operations in the Mediterranean. A period of Leigh Light training followed and then on 13 and 14 February anti-submarine patrols were mounted between Cape St Vincent and Lisbon. With the sea almost entirely devoid of enemy shipping the Wellington crews were now virtually on a training status, although convoy patrols of seven hours' duration were still the order of the day as the war drew to a close.

At this time it was decided that a detachment of seven Wellingtons would be maintained at Rosignano, near Leghorn, for anti-shipping strikes in co-operation with naval coastal forces in the Gulf of Genoa. Part of 38 Squadron was despatched to Rosignano while the rest of the squadron was to operate from Foggia on similar operations along the coasts of Venice and Trieste in the northern Adriatic. On 6 February 38 Squadron flew its Wellington XIIIs to Blida, near Algiers, where it swapped them for the Mk XIV. This version was equipped with the very latest radar and radar altimeters, accurate to one foot, which registered the height of the waves. For operations low over the sea this meant that the pilot could set fifty feet and keep in the 'traffic lights' (amber) if the Wellington was too low. Green meant they were too high. On 21 February the squadron flew an armed reconnaissance over the Genoa-La Spezia area off the west coast of Italy. Their quarry was German shipping. Most of the enemy's larger vessels were either disabled or sunk so the squadron's targets were by now primarily barges, small coasters and E- and F-boats, although on the western side of the Gulf of Genoa, where there was much greater freedom of action so far as shore installations were concerned, the occasional KT ship was also found.

At this stage of the war the Germans were forced to move their supplies in barges along the west coast of Italy by night because by day their road convoys were mercilessly attacked and strafed by Beaufighters. The barges were often escorted by E-boats which developed a technique of firing vertically when Wellingtons were overhead. The Wellington crews also employed a technique, whereby one aircraft flew a course 8,000 feet in a straight line while another flew a head-on course in the opposite direction at 5,000 feet. Henry Fawcett recalls:

'I remember one Wellington that swished past over the top of me at fifty feet!' The Wellington crews worked in close co-operation with the Royal Navy MTBs in the night attacks on barges. To Henry Fawcett the MTBs, with their three Merlin engines, were 'magnificent little beasts'.

Success depended on the close co-operation of the Wellington and MTB crews. One night Fawcett's crew were to be accompanied by a Chief Petty Officer from the Royal Navy. 'Before the Petty Officer ventured on an actual operation he wished to fly a practice flight first. We took him up on an air test. This usually involved a flight up the coast, a few turns around the leaning tower of Pisa, return and then a beat-up of the beach where the lads were. I quite forgot about the Chief Petty Officer. Quite green, he went off at lunch time and I never saw him again. On the night of 27 February we hit one of these 'glorified' barges. Hits didn't do much damage so we aimed for bomb pressure damage. Usually, we dropped sticks of 250lb bombs to go off at thirty feet above sea level. On this occasion, two hit. I went into a steep turn and all I saw was a tiny bit of burning debris. The barge was gone in seconds.

'On 21 March Jack Dougary, the radar operator, found a convoy of five ships. We went safely out to sea and came in at 1,000 feet. We homed in on the ships, which were sailing along like a ghostly convoy, climbed to 8,000 feet and dropped through the thick cloud. I had no idea where our bombs went. We came in and found the convoy again. Flying level, we flew alongside and my gunners strafed the ships. There was no response at all. The first sighting report had been sent off and a second Wellington was coming in. I climbed very fast into the cloud, just as our starboard engine stopped near La Spezia. We had to fly for an hour on one engine back to Rosignano. Next day we discovered that the engine had partially seized climbing to 8,000 feet so rapidly. On 2 April at Falconara near Ancona, we hit miniature U-boats, crewed by six-man sabotage teams. One was surfaced and abandoned. We went back to refuel and re-arm, returned and got another contact. It was the six survivors. We flew around while a Walrus picked them up. Next day we dropped nine 250lb depth charges on another. We saw plenty of planks, oil and dead fish but we received no credit for sinking the boat this time. We made no mistake on 10 April when we sank a 1,000-ton barge. On 23 April we attacked a small convoy with eleven 250lb bombs but missed hitting any ships. Then it was leave to Sorrento for two weeks. We returned to the squadron to begin mine spotting. Off Yugoslavia we flew at fifty feet for four hours fifty minutes. In that time the navigator plotted fifty mines.'

The detached flight of 38 Squadron was transferred to Falconara and the entire squadron was able to celebrate VE-Day together. On VE-Day 458 Squadron flew the last official anti-U-boat operation, although a number of ASR missions were flown throughout the rest of the month. After all the excitement, in June 458 Squadron was disbanded. In July 1945 38 Squadron transferred to Malta and exchanged its Wellingtons for Warwicks for ASR duties. On 25 August 1945 221 Squadron was disbanded in North Africa.

Once again, the Wellington had proved its worth in a diversity of roles from minelaying and supply dropping, to bombing operations, torpedo-bombing and anti-submarine work. These relatively unknown maritime operations carried out by the Wellington squadrons undoubtedly contributed to the downfall of the German naval and air forces in the Mediterranean Theatre of war. The same could also be said of their involvement in all other theatres of the war.

Footnote

137 Ernie Payne never saw action on Wellingtons; he was posted to a Warwick unit.
138 Between 1 and 3 May U-582 was attacked by six Wellingtons on 621 Squadron; on 1 May by JA107/E flown by Flight Lieutenant Mitchell and on 2 May by JA184/F (F/O E W Read); JA389/D (W/O J P Ryall RCAF and HZ040/T (F/L J Y Wade) and on 3 May by JA413/G (F/O J R Forrester RCAF). *U-boat Fact File* by Peter Sharpe (Midland Publishing Ltd 1998).
139 See *Hitler's U-boat War: The Hunted, 1942-1945* by Clay Blair (Random House 1998).

Appendices

Appendix 1
Wellington movements RAF Coastal Command October 1942- November 1944

Date	Squadron	Remarks
1942:		
October 21	547	Established at Holmsley South as maritime recce unit with Wellington XVIII
December 5	612 (RAFA)	Replaces Whitley with Leigh Light Wellington
December 13	612	Begins Coastal Command operations
December 17	547	Begins Coastal Command operations at Chivenor
1943:		
January 29	407 (Demon) RCAF	Equipped with Leigh Light Wellingtons at Docking, Norfolk
April 1	407 (Demon) RCAF	Begins anti-shipping operations
June	311 (Czech)	Converted to the Liberator
June	407 (Demon) RCAF	Receives Wellington XIV
August	172	Receives Wellington XIV
September	415 (Swordfish) RCAF	Receives Wellington VIII fitted with Leigh Light
1944:		
April 30	524	Begins anti-shipping role with Wellington XIIIs off French coast
July	415 RCAF	To Bomber Command
September 26	36	Joins Coastal Command (Chivenor)
October 24	14	Joins Coastal Command (Chivenor) using the Wellington GR.XIV fitted with the Leigh Light
November	179	Converted to the Warwick

Appendix 2
RCAF/RAAF Wellington Squadron Dispositions Bomber Command December 1942-November 1943

Date	Squadron	Group	Station	Remarks
1942:				
December 14	427 (Lion) RCAF	6	Croft	Debut, mine-laying off Friesians
1943:				
January 13	466 (RAAF)	4	Leconfield	Debut, mine-laying off Friesians
January 14/15	426 (Thunderbird)	6	Linton-on-Ouse	Debut, Lorient

Date	Squadron		Airfield	Remarks
January 15/16	424 (Tiger) RCAF	6	Topcliffe	Bombing debut, Lorient
January 15/16	466 (RAAF)	6	Leconfield	Bombing debut, Lorient
January 15/16	427 (Lion) RCAF	6	Croft	Bombing debut, Lorient
January 21	429 (Bison) RCAF	4*	East Moor	Debut, Mk III
January 26/27	428 (Ghost) RCAF	6	Dalton	Debut, 5 a/c to Lorient
March 2/3	431 (Iroquois) RCAF	6	Burn	Debut, 8 Mk X mines off Friesians
March 5/6	431 (Iroquois) RCAF	6	Burn	Bombing debut, Essen
May 23/24	432 (Leaside) RCAF	6	Skipton-on-Swale	Bombing debut 14 Mk X to Dortmund
October 5/6	425 (Alouette) RCAF	6	Dishforth	Debut 4 a/c to Aachen
November 6	419 (Moose) RCAF	6	Croft	Last op, 3 a/c on 'moling' to Wilhelmshaven before conversion to Halifax II

* Transferred to 6 Group 1 April 1943

Appendix 3
Wellington movements Bomber Command May 1942-October 1944

Date	Squadron	Remarks
1942:		
May	304 (Silesian)	To Coastal Command
June	158	Converted to the Halifax
July	103	Converted to the Halifax
August	9	Converted to the Lancaster
September	57	Converted to the Lancaster
September	460 (RAAF)	Converted to the Halifax
October	101	Converted to the Lancaster
November	12	Converted to the Lancaster
November	75 RNZAF	Converted to the Stirling
November	419 (Moose) RCAF	Converted to the Halifax
December 6/7	199	Op debut, 5 bomb Mannheim
1943:		
January 27/28	166	Op debut, 7 Mk IIIs (mines)
January 29/30	166	Op bombing debut, Lorient
January	156	Converted to the Lancaster
February 4/5	196	Op bomb debut, Lorient
March	301 (Pomeranian)	To 38 (SD) Squadron
April	425 (Alouette) RCAF	To North Africa
May	424 (Tiger) RCAF	To Algeria
May	427 (Lion) RCAF	Converted to the Halifax
June	426 (Thunderbird) RCAF	Converted to the Lancaster
June	428 (Ghost) RCAF	Converted to the Halifax
June	199	Converted to the Stirling
July	196	Converted to the Stirling
July	431 (Iroquois) RCAF	Converted to the Halifax

August	429 (Bison) RCAF	Converted to the Lancaster
August	305 (Ziemia Wielkopolska)	Converted to the Mitchell
September	466 (RAAF)	Converted to the Halifax
September	166	Converted to the Lancaster
October	424 (Tiger) RCAF	Converted to the Halifax
Oct/Nov	425 (Alouette) RCAF	Returns to UK to rejoin 6 Group

1944:

Feb 19/20	425 (Alouette) RCAF	Resumes bombing ops
April	300 (Masovian)	Converted to the Lancaster
October	425 (Alouette) RCAF	Converted to the Halifax
October	150	Converted to the Lancaster
October	432 (Leaside) RCAF	Converted to the Lancaster

Further reading

419 (Canadian) Squadron Unit History Blida's Bombers, Squadron Leader Eric M. Summers MM, 1943
Bomber Command War Diaries, Martin Middlebrook
Bomber Squadrons of the RAF, Phillip Moyes, Macdonald 1964
British Bomber Since 1941, The, Peter Lewis, Putnam 1967
East Anglian Crash Logs, R. J. Collis, unpublished
Famous Bomber Aircraft, Martin W. Bowman, Patrick Stephens 1989
History of RAF Mildenhall, A, Dr. Colin Dring, Mildenhall Museum Publications 1980
Royal Air Force 1939-45, Denis Richards and Hilary St G. Saunders, HMSO 1974
Story of another Loch Ness Monster, The, Robin Holmes, The Loch Ness Wellington Association Ltd

Index

2nd Tactical Air Force   19, 143

Aachen   73
Aalborg   65
Abel, Oberleutnant zur see Dr. Ulrich   53
Abigail Rachael, Operation   86
Ackerman, Alan   204
Active HMS   49
Adams, John F.   53
Akyab airfield   134
Alconbury   90, 134, 137
Aldergrove   39
Alexandria   148
Alghero   214
Allerton Park   142
Amendola   190., 192
Angell, Squadron Leader E. E. M.   56, 58
Antoniewicz, Flight Lieutenant L.   55-56
Anzio   187
Archer, J. C.   48
Armstrong Pilot Officer W. N. DFC   51-52
Arthurs, Pilot Officer Kenneth Norman   91
Ary Sheffer   41
Asansol   132
Astell, Pilot Officer Bill   148-150
Aviles, Spain   41

Baden-Baden   77
Bailey, John   25
Balaton, Lake   193, 195-196
Baldwin, AVM J. E. A. 'Jackie'   31
Barber, Pilot Officer Frederick Edward   65
Bari   215
Barnard, Flight Lieutenant Seymour Preston 'Barney'   113-114
Barnstable   50
Barr, Pilot Officer   79-80
Barton Bendish   24-25, 115, 135
Bassingbourn   90
Bateman, Flight Lieutenant L. J. DFC RCAF   54
Bathurst   43
Beaty, Flight Lieutenant A. David DFC   53
Beccles   25
Becker, Oberleutnant Ludwig   115, 118

Belgrade   198, 203
Benghazi   145, 149, 153, 157-160, 162-163, 166, 170, 210-211, 215
Bergen   65
Berlin   79-80, 83, 112, 114-115, 128-129, 191
Bernhard, Prince   179
Bickerstaff, Corporal A.   30
Biddle, Flying Officer Gord   56-58
Bielby, Derek   50-51
Billancourt   135
Bircham Newton   13, 50, 83
Bizerta   155, 167-168, 173, 176-182
Blida   175-177, 179-182, 184, 188, 211, 217
Blum, Otto-Ulrich   48
Bock Island USS   51-52
Boehmer, Wolfgang   53
Bogue USS   53
Bone   214
Booth, Charles   209-210
Bordeaux   81
Bordeaux/Merignac   93
Boscombe Down   12
Bottomley, Air Commodore Norman   31
Boulogne   89, 91
Bowhill, Air Chief Marshal DFC, KCB CMG DSO   16-17, 38
Brace, Sergeant Richard Henry James   30
Brandi, Kapitänleutnant Albrecht   49
Brauel, Oberleutnant zur see Wilhelm   53
Bremen   79, 81, 90, 100, 109-110, 128, 141-142
Brest   46, 53, 55, 89, 91, 93, 95-96, 114
Bretherton, D.   53
Briden, Flying Officer Michael Franklin   33
Bronini, Pilot Officer W. H.   49
Brooklands   10-11
Brooks, Flight Lieutenant Ronnie DFC   176
Brooks, John   19
Brooks, Stan   74-75
Brosin, Kapitänleutnant Hans-Günther   48
Brown, Stuart   143
Brownsill, Flight Lieutenant Antony G.   59

Bruce, Don   96-99
Brunswick   112
Bryant, Pilot Officer Francis Egerton   100
Buckingham, Geoff T.   109-110
Budapest   192-194,197-198, 200, 204
Budapest-Rakos   198
Bufton, Squadron Leader Hal   15-16
Bugs, Oberleutnant zur see
   Hans-Helmuth   53
Bulmer, USS   52
Burnell, Flying Officer   66
Bury, George   79-80
Butler, Flight Lieutenant Sidney W. DFC   52
Butler, Flying Officer I. B. DFC   46

Cagliari-Elmas aerodrome   178-179
Calumba HMS   206
Cambridge   90
Cape Finisterre   48-49
Cape Ortegal   54
Casablanca   43, 53
Castel Benito   82, 146-147
Castrop-Rauxel   73
Catania   147
Cerignola   187
Challen, Steve   157-158
Chamberlain, Neville   26
Chandler, Flying Officer John   28
Chandler, Sergeant R. F. 'Chan'   99-100
Chaplin, Wing Commander John   211
Child, Norman   176
Chittagong   133
Chivenor   18, 50, 54, 59
Chivers, Flight Lieutenant Eugene
   George F.   81
Churchill, Winston   28, 80, 134, 139, 141, 189, 192
Clarke, Flight Lieutenant Irwin A. F.   48
Clarke, Flying Officer Lyn   188, 193, 198
Coester, Oberleutnant zur see
   Christian-Brandt   50
Collett, L. W.   19
Collins, Flying Officer John Noel RNZAF   75
Cologne   73, 79-80, 92, 99, 108, 129, 132, 138-142
Coltishall   33, 112
Comiso   147
Cook, Flight Sergeant Neil Caldwell   111

Cooling, Rupert 'Tiny'   66-73, 183-187
Cooper, Flying Officer John Arkell
   Harding   30
Coote, Pilot Officer William   89, 152-153, 196-197
Copley, Corporal   29
Cornish, Flight Sergeant Donald M.   50, 61
Corona, SS   216
Coumbis, Flight Sergeant Alex   46
Coventry   86
Crank-Benson, Sergeant Jim 'Cranky'   154-156, 158, 162
Crete   214
Crisp, Robert   81
Croft   142
Croome HMS   44
Crosby, Pilot Officer George Lesley   65

Dale   39
Damerow, Oberleutnant zur see
   Wolf-Dietrich   48
Davidson, Flying Officer W. F. M.   51
Davidstowe Moor   54
Day, Eric   13-15
Dearden, Sergeant Frederick Harry
   Ewart   128
Debden, Flying Officer H. J.   48, 55
Dick, LAC G,   66
Dickore, Hauptmann   29
Directional Wireless Installation   11-13, 17-18
Dishforth   142
Dobberstein, Oberleutnant zur see   56
Doolittle, Major General James H.   179, 181
Dorken, Fred   50
Dortmund   73, 102
Douglas, 'Duggie'   66-71
Downey, Flight Sergeant William
   Howarth   30
Downham Market   135
Drewitz, Kapitänleutnant Hans-Joachim   52
Driffield   90, 99, 106, 137
Dugard D. A.   7
Duguid, Flight Lieutenant A. G.   28, 32
Duisburg   128
Dunkirk   72, 75, 137
Düsseldorf   93, 128
East Wretham   135-136
Ebert, Kapitänleutnant Jürgen   59

Eck, Heinz   214-215
Edwards, AVM   136
Ehle, Hauptmann Walter   100, 117
Ehrang   81
El Alamein   148, 166, 211
El Ferrol   48
Ellis, Flying Officer Arthur H. DFC   49
Ellis, Sergeant Leonard Harold   115
Elmas aerodrome   177-178
Emden   83, 93, 109, 131,137, 141
English, Sergeant Duncan   83
Ercolani, Pilot Officer Lucian Brett
    129-131, 143-144
Erith   8
Esbjerg   27
Essen   112, 134-136, 140-142
Eukirchen   73
Evans-Evans, Wing Commander
    Anthony Caron   90, 115

Falconara   216, 218
Falmouth, HMS   214
Farnborough   13, 17
Farrell, Squadron Leader   54
Fawcett, Sergeant Henry   212-213,
    215-217
Feltwell   24, 31, 67, 78, 83, 91
Field, Group Captain R. M.   77
Finlayson, Pilot Officer William John   83
Finnessey, Flying Officer John P.   53
Finningley   90
Firestone, Flight Sergeant Harvey   56-58
Fisher, Flying Officer E. J.   47
Fleetwood HMS   49
Foggia   189
Fone, Sergeant Alfred   137
Fornebu   65
Foss, Squadron Leader Patrick   82
Fox, Charles   132-134
Fraas, Flying Officer Ronnie   102-103, 117
Frank, Oberleutnant Hans-Dieter   136
Frankfurt   112-113
Franks, Pilot Officer John Henry   93
Froyennes   74
Fulton, Wing Commander John 'Moose'
    DSO DFC AFC   137
Furious HMS   37

Gambut   153
Gaul, Wally   145, 154-165
Gaunt, Sergeant 'Tubby'   204-206

Gayford, Pilot Officer Roy Allen   65
Gee, Sergeant Tony   110
Gelsenkirchen   81, 85
Gennevilliers   138-139
Genoa   77, 201
Gerry, Pilot Officer Reginald Torrance
    79
Gibbes, Wing Commander Rodney DFC
    81, 84
Gibraltar   43, 48-49, 54-55
Gildner, Oberleutnant Paul   127-128
Gill, Pilot Officer Alan   176
Gneisenau   26, 91, 93, 111, 134
Grant, Flight Lieutenant Peter   27, 31
Gravesend   90
Great Yarmouth   29, 77
Gresens, Oberleutnant   33
Greswell Squadron Leader J. H.   40-41
Gribble, Leonard R.   39
Griffiths, Wing Commander J. F.   29-30
Grimsby   175
Gristwood, Roy   188-189, 193-194, 198
Gunn, Warrant Officer Ian D.   50
Guthrie, Squadron Leader Archibald
    28, 33

Haddock, Gordon   58-59
Hakala, Sergeant A. S.   39
Hallam, Les   190, 198-199, 202, 208
Halton, RAF   22
Hamburg   65, 73, 79, 83, 96-97, 136,
    138, 143, 215
Hamm   79
Hamm, Horst   46
Hanbury, Flying Officer Reader D.   48
Hannover   27, 90, 112, 143
Harris, L.   56
Harris, Sir Arthur CB OBE   38-39, 64, 134,
    136, 138-141
Harris, Squadron Leader Paul   28-29,
    31, 33
Harrow, Handley Page   21
Hartmann, Kapitänleutnant Klaus   55
Harwell   24, 85, 133, 154, 156
Hashagen, Berthold   54
Hassani airfield   215
Hauptmann, Hans-Jürgen   46
Hause, Karl   48
Haverfield HMCS   53
Healy, Flight Sergeant James Ernest
    Kirby   30

Heap, John   153
Heard, Flying Officer H. B. W.   51-52
Heligoland   28-30
Heliopolis   147
Helmore, Group Captain   17-18
Hemswell   14, 204
Hendon, Fairey   21-22
Hendon, RAF Museum   19
Hendon, RAF   10
Heron, Flying Officer P. W. DFC   52
Hetherington Flight Lieutenant Eugene John   30-31
Hewitt, Sergeant Bob   33
Heyda, Kapitänleutnant Wolfgang   48
Heydemann Oberleutnant zur see Ernst   45-46
Heyford bomber   15
High Wycombe   129
Hill, W. J.   54
Hitchmough, Bill   83
Hobson HMCS   53
Hodgkinson, Squadron Leader D. B. DFC   49
Holme-on-Spalding Moor   132, 134, 209
Honington   24, 28, 31, 34, 66-67, 70, 80, 136
Horsham St Faith   93
Howell, Pilot Officer Wiley B.   41
Hull, Sergeant Arthur Robert   115
Hunkin, Pilot Officer W. H. C.   79
Hurn   134
Husky, Operation   182

Imphal Plain   19
Imphal   133
Ismailia   147

Jade HMS   147
Jaffa   44
James, Flying Officer H. W.   201
Jarman, Squadron Leader L. E.   34
Jarmarker, Kapitänleutnant Walter   45
Jenner, Sergeant Alfred   85-86, 89-90, 93-95
Jennings, Flying Officer W. H. T.   47
Jever   30
Johnson, E. C. 'Johnnie'   21-26, 80-82
Jones, LAC Harry   32-33
Joubert, Air Chief Marshal Sir Philip B. De la Ferte KCB CMG DSO   17-18, 38, 40
Jung, Hauptmann Rolf   90

Kabrit   148-149, 157, 159, 162-165,
Kalinowski, Feldwebel Ernst   115
Kark, Leslie   120
Karlsruhe   112
Kellett, Wing Commander Richard AFC   28-29, 31, 33, 35
Kidney, Harry   153-154
Kiel   45, 81, 95
Kietz, Siegfried   46
King, Flying Officer John   150-152, 164
King's Lynn   21, 31, 90
Kinloss   65
Kirmington   175
Kirwan Wing Commander J. D. DFC   177, 180
Klaus, Hans-Joachim   49
Köhl, Oberleutnant zur see Kurt   48
Köln   65
Königsberg   65
Krahn, Pilot Officer G. H.   56
Krause, Leutnant Hans   191-192, 194-195, 208

La Pallice   111
La Rochelle   41
La Spezia   46, 212, 215, 217-218
Lamb, Squadron Leader Lennox   28
Lamby, Hermann   46
Lampedusa   169, 183, 187-188
Langham   59
Larkman, Sergeant Donald Ewart   83
Larney, Flying Officer 'Joe'   78, 83
Le Havre   89
Leigh Light   17-19, 41, 44, 214-215, 217
Leigh, Squadron Leader Humphrey de Verde   17-18
Leipzig   29
Lemon Flying Officer P. C. 'Cheese'   33, 36
Leopardi, MV   213
Lewis, Pilot Officer Norman Leonard   30
Lilley, LAC Walter   33
Limavady   59
Lindholme   90
Lippe-Weissenfeld, Oberleutnant Egmont Prinz zur   83, 110, 118
Lisbon   217
Little Rissington   20, 23
Longmore, AM Sir Arthur   145
Lorient   48, 52
Lossiemouth   65, 67, 90
Lübeck   136-137

Luigi Torelli 39-41
Lundon, Flying Officer G. D. 46
Luqa 82, 146, 148, 154, 156, 162, 167-170, 209, 211

MacFarlane, Geoffrey 16
Macrae, Flying Officer William John RCAF 36
Magdeburg 83, 112
Maison Blanche 176-177
Máleme 214
Malta 81
Mannesmann, Kapitänleutnant Dr. Gert 52
Mannheim 79, 86, 111-113
Mansfield, The Right Hon. Terence 110, 115-116
Manston 114
Marczak, Warrant Officer R. 59
Marham 21, 23-25, 28, 65-67, 74, 77, 79-83, 89-90, 93, 96, 109, 112, 128, 131, 135-136, 139, 145
Marks, Kapitänleutnant Friedrich-Karl 46
Marsden, Sergeant J. A. 46
Marseilles 77
Martin, Flight Sergeant A. D. S. DFM 45
Martlesham Heath 11, 113
Masters, Eric 92, 95-96, 108-109
Mather, Philip DFC 173-174
Matthews, Sergeant Oswald Arthur 102
May, Sergeant T. 33
Maydown RNAS 59
McGaw, Flying Officer 'Mac' 212
McKay, Pilot Officer J. W. RAAF 49, 52
McKee, Squadron Leader Andrew 'Square' 29-30, 66, 68
McKenzie, Sergeant M. G. A. 102-108
McLellan, Eric 146
McRae, Flying Officer Donald F. 48
McSweyn, Pilot Officer Alan 100-101
McTeer, Sergeant Anthony 193, 195
Merseburg 81
Methwold 102
Middleton St George 142
Milan 77
Mildenhall 21, 24-25, 27-28, 31, 64-65, 81, 110, 116, 134-135, 137, 208
Minakowski, Flight Lieutenant 44-45
Mitchell, Flight Lieutenant H. Roy 214-215, 218

Modin, Group Captain 78
Molesworth 136
Mönchengladbach 73, 112
Moore, Flight Lieutenant Kenneth Owen 'Kayo' 62
Morris, Sergeant Lionel Austin 77
Mors 78
Morson, Sergeant H. J. 82
Morton, Warrant Officer W. F. 52
Münster 102, 109
Mussolini, Benito 77
Musson, Wing Commander Rowland G. 47-48

Nantes 46
Naples 82, 146-147, 182, 185, 199, 207
Netheravon 27
Neumann, Hans-Joachim 44
Newmarket Hospital 31
Newmarket 24, 29, 67, 85, 90, 92
Ney, Feldwebel Siegfried 112
Ney, Günther 52
Nice 214
Nolan, Squadron Leader Maurice 65
Nürnburg 29, 128
Nyult, Flying Officer J. 42

O'Donnell Pilot Officer E. M. DFC 48-49, 52
Oakington 82, 99
Oboe 16
Odoire, Sergeant 29
Oliphant, Stephen A. 209
Orkan 47
Osnabrück 81, 141
Ostend 56, 75, 83, 131
Otto, Kapitänleutnant Paul-Friedrich 56

Palmgren, Oberleutnant zur see Gerhard 53
Pandeveswar 132
Pantellaria 183-185, 187
Paris 85
Parrott, USS 52
Pattie, Donald A. 53
Payne, Ernie 212, 218
Paynter, Flying Officer 'Max' 49, 52-54
Peirse, Sir Richard KCB DSO AFC 128, 134-135, 144
Peleus 214-215
Pelton HMS 82

Pemberton, Sergeant Gordon G.   192-195
Petts, Sergeant Frank   33
Pickard, Flight Lieutenant Percy   77, 84
Pierson, Rex K.   9
Ploesti   202, 206
Pocklington   102
Pola   205, 207, 217
Port Reitz, Kenya   212
Portal, AM Sir Charles GCB DSO MC   134, 179
Porto Lagos   215
Portreath   45, 175
Powell, Flight Sergeant G. A.   65
Powell, Group Captain John Alexander 'Speedy' DSO OBE   182, 184-185
Pratt, H. B.   8
Predannack   54
Prince Rupert HMCS   53
Pringle, Flight Lieutenant Alec Edward DFC   73
Prinz Eugen   91, 111
Pugh, Joe   154
Pughe-Lloyd, AVM Hugh   147, 162
Punta Estace   50

Rahn, Oberleutnant zur see Wolfgang   51
Ramshaw, Sergeant John R.   33
Rasper, Oberfeldwebel Hans   91, 116
Rawlings, Arthur   56, 59
Redpath, Flight Sergeant   193-195
Rees   73
Richards, Flight Sergeant L. D.   52
Robinson, Albert E.   86-89, 120-128
Rogers, Flight Sergeant J. M. RAAF   43-44
Rogers, Pilot Officer Harold Humphrey   81, 90
Roithberg, Kapitänleutnant Hardo Rodler von   54
Rommel, Erwin   132, 145-149, 153-154, 163, 165, 175-176, 179
Rosenstiel, Kapitänleutnant Jürgen von   41
Rostock   137, 139
Rotterdam   89-90, 93, 102
Rowley Mile racecourse   24-25
Runagall Pilot Officer Percy DFC   135
Ruse, Sergeant Herbie   32, 35-36
Rye   65

Saffron Walden   90
Saich, Sergeant Jack Cyril   110-111

Salmon HMS   29
Salon   77
Sandell, Sergeant Maurice 'Scats'   204-206
Sanders, Bruce   41
Sapiston Water Mill   28
Saxelby, Pilot Officer   83
Scharnhorst   26, 91, 111-112, 134
Schumacher, Oberstleutnant Karl   32
Sealion Operation   80
Shallufa   208
Sharpe, Pilot Officer Douglas   99-100
Shearing, Sergeant Kenneth Charles   112
Shepherd, Sergeant Robert   78-79, 83
Sicily   82, 178
Sikh HMS   44
Simmans, Sergeant Albert Edward 'Sim'   137
Singerton, Sergeant Albert Edward   136
Siska, Alois   41-42
Skipton-on-Swale   142
Skitten   44
Smith, Alan   212
Snowden, Warrant Officer J. W. B.   120-122, 143
Soest   79
Sorley, Flying Officer H. C.   52
South Pickenham   79
Southampton   86
Specht, Leutnant Günther   29
Speirs, Flying Officer James Heggie Cumming   33
Squires Gate   14
St Nazaire   46
St. Vincent   217
Stanton Harcourt   209
Stavanger   65
Sterkrade   73
Stettin   115
Stewart, Flight Lieutenant J. B.   28-29
Stradishall   77, 135
Strater, Kapitänleutnant Wolfgang   47
Straub, Siegfried   52
Streib, Hauptmann Werner   111
Strelow, Siegfried   47
Strembridge, Flying Officer Peter H.   46
Stuttgart   138
Summers, Captain J. 'Mutt'   10
Summers, Sergeant Edward 'Slim'   34-35
Sylt   32, 138

Talbenny 42
Tangmere 90
Taranto Harbour 82, 146-147, 216
Targowski, Flying Officer Stanislas 44-45
Tedder, ACM Sir Arthur W. GCB 180
Tempsford 15
Tetcott HMS 44
Thackeray, Flight Lieutenant Reg 165-172
Thorney Island 129
Thousand Bomber Raids 138-142
Tipper, Sergeant Frederick Birkett 109-110
Tiree 39
Tirpitz 89, 99
Tobruk 133, 146, 148, 150, 153, 165-167, 173, 211
Torkington-Leach, Flying Officer Peter 28
Torrens, Squadron Leader David C. 93
Tortorella 197, 204, 207
Trapani 168, 170-171, 179, 182
Travell, Flying Officer Wilfred R. DFC 53
Tripoli 147-148, 153, 169-172
Tunis docks 180
Turin 77
Tweddle, J. W. 52

Upavon 132
Upper Heyford 15
Ushant 55

Valona 149
Varley, N. A. 63-64
Varsity, Vickers 19
Vegasack 109
Vella, Flying Officer J. DFC 42
Vild, Flight Lieutenant Miroslav 41-43, 60
Volker, Leutnant Heinz 93
Von Bonin Leutnant Eckart-Wilhelm 97-98, 117
Waalhaven 68-71, 73
Waddington 116

Waldringfield 11
Wallis, Dr. Barnes Neville 8, 10
Walmsley, Flight Lieutenant 56
Waltham 175
Wangerooge 30
Ward, Sergeant James RNZAF VC 108
Warwick, Vickers 10, 20
Waterbeach 92-93, 95, 132
Weekley, Jack 200-204, 207-208
Wellesley aircraft 8
Wells 79
Welsh, AM Sir W. KCB 175
Wenzel, Kapitänleutnant Wolfgang 51-52
Werner, Oberleutnant zur see 54-55
Wesel 73
West Raynham 113
Westbrook, Trevor 10
Weybridge 8
White, Denys 192, 199
Whiteley, Pilot Officer G. H. 46
Whittaker, Sergeant Henry 201-202
Whyte, Flying Officer J. 47
Wickenkamp, Pilot Officer Estelles Arthur MBE 65
Widdowson, Squadron Leader R. P. 108
Wilamowitz-Mollendorf, Korvettenkapitän Georg von 47
Wilhelmshaven 29, 31, 89
Williams, Wing Commander W. T. S. DSC 64
Wiltan HMS 207
Wingham, Fred 187-188
Witherington HMS 49
Withernsea 90
Wolf, Oberleutnant zur see Eckhart 49
Woltersdorf, Oberleutnant Helmut 102, 117
Wyton 90
Yugoslavia 82
Ziebarth, Feldwebel Ernst 91

Zulu HMS 44

229